THE
PROBLEM OF ORDER

THE
PROBLEM
OF
ORDER

WHAT UNITES
AND DIVIDES SOCIETY

DENNIS H. WRONG

THE FREE PRESS
A Division of Macmillan, Inc.
NEW YORK

Maxwell Macmillan Canada
TORONTO

Maxwell Macmillan International
NEW YORK   OXFORD   SINGAPORE   SYDNEY

The Free Press
A Division of Macmillan, Inc.
866 Third Avenue, New York, N.Y. 10022

Maxwell Macmillan Canada, Inc.
1200 Eglinton Avenue East
Suite 200
Don Mills, Ontario M3C 3N1

Macmillan, Inc. is part of the Maxwell Communication
Group of Companies.

Printed in the United States of America

printing number
1 2 3 4 5 6 7 8 9 10

Library of Congress Cataloging-in-Publication Data

Wrong, Dennis Hume
    The problem of order : what unites and divides society / Dennis H.
Wrong.
        p.   cm.
    Includes bibliographical references and index.
    ISBN 0-02-935515-X
    1. Solidarity. 2. Social conflict. 3. Social structure.
4. Sociology—Philosophy. I. Title.
HM126.W76 1994
303.6—dc20   93-33201
                                                        CIP

To Jackie

CONTENTS

ACKNOWLEDGMENTS

I should perhaps have written this book some thirty years ago for it is a sequel to, or enlargement upon, my article "The Oversocialized Conception of Man in Modern Sociology" (*American Sociological Review*, 26 [April 1961], pp. 183–193). This article achieved a certain celebrity among sociologists—it has been many times reprinted—as a criticism of the dominant tendencies in the field at that time. I was less than happy when a few years later my argument was too readily assimilated to the radical and countercultural ethos inextricably associated today with the 1960s, an ethos that loomed large in the academy in general and in sociology in particular. My own views remained intellectually and politically moderate, and as skeptical of the dogmatism and utopian transports of the period as I was of the complacently positive attitude toward human nature, social order, and social conformity that the article assailed. I should like to think that the present book is better than it would have been had it been written earlier and inevitably been caught up in controversies that have since faded.

I have incorporated into Chapter 2 an essay, "Hobbes, Darwinism, and the Problem of Order," that was originally published in *Conflict and Consensus: A Festschrift in Honor of Lewis A. Coser*, edited by Walter A. Powell and Richard Robbins (New York: The Free Press, 1984, pp. 204–217). Most of the book was written during two sabbatical leaves. I am grateful to New York University for its generous sabbatical leave policy, to the John Simon Guggenheim Memorial Foundation for awarding me a fellowship in 1984–85, and to the Woodrow Wilson Center for International Scholars for granting me a resident fellowship in 1991–92.

The following persons read at least one chapter, several of

them more than one, of the manuscript: Donald Carveth, Jacqueline Conrath, Jonathan Imber, Howard Kaye, Michael Lacey, Edward W. Lehman, Sheila Mehta, Jerry Muller, and James Rule. I profited from their comments and suggestions. I also learned from the responses of audiences at the District of Columbia Sociological Society, Franklin and Marshall College, the University of Virginia, and several at the Wilson Center in Washington, D.C. I should like to thank Alan Ryan and Norbert Wiley for helping me with the references, Alan for providing me with his own first-rate but scattered papers on Hobbes and Rousseau. The staff of the Woodrow Wilson Center was unfailingly helpful during my stay there, in the course of which I wrote just over half of the book.

Last but probably first in importance, my editor, Joyce Seltzer, encouraged me to write this book from its earliest conception and made numerous wise and helpful suggestions in addition to her always valuable textual contributions. I am greatly in her debt. I also appreciate the support I received from Erwin Glikes, President of The Free Press.

CHAPTER ONE

THE MANY-SIDED PROBLEM OF ORDER

People everywhere live in everyday association with each other. This banal observation sums up what essentially is meant by assertions that human beings live "in society," "form groups," or are "social animals." If the most fundamental question about anything is Leibniz's "Why is there something rather than nothing?" the most fundamental question for social theory is surely "Why do human beings maintain a regular social life rather than only minimal and occasional contacts with one another?" The biological survival of mammalian species requires intermittent association for purposes of mating and parenthood, but there are mammals who with these exceptions live relatively solitary lives.

Some past thinkers have believed that the human species once lived in a "state of nature" that involved a primarily non-social way of life. Aristotle held the contrary view in famously describing man as a "social animal."[1] His "social" is often rendered as "political," which meant more or less the same thing to him that we understand today by "social." To Aristotle, humans form families, villages that are unions of families, and states or political communities that are unions of villages. All of these groups he saw as "creations of nature" resulting from the presence in man* of a "social instinct." However, he carefully distinguished

---

*Used, of course, here and elsewhere in the generic sense of "human being" to include both genders.

between "natural" social relations and those created by "law and custom," devoting considerable effort, notably in his discussion of slavery, to deciding which was which.

Although contemporary sociologists could be said to see man as possessing a "social nature," no particular social relation—certainly not slavery and not even relations between males and females or parents and children—is today regarded as determined by "nature" and therefore invariant and universal for the species. Nor is the notion of a social, or what nineteenth-century writers called a "gregarious," instinct thought to have any explanatory value whatever in accounting for the ubiquity of human society. Attachment to and dependence on others are themselves regarded as consequences of undetermined behavioral endowments rather than products of innate disposition. To be sure, the biological fact of the helplessness of human infants at birth and for some time afterward necessitates a long period of nearly total dependence on parental, or at least adult, nurturance and protection. Infantile dependence is a precondition for both habituation to life with others and extensive learning from them, but the very absence of instinctive dispositions, including inborn social responses, is the cause of the dependence, that is, endows it with critical survival value in evolutionary terms.

Aristotle regarded societies as natural wholes, with individuals, smaller groups, and families as their subordinate parts. To Thomas Hobbes, on the other hand, societies were "artificiall" entities, mere aggregates of individuals together by collectively willed or "covenanted" consensus requiring coercion to sustain them. Yet both Aristotle and Hobbes remarked on the difference between human and insect societies. Both of them saw human societies as based not on mere mechanical impulsive behavior but on man's unique capacity for speech and reason endowing him with the freedom to choose and thus to entertain different conceptions of social order. Both philosophers understood that if human societies were as fully integrated and automatically self-reproducing as insect societies, questions about what constituted good and evil, justice and injustice, and the most worthy and effective forms of social and political organization would not even arise.

Nor would questions about what holds societies together, however imperfectly, or why their interdependent parts—individuals and groups—do not break away and become independent, dissolving the larger whole into its diverse components. Individuals and groups do, after all, sometimes separate themselves from larger social units and even, as Hobbes in particular recognized and deplored, engage in deadly conflicts with one another. The most superficial survey of the historical record leaves no doubt on this score.

A further consideration is that individuals often feel their attachments and obligations to others as a burden, a painful constraint preventing them from pursuing desires and interests of their own. Indeed, the choice of duty over self-interest or impulse, of the normatively desirable over the actually desired, was defined by Kant as the very essence of moral conduct. Conflict within the individual, as well as conflict among individuals and between the individual and the demands of society, is from this perspective a human universal. And, of course, some individuals in all societies resolve conflicts between duty and desire in favor of the latter. Moreover, some people, whose number may on occasion be quite considerable, lack any regard for rules or morality as such and abide by them solely out of expediency or fear of punishment. The possibility and not infrequent actuality of deviation from social demands in the form of moral rules is implied by the very existence of the rules. So is the prospect of creating and enforcing new rules, acknowledged by Aristotle in his attempt to separate what was natural from what was law or custom, although he was less inclined than Hobbes to regard the latter as artificial and precarious.

Human societies, in short, always contain tensions that make them vulnerable to possible dissolution. Awareness of this has repeatedly led theorists to proclaim such questions as "What holds societies together?" or "What accounts for social cohesion?" as fundamental and even as the obvious and necessary starting point for social theory itself. The question is posed in a number of different forms, usually so broadly as to blur and run together several distinct issues. Often it is stated in highly metaphorical terms. "Cement"—sometimes "social cement"—

"glue," "magnetic forces," "ties that bind," "the fabric of society," or the "social bond" are invoked and questions are asked about their nature and their strength, that is, the degree to which they are successful in "holding society together," preventing it from "breaking down," "falling apart," "disintegrating," or succumbing to powerful "centrifugal tendencies." Such language is redolent of physical, mechanical, chemical, and biological imagery, whether drawn from science or from everyday life. All language, to be sure, is metaphorical, but some language, it can be argued, is more metaphorical than other language. In any case, even the basic concept of "social structure," often identified as the fundamental subject matter of sociology, suggests a spatial arrangement of parts. The term "structure," however, is so widely used in all disciplines with reference to any and all entities and phenomena that it has acquired an abstractness obscuring its metaphorical character.

The conception of a problem of order, or of social order, is preferable, I believe, to the other formulations I have mentioned, although it is not without ambiguities of its own. However, it is less blatantly metaphorical than most of the other versions. It was named as the basic question for social theory by Talcott Parsons in 1937.[2] He, elaborating on the work of Élie Halévy, identified Hobbes as the first thinker clearly to formulate it in describing a putative state of nature characterized by universal conflict as the condition human beings had to overcome in order to pursue a collective mode of existence. Four different aspects or dimensions of the problem of order, conflated in many or most discussions, should be distinguished.

COGNITION AND MOTIVATION

At the level of human nature or the universally human, cognitive and motivational versions of the problem of order need to be differentiated. Shared understandings of the world, on the one hand, and shared emotional attachments of individuals to one another singly or collectively and/or shared commitments to rules of conduct, on the other, are not the same thing. Georg Simmel gave a Kantian twist to the problem of order, emphasizing knowledge rather than purposes or motives, in asking "How is society possible?"[3] The accent here is not on human motivations, nor on conditions giving rise to cooperation or conflict, but rather on the nature and source of shared cognitive and—especially nowadays—linguistic skills making possible mutual understandings, or the capacity of human beings to communicate in terms of a world of common meanings. Chaos or randomness rather than violent conflict or limited association with others constitutes the negation of order in this view. Order consists of the predictability of human conduct on the basis of common and stable expectations. This approach is primarily concerned with the shared meanings that make possible stable, recurrent, and cooperative social interaction. But its cognitivist conception of order readily merges into the general question of how *any* common perceptions of regularities, whether in nature or in society, are possible for human beings as a precondition for both everyday practical knowledge and for science. When order, regularity, and predictability as such are seen as dependent on socially acquired categories of understanding—as they have been by such thinkers as Durkheim, Mannheim, and Wittgenstein—the problem of knowledge or epistemology itself becomes a version of the problem of order. The specific issue of *social* order, of how human beings with their particular endowments and capacities, including their motivational repertories, manage to create regular and recurrent patterns of interaction with one another, is lost at such a level of generality. The problem of order as a problem of cognition therefore needs to be complemented by and differentiated from consideration of what *motivates* human beings to interact and achieve consensus on common goals.

WHAT ARE THE RELEVANT UNITS?

Definitions of human nature focus on the transcultural and transhistorical—though not necessarily biological—endowments, capacities, and dispositions of individual human beings, on "the" generic individual. This raises the question of what units are integrated or bound together in the formation and structure of societies—individuals, dyads, families, small groups, local communities, politically organized associations, or "imagined communities."[4] It may be obvious that the nature of human nature, on the one hand, and the sociology of group formation, differentiation, and cooperation or conflict, on the other, are quite different processes, but the distinction is often ignored in discussions of the problem of order.

If the problem of order is seen as embracing units ranging from single individuals to organized political communities including millions of people, it spans the entire continuum from face-to-face encounters between individuals to the relations between great powers in world politics.[5] Levels of analysis are not distinguished: the psychological, or the nature of human nature including the intrapsychic; the social psychological, or micro-social relations among persons; the sociological in the strict sense, or how social groups form and sustain themselves in what has often been called "civil society"; and the political, including both the internal conflicts that make up the content of politics within nation-states and international relations. Obviously, all these different levels need at some point to be recognized and considered separately in their own right.

At the level of the individual or human nature, the problem of order merges into the venerable issue of the "relation between the individual and society," often seen as centering on the question of how "biologic individuals," as G. H. Mead called them, driven by purely self-centered passions, succeed in overcoming their egoism and combining to form relatively stable and permanent social groups. In the history of social thought, conceptions of society have again and again—starting with Aristotle—depicted the individual-society relation as a part-whole relation, often drawing analogies between societies and biological organisms, machines, or, more abstractly, systems. But individual human beings are clearly more separable from their relations with their fellows than leaves from trees, cells from organisms, or single points from any overall pattern they may form. This is the fundamental justification for the standpoint of methodological individualism, which in no way entails the assumption that individuals are fully formed independently of their relations with one another, or that when considered collectively they constitute nothing more than an aggregate of randomly or accidentally assembled units. It might be legitimate to regard some insect societies as larger organisms in which the genetically programmed specialized individuals are the equivalent of cells, but, as we have seen, even Aristotle recognized the essential difference between human and insect societies. The problem of order, therefore, cannot ignore human nature and the processes by which it is formed through contacts with others. There is certainly a sense in which the groups or social structures—and also the cultures, or patterns of belief and symbolic expression—that humans produce can be described and analysed in their interrelations as *sui generis* realities, in Durkheim's famous phrase, apart from the process of formation of the underlying capacities and dispositions of the individuals that create and sustain these realities. But insofar as the problem of order is truly the most fundamental and general question in social theory, it cannot ignore this process. It must, in short, be posed at the levels of both the individual and the larger society, considering both how individuals manage to form groups and how separate groups manage to coexist within larger internally differentiated collectivities.

Yet a surprising number of discussions of the problem of order fail to distinguish between the problem as it applies to individuals and as it applies to social groups within a wider social context. The relevant units are either not specified or defined so broadly as to include individuals and any and all varieties of group or collectivity. Anarchy and anomie, crime waves, insurrections, revolutions and civil wars, riots, mob violence, and other kinds of unconventional behavior by large numbers of people acting in concert studied by sociologists under the rubric of "collective behavior"—all of these are seen as instances of social breakdown and the collapse of order. Hobbes's famous account of the "war of all against all," or *bellum omnium contra omnes,* has been indiscriminately applied to situations ranging from strictly individual behavior such as the brutal "dehumanization" of prisoners subject to total domination and oppression in Auschwitz as described by Primo Levi[6] and the greater incivility in public reported in contemporary American cities,[7] to such collective processes as capitalist economic competition, the Marxist class struggle, the threatened dissolution of multinational states confronted with separatist demands by ethnic minorities, and international relations including full-scale wars between nations. Obviously, the units involved in these situations are utterly diverse, embracing single individuals at one extreme and organized political communities containing millions of people at the other.

Both Aristotle and Hobbes regarded the family, essentially the nuclear family, as more "natural" and its unity as less variable and problematic than that of larger groups.[8] The notion of "society" or "social order" should be understood, however, to refer inclusively to any and all stable human social relations and groups, rather than only to large-scale internally differentiated territorially concentrated associations of persons sharing a common culture and set of institutions. The very notion of plural societies as distinct, discrete entities forming coherent wholes or systems has been widely and justly criticized.[9] The classical problem of order must be understood in terms that apply to the social life of man in general, including the family. To put it in more archaic terms, civil society must be seen (in contrast to both Hegel and Hobbes) as including families as well as other associations.

THE PROBLEM OF ORDER AND ITS SOLUTIONS

A number of different solutions to the problem of order have been advanced which should be clearly distinguished from the problem itself. This is particularly important because solutions are sometimes so presented as to suggest that the problem is a false one based on misconception rather than a real condition confronted by real human societies. Alternatively, the problem is stated with tautological overtones by defining it in such a way as to equate a particular solution with the problem itself. For example, the problem is said to be one of forging solidarity or social cohesion, which equates the achievement of a sense of collective unity and group identity, one possible solution to the problem of order, with the very definition of the problem. There is no reason to assume at the outset that the members of a group or society must be aware of and ascribe value to themselves as a supra-individual collectivity in order to attain order. The repeated interactions of individuals that constitute them as a group may be motivated by fear or narrowly instrumental self-interest, rather than by any positive emotional attraction or normative commitment.

It is a simplification but hardly a gross one to identify the three widely recognized solutions (that is, nontheological and nonbiological solutions) to the problem of order[10] with the three major thinkers who argued that a social contract was necessary to overcome a prior presocial and/or prepolitical state of nature. Hobbes's solution was coercive, Locke's stressed mutual self-interest, and the Rousseau of *The Social Contract* gave primacy to normative consensus.[11] Precisely because there is no justification for assuming that one solution precludes or subsumes the others, but that on the contrary all three may operate conjointly in concrete human societies, it is important not to identify the problem of order with any of its proposed solutions. If the characteristic error of sociologists, most notably of Durkheim and Parsons, has been to overemphasize consensus on norms and values as the solution, the Machiavellian-Hobbesian tradition in political thought has tended to exaggerate the role of force, and economists, including Marx, have notoriously overstressed economic interest. Any emphasis on a single solution to the problem of order to the exclusion of others tends so to deny the complexity and variety of human nature as to challenge the meaningfulness of the problem. The very completeness and definitiveness of the answer to the question succeeds in casting doubt on the rationale for the question itself. Although by crediting Hobbes with first formulating the problem of order Parsons clearly did not confuse the problem with its solutions, since he did not accept Hobbes's coercive solution, his own normative solution sometimes seemed so monolithic and all-encompassing as to efface the reality of the problem he had initially identified.[12]

DISORDER OR THE LACK OF ORDER

Like virtually all conceptualizations of social relations, social order is a matter of degree. Order is never so fully present in concrete social reality as to exclude all deviations, unpredictabilities, mistaken perceptions, and accidents. Nor is it ever so utterly absent that completely random behavior, unremitting total conflict, or social interaction confined to the minimum required by biological necessity prevails. Whether regarding disorder as a condition that was presocial and prehistorical—a state of nature—or as a dangerous potential covertly present within even the seemingly most orderly of societies, the thinkers who have been most preoccupied with order and disorder as polarities have at least tacitly seen them as forming a continuum, or as "dialectically" entailing one another's existence as opposites. This does not exempt them from criticism for overemphasis and exaggeration, but neither Hobbes, Locke, nor Rousseau, nor, for that matter, Parsons, was quite as naive as their critics have sometimes assumed in denying the mixtures of order and disorder, stability and change, consensus or cooperation and conflict—whichever set of polar terms is preferred—that all societies present.

The most common representation of the absence of order is as universal violence, as anarchy inducing omnipresent fear of physical assault and violent death at the hands of other human beings. Hobbes's fame as a social and political thinker is the result of his having tapped into a deep fear of violence that he himself felt and articulated in response to the threat and reality of civil war in England. A sense of the precariousness of peace and good will among men, the instability of cooperative endeavors, the thinness of the crust of civility manifest in overt human relations, seems to be widely present in the consciousness of men and women, at least in large-scale or "civilized" societies. When asked how they envisage the "collapse" or "breakdown" of society, most people will immediately refer to violence in the streets directed against persons and property, proceeding, at least if they are well-informed late twentieth-century North Americans, to recall such situations as the widespread looting and vandalism that took place during the police strike in Montreal and the electrical blackout in New York City in the 1970s, the devastating sectarian warfare in Beirut through the 1980s, and "ethnic cleansing" in Bosnia in the 1990s.[13] It should be noted that these visions of disorder do not distinguish between outbreaks of individual crime and violence and group conflict between organized religious, political, or ethnic communities that must be pacified if order is to be achieved.

Hobbes and Parsons, then, were hardly being idiosyncratic in regarding universal violence where "every man's hand is raised against every other man" as the inverse or negation of social order. Yet the absence of order need not connote solely such a situation. The possible lack of intersubjective understanding at the cognitive level has also been seen as a lack of order. Universal solipsism or incommunicability parallels at the level of cognition universal conflict at the behavioral level in the Hobbesian version of lack of order. G. H. Mead's identification of symbolic communication as a prerequisite for "taking the role of the other" and Alfred Schutz's notion of the "reciprocity of perspectives" as the basis of intersubjectivity addressed the problem of order as a problem of cognition of other selves.

At a more general level, lack of order is often equated with randomness or chaos, with the absence of any perceived regularities in or patterning of social experience. Jeffrey Alexander, for example, writes: "The problem of order is the problem of how individual units, of whatever motivation, are arranged in nonrandom social patterns. Defined in such a generic manner, as the neutral problem of 'arrangement' or 'pattern,' it is clear that every social theory must address the order question."[14] However, the problem of order so defined is in no way specific to *social* order but applies to all knowledge, to anything that is knowable. It is, in effect, the problem of knowledge or epistemology *per se* and is therefore hardly peculiar to social theory. And Alexander, indeed, moves from this statement directly to a discussion of the philosophy of science in general.

A third version of the absence of social order should be based on recognition that lack of association does not necessarily entail conflict. Hobbes's first adjective in his famous description of the state of nature is "solitary," which clearly might obtain independently of his third adjective, "nasty," or his fourth, "brutish." People may "have no pleasure. . .in keeping company"[15] for reasons other than fear: out of lack of interest or motivation to maintain social ties beyond the minimal ones dictated by biological necessity. This essentially describes Rousseau's much-misrepresented Noble Savage and the state of nature in which he lives (apart from the social implications of Rousseau's assumption of an instinct of pity that he saw as also possessed by animals other than man).

The point that an asocial, not necessarily antisocial, existence also constitutes a lack of order may seem to be a trivial one. But it needs to be made because of the tendency of so many writers to equate the absence of universal conflict as pictured by Hobbes with the *presence* of cooperative social ties and the collective goals their existence implies. Jon Elster, for example, identifies "two problems of order: that of stable, regular, predictable patterns of behavior and that of cooperative behavior." The first of these is the cognitive problem of order previously discussed, but he goes on explicitly to identify "disorder as absence of cooperation" with "Hobbes's vision of life in the state of nature."[16] Clearly, this excludes the possibility of a solitary mode of life characterized by neither cooperation nor conflict, precisely the way of life that Rousseau saw as the state of nature. "Disorder" is a misnomer for it—it was a secure and happy condition according to Rousseau—but it certainly involved a lack of *social* order since individuals led lives of relative isolation.

THE PROBLEM OF ORDER AND CONSERVATISM

The assertion of order as necessary for the existence of society has often been equated with a conservative opposition to social change and to group conflict as a source of change. The proclaimed aim of "restoring law and order" sometimes professed by political authorities when confronted with outbreaks of civil violence partly explains this false equation. Among recent sociologists, the widespread but erroneous belief that Talcott Parsons was a conservative and the creator of a theory that was not concerned with change and was allegedly unable to account for it has contributed to conceiving of order in static, self-maintaining terms. Moreover, Hobbes himself has often, perhaps anachronistically, been classified as a conservative because of his royalism and his insistence on the absolute obedience short of the sacrifice of life itself owed to an effective ruler.

But there is no inconsistency in regarding order as intrinsic to social existence and acknowledging the universal occurrence of social change. Indeed, "orderly" social change may be a prerequisite for the maintenance of order understood as the avoidance of massive and violent group conflict. Only such conflict, or the actual physical dispersion of the individual members of a society, would amount to the total negation of social order. Short of that, societies can stand a great deal of individual deviance and severe strife among individuals and groups without actually dissolving. Such deviance and conflict may serve to initiate far-reaching social change without the society "breaking down," or falling into "disorder." Thus there is no reason to identify the problem of order with conservative opposition to dissent, nonconformity, and social change.

Order, then, is always a matter of degree. It coexists with, and influences and is influenced by, individual deviance, group conflict, social change, and cultural innovation.[17] Theorists of order from Hobbes to the present day have conflated different problematic aspects of it, and often mistakenly identified its negation with conditions that are not incompatible with its persistence. The aim of the present book is less to review comprehensively past discussions of the problem than to present a new, conceptually sharper statement of it. I have chosen to do so, however, partly through the critical examination of a number of individual thinkers and the theoretical traditions with which they are associated.

CHAPTER TWO

THE PROBLEM OF ORDER FROM HOBBES TO THE PRESENT

Thomas Hobbes's description of the "state of nature" as a human condition in which life is "solitary, poore, nasty, brutish and short" is perhaps the most frequently quoted passage in the entire corpus of Western social and political theory. Writing during Cromwell's Protectorate after the English Civil War of the 1640s and in response to those climactic events that had forced him into French exile, Hobbes was describing the dire prospect he thought both had preceded the creation of any political authority and would be restored if existing authority were destroyed. Human beings, however, are capable of avoiding such disasters because they differ from animals in possessing, according to Hobbes, the faculty of reason, which entails the capacity to foresee the consequences of their own actions. This capacity enables them to think themselves, as it were, out of the perilous situation of never-ending conflict that the state of nature involves. They do this by coming together and contracting to renounce the freedom to use violence and deception in their relations with one another. Yet they recognize that a mere collective resolution to forego force and fraud will not eliminate individual temptations to resort to these often effective expedients and the at least occasional giving-in to temptation. "Covenants without the Sword are but Words, and of no strength to secure a man at all."[1] The social contract, therefore, also includes vesting in one person or group the exclusive authority to use coercion to maintain the peace by restraining wayward individuals from resorting to force on their own initiative in pursuit of their ends. Thus Leviathan or the state comes into being, possessing, in Max Weber's well-known formulation of nearly three centuries later, a monopoly over the legitimate use of physical force.

The first adjective in Hobbes's description of the state of nature is "solitary," which makes plain that he conceives of it as a presocial state in which "men have no pleasure, (but on the contrary a great deale of grief) in keeping company,"[2] as he remarked a few paragraphs earlier in the famous Chapter 13 of *Leviathan* that contains his account of the state of nature. The vivid adjectival passage, moreover, comes as a conclusion to an immediately preceding enumeration of human activities and achievements that are lacking when an established, or "civil," society is absent:

> In such condition, there is no place for Industry; because the fruit thereof is uncertain: and consequently no Culture of the Earth; no Navigation, nor use of the commo-dities that may be imported by Sea; no commodious Building; no Instruments of moving and removing such things as require much force; no knowledge of the face of the Earth; no account of Time; no Arts; no Letters; no Society. . .

This list of human practices and their products missing in the state of nature bears considerable resemblance to E. B. Tylor's famous "portmanteau" definition of culture as "that complex whole which includes knowledge, belief, art, morals, law, custom, and any other capabilities and habits acquired by man as a member of society."[3] Culture, to Hobbes, clearly presupposes the prior existence of society, just as it does for contemporary social scientists.

Later social and political thinkers criticized Hobbes on a variety of grounds. Locke wondered why rational men would willingly submit to the absolute power of a sovereign merely to gain protection from the much more limited powers with which each of them was capable of harassing one another. Vico thought that only men who had already learned to reason in a highly developed society could be capable of formulating Hobbes's covenant.

Montesquieu contended that a presocial state of nature could never have existed, for men had always lived in societies and were social by nature. Rousseau, on the other hand, did not doubt that men had once lived in a presocial state of nature, but he argued that Hobbes had wrongly endowed them with evil and vicious qualities that they could only have acquired from living in society.

Hobbes's belief that society and culture could only flourish after the creation of a political authority or state which liberated men from the anarchic state of nature is the exact inverse of the sociological outlook formed in the eighteenth and nineteenth centuries. From its perspective, the state is an outgrowth of a preexisting society and reflects the continuous operation of deeper, autonomous "social forces" at work in that society, whether these forces are conceived of as spiritual or material. Hobbes's state of nature or "natural condition of mankind" is the most famous image of what human life might be like in the absence of a stable and organized society. The Hobbesian "war of all against all" is the total contradiction of what we mean by "society," that is, cooperative relations among individuals and their common observance of rules governing their conduct toward one another. Hobbes saw the war as a hypothetical construct rather than as a condition that had at one time generally existed in human history but had been overcome by the implementation of a social contract.[4] True, he referred to accounts of the lives of primitive peoples, notably the Indians of North America, as suggesting that the war of all against all, or at least of small families against one another, had once been widely prevalent. He also noted the pervasive mistrust among men in established societies, the occurrence of rebellions and civil wars, and the ubiquity of international conflicts as evidence for the state of nature even under conditions of civilized life. But his view of these as usually no more than tendencies or latent possibilities, and his recognition that most states had been created "by acquisition" through conquest, rather than "by institution" as the result of a founding social contract, indicate that he fundamentally conceived of both the state of nature and the social contract as theoretical "models" or Weberian "ideal types"; at most, the war of all against all represented a limiting condition toward which all societies tended in times of weakened political authority and internal conflict.

Hobbes's model of the state of nature and the social contract that overcomes it has been described as a "a Galilean experiment of an imaginary sort."[5] The most direct suggestion of his analytical model-building rationale has often been noticed and quoted despite its being a more or less incidental comment in a late chapter of *De Cive* (a shorter work written some years before *Leviathan*) on the specific subject of the obligations of servants to masters: "Let us return again to the state of nature, and consider men as if but even now sprung out of the earth, and suddenly (like mushrooms) come to full maturity, without all kind of engagement to each other."[6] A contemporary reader is instantly reminded of John Rawls's "original position" and "veil of ignorance." Like Hobbes, Locke also cited reports of the behavior of primitive men to support his different conception of the state of nature, although he too was clearly less concerned with accurate empirical description than with abstracting from reality in order to justify his normative principles about the proper role of government.

HOBBES AND ROUSSEAU

In contrast to Hobbes and Locke, Rousseau thought of the state of nature as a real historical—or, rather, prehistorical—condition that had once prevailed at the very beginning of the long and painful process of development toward civilization that men had followed. In the *Discourse on Inequality* Rousseau drew on comparative anatomy, medical knowledge, naturalists' descriptions of animal behavior and early anthropological accounts of primitive peoples to support his inferences about the state of nature.[7] "Rousseau is the first great exponent of social evolution," Bertrand de Jouvenel observes. "His was the first attempt to depict systematically the historical progress of human society: here he precedes Condorcet, Saint-Simon, Comte, Marx-Engels and all those who sought to systematize views of social evolution."[8]

Rousseau, to be sure, regarded the transition from the state of nature to an inegalitarian social order upheld by a despotic ruler as moral decline or degeneration rather than as progress. Yet his sequence of stages through which mankind had passed, reflecting improvements in technology and the more complex division of labor that resulted, bears considerable resemblance to those of Marx and Engels and of many post-Darwinian "materialistic" reconstructions of social development.[9] Nor is it markedly inferior, though antedating them by a century or more. Rousseau clearly displays the historical consciousness that distinguishes social thought in the modern epoch. In this respect, he differs strikingly from such seventeenth-century thinkers as Hobbes and Locke. If Rousseau anticipates nineteenth-century social evolutionism, Hobbes and Locke, paradoxically, strike an even more "modern" note in their anticipation of theoretical model-building. They were reflecting the influence of classical mechanics and, particularly in Hobbes's case, the paradigmatic example of geometrical reasoning. One could argue that Hobbes's and, more doubtfully, Locke's conceptions of the state of nature and the social contract are less open to objection than Rousseau's because they were not thought of as recording actual conditions or events in the history of real human societies.

Yet Rousseau's argument that Hobbes's war of all against all necessarily implies the prior existence of society rather than a nonsocial state of nature is well taken. Hobbes's state of nature is the negative mirror image of social order. It is intended to depict *disorder* as the opposite of order: conflict rather than cooperation, individual goals at odds with one another rather than converging or aggregating to become common or collectively shared goals, fear and distrust among men rather than solidarity and sociability. To buttress his overall case against the corruption he saw as endemic to civilized societies, Rousseau wanted to show that the vicious features of Hobbes's state of nature could only have originated within a fully developed society. He was right in seeing—like Sumner, Simmel, Weber, Park, and many later sociologists—that conflict is a social relation just as much as cooperation; also, in understanding that the motivations for engaging in it, especially the wish to excel in the eyes of others, could only arise in a social context.

If Hobbes's state of nature is the contrary of social order, Rousseau's state of nature is the total negation of society, the complete absence of all social ties and of all motivations directed toward others, even those of a negative or "antisocial" character. Hobbes still followed Aristotle in assuming the existence of the family as part of a natural and "private" realm in contrast to the "artificial"—today we would say "socially constructed"—and "public" realm of the political community or polis. Rousseau, on the other hand, eliminated even the family from his state of nature, reducing social contacts to the absolute minimum necessary for mating and the maternal care of very young children. Rousseau's state of nature is a fully nonsocial mode of existence in which the lives of men are truly solitary if by no means poor, nasty, brutish, and short.

Hobbes's inconsistencies and ambiguities about the state of nature may well have resulted from the fact that his primary interest in it was always as a state toward which men tended in times of civil war and the collapse of political authority rather than, as for Rousseau, a pristine original condition at the beginning of history. Despite familiar clichés about Rousseau's supposed glorification of the Noble Savage, he did not believe a return to the animal-like existence of man in the state of nature to be even conceivable, let alone desirable. His ideal was, rather, what he called "nascent society," an early stage of social development in which men lived in families that provided equally for their own needs with simple tools, maintaining wider social ties but without either government or the dependent relations produced by the division of labor. Rousseau's concrete exemplar was the farming communities of the Swiss canton of Vaud; his ideal influenced Jefferson's preference for a republic of independent yeoman farmers, free from the inevitable corruptions of city life.

For Hobbes, the solitariness of the state of nature was overcome only after the creation of a political sovereign permitting men to live thereafter at peace in society. For Rousseau, too, the state of nature was both presocial and prepolitical, but the social contract that established the state was entered into *after* men had adopted a thoroughly social way of life that had already gone through several stages of development. The last prepolitical stage was marked by internecine conflict resulting from social inequality that, in Rousseau's view, Hobbes had mistakenly attributed to the presocial state of nature. Rousseau clearly stands closer than Hobbes to the views of later sociologists and of Marxists in seeing society as preceding political institutions, which constitute an effort to overcome the conflict resulting from the division of labor and the antagonistic classes it brings into being.

Rousseau's conception of the original state of nature was, as he fully recognized, purely speculative. Since he thought of it as a condition that might have actually existed in the distant past, he is more vulnerable to empirical objections to its very possibility than is Hobbes, whose parallel conception was framed in a more hypothetical mode patterned after the physicist's idea of a vacuum or the geometer's of a perfect figure.[10] Even the limited mental, moral, and tool-making capacities with which Rousseau endowed human beings in the state of nature could not have existed in the absence of regular social life. Rousseau's view of original human nature is more radically "undersocialized" than Hobbes's, given the latter's traditional assumption that the family was a universal natural association. Rousseau did impute to human beings in the state of nature one "natural virtue" involving a minimal social bond that he accused Hobbes of overlooking: compassion or a sense of pity when confronted with the suffering of one's fellows. However, he thought this trait was also possessed by lower animals, including horses and cattle. From a latter-day social psychological standpoint, it is hard to see how or why such sympathetic identification with others could have come into existence among creatures whose contacts with one another were as few and ephemeral as those of Rousseau's savages in the state of nature. Perhaps it might be accounted for by the genetic selection of altruistic behavior toward kin postulated by contemporary sociobiologists, but Rousseau could hardly have had recourse to an explanation in such terms.

THE HISTORICAL RELATIVIZATION OF HOBBES

The essence of the sociological perspective as it developed in the late eighteenth and early nineteenth centuries amounted to a denial of two of Hobbes's basic assumptions: first, that individuals with the attributes he ascribed to them could possibly exist outside of a preexisting society that had powerfully formed their natures; and second, that society depended upon the prior establishment of the coercive political authority of the state. The "revolt against individualism" and the assertion of the priority of society over the state are hallmarks of "the sociological tradition,"[11] surviving even today as central tenets of most academic sociology. The concepts of state of nature and social contract, though endowed with different contents by Hobbes, Locke, and Rousseau, provided foils for both conservative and socialist forerunners and founders of sociology, even before the influence of Malthus and especially Darwin revived in biologistic rather than utilitarian terms the conception of society as a mere aggregate of competing individuals.

Malthus's theory of a continual struggle for subsistence resulting in permanently high death rates first suggested to Darwin the idea of natural selection, so the link between classical economics, and Darwinism was a direct one. Hobbes and Locke have long been regarded as precursors of classical economics and even as preindustrial prophets of the rise of capitalist market society. Hobbes's depiction of autonomous individuals relentlessly pursuing their own interests at odds with one another is readily seen as a theoretical reflection of the erosion of medieval and feudal ties and the rise in the numbers of "masterless men" (his phrase) in the post-Renaissance and post-Reformation world of emerging bourgeois society.

The most impressive recent reinterpretation of Hobbes (and Locke) as early anatomists of bourgeois society is that of C. B. Macpherson.[12] Hobbes, he argued, described the "possessive individualism" of the new bourgeoisie in the emerging capitalist economic order of seventeenth-century England. Far from picturing human nature *in vacuo* as it might manifest itself in a hypothetical presocial state of nature, Hobbes was an accurate observer of his own time. Macpherson convincingly shows that many of Hobbes's inferences about human nature are drawn from life in established and orderly civil society *after* the transcendence of the state of nature as a result of the social contract. The most striking instance of this is the passage immediately following Hobbes's famous characterization of life in the state of nature in which he suggests that the doubting reader simply look around him if he seeks confirmation of Hobbes's less-than-exalted view of mankind:

> Let him therefore consider with himself, when taking journey, he armes himself, and seeks to go well accompanied; when going to sleep, he locks his dores; when even in his house he locks his chests; and this when he knows there bee Lawes, and publike officers, armed to revenge all injuries shall bee done him; what opinion he has of his fellow subjects, when he rides armed; of his fellow citizens, when he locks his dores; and of his children, and servants, when he locks his chests. Does he not there as much accuse mankind by his actions, as I do by my words?[13]

Obviously, Hobbes's suggested observational test is based on the evidence of everyday conduct in a society that has long benefited from the creation of Leviathan, the coercive power of the state that keeps men in peace and order by suppressing the war of all against all. (As I have occasionally remarked in the classroom, he sounds as if he might be describing certain neighborhoods in New York City!)

Macpherson is unquestionably right in insisting that Hobbes's argument rests on observation of men in civil society rather than on abstract deductions or speculations about a putative presocial state of nature. Accordingly, Macpherson defends Hobbes against the frequent and often patronizing view of such a presocial condition as a foil to a sociological view of human nature as fundamentally socialized and of society as the medium in which men live just as "naturally" as fish live in water. But Macpherson's claim that Hobbes was describing early capitalism rather than, at the very least, a still earlier condition of England or, at most, tendencies present in all societies, remains open to question. Critics of Macpherson have pointed out that Hobbes's beliefs and values on a variety of matters were more aristocratic or traditional than bourgeois,[14] and that the social and economic life of England in the middle of the seventeenth century was still far more traditionalist and medieval than capitalist or market-centered.[15] Moreover, in imputing to Hobbes a vision of a world dominated by the values of possessive individualism, Macpherson places disproportionate emphasis on Hobbes's occasional references to "commodious living"—material comforts augmented by technical progress—as a gain secured by subjection to a sovereign political authority.[16] Security of possessions and opportunities to increase them play a considerably lesser part in Hobbes's argument than his repeated insistence on the need to safeguard life itself through avoidance of violent death at the hands of others. The suspicious, fearful, and malevolent men who confront one another in the state of nature do not bear much resemblance to the sober, prudential, acquisitive bourgeois economic man calculating his gains and losses in the marketplace.[17] Indeed, as Albert O. Hirschmann has shown, an increase in material acquisitiveness through trade and commerce was widely regarded in the later seventeenth and eighteenth centuries as a pacifying and even "sweetening" influence, tempering the passions for war and armed conflict that had previously been so prominent.[18] Hobbes's view of human nature unmistakably gives priority to the passions conducive to violence rather than to the interests encouraging peaceful commerce.

Macpherson's argument nevertheless is textually well-founded and attests to the iron consistency of Hobbes's "geometrical method" in deriving his entire theory from a few simple premises about human nature. Yet, despite his formal deductive rigor, Hobbes's constant stress on vainglory, pride, and striving for recognized preeminence strongly implies that men are often as much concerned with what others think of them as with the physical—and, for that matter, economic—security that he postulates as their overriding interest. Hobbes repeatedly notes that the intensity of the desire for glory varies among men, inducing some of them to seek even more power than their security requires. All men are compelled to seek power to obtain the means of life under conditions of scarcity and also for defensive reasons, but an additional source of conflict among them is created by the desire of some of them for the greater glory to be attained by besting others. Men, in short, are often "antagonistic cooperators" (in William Graham Sumner's phrase) rather than purely solitary beings. If power and glory are both originally sought as a means to preserve life, they are surely capable of coming to be desired for their own sakes even at a risk to life itself.[19]

If Hobbes failed to develop this point explicitly, it is also, however, a criticism of Macpherson, for men who "use Violence. . .for trifles, as a word, a smile, a different opinion, and any other signe of undervalue, either direct in their Persons or by reflexion in their Kindred, their Friends, their Nation, their Profession, or their Name"[20] are not accurately described as possessive individualists protectively hoarding the wealth they are constantly engaged in accumulating by exploiting the labor of others. In addition, whatever importance Hobbes accorded to fame as the spur goading at least *some* men, he regarded *all* men as driven to seek power, and eventually to agree to subordinate themselves to a common power, neither for glory nor to increase their opportunities for economic exploitation but rather for security against the depredations of others.[21] A life free from the fear of death by violence is a more elemental and universal desideratum than either gain or glory in Hobbes's conception of human motivation.

Regardless of whether Hobbes's view of human nature was aristocratic or bourgeois, his stark picture of human relations dominated by distrust and envy may have applied with particular force to the lower classes in late sixteenth- and early seventeenth-century England, even in their most intimate personal relations. Lawrence Stone writes of this period:

> The extraordinary amount of casual interpersonal physical and verbal violence, as recorded in legal and other records, shows clearly that at all levels men and women were extremely short-tempered. The most trivial disagreements tended to lead rapidly to blows, and most people carried a potential weapon, if only a knife to cut their meat. As a result, the courts were clogged with cases of assault and battery. . ... The Elizabethan village was a place filled with malice and hatred, its only unifying bond being the occasional episode of mass hysteria, which temporarily bound together the majority in order to persecute and harry the local witch.[22]

Stone concludes:

> What is being postulated for the sixteenth and early seventeenth centuries is a society in which a majority of the individuals that composed it found it very difficult to establish close emotional ties to any other person. Children were neglected, brutally treated, and even killed; adults treated each other with suspicion and hostility; affect was low, and hard to find. To an anthropologist, there would be nothing very surprising about such a society, which closely resembles the Mundugumor in New Guinea in the twentieth century as described by Margaret Mead. [23]

Alan MacFarlane, himself an anthropologist, vehemently challenges Stone's assertion that an anthropologist would find "nothing very surprising" about a society like that of the Mundugumor; he insists that anthropologists were very surprised by Mead's account, finding her description strikingly deviant from most reports on primitive societies.[24] Stone's statement is undoubtedly an exaggeration, but there are other examples in the anthropological literature of "Hobbesian" societies, granting that they deviate from the norm for most primitive societies. Perhaps the best-known case is that of the Dobu of Melanesiato "to whom all existence appears. . .as a cut-throat struggle" studied by Reo F. Fortune,[25] whose account was summarized in Ruth Benedict's famous *Patterns of Culture*.[26] A more recent and even more extreme example of a society rent by mutual enmity is Colin Turnbull's account of the Ik tribe of Uganda in *The Mountain People*.[27] The Ik, however, are not as pure a case as the Mundugumor or the Dobu, because their Hobbesian condition resulted from the loss of their traditional hunting grounds to a national park. There are also the people of Alor in the South Pacific studied by Cora Du Bois,[28] of whose society Abram Kardiner observed: "It is not even anarchic, because to be anarchic strong destructive forces must be unleashed which have a firm psychic underpinning. While everyone is against everyone else, this attitude cannot be implemented by enough organized aggression to do any real damage."[29]

Hobbes's political writings were composed shortly after the

end of the period when, according to Stone, hostility dominated personal relations—from roughly 1450 to 1630—when Hobbes was already middle-aged, but Stone's own citations suggest that many of the period's features survived into the eighteenth century. After 1640, however, Stone discerns a tempering of the hostile tone of personal relations, especially within the nuclear family, with the rise of what he calls "affective individualism." Whatever questions may be raised about Stone's periodization,[30] it is surely the case that his earlier period, which Hobbes's views seem to reflect, is unlikely to have been *more* capitalist and expressive of a bourgeois outlook or pervaded by the competitiveness of a market society than the later period after the Whig compromise of 1688. Stone, in fact, asserts a correlation between the growth of affective individualism and the spread of market relations, including the market for labor on which Macpherson places special stress;[31] he even uses Macpherson's term "possessive individualism" in this connection.[32] Individualism in both its intrafamilial affective aspects and its possessive market-oriented manifestations may be viewed as the expression of a distinctive and essentially bourgeois ethos. But the period before the middle of the seventeenth century has usually been considered less individualistic. If life, even for people in the higher ranks, was rather more poor, nasty, brutish, and short than at a later date, it was by no means solitary. Individual interests, according to Stone, were subordinated to the extended kinship group and to clientage, although these ties were based on convenience and mutual dependence rather than on personal feelings. Even the word "friends" implied "advisors, associates, and backers" rather than people with whom one sustained personal affectional bonds.[33]

Alan MacFarlane has challenged the widely accepted view that England underwent a great transformation in the seventeenth century from a traditionalist, kin-centered peasant society toward a greater individualism identified with the rise of capitalism and the bourgeoisie, a view held by thinkers and scholars ranging from Macauley, Marx, Durkheim, and Weber, to contemporary British historians of late medieval England.[34] MacFarlane's primary thesis, based chiefly on records indicating highly individualistic property rights, especially in land, is that as early as the thirteenth century England already had many of the attributes of what came to be called "bourgeois society": a market economy, wage labor, high population mobility, a relatively autonomous nuclear family, and even considerable legal equality between the sexes. Nor does he picture this society in Hobbesian terms: In his critical review of Stone, he cites, *inter alia,* the very same two passages I have quoted and specifically rejects their conclusions about the pervasive hostility of the time.[35]

MacFarlane's bold claims for a far-reaching English exceptionalism have, as one would expect, been cautiously received by those whose assumptions he has criticized.[36] However, should his revised view of English social and economic history ultimately supplant the idea of an epochal transition at the end of the Middle Ages, one might still conclude that Hobbes was essentially describing, if in exaggeratedly negative terms, the society in which he lived, as Macpherson has argued. But if this society was one that had not significantly changed for several centuries, Macpherson's insistence that Hobbes was the first to see the outlines of a rising capitalism would have to be rejected.

It is difficult therefore to accept Macpherson's claim that Hobbes's theory of human nature reflected "the behavior of men toward each other in a specific kind of society," namely, "a possessive market society. . .similar to the concepts of bourgeois or capitalist society used by Marx, Weber, Sombart, and others who have made the existence of a market in labor a criterion of capitalism."[37] Hobbes certainly drew on the life of seventeenth-century England to support his description of human nature, but he clearly regarded his account as of universal applicability to all men in all societies. Nor have sociologists been mistaken in treating the problem of order as a transhistorical problem inherent in the very existence of human societies. William Letwin's conclusion can scarcely be improved upon:

> Hobbes may have drawn upon his own immediate experience; he could not have helped doing that; but he knew enough about other times and places—a knowledge of which was and is available in any society which remembers some history and meets some foreigners—to draw on their experience as well. His premises, in

short, are universal statements about the nature of man. Insofar as
they are true at all, they are more or less equally true of all men at
all times.[38]

SOCIAL DARWINISM REVIVES THE HOBBESIAN PROBLEM

If Rousseau was a precursor of later theories of social evolution,
Hobbes's war of all against all resembled the struggle for survival
among individual members of animal species that Darwin identified as the mechanism setting in motion biological evolution. The
Darwinian vision of the "struggle for survival" and "nature red
in tooth and claw" revived and gave new relevance to the
Hobbesian problem of how asocial, self-preserving human beings
manage to create and maintain cooperative and rule-governed
social relations at all. If one may doubt that Hobbes's state of
nature was actually a description or even a prescient anticipation
of a new bourgeois society dominated by capitalist economic
relations, there can be little doubt that the Social Darwinism of
the late nineteenth century both legitimated and partially mir-
rored such a society and thus appealed to businessmen and their
supporters in late Victorian England and America.[39] Marx and
Engels themselves saw this with utter clarity at the time.[40] The
obsessive search by social evolutionists for "social origins" was
also reminiscent of Hobbes's hypothesis of a transition from the
state of nature to civil society by means of a social contract,
although the evolutionists, anticipated as we have seen by
Rousseau, sought to discover or imagine a real if remote historical or prehistorical past rather than an imagined contract intended to disclose the true nature of political authority. There is also a
striking similarity between Hobbes's emphasis on security or self-
preservation as the dominant human motive and the Darwinian
stress on survival as the sole measure of value in the world of living organisms.[41] Yet whatever the line of intellectual descent from
Hobbes and Locke through Adam Smith, Malthus, and the
Utilitarians to the Social Darwinists, it needs to be emphasized
that to Hobbes—and in a different way to Locke—the state of
nature was a condition to be overcome or escaped from rather

than, as it was to the Social Darwinists, a struggle for survival dictated by ineluctable laws of nature to which mankind had no choice but to conform. As Talcott Parsons has pointed out, Social Darwinism dissolved the tension between the state of nature and its transcendence through the exercise of man's reason that was central to Hobbes by making reason itself merely an instrument in the insurmountable struggle for existence. More recent interpreters of Hobbes have noted the fundamental ambiguity in his conception of "natural law," which left an opening for the biological reductionism of Social Darwinism as an apparent resolution of the tension between nature and reason that is still visible and even salient in Hobbes's thought.[42] The ambiguity essentially lies in Hobbes's conflation of *causes* and normative *reasons* in human action, in, as Jürgen Habermas puts it, his "transference of juridical categories to nature as a whole," leading him to "demand of the causal order in the state of nature those norms he required for the foundation of his civil state."[43]

Parsons is certainly correct in arguing that with the "disappearance of the normative aspects of the utilitarian system, ends and rationality" in Social Darwinism, "the problem of order. . .evaporates." But this is true only at the formal theoretical level: The Darwinian emphasis on intraspecific competition and conflict posed even more sharply the problem of the origins and nature of ethical and political restraints on human self-seeking, even to those like Walter Bagehot who identified themselves as thoroughgoing Social Darwinists. Gertrude Himmelfarb argues that "Bagehot's work comes close to being a travesty of Darwinism,"[44] because, although she does not refer to Hobbes in pointing this out, he presents in effect a Hobbesian account of the origin of society rather than one stemming from natural selection. Bagehot insisted on the necessity of a single absolute and binding authority serving to create a "cake of custom" that held in check the competition that would otherwise threaten the survival of society. There have, of course, been many efforts to resolve the problem of order itself in biologistic terms: the treatment of groups or societies as unitary organisms with individuals as their "cells," the stress on "mutual aid" as a factor in evolutionary survival and progress, the numerous social psychologies that have postulated "gregarious instincts" or innate sentiments of "sympathy" or "consciousness of kind" as the source of the social bond.[45] Rousseau's natural sense of pity was the ancestor of these psychological conceptions. The interest shown by contemporary sociobiologists in the "altruistic gene" is a latter-day version.

The attempt to develop less deterministic and conflict-ridden versions of evolution and natural selection in the realm of human society and history was a major theme of late nineteenth-and early twentieth-century Anglo-American social thought, usually in the form of a dialogue with Herbert Spencer and William Graham Sumner, the two leading sociological Social Darwinists. With the exception of Sumner, all of the early American sociologists were centrally concerned with advancing a more cooperative, benign, and goal-directed view of social evolution and the relation of the individual to society than that presented by Social Darwinism and by the defenders of laissez-faire capitalism who made heavy ideological use of Social Darwinist arguments.[46] By the end of the 1930s the largely successful discrediting of biologism and evolutionism in the social sciences—greatly aided, of course, by the reaction against Nazi racialism—made it possible for Thomas Hobbes to be rediscovered as a more "modern" and conceptually sophisticated thinker than the Social Darwinists who had overgeneralized Darwin's biological theories. Yet the Darwinian focus on the individual as the unit of the species had also brought renewed attention to the problem of how these units succeeded in subordinating their own strivings to a shared set of rules, the question first raised by Hobbes with such rigor and clarity in the seventeenth century.

It is worth noting that American popular speech has long been full of phrases and maxims suggesting a Hobbesian or Social Darwinist view of human existence: characterizations of the social world as a "jungle," a "rat race," a "dog-eat-dog" struggle; expressions of "pavement cynicism" to the effect that everyone is "out for himself," seeking the "main chance," "looking out for number one," concerned only with "getting ahead" at the expense of others or "chasing the almighty dollar."[47] These views are the underside of the "Horatio Alger myth," which has long been seen as definitive of the American ethos. They can obviously be understood as a veiled, unsentimentally fatalistic legitimation of the realities of the competitive individualism of capitalist society, yet at the same time as a protest, if often a wistful and despairing one, against those realities.

No doubt these maxims owe something to affirmations of "rugged individualism" often upheld through the 1920s in Social Darwinist accents. And the note of protest they sometimes articulate echoes the countervalues of the Progressives, the early socialist movement, and the New Deal, in which many sociologists, including prominent ones, participated. The identification of sociology with an emphasis on the values of cooperation as opposed to competition, collectivism as opposed to individualism, and community as opposed to privatism is not peculiar to Europe but has long been present in America as well. Note the following dialogue in a popular novel of more than fifty years ago, whose title entered the language as an idiomatic phrase, Budd Schulberg's *What Makes Sammy Run?*:

> So I switched to my sociological approach."Sammy," I began wisely, "society isn't just a bunch of individuals living alongside of each other. As a member of society, man is interdependent. Not independent, Sammy, interdependent. Life is too complex for there to be any truth in the old slogan of every man for himself. We share the benefits of social institutions, like take hospitals, the cops and garbage collection. Why, the art of conversation itself is a social invention. We can't live in this world like a lot of cannibals trying to swallow each other. Learn to give the other fellow a break and we'll *all* live longer."[48]

What Makes Sammy Run? was first published in 1941, four years after *The Structure of Social Action* in which Talcott Parsons named the "problem of order" as the fundamental theoretical problem of sociology, identified Hobbes as the first thinker to formulate it explicitly, and proposed his own "voluntaristic theory of action" with its stress on autonomous normative values restraining egoism as a solution to it. Conceivably Schulberg, who graduated from Dartmouth in 1936, had been exposed to some of Parsons's ideas in undergraduate sociology courses taught by former students or colleagues of Parsons who had heard them from him before the publication of his first and still most influential book.[49] It seems, to put it mildly, a bit unlikely that the book was widely read in Hollywood, where Schulberg worked as a scriptwriter after his graduation—not the sort of reading matter likely to be found gracing Beverly Hills coffee tables. More probably, Schulberg's identification of the "sociological approach" with the assertion of a common interest in rules restraining individual selfishness was already general intellectual currency long before Parsons. One recalls that Schulberg was for a few years a member of the Communist Party, which was influential in the movie colony during this period, and Marxism, of course, is a kind of sociology and a notoriously anti-individualistic one.

So is classical conservatism. The first two books to be published in the United States with the word "sociology" in their titles were written in the decade before the Civil War by Southern defenders of slavery and drew heavily on the anti-individualist and anticapitalist thought of the French Counter-Enlightenment.[50] The author of one of them, Henry Hughes, had on a visit to France met Auguste Comte himself,[51] whose debt to the reactionaries de Bonald and de Maistre he always acknowledged, although he did not share their passionate longing for a restoration of the *ancien régime*. Hughes's better-known contemporary, George Fitzhugh, defended the doomed institutions of the Old South against the dehumanizing rapacity of expanding Northern and world capitalism.[52]

If defenders of slavery against free labor like Fitzhugh often seemed to speak in Marxist accents,[53] contemporary "Western" Marxists frequently sound like classical conservatives when they deplore the erosion of community, the destruction of nature, and the nihilism of the "instrumental rationality" they attribute to capitalism.[54] A disposition to regard capitalist market relations and bourgeois individualism as historical aberrations is shared by traditionalist conservatives and Marxists, the former viewing them as transitory departures from the stable hierarchical societies of the past, the latter as a stage to be superseded by the socialist and ultimately communist social order of the future. The historical relativization of the problem of order is congruent with both conservative and Marxist sentiments: The problem of order is essentially the problem of a competitive liberal market society; it reflects the inclinations of "bourgeois man" rather than of human nature in general. Macpherson's Marxist interpretation of Hobbes is, in fact, a development of Leo Strauss's earlier thesis that *Leviathan* is essentially an attempt to provide grounding for a new bourgeois moral philosophy.[55] Strauss, far from being a Marxist, was a natural law conservative, finding the greatest wisdom in the ancients and highly critical of all modern political creeds whether bourgeois or nonbourgeois. In Strauss's later work on natural right, he treated Hobbes, Locke, and Rousseau as the major figures in the liberal tradition of absolutizing the rights of the individual over and against the claims of the "public" realm.[56] Hannah Arendt, who resembled Strauss in her veneration for classical thinkers and her antimodernism, described Hobbes as "the only great philosopher to whom the bourgeoisie can rightly and exclusively lay claim."[57]

THE NORMATIVE SOLUTION

Once belief in a preestablished harmony among individuals, whether grounded in divine commandment, natural law, or innate biological disposition, lost all credibility, the problem of order inevitably became at least an implicit issue in social theory. To Parsons, Hobbes's war of all against all is defined by the absence of common ends combined with the freedom of individuals to use any and all means in pursuit of their separate—"discrete and unrelated"—ends; since power over others achieved through the use of force or fraud is "the most immediately efficient means," continual conflict is inescapable. Parsons acknowledged that Locke's version of the state of nature characterized by a "natural identity of interests," in Élie Halévy's choice phrase, was "factually the more nearly right" compared to Hobbes's version. However, Locke was "right but gave wrong reasons"[58] in failing to articulate "his implicit normative assumptions," whereas Hobbes's rigorous consistency enabled him to demonstrate not only that a society without common norms and values was impossible, even a contradiction in terms, but that such a condition would inevitably lead to every man's hand being raised against his neighbor. Parsons does not mention at all Rousseau's nonsocial but pacific conception of the state of nature. The problem of order is totally identified with the avoidance of a war of all against all.

Since Parsons named the Hobbesian problem of order, it often seems to be inseparably linked to his normative solution to it: the institutionalization of a common value-system proscribing resort to force and fraud and creating ultimate ends held in common. Parsons gave short shrift to Hobbes's own solution, the enforcement of order by a sovereign state monopolizing the use of force, without actually denying that it might make some contribution to order. A standard criticism of Parsons has, of course, charged him with unduly minimizing the role of force in society. Parsons also criticized at greater length the Lockean solution to the problem of order, the emergence of mutually beneficial exchange relations among individuals, in striving to differentiate the conceptual focus of sociology from that of classical economics. Parsons, in contrast to the writers who relativize the problem of order by treating it as a reflection or anticipation of bourgeois society, not only saw the problem as universal but insisted that his normative solution was also necessarily universal because it was by far the primary, if not the only, solution possible. If he was right to regard the problem as universal, it does not follow that different, historically variable, combinations of the Hobbesian stress on force, the Lockean assumption of complementary individual interests, and the Durkheim-Parsons emphasis on common values might not succeed in maintaining social order.[59]

If the problem of order arises out of the necessity of taming or eliminating motivations and actions that lead to conflict, it represents at least a special case of the larger "age-old question" or "classic debate" about the relation of "the" individual and society.[60] How are individuals shaped and controlled to avoid destructive conflict? How and to what degree are individuals socialized, in the language of contemporary sociologists? More broadly, the physical and mental discreteness of individuals, their separability as distinct entities in both reality and thought, makes the question of how they succeed in combining and coordinating their activities to maintain enduring common enterprises inherently problematic. But this also applies to species of social insects, as Hobbes himself fully recognized. He argued that bees and ants differ from human beings in that the absence among them of conflict is "Naturall," whereas the suppression of conflict among men "is by Covenant only, which is Artificiall."[61] Hobbes's frequent insistence on the "artificiality" of the obligations of men toward one another can be read as a recognition that human society is largely a product of what we today call "culture" rather than of nature.

That human nature, whether innate or acquired, contains impulses and passions that lead to conflict among individuals, often with deadly results, was, of course, recognized long before the beginnings of modern social theory. The conflict between man's disposition to original sin and his responsiveness to divine command was central to Christianity. Some recent interpreters of Hobbes have argued that he was restating in nontheological language an essentially Christian view of natural law governing man's conduct in society, but Quentin Skinner has shown that such an interpretation is utterly discrepant with how Hobbes's contemporaries understood him.[62] There is in any case nothing peculiarly Christian or even Western in the idea that humans have a general inclination both to oppose and to cooperate with their fellows and to feel both love and hate toward them. Note the Islamic saying that seems to echo Hobbes himself: "Sixty years of tyranny are better than one hour of civil strife."[63] If divine commandment, Aristotelian entelechy or telos, natural law or innate biological disposition have often been invoked to account for the palpable fact that men do establish secure and highly valued social bonds, the existence of a "negative element"[64] offering resistance to the stability and continuity of society is at least tacitly acknowledged when actual or potential conflict between individual impulses and social imperatives has been treated as rooted in human nature as such.

Hobbes elevated this negative element to a position of equality with the forces conducive to the formation of social attachments. It has long been argued that he attributed primacy rather than equality to man's hostile and antisocial tendencies, thus making it less than credible that men constituted as Hobbes described them could ever through their own efforts have escaped from a state of nature in which a war of all against all prevailed. Hobbes can indeed be considered as having held an undersocialized conception of human nature. Yet his view anticipates in several respects Freud's more complex theory of nearly three centuries later and, in contrast to vulgar Darwinists and Nietzscheans, his combination of the socializing and antisocial elements of human nature gives weight to both elements and to their interaction in the creation and maintenance of human society.[65]

In addition, Hobbes's emphasis on scarcity as a constant in the human situation makes him more than simply an anatomist of human nature. J. L. Mackie, one of the most recent contributors to the analysis of ethical reasoning as developed by British analytic philosophers, has contended that morality itself must be seen as an attempt to solve the problem of "limited resources and limited sympathies [which] together generate both competition leading to conflict and an absence of what would be mutually beneficial cooperation."[66] Mackie sees Hobbes as a major forerunner of this view, which locates in the human condition the necessity of "inventing right and wrong," the subtitle of Mackie's book. The problem of order arises out of the dual circumstance that human beings have limited (though not nonexistent) capacities for sympathy with their fellows and that they inhabit an environment that fails to provide them with sufficient resources to satisfy fully the needs of all of them. The problem of order is therefore a genuinely transhistorical problem rooted in inescapable conflict between the interests and desires of individuals and the requirements of society: to wit, the pacification of violent strife among men and the secure establishment of cooperative social relations making possible the pursuit of collective goals.

CHAPTER THREE

ORDER AS REGULARITY AND AS RULE

The "problem of order" has come to be widely recognized as a major, often as *the* major, perennial issue of social theory. The phrase has become commonplace to such an extent that its meaning is often blurred and broadened to the point of vacuity. Frequently, it is used so generally that it effaces the difference between the social and natural sciences, both of which presuppose a world of orderliness or uniformity as a necessary condition for the acquisition of reliable and useful knowledge. "Order" *means* regularity, predictability, and system as opposed to randomness, chance, and chaos. All science, even all intellectual inquiry, both implies belief in orderliness and seeks to establish its specific forms in different object domains. The social sciences are in no way distinctive in this respect. It is otiose therefore to identify the problem of order in human society with the search for regularities and recurrences, for at this general level the problem applies to the study of stars, atoms, chemical compounds, or organisms as much as to the understanding of human beings and the groups, societies, and cultures they create. The claim is often made that the social sciences find it harder to discover regularities because their subject matter is vastly more complex and open to the influence of many more "variables" than the subject matter of the natural sciences. But if this is true, the problem of order then differs only in degree, in its greater magnitude, in the social sciences as compared to the natural sciences. Greater complexity does not imply anything qualitatively peculiar to human societies as such.

Talcott Parsons named the "problem of order" the fundamental theoretical problem of sociology and identified Thomas Hobbes as the first thinker to formulate it explicitly. He did not equate order with the existence of regularities in human conduct similar to the regularities reported by the natural sciences, but rather defined social order substantively as the absence of universal conflict among individuals maintaining social relations with each other, as the inversion or contrary, in effect, of the Hobbesian "war of all against all." Parsons explicitly noted that conflict among individuals might conform to a "factual order" exhibiting uniformities permitting an observer to make reliable generalizations and predictions. He stressed the difference between such a factual order and "normative order," that is, order resulting from the common observance by individuals of shared rules by which they govern their conduct. Such a normative order also constitutes a reliable factual order insofar as its rules are generally lived up to in behavior, but a factual order might exist in the absence of normative order.[1]

The most familiar criticism of Parsons has always been that in accounting for social order he gave insufficient weight both to the domination of some by others and to the rational adjustments of their interests negotiated by individuals and groups as against the overriding priority he ascribed to the presence within a group of normative consensus, of shared values and moralities, profoundly shaping its members' conduct. Yet such a criticism of Parsons's preferred resolution of the problem of order in no way reduces it to no more than the precondition for the discovery of scientific laws that permit predictive (or retrodictive) statements. Parsons's major aim in *The Structure of Social Action* was the more specific one of affirming the autonomy of human ends or purposes, and the impossibility of reducing them to the dictates of biology or the directly imposed constraints of the external nonhuman environment. The freedom to choose or create goals and affirm values was primary to Parsons, hence his choice of the "voluntaristic theory of action" to designate his conception of the basic subject matter of social science. By "voluntaristic' Parsons did not mean "free will" exercised by individuals but the collective choice and institutionalization of goals and norms undetermined by biology or the natural environment. His position therefore does not exclude a cultural or social determinism.[2] It can be argued that Parsons ties his view of human action, defined by its teleological and voluntary character, too closely to his normative resolution of the problem of order, at times virtually conflating two quite separate theoretical issues.[3] But this criticism actually presupposes Parsons's recognition of the nonreducibility of the problem of order to the mere presence or absence of regularities in human actions and interactions.

The familiar claim that human affairs are more complex and variable than natural processes is both unclear and doubtfully true. But even if true, it does not necessarily follow from it that human actions are invariably less predictable than presumptively simpler nonhuman events. Human actions are often quite evidently more repetitive and predictable than some natural processes—the notorious uncertainties plaguing meteorology are the standard example. To refute the idea that human conduct is so variable and capricious as to pose an obstacle to the discovery of the regularities that are the *sine qua non* of science, Robert K. Merton used to gesture toward the class in front of him and exclaim "Consider the miracle that you are all here!" This was intended to be a dramatic refutation of the notion that their possession of "free will" made the actions of human beings unpredictable; obviously, the fact that everyone present was able to count on the appearance of Merton himself and at least most of the students at exactly the same time and place each week for a specified number of months was evidence of prodigious feats of precise and successful prediction indicating a degree of orderliness in human conduct equaling if not exceeding that reported by the so-called exact sciences.

Merton, a brilliant teacher, wished to impress vividly upon his students the uncharted possibilities of sociology. Accordingly, he did not go on to point out that the "miracle" of our mutually predicted collective presence in the classroom depended in no way whatever on the achievements of social science. His example might just as plausibly have been invoked to argue that since such extraordinary results could be achieved without it, "Who needs social science?" The charge that sociology does no more than proclaim the obvious, that it merely tells us in polysyllabic language what everyone already knows, has always been a much more devastating argument against its scientific pretensions than the wistful belief that free will is a guarantee of unforeseen and possibly liberating eruptions in human conduct. "Astonish me!" is one of our major expectations of "real" science, as Stuart Hampshire has noted.[4] The failure of sociology to live up to what Anthony Giddens has called the "revelatory model" of the natural sciences[5] has been a persistent reason for doubting its scientific status, both within and outside of the discipline. The purported technical language of social scientists is often ridiculed as a pathetic aping of the specialized language of natural science in a vain effort to borrow from its prestige, as well as a strategic concealment of the fact that little is being said that could not be expressed just as precisely in ordinary language reflecting the "common sense" of someone quite untutored in the social sciences.

Such complaints used to be the special province of outside critics and debunkers of the claims of the social sciences—"men of affairs," the clergy, literary intellectuals, professors of the humanities. More recently, they have become widespread among social scientists themselves as "positivism" has fallen into disfavor and been assailed from a variety of perspectives within the social science disciplines. Antipositivists, unfortunately, are not noticeably inclined to use simpler, less specialized, or more precise language. Their preoccupations have usually been epistemological or methodological to just as great an extent as those of the programmatic positivists of whom a French physicist and philosopher of science once famously complained that they always seemed to be packing a suitcase for a journey on which they never set out.

It is obviously legitimate to invoke the predictability of everyday human conduct in order to make an epistemological point in the manner of Merton. But even the most ardent and naive believer in the unity of natural and social science would hardly put forward the successful predictions we make as a matter of course in everyday life as candidates for the status of social laws methodologically comparable to the laws formulated by natural scientists. These predictions depend for the most part on the intentional acts of individuals striving to realize their various purposes. As Giddens remarks, mentioning stopping at traffic lights as an example, "The fact that such examples are not talked of as laws, even though the behavior involved is very regular, indicates that the problem of laws in social science is very much bound up with unintended consequences, unacknowledged conditions and constraint."[6]

Yet apart from the strictly epistemological significance of the existence of regularities in human conduct, it is worth examining further the fact, whether it is regarded as miraculous or not, that people manage routinely to make successful predictions about one another in ordinary social life. Reflection on the predictability of human conduct can lead to a consideration of the problem of order that synthesizes order as regularity and order as rule, or factual and normative order in Parsons's terms.

When people predict that classes will be held at regular times and places, that the buses will run and follow fixed routes, that stores will be open for commerce in the daytime, and that cars will stop at red lights, these predictions are scarcely less reliable than the predictions made by the same people that the sun will rise in the east, the flowers will bloom in the spring, water will flow downhill and produce steam when boiled. Their predictions about human conduct, however, are based (at least in the examples given and in many others that might have been) on assumptions about intentional acts carried out by individual human beings. Society is constituted by an immense series of interlocking intentional acts performed by a multitude of people. Social order is nothing more than this series.

The sociological observer's account of what is happening in social interaction necessarily includes reference to the predictions in the minds of the actors under observation. This is what distinguishes it from physical science whose objects do not themselves make predictions about their own behavior.[7] All social theories are necessarily theories about theories, interpretations of interpretations, predictions or expectations of predictions or expectations.[8] If the social world of the actors is unknown to the social scientist's audience, the audience may find the social scientist's account genuinely "revelatory" or even "astonishing," as in the case of early ethnographic reports emphasizing the strange, bizarre, esoteric practices of primitive tribes. If the audience is familiar, however, with the social world presented by the social scientist, it may find the description less than enlightening and even see it as an "elaboration of the obvious." Hence the greater skepticism so often displayed toward the claims of sociology in contrast to those of anthropology and history.

The crucial point is that the predictability of social life does not represent or reflect an order discovered by the social scientist, but "is in many of its aspects made to happen by social actors; it does not happen in spite of the reasons they have for their conduct."[9] Social order is to a considerable degree the conscious creation of those who exhibit and sustain it. For all of his insistence on the necessity of taking into account the point of view of the actor, it may be that Parsons, as Schutz contended,[10] was too disposed to use a standard set of what he saw as objective categories to describe the subjective orientation of the actors; he stopped short therefore of fully explicating just how order is generated, or "socially constructed," out of the interacting subjectivities of a plurality of actors.

THE DUALITY OF EXPECTATIONS

There is an ambiguity in the use of the term expectation that is not present in prediction. The former term brings out the jointly created character of ongoing social interaction in a way that the latter does not. In one sense, expectation is no more than a synonym for prediction or anticipation. The phrase "anticipated reactions" has figured prominently in conceptual analysis of a particular form of social interaction, namely, that involving unequal power relations between the actors.[11] We expect the class to be held on schedule, stores to be closed on holidays, and so on, just as we expect it to turn cold in the winter, a full moon to be visible once a month, and the like. In both cases, we successfully predict or correctly anticipate certain recurring events, certain regularities and uniformities in the behavior of various objects in different reqions of our world. The ambiguity of expectation becomes apparent only when we consider its use in communications such as that of a mother telling her child that she "expects" obedience at school to the teacher, or of the admiral addressing the fleet who affirms that "England expects every man to do his duty."[12]

The mother and the admiral are not simply predicting out loud future events of common interest, as they would be in announcing that they expected it to rain tomorrow. Their utterances to the child and to the assembled fleet are in the imperative mode: the expectations asserted are intended to bring about the conduct they claim to be anticipating. One might interpret these assertions as threats veiled by being expressed as expectations, as "mere" predictions of future events. The child, after all, knows, and the mother knows the child knows, that disobedience at school will be reported at home and lead to possibly unpleasant results. The sailors are fully aware that the harsh code of the British navy ensures they will be severely punished, perhaps even with death, should they fail to do their duty. Obviously, the mother and the admiral occupy dominant or superordinate positions in power relationships vis-a-vis the child and the sailors of the fleet. But it would be a mistake to regard their expressed expectations as nothing but thinly veiled threats. Nelson's address to the fleet before Trafalgar is commonly regarded as having been inspirational rather than threatening. The mother's tone of voice may be prideful or admonitory. Despite the unequal power relationship, the expectations communicated may be regarded less as threats than as efforts at what Parsons called the "activation of commitments,"[13] that is, as moral appeals or exhortations.

Indeed, since an expectation that is communicated is often an attempt to influence or control the behavior of another person, it may exemplify any of the diverse forms of influence or power ranging from the unambiguously coercive utterance of a threat to an effort to persuade within an entirely reciprocal and egalitarian relationship between two actors. Or the pronounced expectation may be a blend combining elements of coercion, appeal to duty, and rational persuasion.[14] The crucial point is that the stated expectation is not a mere prediction of occurrences that are seen as bound to take place in any event but an intentional effort to *make happen* or bring about certain behavior by other persons as a result of influencing their minds and wills. The verbalized expectation might be regarded as a prophecy that is intended to be self-fulfilling, in contrast to one that produces effects on the behavior of those who hear or learn of it that were unintended and unforeseen by the prophet as in Merton's well-known discussion.[15] In any case, the warranted predictions of everyday social life that create and constitute a stable social order are quite different from similarly routine predictions about the physical world insofar as the former are the products of the reciprocal awareness and interacting intentions of social actors.

But the attempt of some actors to exercise power over others by making known to them their expectations so that these may operate as concealed imperatives is only a special or polar case of a more general phenomenon. I have chosen to stress a certain ambiguity in the use of the term "expectation," not primarily in order to call attention to power relations among persons, but rather to bring out the much more general circumstance that awareness of the expectations of others in itself may provide these expectations with a normative aura, may serve to endow them with an imperative character that constrains the actor who is conscious of them to fulfill or conform to them.[16] Expectations may in this sense possess self-fulfilling properties even if those who hold them are innocent of any intent to wield power or to impose their will on others. The power of the group over the individual, of the Many over the One, through the effective psychological medium of what George Herbert Mead called the "generalized other," is usually more ubiquitous and more successful in inducing conformity than the efforts of particular persons to control the conduct of others. The rule of expectations in this broad sense is basic to the achievement of social order.

Durkheim said—seemingly at variance with his earlier insistence on the "thing-like" character of "social facts"—that society exists only in the minds of its component individuals. In order to rid my students of their tendency to regard "society" as a substantial entity rather than as a process or a fluctuating set of events unevenly distributed in space and time, I used to pose the question of whether society could be said to exist at all at three o'clock in the morning when nearly everyone was asleep. Or, with reference to specific social structures, in what sense does Congress still exist when it is not in session, or New York University during Christmas vacation? My conclusion was that society, as well as the particular social formations in question, existed on such occasions only in latent form, or dispositionally, as the expectations individuals held about one another's actions in particular circumstances, whether those circumstances were immediately present or not, expectations that past experience had generally shown to be warranted.

Society is nothing but a web of social relations that is constantly being spun, broken, and spun again, invariably (unlike a spider's web) in slightly different form. Society is not only its members' expectations, though they are all it may be when everyone is asleep or when the members of a group or collectivity are temporarily dispersed. But society should also be understood as including the actual interactions shaped by the expectations of the participants; it is therefore something more than simply an idea in the minds of its members. Society is both the web that is spun and the expectations out of which it is spun. The web is made of flimsy gossamer, "merely" mental stuff, yet, as we well know, it binds like chains of steel, often with a power and force equal to that of laws of nature, as Durkheim recognized in his famous identification of social facts with "exteriority and constraint," that social facts are both external to the individual just like physical facts and that he or she is similarly forced to take them into account when acting.

Nevertheless, the insubstantial, evanescent, here-one-moment-gone-the-next attributes of the social order induce the sense of its fragility that plagues anxious conservatives and lends initial plausibility to the utopian fantasies of radicals envisaging its reconstitution along utterly different lines as a result of an instantaneous, overnight "change of heart." The resonance of the phrase "social construction of reality" to young sociologists influenced by protest movements of the left in the 1960s stemmed from its suggestion of the vulnerability of the social order to radical change even though the two writers chiefly associated with the phrase were conservatives strongly disposed to emphasize the human "need for order."[17] One recalls also the awareness of the apparently transient character of social existence possessed by statesmen and bankers who build (or at least used to) unusually massive and solid buildings in which to carry on their institutional activities.

Expectations may, I have argued, function as imperatives, as normative demands constraining the human objects of expectation to conform to them. This is most obviously true of expectations that reflect explicit, articulated rules, such as stopping at red lights, wearing clothes in public, and eating at specified times and places. As expectations that guide and constrain action, these exemplify what sociologists call "social norms." They have been previously formulated by the actors as rules, or symbolized models of conduct, in advance of the situations in which they regulate action; their status as rules may also be invoked retrospectively by the actors as "reasons" for having so acted. But what of nonverbalized expectations existing only at the level of inarticulate awareness?[18] Are they also to be considered social norms even though they are not transmitted through prior instruction or exhortation, nor stated explicitly to explain, justify, or account for action afterward? Such expectations are unmistakably part of Goffman's "interaction order,"[19] without necessarily belonging to a coherent normative order consisting of an articulated set of rules.

The ubiquity of such situationally rooted or context-bound expectations in social life explains why direct social observation, or even active participation, is often necessary in order to understand a social world; one cannot rest content with simply asking people why they act as they do, let alone with consulting a formal rulebook should one exist. The subtle interplay of tacit understandings and nonverbalized expectations in face-to-face encounters endows social life with its varied and spontaneous character, its quality, except in special cases such as ritual behavior, of never being completely reducible to a manifestation of pregiven cultural patterns reflecting standardized norms and roles. Recent microsociological perspectives in sociology have often originated in protests against the implicit determinism of approaches that appear to regard preexisting norms, roles, or value-patterns as entirely capable of accounting for most concrete social behavior. Such views have stressed not the randomness or unpredictability of behavior supposedly subject only to the free will of its agent, but rather the particularized, context-specific nature of mutual expectations and their emergence and openness to *ad hoc* adjustments within the course of interaction itself. The pattern of interaction is seen as self-determining rather than as predetermined by the norms, values, and role-expectations brought to it by the actors.

Expectations approximate to norms when they are perceived by actors sensitized to them as imperatives imposing limits on choice and action. Clearly, action subject to such constraints is "rule-governed"—guided by mental models of possible actions— in the Wittgensteinian sense; it may even possess the force of obligation, of "oughtness," associated with full-fledged moral norms. If this is true of the actor conforming to expectations, it also applies to the actor who conveys, albeit inarticulately, his expectations to another. The expectations so communicated may be normatively weighted in that failure of the other to live up to them will induce at least some irritation or even moral disapproval on the part of the communicator.[20]

All concepts pertaining to human actions and interactions are efforts to make distinctions between matters of degree, to identify variations that are continuous rather than discrete. At one pole, the expectations that actors both hold and orient themselves to in interaction are capable of full statement by any of them. The other pole is that of unthinking, reflex-like habits, exemplified by interaction exhibiting the "corpse-like obedience" that the old Prussian army strove to instill in its recruits. The continuum runs from conscious adherence to clear-cut norms to the sheer automatism of "blind" habit.

STABLE AND CHANGING EXPECTATIONS

Habits develop in interaction that involve neither reflex-like obedience to commands nor conscious conformity to formal rules, but that emerge from the complex, subtle, often nonverbal and not fully conscious adaptations of people to one another. Such habits become expectations when actors acquire a tacit awareness of them with the result that they constrain the conduct of participants in interaction. If "social norms" are to be equated with rules capable of explicit statement by the actors, then the expectations that arise concerning habits emerging and crystallizing in the course of repeated interactions might be regarded as *latent norms*. Conversely, norms that are effective in guiding and constraining action are necessarily embodied in expectations that in turn are converted into actual behavior. The continuum from habits to expectations to articulated norms can be explored conceptually from either end.

Social conduct that conforms to well-understood norms, conduct that is "patterned," as it is sometimes put, involves norms capable of explicit formulation governing the situated expectations of actors in interaction, which results in overt behavior in accordance with the norms. Norm, expectation, and action constitute a tight, interlocking unity. There is no conflict or divergence between the normative order and the factual order. Or, to put it another way, "norm" understood in the purely statistical sense as the modal behavior of group members or incumbents of a role, on the one hand, and "norm" as a rule or standard for behavior proclaimed and affirmed by the group, on the other, are in no way at variance at the level of concrete, observable behavior.

Instead of thinking of habit-expectation-norm as a seamless structured unity of simultaneously present elements or aspects, one might think of it as a sequence emerging in the course of time. Repeated interactions give rise to habits. They are perceived by the actors and become expectations in the sense of predictions or anticipations of behavior. Aware of what is expected by the other, each actor feels constrained to live up to the expectation, partly out of a feeling that the other will be irritated, offended, or disappointed if the expectation is not fulfilled. In short, interaction generates habits; perceived, they become reciprocal expectations; in addition to their purely predictive and anticipatory nature, sensitivity to them endows them with a constraining or even an obligatory character. This entire process is in no sense willed or even fully foreseen by either party. It is a *sui generis* resultant of their recurrent situated interaction. Whatever the needs, motives, and interests underlying this interaction, its continuation has precipitated mutually binding sets of expectations. Thus do norms grow in unplanned fashion out of ongoing interaction.

This sequence of habits becoming expectations that acquire normative force as a result of the actors feeling constrained to live up to them describes how norms originate within the process of social interaction. One might say that interaction among human beings sensitized to one another's expectations precipitates norms as "naturally" as contact between moving physical bodies creates friction. Human beings are able to perceive the particularities of a situation and the novelty and change, it may exhibit. By altering their behavior in response to perceived particularity, novelty, and change they are able to generate new expectations with the potentiality of becoming new norms. Thus the possibility of change is inherent in human interaction. Obviously, no two individuals or situations are entirely alike, and new and problematic circumstances inevitably arise for which predefined rules are inadequate. But particularity and novelty make a difference only because human beings are capable of perceiving them and attaching significance to them.

The emphasis of such sociologists as Herbert Blumer and many of his fellow "symbolic interactionists" is on spontaneity, processs, and innovation as intrinsic to interaction. Their polemical orientation is directed against sociologists who stress "role-taking" over "role-making," conformity to preexisting rules over improvisation and negotiation: "It is the social process in group life that creates and upholds the rules, not the rules that create and uphold group life," in Blumer's words.[21] Other sociologists have chosen to stress how expectations created or produced in the course of interaction react back upon interaction when it recurs, giving it form, stability, and predictability. For centuries thinkers have imagined a state of nature, well before that seventeenth-century term came into use, in which men were thrown together unencumbered by any cultural and institutional baggage. The Robinson Crusoe experience and variations on it, the idea of one or more persons finding themselves castaways in an

utterly new and unfamiliar environment, has long had a hold on
the Western imagination. The attraction of such conceptions has
often derived from the belief that such situations reveal man's
"original nature" divested of the superstructure resulting from
life in a particular society with its distinctive historical culture.[22]
But sometimes the focus of interest has been on the process
whereby new norms, institutions, and cultures adapted to the
specificities of the new environment are created and perpetuated
by castaways or refugees from "civilization." Peter Berger and
Thomas Luckmann, for example, in their influential *The Social
Construction of Reality*, make ample use (with a considerable
touch of whimsy) of the desert island scenario in attempting to
show just how recurrent interaction creates expectations—or
"typifications" in their terminology—that then become articulated, transmitted to new members of the group such as children
born into it, and elaborated in the form of mythological legitima-
tions with all sorts of ritual and ceremonial embellishments as in
rites de passage, funeral ceremonies, and the worship of gods
seen as mandating existing norms and institutions. Berger and
Luckmann's interest is not so much in the flux of interaction
itself as in the way in which the purely subjective consciousnesses
of the actors are externalized in action and ultimately objectified
in a stable institutional order consisting of rules and roles which
the actors themselves, especially those who are initiated into the
order without having been "present at the creation," eventually
perceive as a massive, objective, powerfully constraining external
reality.

   The process by which interaction creates new expectations
with the potentiality of becoming explicit norms must be regarded as one that occurs continuously in the most ordinary recurrent
experiences of everyday life. It is not a process confined to dra-
matically new situations for which established expectations and
norms provide no orientation; not, that is, a process, the understanding of which primarily illuminates the social origins of the
normative order that finally confronts each separate individual as
an imposing set of constraints limiting, channeling, and sometimes directly prescribing his or her choices and decisions. Berger
and Luckmann are fundamentally concerned with institutional-

ization, with how a stable, apparently solid, collective order of norms and roles is nevertheless produced by the intersecting intentional actions of individuals, of women and men working out adaptations to each other in the various circumstances in which they find themselves. Blumer and his symbolic interactionist followers, on the other hand, are not so much concerned with the construction of a stable social order as with emphasizing the indeterminacy, fluidity, and context-specific nature of social interaction itself, which they see as transcending any established order, or at least as possessing qualities that are virtually independent of an order's necessarily abstract and schematic rules for conduct. Obviously, total contingency and novelty would amount to the negation of any order, a denial of the regularity and predictability of human action itself. The insistence by some microsociologists on the spontaneous, improvised character of much interaction scarcely intends to go so far: it is essentially a protest against the abstract, mechanistic overtones of "normative determinism"[23] regarded as implicit in the approaches of Parsons and other normativist theorists.

The emergence of expectations-cum-norms out of recurrent interaction is a process that goes on all the time, if often in trivial and evanescent ways. Two persons meet and establish a relationship that may be brief and casual, or intimate and of a lifetime's duration. They develop expectations about one another based on their unique individual biographies. The relationship indeed is essentially constituted by the special mutual understandings and expectations that develop, although the bulk of them remain inarticulate, existing at the level of practical or active rather than discursive consciousness. To describe such expectations, grounded as they are in the particularities of personal relationships, as latent norms may sound odd, for they do not survive the termination of such a relationship nor do they have any relevance to persons other than the particular individuals forming the relationship. Apart from the individuals themselves, only novelists and psychoanalysts are likely to explore in depth the intricate bonds and fulfillments of personal relations and they are able to do so precisely because of their relative detachment from them. Yet the process by which mutual expectations crystallize and come to constrain the interacting individuals takes place in even the most limited and unstable personal relationship. "It takes two to make a quarrel," as they say, or to sustain a relationship based on enmity. The production of expectations-cum-norms occurs wherever individuals engage in recurrent interaction. The hypothesis of a desert island or a state of nature is a useful intellectual device for isolating and highlighting how the process of norm-creation or institutionalization takes place. And it may be especially useful as a corrective to ahistorical, hyperstructural theoretical approaches that assume the presence of norms, roles, and institutions as given and proceed to treat them as the prime shapers of human action and human nature without reference to the fact that they are also themselves products of human action and human nature. But the precipitation of expectations that become constraining out of recurrent social interaction goes on constantly around us.

Usually it is of little permanent consequence even for those directly involved. Suppose two young male students away from home for the first time attending a residential college meet at a freshman social event. Lonely and disoriented, they agree to go to the movies together the following Saturday night. They repeat the experience for several weeks in succession. Then one of them is offered a "blind date" with a female. He eagerly accepts, but reflects that he will have to break his movie date with his friend, that is, violate what has become an established expectation in their little society of two. No doubt he will have slight compunction about doing so, but he will be sensitive enough to his friend's expectation to feel obliged to express his regrets, conceivably to suggest that he ask his female date if she has an available friend. The simple habit of going to the movies together once a week has become an expectation that carries with it at least the minimal constraint implied by the felt obligation to offer an explanation and apology if the expectation is to be broken.[24] The example is of surpassing triviality; the point, however, is that such cases of expectations becoming latent norms are universal, though lasting only as long as the particular relationship in which they develop among the multitude of dyads and small groups that are constantly forming and dissolving in the midst of life in society.

Occasionally, expectations thrown up in the course of interaction turn out to be nascent rather than merely latent norms. That is, they prove durable to the point of achieving successful institutionalization, understanding by this term the maintenance and perpetuation of expected conduct by persons other than the persons who originally created it. Doubtless this is more likely to happen in the case of small groups than isolated dyads. There is a continuum from emergent expectations that die with the dissolution of the relationship or group within which they developed through deliberate but less than successful efforts to perpetuate them by transmission to new members who may be actively recruited, to more or less full institutionalization attaining its complete form in intergenerational continuity.

There is a good example of the intermediate case in one of the most famous ethnographic community studies of American sociology, William Foote Whyte's *Street Corner Society.*[25] Whyte observed a group of unemployed Italian-American young men who congregated on the same street corner in Cambridge, Massachusetts, and participated together in various recreational activities. The group at one point named itself after Norton Street, its preferred locale; adopted colors and a partial uniform for team sports; found a clubhouse in which to meet regularly; and created a set of formal elective offices—president, vice president, secretary-treasurer. Some effort was made to recruit new members; it was hoped that the now-organized group would continue in existence if and when its founding members became inactive. This did not happen, for, as Whyte makes plain, the group, its regular activities, and its unity and cohesiveness were essentially products of the Depression years of the 1930s when its members were blocked by unemployment from conventional jobs, marriages, and careers.

For an example of successful institutionalization, consider a group of students away from home at university who solve their living arrangements by renting an apartment or a house together, pooling their expenses, and dividing up various housekeeping tasks according to the skills and preferences of the members of the group. When one of them graduates, a replacement is recruited from the larger student body. A new lease is signed and soon there has been a complete turnover of membership. More time passes, a house is purchased, a name for the establishment is chosen, the division of housekeeping chores becomes a set of offices with fixed names, members compete with other similar residential groups to attract new students, financial bequests, and, perhaps, in various games, sports, and scholarly competitions as well. Oxford and Cambridge colleges, and at a later date American Greek-letter fraternities, had their humble beginnings in efforts to cope with the elementary material needs of youthful students away from their homes for purposes of education.[26] They were not created by design at a particular moment in time but evolved to their eventual more-or-less stable form in the course of several generations, even centuries in the case of the Oxbridge colleges. Norms and institutions usually originate and evolve this way, eternal and overpowering though they may appear to those subject to their authority.

These examples of degrees of institutionalization do not involve creation *ex nihilo* as in the desert island case, for the new expectations, norms, and roles emerge against the background of relatively unthinking conformity to a multitude of habitual, fully established patterns of interaction previously learned in the course of socialization. More precisely, new expectations arise and become stable *within* the limits of prescribed norms and roles. Norms and roles do not usually regulate actions in very exact detail; only rituals, rules of etiquette, and perhaps some bureaucratic regulations do that. So, of course, does acting on the stage, which is why the use of the theatrical metaphor of "role" to refer even to conforming, institutionalized behavior can be misleading: we are not most of the time reading from prepared and previously rehearsed scripts. Rather than detailed prescriptions, norms establish a "zone of conformity" within which considerable variation may be possible well short of transgressing the norm.[27] The looseness of most normative prescriptions makes possible both individual variations in conformity and the occurrence of gradual, initially imperceptible changes in prevailing expectations as to what constitutes sufficient conformity. Much social and cultural change involves a process of drift from a strict, near-literalist pole of conformity to a much more "permissive," less demanding pole. There may also be drifts in the reverse direction, although these are probably less common without conscious determination to bring them about.

Consider yet another commonplace example. The norms and role-expectations governing classroom teaching are thoroughly familiar. A group of students sit in front of a single teacher who addresses them for a prescribed period of time, sometimes calling on the students to answer questions or encouraging them to speak up in turn. Students are expected to remain quiet, to present the appearance of listening to the teacher, and to refrain from obviously distracting "side involvements" (as Goffman calls them). Although these broad prescriptions order the classroom situation, great variations exist between one classroom and another. The content of what is taught obviously varies according to the subject of instruction. Yet however standardized their presentation may be, sticking closely perhaps to a textbook, individual teachers vary in what they select or emphasize. The almost infinite combinatory possibilities of language ensure that every one of us says things, at the level at least of the paragraph and even of individual sentences, that have never been said before.[28]

But variations in social behavior rather than in linguistic content are at issue here. Every class creates its own particular social atmosphere, consisting of a set of expectations that become established after the first few meetings of the class. Does the teacher tolerate interruption? Does she or he actively encourage student participation? Is she or he strict in enforcing the appearance of close attention? Does she or he permit smoking, knitting, adjusting the window or heating, leaving the room briefly, presumably to go to the bathroom? I once had a rather old-fashioned colleague who preferred to teach early in the morning, chose classrooms with a dias and podium, locked the door against latecomers, and, fastening his eyes on a point on the back wall well above the last row of students, proceeded to lecture, brooking no interruptions, until the exact end of the period when he immediately departed without any informal contacts with the students. Once a new student interrupted him to ask a question; he was dumbfounded and the rest of the class tittered.

One might regard this colleague as representing the strict pole of the zone of conformity for the role-expectation of classroom teaching at the university level. Delivering a well prepared formal lecture from a position of eminence that was spatial as well as social to a passive, deferential audience was, of course, the traditional form of university teaching in the nineteenth century and earlier (though not in the very earliest medieval universities). The permissive pole is represented by the encouragement of a maximum of student participation, involving even give-and-take exchanges between teacher and student on a plane of apparent equality, with the group resembling a primary group of equals discussing a subject of common interest in an undirected manner, as opposed to the formalized, hierarchical teacher-student confrontation.

I also remember a new teacher of psychology in a graduate program who wished to apply "group dynamics" principles to the classroom situation: everyone sat around a circular table and talked, exchanges taking place among the students as well as between teacher and students. Several students complained to the dean that they felt they were not receiving their money's worth in being denied the opportunity to learn something from someone of superior knowledge by the conversion of the classroom into an open discussion forum, in which the teacher exercised no authority or even direction and was indeed quite invisible. The drift toward a permissive version of roles and behavior had reached a point where, to the complaining students, the defining rules of classroom teaching itself had disintegrated. "Why this is not a class, it's nothing but a bull session!" one of them might have exclaimed, suddenly arriving at a negative redefinition of the situation. Made public, the redefinition might have led either to reaffirmation of the original, stricter interpretation of teaching and the teacher-student relationship, or to defense and acceptance of the new minimizing of the traditional hierarchical aspects of the relationship.

Sudden awareness of the direction of a process of drift may, as in this example, precipitate a crisis, followed by conflict between those who approve the change and those who want to reverse it and reaffirm the old order. If the change has been slow and evolutionary, the sudden consciousness of it may create a need for public response that might be regarded as equivalent to the development of a "revolutionary situation." In general, newly acquired awareness, or the raising to the level of discursive consciousness of what had previously taken place unreflectively at the level of practical consciousness, is likely to lead to some alteration of the expectations guiding interaction. Whyte remarks of his corner boys, "I made them conscious of the nature of their unreflective behavior. To that extent I changed the situation." He then quotes Doc, his chief informant and the leader of the Norton Street gang, as complaining to him that "You've slowed me up plenty since you've been down here. Now when I do something, I have to think what Bill Whyte would want to know about it and how I can explain it. Before I used to do these things by instinct."[29]

Frequently, blatant deviation from an expectation may be necessary for a group to become aware of the extent to which their conduct has been subject to a latent, previously "unspoken" norm. The latent normative weight of expectations at the level of practice suddenly becomes manifest and articulate. This is perhaps a special case of Durkheim's general proposition that an occasional crime, or dramatic violation of a rule, serves to reaffirm the sanctity and authority of the rule for the community whose moral sentiments are outraged by its flouting. However, awareness of departure from a strict, traditional norm may also lead to the legitimation of a new, looser version of conformity to the norm, or even, sometimes, to its abandonment altogether. Durkheim also noted that the deviation of the criminal made possible the deviation of the innovator by exhibiting the openness to change of the norms upheld by the majority of the community.

In conclusion, social order consists of people's expectations which are, by and large, or most of the time, borne out because other people are aware of them and live up to them. Thus the extraordinary precision-like predictability of the actions of total strangers on which we all rely daily and even hourly. When Weber wrote that a social relation "consists entirely and exclusively in the existence of a probability that there will be a meaningful course of social action," he was not making a quasi-statistical estimate from the standpoint of an objective scientific observer, but was assuming that the estimate of probability—the "expectation"—is made by the actors themselves who are also aware of each other's estimates. Weber may not have spelled this out, but it is clearly implied by his corollary definition of "social action" as "action in which the action of each takes into account that of others and is oriented in these terms."[30]

People, of course, bring to association with others expectations based on past experience and on injunctions, directives, and moral commandments that have been transmitted to them by their parents, teachers, peers, and more remote figures of authority. Interaction is guided by these expectations, but the expectations are themselves products of past interactions. The patterning of expectations by established norms and the modification of norms, including the formation of new ones, in the interplay of changing expectations is a process that goes on constantly. Social reality once constructed does not then impose its order in a uniform way on successive generations unless and until some explosive or implosive force shatters and makes possible its reconstruction. Social order always undergoes minute changes, some of them amounting to no more than the individuality of particular exemplifications of an order which do not survive a single embodiment; some of them setting in motion processes of unidirectional drift that at some point lead to a new and conscious redefinition of the relevant norms, roles, and institutions.

These formulations do little more than enlarge upon the familiar proposition that both order and change are inherent in social life or, more fashionably, that the "production and reproduction of society" is a constant process in which the reproductions never exactly match the original production. Change and reproduction take place within the limits set by order and production, yet over time they may break through the original limits. Completely unprecedented situations (for the people involved) requiring radically new and different responses occur more rarely, as does the total disintegration of an established order resulting in the formation of new expectations that acquire normative weight and eventually become embodied in formal institutions, all originating in what was at the beginning a virtual social vacuum.

THE NEGLECT OF MOTIVATION

The precedinq conception of social order as the product of fulfilled reciprocal expectations that emerge in the course of ongoing social life is consistent with interactionist and phenomenological viewpoints in sociology. So is the emphasis on the ubiquity of variations in the different temporal and spatial manifestations of a stable order and on change as a process inherent in
the inevitably imperfect reproductions of such an order. It
would, however, be a great mistake to regard the above account
as even approximating an adequate explanation of social order,
for there is a huge gaping hole in it, an unexamined assumption
or set of assumptions that reduces it at best to no more than a
description of *how* order is both perpetuated and changed,
falling far short of any answer to the question of *why* order
comes into being in the first place. What is omitted is any discussion of motivation, of the human wants, feelings, and
impulses that undergird and set in motion the whole process of
social interaction out of which relatively stable institutions
develop.[31]

Hobbes's conception of order as problematic because of the
constant threat of a war of all against all was essentially based on
his view of human motivation, of fundamental drives and dispositions rooted in a generically human nature. Unquestionably, his
idea of dominant motives was undersocialized in ignoring the
positive attitudes and affective bonds drawing people together
and uniting them in close and permanent association. Parsons, on
the other hand, put forward an oversocialized conception of
human nature in his resolution of the Hobbesian problem of
order. Hobbes's psychological assumptions may well render it
implausible that the war of all against all could ever be overcome
by such ineradicably egoistic and mutually suspicious human
beings. Parsons's assumptions may, by contrast, so minimize the
inherent tensions and antagonisms among people as to make
questionable the fundamental problematic status he himself
accorded to order.[32] But neither Hobbes nor Parsons[33] glossed
over or bypassed the question of the motivational foundations of
social order.[34]

To acknowledge the rootedness of the problem of order in human nature is not to deny the importance of the interactional processes previously described. But, obviously, if Hobbes was right in contending that "men have no pleasure, (but on the contrary a great deale of griefe) in keeping company, where there is no power able to over-awe them all,"[35] mankind might conceivably be a predominantly solitary rather than a social species and there would be no problem of order because there would be no permanent social order at all, that is, no recurrent patterns of cooperative interaction. (Essentially, this was Rousseau's view of the "state of nature.") The issue of motivation, therefore, of the nature of human nature conceived in motivational and affective terms, cannot be avoided.

Many sociologists confine themselves, implicitly at least, to the cognitive rather than the motivational or emotional aspects of interaction, often making tacit assumptions about the latter or simply taking them for granted. Berger and Luckmann explicitly call their vivid account of how actors construct an objective social world that then confronts and constrains them a contribution to the "sociology of knowledge." Presumably, one may legitimately infer from this claim that their theoretical task is a restricted one that needs to be complemented by a sociology of motivation and emotion, for man is clearly more than just a knower or thinker and society is more than a body of knowledge. In this and other works, Berger often asserts that there is a basic human need for "nomos" (or normative order) as well as a deep-rooted fear and even terror of anomie (or normative chaos).[36] He attributes both the need and the fear to man's "world openness" as a fundamental biological trait requiring humans to find substitutes for the fixed instincts they lack in repetitive, socially created and acquired patterns of behavior. The failure of Berger's social psychology to go much beyond these broad statements, in conjunction with his frequent animadversions on psychoanalysis, leaves him open to the charge of an exclusive concentration on knowledge and beliefs that sustains his own version of an oversocialized conception of man.[37]

Symbolic interactionists and ethnomethodologists also display a cognitivist bias that slights motivation or overlooks it altogether. To ethnomethodologists, the problem of order is essentially epistemological:[38] it has become the problem of overcoming the solipsistic consciousnesses of a plurality of individuals rather than, as for Hobbes and Parsons, the problem of controlling the potentiality for destructive conflicts over scarce resources and the domination of human beings by one another in the service of egoistic goals and motives. One ethnomethodologist has redefined ethnomethodology as "cognitive sociology,"[39] which, like Berger and Luckmann's identification of their theorizing with the sociology of knowledge, suggests the limits of its concerns, for man does not live by cognition alone.

Symbolic interactionism has a longer and more strictly sociological history than the various versions of phenomenological sociology, although it, too, had its origins in a late nineteenth- and early twentieth-century school of philosophy, namely, pragmatism, for which, as for other contemporary philosophies, the problem of knowledge, or epistemology, was of primary importance. The influence on American sociologists of George Herbert Mead has been considerable, but they have often overlooked or minimized the fact that Mead was first and foremost a professional philosopher. Herbert Blumer has been Mead's most influential sociological disciple; it was Blumer who changed Mead's phrase "symbolic communication" to "symbolic interaction," a change that reflects the more general concern of sociologists with human social conduct as such, rather than with the epistemological issue of how language entails the intersubjective communication of meanings. Mead had studied philosophy in Germany at the height of the late nineteenth-century neo-Kantian revival and he was preoccupied with many of the same, primarily epistemological, themes that became central to Husserl's phenomenology.

Immanuel Kant wrote:

> That I am conscious of myself is a thought that already contains a twofold self, the I as subject and the I as object. How it might be possible for the I that I think to be an object (of intuition) for me, one that enables me to distinguish me from myself, is absolutely impossible to explain, even though it is an indubitable fact; it indicates, however, a capacity so elevated above sensuous intuition

that, as the basis for the possibility of understanding, it has the effect of separating us from all animals, for which we have no reason for ascribing the ability to say I to themselves, and results in an infinity of self-constituted representations and concepts. But a double personality is not meant by this double I. Only the I that I think and intuit is a person; the object that belongs to the object that is intuited by me is, similarly to other objects outside myself, a thing.[40]

This is a fairly literal translation from Kant's posthumously published German text.[41] Kant is obviously drawing the distinction between what Mead called the "I" and the "me," or the self as thinking, perceiving, willing subject and as object of perception or cognition. Mead clearly set himself the task of trying to explain what Kant declared was "absolutely impossible to explain": the reflexivity of the self, its splitting into an observing and an observed part.[42]

He found his explanation in the workings of language as a system of symbolic communication. In addition to trying to resolve Kant's problem, Mead was also concerned with refuting contemporary behaviorists who denied that human behavior was different in kind rather than in degree from animal behavior. Mead held that the behavior of the psychologist conditioning the rat to run the maze was not simply a more complex combination of the behavioral capacities present in the rat that were subject to experimental manipulation by the psychologist.[43] Here too, Mead was affirming Kant's insistence that it was the "doubling" or splitting of the self into the perceiving and the perceived "I" that crucially differentiated human cognitive powers from those of all animals. At roughly the same time Talcott Parsons was writing *The Structure of Social Action* as, *inter alia*, a tract against behaviorism. But in contrast to Mead he did not focus on language as a form of social behavior. Mead was prepared to concede more to the behaviorists than Parsons, who essentially produced an upgraded version of traditional Idealist and humanist arguments for what Aristotle called the *differentia specifica* of mankind. Mead agreed with the behaviorists that "mind" had its origins in overt behavior, but contended that a repertory of vocal actions or gestures possessing common meanings to the interacting organisms arose specifically out of human social behavior. Hence his self-description as a "social behaviorist."

Language, according to Mead, enables the individual to "take the role of the other" because in addressing the other the individual arouses in himself the same tendency to respond that he is attempting to elicit from the other. In adumbrating the response of the other, he is able both to "get inside" the other's mental processes and to look back on himself, the stimulus to the other's response, as he appears to the other. This process is nascent in the "conversation of gestures" among animals, becomes fully realized in interaction by means of vocal gestures transformed into "significant symbols" that emerges as true "symbolic" or linguistic communication among humans, and is "interiorized" by individuals in the form of an inner dialogue between their "I" and their "me." The latter constitutes mind or thought. Although Mead does not fully discuss this process, the ability to objectify oneself to oneself is presumably a consequence of the existence of words or linguistic signs that signify or symbolize both the actions of others as directly perceived and one's own actions inferred as similar or identical as a result of the naming of them by others in communication. This is surely the foundation of both selfhood and the "consciousness of kind" making possible imitation and identification that are distinctively human capacities.[44] The assessment of the "me" by the expectations or normative standards of the community at large, or what Mead often calls the "generalized other," is a precondition for choosing to conform to these expectations and standards. It is also a precondition for conscience, or the motivation to do one's duty by living up to standards that may have long since become dissociated in the individual's mind from their origins in parental injunctions or the norms of groups to which he or she may once have belonged.

Mead's concerns were first and foremost with the philosophical or epistemological puzzles coming out of the Kantian tradition. How is the self capable of becoming both subject and object to itself? How do we overcome complete solipsism and acquire knowledge, however incomplete and imperfect, of other selves? What are the fundamental discontinuities between the mental capacities of human beings and the lower animals? How—and here he departed from Kant and was influenced by both Darwinism and behaviorism—are man's higher capacities emergent from lesser capacities shared with other animals and all that we possess at birth? These questions are certainly relevant to the nature of human nature, its diverse manifestations, and to the fundamental structures of social interaction, but they are not identical with them and do not necessarily suggest answers to many of the substantive concerns of social theory. There is a fundamental difference between Mead's analysis of the cognitive powers with which language endows us and consideration of human motivation.

The implications for social theory of Mead's derivation of "mind, self and society" from language as a medium of symbolic communication peculiar to human beings are nevertheless vital. The dependence of conceptual thought on language rather than the reverse and the shaping of human consciousness itself by linguistic forms were argued by Mead some time before the celebrated "linguistic turn" in modern philosophy and social thought won general acceptance for these viewpoints. Mead was in advance of his time and he has still not been adequately recognized as a precursor of Wittgenstein, Anglo-American analytic philosophy, and French structuralism.[45] Mead showed that self-consciousness was an inescapable derivative of language as a shared mode of communication in which the emergence of the self as an object of experience makes possible the "reflexivity" of human consciousness that enables it to direct and control human actions in ways that have no parallel in other animal species. The reflexivity of the human mind transforms human action into something more than mere reactive "behavior" in response to a combination of internal and external stimuli. Mead's major achievement was to account for precisely *how* language as a form of social interaction, a means of symbolic communication among organisms, inevitably generates self-consciousness by creating the self as a mental construct modeled on the prior perception of others as selves. The later and better-known philosophers of language did not deal with this problem, although their preoccupation with the epistemological significance of language and with language itself as an autonomous system of meanings was greater than Mead's. Mead's primary interest, consistent with his roots in pragmatism, was in the uses of language in relation to action, especially biologically or socially adaptive action.

Mead was, however, only casually and tangentially interested in the self as a source of motivational energy, or as an object of affective attachment. His concern was with the self as a cognitive structure and the conditions under which it emerged.[46] He was quite unambiguous on this score, writing that "self-consciousness rather than affective experience with its motor accompaniments, provides the core and primary structure of the self, which is thus essentially a cognitive rather than an emotional phenomenon." A few lines later, Mead reiterates that "the essence of the self, as we have said, is cognitive" and proceeds to equate this essence with "thought or reflection."[47]

Sociologists, in reading Mead entirely as a social psychologist, have tended to ignore or gloss over his essentially cognitive conception of the self reflecting his epistemological concerns as a philosopher. They have smuggled motivation and affect into the Meadian concepts, assuming that because the "me," the self as object, is assessed in relation to the "generalized other," this is equivalent to being motivated to conform to the norms and expectations of that other. Since sociologists and psychologists are concerned first and foremost with the variable empirical content of human behavior, they are well aware that all of the "others" with whom an individual comes into contact are not equally influential, especially in large-scale heterogeneous modern societies with a diversity of groups and subcultures. They have, therefore, treated the concept of "significant other," which they attribute to Mead, as a complement to his "generalized other." But this concept, one of several of sociological provenance that have recently passed into popular jargon, is not to be found in Mead; its source is Harry Stack Sullivan, who as a psychiatrist was preoccupied with the emotional underpinnings of interpersonal relations and had in mind in coining it, not surprisingly, parents, siblings, peers, and lovers.[48] Mead's concern was confined to the universal capacity of the human mind to acquire knowledge and with the relation of that knowledge to adaptive or instrumental action; he was not primarily interested in the varying details of human activity and experience that, at different levels, constitute the subject matter of the sociologist, cultural anthropologist, and psychiatrist.[49]

What is the bearing of this difference on motivation? Anyone who has learned a language possesses a mind and a self, is capable of thought and memory, knows the attributes of the "generalized other," and engages in an internal dialogue between the "I" and the "me" that may be a mental rehearsal of possible options for action or be carried on within the mind simply for its own sake. All these capacities have been acquired through symbolic communication in interaction with others. Individuals differ enormously in their attitudes toward and their feelings about themselves; cultures differ enormously in the degree to which they perceive the self as a unique object of value. But all human beings who have learned to speak have minds and selves, that is, are capable of mentally anticipating a range of possible actions open to them before choosing any one of them—or, for that matter, opting for inaction—and are able to gauge the expectations and likely actions of other people. These are cognitive capacities and imply nothing whatever about attitudes and feelings toward self or toward others and their expectations.

A confidence man may be a skilled diagnostician of the expectations of the "generalized other," but he is not motivated to conform to them in order to win approval—he conforms in appearance only in order the better to deceive and manipulate his "marks" to his own advantage.[50] He has a mind and a self that are of social origin, products of early socialization, but his conformity to the expectations of the people he manipulates is "cold and calculated," strictly instrumental to his self-interested purpose. Then there is the category, even more significant though imperfectly understood, of persons classified as "psychopaths" or "sociopaths," who evidently lack the inner capacity to delay and control their own impulses or to feel remorse or guilt or even genuine sympathy for victims of their actions, although they are able to function most of the time as apparently "normal" members of the community. They give evidence of lacking superegos—internalized moral restraints—in the Freudian sense,[51] but they are entirely capable of communicating symbolically with others and clearly do not lack minds and selves in the Meadian sense. One must conclude that Meadian socialization, centered on the acquisition of language through interaction with others, is essentially *cognitive*. Freudian socialization, involving emotional identification with others and the introjection or internalization of their attitudes both as models to strive to emulate and as restrictions on options for action, is an *affective* and *motivational* process. The former is a necessary but not a sufficient condition for the latter.

WHY DO PEOPLE INTERACT?

My account of the genesis of norms in common expectations that arise in recurrent social interactions rests primarily on claims about the knowledge possessed or acquired by social actors. Actors make "predictions," or hold "expectations," about one another's behavior that are not different except for their objects from the predictions or expectations they cherish about natural events. Such phrases as actors' "perceptions," "mutual awareness," "sensitivity to," "practical" and "discursive consciousness," "redefinitions of the situation," and the like reveal a language of cognition, not of emotion or motivation.

The expectations actors develop about one another's conduct do not always remain purely cognitive but may become binding in acquiring the force of imperatives governing the action of those who initially perceive the expectations as present in the consciousness of others. This unmistakably implies that expectations achieve the power to motivate the behavior of others to conform to them. I do not mean to suggest that someone's mere awareness of another's expectations of his or her behavior induces "automatic" conformity to those expectations by a psychological process akin, perhaps, to posthypnotic suggestion. Sociologists conventionally maintain that social norms are enforced by "sanctions." But sanctions are rewards or punishments expected to result from conformity to or deviation from a norm (or expectation) and directly imply motivation: a wish to obtain a reward or avoid a penalty. Desire for approval and fear of disapproval are the most general and "diffuse" sanctions assumed by sociologists; they clearly assume a theory of human motivation whether or not it is explicitly formulated. Why, in short, do people so desperately want others to think well of them? Or, more commonly, merely not to show disapproval of them? The answer is not self-evident.

Moreover, this does not suggest either that *all* expectations are self-fulfilling, or, more specifically, that *all* perceptions of the expectations of others create a motivation to conform to them. Many expectations about other people, indeed the majority we hold, clearly do not differ at all from our expectations about natural events. Much of the time others are not merely indifferent to but quite unaware of our expectations and thus incapable of being influenced by them, as we well know. Sometimes, far from wanting others to confirm them, we hold our expectations regretfully. We privately expect a marriage to fail though presenting a public facade of cheerful optimism, all the while wistfully hoping that our assessment of the clashing temperaments of the couple may prove to be one-sided or mistaken. We expect a stranger approaching us on a deserted street at night to rob us and are pleasantly surprised when he passes by peacefully. Knowing that our friend expects his or her anger to elicit ours, we choose instead to act on the maxim "a soft answer turneth away wrath."

This last example involves unlike the previous ones full awareness of the other's expectations, although we resolve to falsify rather than to confirm them. Such suicidal or self-defeating prophecies are counterparts of the self-fulfilling cases in which expectations possess a normative aura that induces conformity to them. There are less benign examples in which conflict or hostility dictates the response to the perceived expectation. Actors sometimes wish to gauge the expectations of others precisely in order to flout them out of a wish, perhaps, to *épater le bourgeois*, or an inclination toward "doing the reverse on all occasions till you catch the same disease," as Auden characterized compulsive rebellion against parental authority.[52]

I recall a colleague who suddenly went around asking everyone in a puzzled way, "Why do people interact?" A silly question with an obvious answer was one's first reaction—after all, the whole field of sociology is premised on the assumption of the universality of interaction, as indeed is social science in general. But on second thought the question is fundamental and inescapable. Man might be a solitary species, a possibility suggested by Hobbes in his imaginary model of the state of nature and by Rousseau who thought that men had kept greater distance from one another in the remote past and were the happier for it. Why should people seek to associate with others? If the need for "social approval" is, as so many sociologists and social psychologists have long contended, the basic motivational force making possible the socialization, or domestication, of human beings, where does this need, evidently not present in infants and animals, come from, and why is it so powerful? Why should people care at all what other people think of them, so long as they are not physically molested by them?

Sociologists and social psychologists have, of course, provided plausible and empirically convincing answers to these questions. I have the impression, however, that the questions have become less salient in recent years, partly because of disciplinary biases that view "psychologizing" with suspicion and have become more pronounced with the expansion of sociology that has made it possible for some people to live (*horribile dictu!*) their entire intellectual lives within its confines, partly because of the manifest cognitivist emphasis of the most prominent recent movements and tendencies in social thought such as social phenomenology, ethnomethodology, and neosymbolic interactionism. These movements and tendencies have often corrected a previous neglect or oversimplification of the complexity and creativity of human cognitive capacities, but, inevitably, they have in turn fostered a one-sided outlook. Adepts of the various versions of structuralism, poststructuralism, and deconstruction have certainly attempted to supply motivational underpinnings for their worldview, drawing in particular on Nietzsche and Freud. Their starting point, however, has been structural linguistics as the foundation of the cognitive performances of the human mind. But reflection on the problem of order necessarily begins with consideration of the motives, feelings, interests, needs, and aspirations of men and women.

CHAPTER FOUR

SOCIAL AND ANTISOCIAL ELEMENTS IN HUMAN NATURE

Muy account of how norms, roles, and institutions emerge from expectations generated in the course of recurrent social interaction takes largely for granted that people *want* to interact, to maintain association with one another, even to cooperate on common projects. But the motivations leading them to seek and strive to sustain relations with others are not self-evident. If they were, there would be no problem of order. The problem is a real one because human beings are also often motivated to ignore and resist other people and their demands. Human nature contains social, asocial, and antisocial dispositions, although thinkers have differed on the relative importance they have assigned to each. The Hobbesian war of all against all is an image not of an asocial or nonsocial state in which individuals lead relatively solitary lives, but of an antisocial condition in which they interact only by engaging in unrestrained violent conflict with one another.

The social contract theorists employed the conception of a state of nature as an intellectual device for highlighting the asocial and anti-social motivations of human beings, whether or not they regarded it as a real condition that had once generally prevailed, a latent potentiality inherent in all societies, or as no more than a conceptual ideal type. Hobbes emphasized the fear and mistrust men felt toward one another. Locke regarded the state of nature as a prepolitical but not a presocial condition; for him, a social contract establishing law and government was essentially a convenience serving antecedent common or complementary interests and purposes. Rousseau treated both social and antisocial motivations as later superimpositions on a fundamentally asocial human nature. In contrast to Hobbes, he did not regard society as the product of a social contract, but rather as the unintended and unforeseen result of technological and demographic changes producing further changes in human nature itself.

Whether or not these thinkers believed that basic human motivations and cognitive capacities are acquired independently of and remain uninfluenced by social life is a separate issue from their account of those motivations and capacities. It may be, as Robert Nisbet claims, that they had an "image of the individual mind, separate and aloof from, basically undirected by, social structures and mechanisms."[1] If so, they are subject to Steven Lukes's judgment that "the abstract conception of the individual. . . directly contradicts all the accumulated lessons of sociology and social anthropology and of social psychology."[2] The fallacy that there ever was or ever could be such a thing as a "natural man" capable of living in relative isolation from his fellows has been conventionally imputed to the social contract theorists by generations of sociologists and anthropologists. But these theorists were not as naively antisociological as this view implies. Evidence can be found in their writings that at least suggests they were no less aware of man's basically social nature than contemporary contractarian thinkers like Rawls, Nozick, and Dworkin. In a different vein, Habermas and Coleman too have made use of notions comparable to the state of nature and the social contract as limiting conditions or abstract or ideal-typical possibilities in arguing for their particular normative conceptions of justice, human rights, procedural democracy, and the like. Rousseau is the most ambiguous case.

HOBBES ON THE PASSIONS, POWER, AND CONFLICT

Hobbes was less preoccupied with the content and variety of human motives than with the *form* of motivation in his effort to incorporate humans and their actions into his mechanistic and materialistic general philosophy. His primary concern in Chapter 6 of *Leviathan* devoted to "the interior beginnings of Voluntary Motions, commonly called Passions" is with motives or passions as the triggers, the internal movers, setting the human machine in motion in the same manner as the impact of external bodies upon one another causes motion in classical mechanics. The degree to which his political thought, including his political psychology, depended on his materialistic general philosophy has been a matter of dispute among his interpreters which need not concern us here.

Self-preservation is the motive to which Hobbes assigned primacy, like the Social Darwinists two centuries later. But, as John Dewey pointed out (with the Darwinists rather than Hobbes in mind), self-preservation is not really a separate motive stirring people to activity in concrete situations; it is, rather, an outcome that all elemental motives promote or subserve.[3] Whatever the primacy accorded to self-preservation, in effect to the maintenance of life itself, motives have generally been regarded as plural rather than singular at the level of action, including hunger, lust, fear, aggression, love, vanity, and so on. Hobbes is no exception, naming several specific passions, all of which presumably contribute to self-preservation. The desire for gain, for security, and for reputation are the motives he mentions that bring men into conflict in seeking to gratify them.

Gain embraces all the material needs that man must satisfy in order to sustain life. The niggardliness of nature, the scarcity of the necessary means of subsistence, is assumed by Hobbes in contrast to Rousseau who argued that needs were few, simple, and readily satisfied in the state of nature. Sartre is only one of many later writers who have seen economic scarcity as the fundamental human condition eternally predisposing men to conflict.[4] In referring to the desire for "Gain" and for "Riches" as a source of conflict among men rather than merely to material need under conditions of scarcity, Hobbes lends credibility to the claim by some interpreters that he was articulating a distinctively "bourgeois" view of life dominated by insatiable acquisitiveness or "possessive individualism." Scarcity of the things that satisfy human desires remains the fundamental circumstance conducive to conflict, whether the desires are moderate or inordinate. Hobbes repeatedly states that men differ in their appetites and aspirations, some keeping them "within modest bounds" while others are driven to pursue power "farther than their security requires."[5] Although he nowhere refers to population growth, Hobbes's insistence that there is a constant struggle for survival because nature never provides enough to meet the needs of everyone foreshadows, as Parsons noted, Malthus, whose "principle of population" inspired Darwin's theory of natural selection.

Parsons maintained that Marx's claim that the struggle between classes over the material means of life was the motor of history amounted to a collectivization of Hobbes's war of all against all[6] and Sartre advanced a not dissimilar view. Marx's fully realized communist utopia at the end of history is specifically characterized as a society in which the forces of production have progressed to the point of eliminating material scarcity so that the old socialist maxim "from each according to his quality, to each according to his need" can be fully realized. It has often been argued that economic conflict between individuals and groups is chiefly waged over the distribution of an economic surplus over and above immediate subsistence needs.[7] The existence of such a surplus presupposes productivity resulting from the development of the forces of production beyond the rudimentary technological level exhibited by "primitive" societies. Such societies still living at or close to the subsistence level avoid conflict by institutionalizing more or less equal distribution.[8] Rousseau had such societies in mind, notably the Indians of the Caribbean, although he erred in regarding them as more "natural" than societies with a more complex technology and a division of labor and, indeed, in picturing the state of nature as a nonsocial condition in which humans lived in relative solitude. Marx's view of history has often been depicted as a spiral movement in which the utopian end of history represents a return at a level of abundance to the equality of "primitive communism" under the conditions of scarcity that prevailed at the beginning of history.

The desire for what Hobbes calls "Safety" leading to "Diffidence" as the second cause of "quarrell" among men directly follows from self-preservation as the underlying master interest of men. The avoidance of death by violence at the hands of others inevitably has top priority. Michael Oakeshott has noted that in *Leviathan* death in itself is the *summum malum*, the greatest evil, whereas in *De Cive* and elsewhere in Hobbes's writings "the greatest evil is *violent* death at the hands of another." Essentially, this is because "the death to be most greatly feared is that which no foresight can guard against—sudden death."[9] The passage from Hobbes most frequently quoted after his summary adjectival characterization of the state of nature is from Chapter 11: "So that in the first place, I put for a general inclination of all mankind, a perpetual and restless desire of Power after power that ceaseth only in Death."[10] In the very next sentence Hobbes unambiguously asserts: "And the cause of this, is not always that a man hopes for a more intensive delight, than he has already attained to; or that he cannot be content with a moderate power: but because he cannot assure the power and means to live well, which he hath present, without the acquisition of more."

Hobbes is saying that a good offense is the best defense, that one has to keep running to stay in the same place, always strive for more power merely to protect what one has already attained. He is far from saying that men are constantly driven by a deeply rooted and irresistible will to power, or by, as those writers who have seen Hobbes as expressing a quintessentially bourgeois outlook have contended, an insatiable drive to accumulate more material possessions. He specifically says that men do not necessarily strive for a "more intensive delight" (though he implies that there are some who do), nor are they discontented with a limited quotient of power or gain.[11] To be sure, as I noted above, the motive of "gain" (or "riches" as its object) itself seems to imply a competitive striving beyond mere need or moderate satisfaction. Yet the fear of losing what they possess, however modest, compels men nevertheless always to keep their powder dry.

Consideration of Hobbes's definition of power at the very beginning of Chapter 10 of *Leviathan*, the chapter preceding the chapter in which he imputes a perpetual desire for power to mankind, reinforces the point: "The Power of a Man, (to take it Universally,) is his present means, to obtain some future apparent Good."[12] The much-quoted passage in the following chapter, then, asserts that so long as people are still alive they are engaged in a ceaseless quest to obtain the means for satisfying their wants, whatever those wants—the "future apparent Good" they seek to obtain—may happen to be. (One can see why Parsons regarded Hobbes as a Utilitarian, if mistakenly.) What Hobbes called "Felicity," or the full and permanent satiation of desires, is never achieved. Life, he is saying, is constant striving and struggle that ends only with the extinction of desire at death. Hobbes's tone is close to that of the T-shirt slogan "Life is a bitch and then you die." But this is hardly the same thing as insisting that human existence is simply a jungle in which men are driven to prey on one another all the time. To say that they seek the power to satisfy their wants, or the means or resources enabling them to do so, is simply another way of saying that they *have* wants, or at least that they want to get what they want. For to have wants entails wanting to satisfy them and thus wanting to possess the means to satisfy them, given that instant, effortless satisfaction is not the human lot, though it is approximated in early infancy. Power *is* possession of the means and resources that are instruments for the gratification of desires and/or the achievement of ends.[13]

Hobbes's definition of power encompasses power over nature and over the self as well as power over other humans. It resembles Bertrand Russell's definition three centuries later that power is "the production of intended effects."[14] Both are very broad definitions that include but are not confined to social relationships and behavior. They are versions of definitions that stress the "power to" obtain any and all objects of desire as distinct from narrower definitions centering on "power over" others, which define power as a unilateral or asymmetrical social relationship. The latter kind of definition constitutes a special case of the former, although of obvious particular relevance to political and social theory. I have elsewhere adapted Russell's definition to apply to social relations as "the capacity of some persons to produce intended and foreseen effects on others."[15]

To Hobbes, conflict follows from universal striving for power as he defines it primarily because of scarcity rather than because humans are endowed with an inherent drive to acquire power for its own sake. Power is of strictly instrumental value rather than something that is pursued as an end in itself, an intrinsic or terminal source of satisfaction. True, after his assertion of the general inclination of mankind perpetually to desire power, he proceeds to observe that even kings, "whose power is greatest," seldom rest content with what they have but are driven to seek new conquests and greater fame. He then notes that "Love of Contention" follows from "competition of Riches, Honour, Command, or other power" inducing competitors "to kill, subdue, supplant, or repel the other." Thus the war of all against all. But though kings and other powerful men may be subject to the temptation of further competition and contention, this is not because they share with all men an innate power drive.[16] Ordinary men must nevertheless strive to augment their power because of the scarcity of all objects of desire. The priority Hobbes accords to scarcity as a source of conflict is even more evident in *De Cive* than in his better-known statement in the famous Chapter 13 of *Leviathan*:

> But the most frequent reason why men desire to hurt each other, ariseth hence, that many men at the same time have an appetite to the same thing; which yet very often they can neither enjoy in common, nor yet divide it; whence it follows that the trongest must have it, and who is strongest must be decided by the sword.[17]

Hobbes's view of human nature is certainly far from a pacific one, but he stops short of picturing human beings as sadists who actually enjoy inflicting pain and death upon their fellows.

The cynical Machiavellian tradition of thinking about power (whether or not it is truly applicable to Machiavelli himself) often acquires its plausibility from its obscuring of the distinction between "power to" and "power over." To insist that all men seek power is virtually a truism, even a tautology, if one takes absolutely literally "power to" definitions such as Hobbes's and Russell's. Nor does it in any way imply that people get pleasure from "power over" others in relations of domination and subjection. The power of some over others, however, *does* imply hierarchical inequality and at least suggests the possibility of exploitation and victimization. The cynical, pessimistic, and even demonic aura that surrounds the suggestion that the desire for power is a basic human drive rests on conflating "power to" with "power over" and is the stock-in-trade of the Machiavellian tradition. Perhaps I should update it by calling it the Foucaultian tradition, for Foucault's conception of power as present in all human relations acquires its appeal from the *frisson* evoked by such a conflation.[18]

Hobbes's third motive for conflict, "Glory," and the object it induces men to strive to obtain, "Reputation," raise a number of more complex problems. This is clearly a desire for *psychic* rather than primarily material or physical satisfactions like the quests for possessions and for security from violence. Nor do the latter two desiderata in themselves imply any necessary association with other persons, leading indeed to the avoidance of all association where covetousness and violence govern the relations among men as in Hobbes's state of nature. Glory and reputation, on the other hand, unmistakably suggest others' evaluations of oneself and the effort to influence them, what Goffman called "impression management." They therefore presuppose at least a minimal social relationship. Hobbes contends that the reputation men seek is a reputation for power that will stay the hand of potential invaders because they will fear successful resistance. Reputation serves to deter attack and thus protects the individual from the risk of violent death at the hands of others. It symbolically conveys the message "Don't mess with me," or "When you say that, pardner, smile!" Hobbes, in short, reduces reputation to an additional means of defending oneself against the possible depredations of others, although it is a means that implies some recognition of and contact with others and some ability to communicate with them.

This view poses problems if one reflects in greater depth on "glory" as a passion or motive, especially when taking into account the role it has played in the thought of earlier writers, notably Machiavelli. To seek glory is to seek the recognition, even the celebration, by others of one's extraordinary achievements or exceptional qualities, of one's manifest superiority to others. If it is inherently relational in depending on the judgment

of others, it is also inherently agonistic when all individuals passionately seek it, for it pits individuals against one another in
intense competition. It is not hard to see why Hobbes saw it as a
major instigator of contention among men. Moreover, glory is
scarce by definition since it implies individual preeminence in
comparison with others.[19] Whereas it is possible to imagine a
world without material scarcity and also one of security from
physical violence, it is a contradiction in terms to conceive of a
world in which all are equally glorious—at least simultaneously,
recalling Andy Warhol's much-cited aphorism that in America
everyone can be famous for fifteen minutes. Of the three basic
human desires that cause conflict, Hobbes recognized that economic progress could mitigate the quest for gain, the absolute
sovereign he favored would ensure greater security (which is, of
course, why he favored one), but pride, the most social and even
"socializing" of the desires, was intransigent and immutable precisely because of its inherently comparative nature.[20]

Machiavelli also saw glory as an object of passionate striving,
at least by princes. But in contrast to Hobbes he saw it as a quality that could be attained or possessed by groups, specifically by
principalities, as well as by individuals. This is one of the ambiguities in Machiavelli that has given rise to the long-standing
controversies over the meaning of his work. In recommending to
princes the adoption of apparently unrestricted, even "immoral"
means in the pursuit and maintenance of their power, was he
advising utter ruthlessness on the part of the individual power
seeker, or was he realistically acknowledging that the interests of
the state, of the collectivity, often required deviation from the
hallowed principles of Christian morality? Even in *The Prince*,
his most famous and most scandalous work, which is directly
about individual political leaders, he states in Chapter 8 after
recounting the cruelties and deceptions practiced by Agathocles
of Sicily that "These ways can win a prince power but not
glory."[21] His later work was clearly more concerned with principalities, specifically with Florence, than with princes, that is, with
individuals. In Max Weber's great essay "Politics as a Vocation,"
he praised Machiavelli for having valued the glory and greatness
of his native city over the salvation of his soul. So for Machiavelli

the quest for glory both imposes limits on the choice of means by individuals and can also be a collective goal to which individuals may commit themselves over and above their purely self-interested concerns.

Hobbes's statements about glory, reputation, and the several synonyms he uses for them ignore or play down both the real if limited dependence on the judgments of others that the striving for them of individuals involves and their possible extension to groups in a world of competing groups. He can be criticized for reducing power to coercion, or for equating power over others with force or the threat of force. If reputation is sought simply for its deterrent effects, it is the equivalent of a display of bulging biceps or of a visible weapon for the purpose of warning off a possible aggressor. Even the minimal socializing tendency implied by the desire to elicit admiration from others is absent in this conception.

Yet Hobbes's frequent shrewd and sardonic remarks on the inclination of men to want others to accept them at their own high valuation and their disappointment and rage when such acceptance is not forthcoming suggest a different view. If men are so quick to anger over minor slights, "a word, a smile, a different opinion, and any other sign of undervalue," is it not possible that they may dread disgrace and dishonor even more than death itself?[22] If so, then glory, honor, and reputation are sought for their own sakes and not simply as an economical means of deterring physical assault by others. Oakeshott goes so far as to maintain that for Hobbes violent death is feared not so much in its own right but *because* it brings dishonor: "And whereas with animals the ultimate dread is death in any manner, the ultimate fear in man is the dread of violent (or untimely) death at the hand of another man; for this is dishonour, the emblem of all *human* failure."[23] This view inverts the contention that glory and reputation are primarily sought as defense policies designed to deter physical assault by others.

Hobbes asserts repeatedly that there is a discrepancy between the exalted opinion people have of themselves and what others think of them. This vanity, or "Vaineglory" as Hobbes called it, to which all humans are prone accounts considerably for the fact that "men have no pleasure in keeping company" when others decline to accept them at their own estimation. It might induce them to keep to themselves, to live contentedly in their own minds, *in foro interno* as Hobbes put it, basking in narcissistic self-adoration. The fact that the desire for glory is a desire for psychic rather than physical satisfaction makes this possible in contrast to material desires which impel the individual to seek out objects in the world and the desire for security from violent death which requires facing up to external physical dangers. The gratification of vanity, on the other hand, might very well produce a population of narcissists luxuriating in the passive contemplation of their navels, or perhaps a population of psychotics withdrawing from the world in cultivation of delusions of grandeur.

But if this were so, glory and reputation would not be a source of contention among men equal to if not greater than the desires for gain and security. Clearly, men are motivated to induce others to accept them at their own self-estimation. As Leo Strauss put it: "The vain man, who, in his imagination believes himself superior to others, cannot convince himself of the rightness of his estimate of himself; he requires the recognition of his superiority by others. He therefore steps outside his imaginary world."[24] Since men usually fail to achieve such recognition, they "have no pleasure in keeping company" but are driven nevertheless to keep it. As Oakeshott observes:

> They are enemies but they also need one another. And this for two reasons: without others there is no recognition of superiority and therefore no notable felicity; and many, perhaps most of the satisfactions which constitute a man's felicity are in the responses he may wring from others. The pursuit of felicity, in respect of a large part of it, is a procedure of bargaining with others in which one seeks what another has got and for which he must offer a satisfaction in turn.[25]

One is reminded of Schopenhauer's parable of the porcupines cited by both Freud and Oakeshott,[26] in which human society is compared to a colony of porcupines huddling together to keep warm in winter but then pricking one another with their quills and drawing apart repeatedly until they achieve a balance between the need for warmth and a secure distance from pain. In contrast to the quests for gain and security and to Hobbes's frequent equation of reputation with symbolic physical strength serving to deter assaults by others, the desire for glory, honor, or reputation implies at least a minimal socializing tendency: an agreement among individuals to pay a modicum of attention to one another and a dependence on the evaluations of others that promotes conformity to the standards by which they render favorable judgments. This may not amount to much, but it ensures some association of individuals with one another and some presumptive mitigation of the war of all against all. Oakeshott concludes that "the human 'state of nature' is a profoundly 'social' condition,"[27] but the quotation marks around "social" speak for themselves in qualification.

Hobbes's view of human nature, therefore, is not totally lacking in socializing motivations. One might even describe it as dialectical in that the same motive, the wish for glory, promotes both attraction and repulsion among men. Or perhaps it recognizes, as have many classical sociological thinkers, that conflict in contrast to simple avoidance is itself a form of social contact, a mode of interacting with others. Moreover, such conflict may be orderly, may constitute a stable factual order in Parsons's sense, from the standpoint of an observer even though it confronts each individual actor with terrifying uncertainty as to both its incidence and its outcome. Viewed from the outside as a general state of affairs, the war of all against all may present a highly predictable factual order characterized by unchanging, seemingly eternal monotony. Indeed, this appears to be how Hobbes himself saw the state of nature in his famous negative description of it. But from the standpoint of the individual actor, such a world is a world of terrifying uncertainty: the constant threat of surprise attack or deception by others disrupts any stable expectations and frustrates his or her best-laid plans. Doubtless it is tacit identification with the plight of the concrete actor in the war of all against all that greatly accounts for the tendency of so many writers on the problem of order to equate universal conflict with randomness, lack of regularity, and unpredictability in human behavior. Not only is the perspective of the concrete individual actor adopted rather than that of the total situation as it might be perceived by an Olympian observer (say a generalizing social scientist), but epistemological disorder to the point of universal solipsism is then confused with a war of all against all stemming from the hostile, antisocial dispositions of human nature.

Despite the presence of minimal socializing elements, Hobbes's view of human nature can still be described as undersocialized. His discussions of gain and glory as sources of contention among men exhibit a striking parallel. He stresses riches as the object of competition among men, which implies that men wish for more than their fellows and may strive to outstrip them by depriving or exploiting them, a point strongly emphasized by Marxist readings of Hobbes like C. B. Macpherson's. Hobbes does not confine himself to mere acknowledgment of the universality of material need and the insufficiency of the environment to supply everyone. For Freud, on the other hand, Ananke (or Necessity), essentially the necessity of work to extract subsistence from the environment, encouraged cooperation and the repression of antisocial impulses.[28] In the case of reputation, Hobbes similarly identifies it with striving for superiority rather than with the universal human desire for favorable recognition by others motivating conformity to their wishes and expectations. In each case the agonistic extreme of a universal human motive is stressed because it promotes competition or conflict, although the most elementary and common form of the motive may, and in the case of the wish for approval must, encourage unity, conformity, and cooperation in the pursuit of common goals.

The wish for an audience of others before whom to disport oneself, while it may promote a limited kind of social life, hardly suffices to motivate men to negotiate a social contract in which they surrender their freedom to use violence and deception in their dealings with one another. Such hostile dependence or "antagonistic cooperation" is scarcely likely to overcome the fear and mistrust prevailing in the state of nature. Hobbes provides no stronger positive force of attraction drawing men together and serving as an incentive for the establishment of a peaceable, cooperative social order. He gives exclusive priority, rather, to the strictly negative desire to avoid violent death.

Self-interested rationality rather than any emotional attachment to others convinces men to renounce force and fraud and empower a ruler to enforce their renunciation. Their interest is the purely defensive and negative one of the protection of their persons from assault and their possessions from appropriation by others. Not surprisingly, the social contract is always precarious in the absence of any positive affective bond uniting men. Since neither other people, nor laws or moral injunctions proscribing violence possess any inherent value, fear of punishment imposed by the sovereign is needed to deter individuals from reverting to their old ways when it seems expedient to do so ("Covenants without the Sword are but words. . ."). Reason alone brings about both the creation of political authority and conformity to its dictates. The original social contract creating Leviathan is reenacted every time someone declines to resort to force in the pursuit of his or her ends.

Critics of Hobbes have long argued that men constituted as he describes them could not possibly have come together and arrived at a consensus that led to the formation of civil society, however acute their powers of reasoning. This criticism usually rests on the assumption that Hobbes sees men as lusting continually after power, wealth, and individual preeminence at the expense of their fellows. But, as we have seen, this was not his view. Though some men may be so driven, situational rather than internal pressures give rise to the war of all against all. In the absence of these pressures, most men would be quite content with modest attainments and with peaceably cultivating their own gardens, adopting a "live and let live" attitude toward their fellows.

In addition, twentieth-century history suggests that fear of violence *can* become a powerful political force. Consider the popular support garnered by authoritarian, often military, regimes offering no more than the restoration of "law and order" in times of social unrest,[29] and even the electoral effectiveness of promises to fight crime in stable democratic societies. To be sure, the political effects of fear of violence often prove quite transitory: authoritarian dictatorships crumble when relative social and political peace has been regained and politicians whose main appeal has been their proclaimed toughness on criminals are soon voted out of office or compelled to diversify their appeals to the electorate. More darkly, authoritarian regimes promising law and order may themselves resort to terrorism and rule by fear, which has happened often enough to earn this century a reputation likely to last forever as the "terrible century." The not infrequent salience of fear as a political motive, however, is consistent with Hobbes's contention that the war of all against all is often latent, as well as with the argument of Macpherson and others that to Hobbes it remained a menacing possibility slumbering below the surface even in societies long habituated to government and the rule of law. Hobbes's critics who doubt that men equipped with the dispositions he imputes to human nature could negotiate a social contract can not infrequently be faulted for underestimating the intensity and political potency of the fear of violence, if not for thinking that Hobbes assigned too exclusive an importance to them.

THE SOCIAL ORIGINS OF MIND, SPEECH, AND SELFHOOD

If some critics have argued that men with the motives Hobbes ascribed to them could not possibly unite to negotiate a social contract, others, ignoring motivational considerations, have argued that they would have to have been already socialized to possess the cognitive capacities he regarded as distinctively human. Both criticisms, however, are usually directed against the "atomistic individualism" imputed to Hobbes, his alleged assumption of a "Naturall condition of Mankind" in which self-sufficient individuals lived in isolation from one another. The argument from cognition is that the negotiators of Hobbes's social contract must have been partially socialized because the very "gift" of reason that induces men to seek a social contract as well as the cognitive and communicative capacities involved in agreeing on the terms of the contract could only have originated in a previously existing society. If reason and language are social products, they cannot be invoked as they are by Hobbes to explain how society comes into being, however plausibly they may account for how political organizations or states monopolizing violence might be created by men who are already social beings. Vico and Rousseau both pointed to the social origin of human cognitive skills in criticizing Hobbes, anticipating a line of criticism that would become commonplace later on, especially after the "linguistic turn" in philosophy and social thought in the present century. Rousseau was one of the first to question Hobbes's assumption that thought was antecedent to speech, which is a medium of communication implying social interaction, a very modern line of argument indeed.[30]

Nevertheless, it is not as obvious as it is often held to be that Hobbes regarded man's cognitive capacities as fully formed independently of society. The insistence that the distinctively human cognitive skills of language and thought can only be acquired in the course of recurrent peaceful social interaction is the ultimate ground on which not only Hobbes but the other social contract theorists are rejected as atomistic individualists unrealistically postulating a human nature that is in no way shaped by social influences. Clearly, neither Hobbes nor the other contract theorists had a developed conception of the origins of "mind, self, and society" in social interaction (Mead), or a notion of the dependence of cognition on ordinary language (Wittgenstein), or a "communicative theory of action" (Habermas). Like the ancients, they (with the partial exception of Rousseau) tended to think of reason as an inborn, uniquely human endowment that preceded the acquisition of language. Yet few commentators on Hobbes have noted the long footnote at the very beginning of the first chapter of *De Cive* in which he defends himself against the charge of "stupidity" because of his alleged denial that "man is a creature born fit for society:"

> Therefore I must more plainly say, that it is true indeed, that to man, or as man, that is, as soon as he is born, solitude is an enemy; for infants have need of others to help them to live, and those of riper years to help them to live well, wherefore I deny not that men (even nature compelling) desire to come to-

gether. . . . .Manifest therefore it is, that all men, because they are
born in infancy, are born unapt for society. . .wherefore man is
made fit for society not by nature, but by education.[31]

There is nothing here to which a modern sociologist or social
psychologist could possibly object. Hobbes's statement of the
inevitable dependence of infants on society is, however, part of an
argument that infants could not have consciously *chosen* to live
in society and therefore have been parties to the social contract.[32]
He went on to argue that their implicit agreement to the contract
had to be asssumed.

The point that the social contract theorists may not have
believed that man's cognitive capacities were formed outside of
society can perhaps be made most strongly with reference to
Locke. Arguing in *The Second Treatise of Government* that men
may make "promises and compacts. . .one with another and yet
still be in a state of nature," he went on to assert in a famous
passage:

> The promises and bargains for truck, etc., between two men in the
> desert island, mentioned by Garcilasso de la Vega, in his history of
> Peru, or between a Swiss and an Indian in the woods of America,
> are binding to them, though they are perfectly in a state of nature
> in reference to one another; for truth and keeping of faith belongs
> to men as men, and not as members of society.[33]

This seems entirely unambiguous: men engage in exchange, "bargain for truck," because it is their nature to do so, quite apart
from their membership of society. The statement has been widely
noticed because there is a direct continuity between it and Adam
Smith's famous assertion in the third chapter of *The Wealth of
Nations* of man's "propensity to truck, barter, and exchange one
thing for another."[34] But consider: Locke is, after all, the thinker
par excellence who saw the mind as a *tabula rasa* and denied the
existence of "innate ideas." He is rightly regarded as the pioneer
advocate of the primacy of nurture over nature, environment
over heredity, in his influential writings on education as well as in
his theory of knowledge. It is implausible that in his political the-

ory he would revert so readily to belief in an inborn human nature dictating the behavior of men toward one another.

Two reasons can be adduced for regarding the contradiction as apparent rather than real. First, both Hobbes and Locke frequently used "state of nature" to describe a relation and did not limit it to the characterization of a general historical or—more plausibly in the case of Hobbes—hypothetical condition of society as a whole. This practice is, in fact, one source of their conflation of interpersonal and intergroup relations to be discussed in a later chapter. Obviously, two strangers meeting as castaways on a desert island or a European and an Indian confronting one another in the forests of the New World are not bound by any previous contract and are not subject therefore to any common political authority. Locke, as a matter of fact, had actual examples from travel literature in mind[35] and his use of the desert island situation as a real illustration of the "state of nature" was similar to that of the later writers who have utilized the Robinson Crusoe example mentioned in Chapter 3.

A second reason for doubting that Locke regarded economic exchange as innate to man involves what he meant by "society." Probably he had in mind "civil society," understood in the seventeenth century as a society subject to government and the rule of law which were clearly lacking in his examples. Locke believed that the state of nature was a condition in which men possesseed natural rights and used their powers of reason in acting on them, but, as opposed to Hobbes's view, this in no way precluded an established and relatively peaceable social life. "Society" to Locke meant a legal and political order, not what we today conceive of as a social order wholly or partially independent of these. Although nowadays the term "civil society" is often invoked as a counter-concept to the state, this was not the case in the seventeenth century.[36] Current usage comes out of the Hegelian and Marxist tradition and cannot be equated with the term as it was understood by Hobbes, Locke, and Rousseau, or, for that matter, by Adam Ferguson, Adam Smith, and the Scottish Moralists.

If the social contract theorists did not necessarily believe in a human nature that was fully formed independently of social influences, they were certainly presociological thinkers in blurring or remaining indifferent to the distinction between the political and the social, between the state and society. The question of whether human nature was innate or shaped by socialization simply was not a matter of concern to them; they described it as they found it and directed their attention to advocating the form of government they regarded as best suited to it, more or less ignoring or taking for granted the "intermediate" groups and institutions (except occasionally religious bodies) that compose what the modern sociologist understands by "social structure." The very term they used, "civil society," reflects their indifference to the distinction between law, on the one hand, and the "folkways," the *conscience collective,* or the normative order central to the sociological tradition, on the other.

Adam Smith, too, is often charged with having believed that the dispositions he imputed to human nature were innate,[37] but this is plainly not the case. He proceeds in the same chapter expressly to doubt whether the propensity to truck and barter "be one of those original principles in human nature of which no further account can be given," stating that "it seems more probable" that it is one of the necessary consequences of "the faculties of reason and speech." The capacity for economic exchange, he suggests, is a distinctively human one, presupposing the ability to put onself mentally in the place of another ("take the role of the other" in Mead's phrase) in order to understand his or her needs. Dogs, he notes, do not bargain and trade in bones. Exchange and the free market to which it gives rise were to Smith human creations for which reason, language, and selfhood were preconditions. Whether the faculties of reason and speech are themselves innate is, of course, a separate question altogether.

Critics of the social contract theorists, making the case against their supposed atomistic individualism, have long contended that the motivation to enter into a contract, and the capacities to reason and communicate involved in making it, could only be attributes of human beings who had already been shaped by the kind of rule-governed social life that the contract is supposed to bring into being. Alessandro Pizzorno has recently given an original and subtle new twist to this general argument in adding to the social motivation, rationality, and language stressed by earlier critics an additional socially acquired attribute as a precondition for the making of the contract.[38] He contends that individuals who possessed no enduring sense of their individual identities transcending particular encounters with others would have no incentive to enter into a contract with others. The reciprocal recognition by others of their durable identities, that is, "recognition of an individual as being the same throughout different interactions,"[39] is necessary for the contract to be in the common interest of individuals intent on their own self-preservation. Otherwise, no one would be sufficiently strongly motivated to renounce force or fraud on future occasions when it seemed to their advantage to do so.[40]

Pizzorno concludes: "The original resource a human being can offer to another is the capacity to recognize the worth of the other to exist—a resource that cannot be produced if it is not shared."[41] This resembles the point made earlier, supported by Leo Strauss and Michael Oakeshott, that people need and seek from others confirmation of their own self-evaluations. But rather than stressing in Hobbesian fashion the inevitable frustration of this need in view of the overweening vanity of humans and the ensuing antagonism among them, Pizzorno stresses its mutuality and sees it as a necessary condition for the existence of social order. He interprets the self-preservation that Hobbes saw as the fundamental motive inducing men to make the social contract as implying not just a wish for bodily survival but literally as a wish for the preservation of the *self*, that is, of a "socially constructed" psychic entity that persists through changes in time and space.

This view is consistent with accepted (or "mainstream") sociological conceptions of social motivation, the self and its formation, although Pizzorno does not spell this out in any detail. The desire for recognition from others (in the form of a "need for social approval") is regarded by sociologists as the prime socializing motive, often as virtually the dominant motive actuating human beings, leading to an oversocialized conception of human nature.[42] The self as an object of consciousness is a product of the reflexivity of language. The individual's emotionally charged self-evaluation is derived from, in the phrase of Harry Stack Sullivan, the only psychiatric theorist to be influenced by the social psychology of G. H. Mead, "the reflected appraisals of others." Pizzorno therefore has advanced a version of the view that men would have to be already socialized to enter into the Hobbesian (or Lockean) social contract. He also makes the secondary point that there would have to have been some sense of limits or boundaries to the population covered by the contract, establishing clearly "who must obey and who is entitled to be protected."[43] Thus in addition to individual identity, an at least latent awareness of group identity would also have to have been present.

The case against Hobbes's "individualistic theory of social order," as Pizzorno has called it, has often been overdone. While rightly criticizing some of the conceptual limitations in Hobbes's views of the origins of man's cognitive capacities, the acuteness of his perception of the role of fear of violence in political life is not always given sufficient credit. And his perception of the workings of human vanity is not only acute but points at least implicitly to a more intimate involvement of individuals with one another than his theory seems to entail. Yet at the very level of motivation where his insights are sharpest, he can also be faulted for their one-sidedness in minimizing the powerful emotional ties and mutual identifications that provide the deep underpinnings of human society.

ROUSSEAU: VANITY, VANITY, ALL IS VANITY

It has long been a commonplace to contrast Hobbes and Rousseau, with Hobbes seen as viewing human nature as evil and society a protection against it while Rousseau regarded men as naturally good but corrupted by society.[44] Like most clichés this is at least a half-truth. Rousseau himself occasionally posed the difference between himself and Hobbes in just these terms: he contended in the *Discourse on Inequality* that Hobbes described man in the state of nature as "naturally evil"[45] and in a famous letter to Malesherbes thirteen years afterward represented his "illumination" on the road to Vincennes as the revelation "that man is naturally good and that it is by their institutions alone that men become wicked."[46] However, Hobbes and Rousseau agreed in virtually identical terms that "good" and "evil," or "right" and "wrong," connoted relations with others and thus presupposed the presence of society. They therefore had no meaning whatever in the state of nature where men lived solitary lives.

The Hobbes-Rousseau contrast is usually drawn in Hobbes's favor. Hobbes may have, it is conceded, exaggerated the nastiness of human beings, but he was a "realist" and the twentieth century has shown just how nasty they can be. Rousseau, on the other hand, is regarded as a sentimental romantic with dangerously proto-totalitarian utopian ideas about the possibility of transforming man and society.[47] The adjective "naive" has so often preceded "Rousseauian" as to seem part of a portmanteau, or at least a hyphenated, word. Most intellectuals and social scientists would rather be thought to possess a jaundiced view of humanity than to be considered "sentimental," "naive," Panglossian, or unrealistically "utopian" in outlook. Rousseau's popular reputation has undoubtedly suffered from this bias.

Rousseau is said to have glorified the Noble Savage, picturing him as following a happy and simple mode of life at peace with his fellows and ruled by benevolent feelings toward them. He has been both scorned for his "primitivism" and hailed as the "father of anthropology" for having affirmed a favorable image of primitive man as the touchstone against which to measure the cruelties, miseries, and hypocrisies of civilization. If the reading of moral lessons from the primitive to the fallen present has not necessarily characterized all anthropology—it hardly applies to Victorian evolutionism, for example—it has been quite salient in this century, especially in the work of Margaret Mead, Ruth Benedict, Edward Sapir, and Claude Lévi-Strauss, the personality and culture theorists of the 1930s and 1940s in general, and the neo-Freudian psychoanalysts who influenced and were influenced by them.[48] Several of these writers became famous beyond the precincts of academic anthropology precisely because they used cultural anthropology as a weapon of social criticism.

The cliché that Rousseau regarded primitive man as good is almost invariably understood as implying that primitive societies are harmonious and cooperative, veritable utopias incarnating altruism and the Christian virtues.[49] But Rousseau's state of nature was a nonsocial condition and he took great pains to emphasize this. Against Aristotle, Hobbes,[50] and Locke, he refused to concede that even the nuclear family was in any sense a "natural" social group. In the *Discourse on Inequality* he specifically stressed the casual, impermanent nature of sexual attraction between males and females, and the limited duration of the mother-child bond. If Hobbes is right that "the wicked man is. . .a robust child," Rousseau asks, why are familial relations not also subject to the war of all against all?[51] He devoted a long endnote to criticizing Locke's argument that the union between male and female in the state of nature is likely to become a lasting one, buttressing his general argument for transitory and promiscuous sexual contacts with zoological information about other species.[52] Since he saw dependent relations as the source of all the evils of the social condition, Rousseau went to considerable lengths to emphasize their absence where, as in the state of nature, needs are simple and mainly physical, nature is abundant, and the population far from dense. Like Hobbes before him, he stressed the fundamental equality of men in the state of nature, ruling out the development of stable ties of bondage among them.

Rousseau divests his men in the state of nature of many distinctively human characteristics assumed by Hobbes and Locke, as he himself explicitly noted.[53] He suggests the interdependence of language and thought, and the extreme unlikelihood of language developing in the absence of a regular social life placing a premium on communication. He does not assume the presence of the human faculty of reason that loomed so large for both Hobbes and Locke (as well, of course, as for the ancients). In a bold and lapidary phrase Rousseau even pronounces that "The man who meditates is a depraved animal."[54] The absence of reason and imagination entails a lack of foresight. Men have no capacity to form ideas of future outcomes and to act in order to realize them—the very essence of human action guided by ends or intentions in the view of Talcott Parsons, John Dewey, G. H. Mead, and contemporary analytic philosophers alike. Like the lower animals, Rousseau's natural men live entirely in the present. Only two attributes distinguish them from animals: free will, meaning no instincts that rigidly determine behavior, and "perfectability" or the faculty of "self-improvement," amounting essentially to the ability to learn new things, although Rousseau is quick to note that what is learned may be—in fact has been—a source of misfortune and degradation, depriving men of the simple satisfactions of their animal-like existence in the state of nature.

Rousseau's savages, as he himself acknowledged, are essentially animals rather than humans; the entire realm of mind and of psychic as against physical need is alien to them. The only quality they possess that might be regarded by human standards as moral is an instinct of pity for the sufferings of their fellows. But far from being peculiarly human, this "noble" attitude is shared with other animal species and is all but extinguished among civilized men. Ruled most completely by their minds and repressive of their feelings, philosophers, Rousseau pointedly remarks, are especially likely to manifest what might be called the Kitty Genovese syndrome by pulling the covers over their ears if their sleep is disturbed by the cries of a murder victim beneath their bedroom windows.[55] Rousseau does not explain why his savages should feel such intense sympathy for the misfortunes of others with whom they only intermittently come into contact.

In arguing that society corrupted the peaceful, simple life of his savages, Rousseau meant "society" in the fullest and most literal sense—not just civilized or modern societies such as eighteenth-century France, nor this or that noxious social institution such as private property or authoritarian government, but the involvement of human beings with one another as such, sociability in and of itself. To be sure, it is a misreading of Rousseau to claim that he celebrated the Noble Savage in the state of nature; "nascent society" was for him "the golden mean between the indolence of the primitive state and the petulant activity of our own pride [that] must have been the happiest epoch and the most lasting."[56] This idealized condition, as anthropologists have pointed out, corresponds roughly to the neolithic era in human history.[57]

The seeds of destruction lie within it, however. With the growth of population, competition for limited resources is intensified. The human capacity for self-improvement leads to the invention of new tools and the resulting greater productivity gives rise to new and more elaborate material needs. The new technology requires more complex skills which accentuate and endow with increased relevance individual differences that previously counted for little.[58] The more talented and energetic individuals acquire greater possessions and positions in the division of labor, rendering others dependent upon them. Inequality is born and with it conflict between the haves and the have-nots. Something resembling Hobbes's war of all against all ensues, but it is the product of social life rather than antedating it as it did for Hobbes. The inventions of metallurgy and agriculture accelerate these trends: "It is iron and wheat which first civilized men and ruined the human race."[59]

But not private property, nor the division of labor, nor even inequality in and of themselves create or constitute the evils of civilization, although many commentators on Rousseau have mistaken one or the other of them as the major culprit.[60] The root of all evil is, rather, vanity, what Rousseau called *amour propre*, the compulsion to compare oneself with others and to strive to elevate one's own position in their eyes on a scale of invidious distinctions. *This* is the worm in the apple, the dog in the manger, the blot on the escutcheon—the fundamental flaw in human nature that produces the exploitation of the poor by the rich, the snobbery of the highly placed toward their inferiors, the cruelty inflicted by the rulers on the ruled—all the miseries of civilization that are absent in the state of nature and at most only latent in nascent society.[61]

Rousseau's fateful *amour propre* is our old friend the quest for glory, so prominent in Machiavelli, Hobbes, and earlier writers, encountered once again. But Rousseau democratizes, as it were, the striving for glory: life in society implants it in Everyman—it is not just the ambition of princes or, as for Hobbes, the dangerous aspiration of "children of pride" forcing everyone else into a hostile defensive posture. Moreover, far from being an innate potential in human nature, it emerges only when men are compelled by technology and the division of labor to live cheek by jowl with one another in relations of interdependence that inevitably become hierarchical, subjecting some, the majority, to the power of others. In Durkheim's theory of the origins of the division of labor which was clearly influenced by Rousseau's, greater "material density" of population resulting from growth in numbers leads to a greater "moral" or "dynamic density" giving rise to occupational differentiation and to a more complex common morality that becomes the foundation of a new and in some ways deeper form of social solidarity.[62] For Rousseau, on the other hand, more frequent social interaction caused people to become preoccupied with the impression they make on others and to strive to enhance it, creating a gap between the reality of what they are and the appearance they try to present to others. Far from producing a new form of social solidarity, the division of labor for Rousseau produces vanity, deceit, and rivalry, binding men together in ties of hostile rather than fraternal dependence.

Hypocrisy and inauthenticity are born as soon as men begin to care obsessively what others think of them and to strive to make a favorable impression. Again and again Rousseau adverts to this; the desire for wealth and power are but expressions of it.[63] Jean Starobinski's interpretation of Rousseau as an existentialist *avant la lettre*[64] has been widely praised; there is indeed a direct line of continuity between Rousseau's denunciation of vanity and the Sartrean theme, still central to French structuralist and post-structuralist thought, that all of us are prisoners of the "gaze of the Other."[65] Or, as Sartre's famous complaint in *Huis clos* (No Exit) had it, "Hell is other people!" Rousseau's objection is to the falsity of the appearances people create to deceive others whereas Sartre's is to the fixity of being regarded by others as no more than the sum of one's past actions despite one's freedom to embrace new projects that transcend and negate the past. Yet in both writers the Other is the enemy with whom one is inescapably and compulsively preoccupied. Despite his reputation for a sentimentally optimistic view of the goodness of man's nature, reiterated by scholars and intellectuals who ought to know better, there is a deep strain of misanthropy in Rousseau, which is altogether congruent with what we know of his personality.[66] (On the other hand, Hobbes, for all his cynicism, was evidently a likeable, even lovable, and gregarious man.)[67]

Both Hobbes and Rousseau gave an agonistic twist to the very motive so many sociologists have identified as the psychological foundation of society itself: the desire to win approval from others. Sociologists and social psychologists have formulated it in a variety of ways: as the need for social validation of one's ideal self-image, as the striving for prestige or status that underlies social stratification, more recently as the quest for identity, both personal and social.[68] Parsons's ego-alter model, in which two actors exhibit a "complementarity of expectations" because of their "need-disposition" to win approval from one another by conforming to norms they hold in common, grounds social order itself in this dominant motive. Nor have social scientists failed to analyze its different forms and nuances. The needs for "respect" and for "love" have been differentiated; W. I. Thomas's antique but once influential social psychology distinguished them as wishes for "recognition" and for "response," two of the four wishes he saw as the motivational forces driving human behavior. Both Hobbes and Rousseau, so often dismissed as abstract individualists insensitive to the dependence of human nature on social life, single out as the source of ubiquitous conflict, contention, and discord among men the same basic motive habitually invoked by sociologists as the psychological basis of the cooperation, conformity, and consensus they regard as the very essence of social order.[69] Elster observes that "many people are simultaneously motivated by the desire to stand out *and* by the norm against sticking one's neck out."[70] Certainly, there is such a norm, but just as the "desire to stand out" corresponds to Hobbes's "glory" and Rousseau's "*amour propre*" as motives, so the desire for the security of unconditional acceptance by others may motivate unadventurous conformity.

Discussions of the problem of order invariably center on Hobbes and completely ignore Rousseau's much more resolutely nonsocial version of the state of nature. The most obvious explanation for this is that Parsons, the dominant figure in sociological theory for several decades, introduced the problem of order and discussed it in relation to Hobbes, Locke, Malthus, and the Social Darwinists without so much as mentioning Rousseau in his entire lengthy and famous book. That Parsons's discussion, with its focus on the Hobbesian war of all against all as the negation of order, became so influential itself requires explanation. A resemblance between Hobbes's state of nature and the relentless competitiveness of capitalism has long been noted and exaggerated. The apocalyptic, catastrophist overtones of the Hobbesian vision of universal conflict undoubtedly catches the imagination of twentieth-century men and women and feeds into real fears of social breakdown. Yet to regard the equation of social dissolution with violent conflict as no more than a reflection of capitalism or the turmoil of this century, and in the West at that, is to be much too present-minded and ethnocentric: as we have already seen, a most Hobbesian-sounding Islamic saying propounds that "Sixty years of tyranny are better than one hour of civil strife."[71] Rousseau's alternative vision, however, of amiable, self-reliant creatures wandering alone in the forest, except for their solitariness rather like the Neanderthal men in William Golding's novel *The Inheritors*, lacks any melodramatic contemporary flair. Hobbesian men are—or at least are thought to be—more like Golding's brutal but intelligent Cro-Magnon men who overpower the Neanderthalers, or, for that matter, like the English schoolboys gone native in his most famous novel, *Lord of the Flies*.

Neither Rousseau's state of nature nor his "golden mean" of self-sufficient farmers much resembles any actual primitive societies, which are typically characterized by considerably tighter bonds of interdependence.[72] At most, they perhaps suggest a few hunting and gathering peoples subsisting in sparsely settled and harsh environments at a lower technological level than neolithic agriculturalists.[73] Although Rousseau's espousal in *The Social Contract* of a new social contract based on the "general will" has been interpreted by a number of recent commentators as a means of regaining the absolute freedom and self-sufficiency of the state of nature described in the *Discourse on Inequality* under conditions of permanent social life, he is not easily represented as a partisan of *Gemeinschaft* bent on overcoming "loss of community" in the impersonal mass society of modern times.[74] Indeed, his solitary and autonomous men, compassionate but indifferent to the opinions of their fellows and disinclined to mingle with them apart from the family ties present in nascent society, resemble if anything the much-attacked "privatization" of contemporary suburban life.[75]

The attention given to Hobbes's war of all against all as the negation of social order and the neglect of Rousseau's more comprehensively nonsocial version may also account for the erroneous conflation of universal conflict with the lack of predictability of human behavior to which I have frequently referred. Robert Edgerton, for example, declares that "the fundamental problem in bringing about social order is to make behavior predictable and controllable."[76] But if people had as little to do with one another as Rousseau's self-sufficient unsavage savages, it would surely not matter much if the behavior of others was not predictable and controllable so long as it posed no threat. Security from violence at the hands of others requires only a limited predictability and such security is all that is needed to avoid Hobbesian universal conflict. The emphasis on social order as predictability of behavior by contemporary theorists tacitly presupposes the "iron cage" of economic interdependence in advanced modern societies: the existence of "hospitals, the cops and garbage collection," as Schulberg's character quoted in Chapter 2 put it.

Nevertheless, Rousseau as much as—in a sense even more than—Hobbes presented a vision of the lack of social order and rooted both its initial absence and the later coming of society in a conception of developing human nature. Order and disorder are matters of degree. This is especially the case where lack of order connotes isolation and indifference rather than hostility and conflict. The absence of wider social ties, the centering of life in a micro-society of family, friends, and neighbors combined with indifference and suspicion toward large organizations and the macro-world of politics and the market in general,[77] is more characteristic of large-scale modern societies, especially the United States, than deepening interindividual and intergroup conflict manifesting itself in outbreaks of crime and violence. Rousseau may be a better guide to this kind of weakening of order than catastrophist readings of Hobbes. Why should the breakdown of society immediately suggest violence and fighting in the streets rather than merely the loosening of social ties and the dispersion, if not of individuals, of dyads, families, and small groups, minding their own business of cultivating their private gardens while apathetic toward any wider social commitments? The many observers who have reported and expressed alarm over a trend to privatization assume the continuance of a high standard of living based on a worldwide complex division of labor and economic interdependence. The Industrial Revolution and the greatly expanded life-chances it made possible for individuals were in no way anticipated by Rousseau who looked backward to an idealized rural past.[78] In this sense he was a premodern thinker, if not quite the celebrant of a virtuous natural man living in fraternity with his fellows that he is so often caricatured as being.

PARSONS ON HOBBES AND THE PROBLEM OF ORDER

Parsons deserves credit for having perceived the superior realism of Hobbes's sense of inherent tensions among men as against Locke's more optimistic belief in a "natural identity of interests,"[79] especially in light of the Lockean assumptions so deeply rooted in American social thought.[80] I recall many years ago when teaching introductory sociology to freshmen I used to ask them how they thought societies had first come into being in the remote past. My ultimate pedagogic intention was to assert that it was a false question, that humans and their proto-human ancestors had always lived in societies and their very biological evolution as a species had been shaped by that fact.[81] Students usually produced some variant of the following response: "Well, suppose there were two families living in caves on opposite sides of a hill. A saber-toothed tiger appeared and threatened one of them. *Naturally* (*sic*!), they joined forces to drive the tiger away." How Lockean can you get? I wondered. Ignoring for the moment that the students saw the existence of families, which surely are at least mini-societies, as nonproblematical, I then would ask them: "Why isn't it just as plausible to imagine that one family egged the tiger on to attack the other, or at least looked on passively while the tiger killed their neighbors, and then occupied the other family's cave and appropriated its material possessions?"

The students thought this Hobbesian suggestion a shockingly cynical one.

Parsons paid little attention to Hobbes's conception and enumeration of the passions, and none at all to the social origins of reason, language, or selfhood. In treating Hobbes as others had before him as a Utilitarian, Parsons's emphasis was on rationality as the efficient linkage of ends and means, what has come to be known as "instrumental reason." His argument was primarily directed against this view of reason so central to classical and neoclassical economic theory with its concentration on the allocation of means or resources among ends assumed to be "discrete and unrelated" and on the particular version of atomistic individualism implicit in this approach.[82] Parsons was seeking a rationale for sociological as distinct from economic theory—indeed for sociology itself as a discipline—that, instead of treating the ends men pursue as residual, would center on their commonality and social origin. Hence his critical assault on the assumption of what he called the "randomness of ends," which is clearly a version of the economist's principle of the noncomparability of utilities or preferences, the assumption that there is no objective standard by which they can be measured and evaluated.[83] Economics becomes the study of how scarce means are allocated among the ends individuals happen to hold and pursue, whether these ends are base or noble, petty or grand, egoistic or altruistic.

Human beings may serve as means to one another's ends. The use of force or fraud by an individual to coerce or manipulate others may be a highly effective way of advancing his or her own ends. The absence of rules proscribing the unrestricted use of human beings as means or instruments is to Parsons the essence of the Hobbesian problem of order and the war of all against all. There is an unmistakable Kantian note in the importance Parsons attaches to the prohibition on the use of human beings as means. Since for Hobbes the social contract was negotiated because it was perceived by reason as an effective "means" to the "end" of individual biological self-preservation, he could be seen as a precursor of the economist's instrumental version of reason and of the individual and "given" nature of the ends it serves.

Hobbes certainly regarded reason as the servant of the passions: "For the Thoughts, are to the Desires, as Scouts and Spies, to range abroad, and find the way to things Desired."[84] But it was the nature of the desires or passions, their thrusting of men into competition and conflict with one another, that caused the war of all against all rather than, as Parsons would have it, the indifference of reason to the selection of means on any grounds other then sheer efficiency. The content of the passions can hardly be regarded as an incidental matter randomly variable among individuals, for their content shapes the particular ends men seek which bring them into conflict with one another. This is clearly true of the quests for glory, intrinsically scarce because it is inherently relational and comparative, and for gain or riches defined as one man's excess over that of another. It is not merely, as Parsons would have it, that men are tempted to use other men in the service of their ends; the very existence of others constitutes an obstacle to realizing the ends each and every one of them pursues given the fact of scarcity. Ends dictated by the passions and objective conditions of scarcity combine to bring about universal conflict rather than conflict resulting from the morally indifferent rational choice of means stressed by Parsons.

Parsons was concerned with ends rather than with motives (or "passions")[85] because he was arguing against both behaviorism and biologism in favor of what would today be called "intentionality" or "agency" in human action: the purposive, teleological, goal-directed nature of human behavior and its capacity to change the situation rather than merely to respond to it passively. Hence his much-debated choice of "voluntaristic" to characterize his theory of action. His position was not essentially different from that of John Dewey, who at roughly the same time was insisting on the reality and autonomy of "ends-in-view" as causes of human action capable of producing effects on the world.[86] In describing the "passions" as "discrete, randomly variant ends of action,"[87] Parsons passed over altogether the distinction between motives and ends or intentions of which recent analytic philosophers have made so much.[88]

For Hobbes it is the passions, to which reason is subordinate, that create the war of all against all, but it is reason in the service of the most general and powerful passion of all, the wish to live, that discovers the "way out" in conceiving and implementing a social contract. For Parsons, on the other hand, the war of all against all is the result of amoral reason blind to any consideration other then effectiveness in achieving ends, whatever the content of the ends. Parsons's focus was on action[89] in the form of the isolated "unit act" involving an actor, a set of unmodifiable conditions including the presence of other people, a given or "random" end, and an array of possible means that might be deployed by the actor to realize the end. His basic thesis was that action *must* be social in the sense that ends are not random but are socially acquired or learned. But Parsons's social action is not equivalent to social *inter*action, although it obviously implies that such interaction has taken place in the past since the ends have been socially acquired. His concern with the social derivation of ends leads him to omit from his account of the unit act any reference to motivation, to the passions that for Hobbes were major causes of the miseries of the state of nature. Hence also Parsons's imputation to Hobbes of the idea of "randomness of ends" for failing to address the commonality of ends shaped by values and norms that the actors acquire from their society.

Parsons contends that to Hobbes and the Utilitarians both the diverse ends pursued by a single individual and the multiple ends pursued by different individuals are random.[90] Parsons means "random in a statistical sense":[91] the pursuit of one end does not increase or decrease the probability of any other end being pursued by another actor or by the same actor on another occasion. In short, there are no connections between ends; they are unrelated in the sense of having been formed independently of one another in the absence of social influence. The randomness of a single individual's ends also implies their lack of grounding in a relatively stable motivational matrix or character structure. But Parsons, at least in *The Structure of Social Action*,[92] was primarily interested in the putative randomness of the ends of different individuals. His major argument, virtually the foundation of his entire subsequent theoretical position, was that the ends of individuals mutually determine each other and are held in common as a result of the actors' sharing a common culture of "value-orientations."

Parsons's use of the term "randomness" was unfortunate for a quite different reason: it lends apparent legitimacy to the readiness of later sociologists to define the problem of order itself as primarily a problem of the specter of irregularity and unpredictability in human behavior and even of total cognitive chaos or solipsism, excluding the possibility of any common stable body of knowledge about the world. Academic men are notoriously inclined to define all problems as resulting from uncertain knowledge, although Parsons himself was not guilty of this in his own original discussion of the problem of order.

Parsons's definition of randomness as lack of causal—or probabilistic—connection among ends clearly excludes the common ends acquired through membership in a group that are his primary concern. But it does not exclude the possibility that individuals might hold *like* as distinct from *common* ends, in Robert MacIver's once well-known distinction.[93] Indeed, it is precisely the fact that men hold like ends as a result of their common psychological constitution and are fated to live under conditions of scarcity ensuring that some will not attain their ends that to Hobbes accounts for the war of all against all. Here Parsons's notion of the randomness of the plural ends held by single individuals leads him to neglect the rootedness for Hobbes of the potential for the war of all against all in human nature, despite Parsons's acknowledgment of scarcity as one of its major preconditions. Parsons's emphasis on universal means both reflects the emphasis of the economists on scarce material means and foreshadows Parsons's later much-discussed parallel between *power* and *money* as means or "media."[94] The seductive appeal of such means in the service of a wide, if not infinite, range of ends is what creates the potentiality of the war of all against all.[95]

If the war of all against all results from the use of force and fraud as means to "random" ends, then it could be averted by preventing the use of these means. Hobbes's solution was to rule out such means by empowering a sovereign to use force against miscreants who resorted to them. For Parsons, the same result was achieved by a moral consensus on the prohibition of their use that is successfully learned ("internalized") by members of the group.[96] Since the lack of any normative limitation on the use of means is what creates the threat of disorder, nothing in Parsons's account excludes the possibility of a social order that institutes norms proscribing force and fraud as means while at the same time most of the ends men pursue continue to be random in Parsons's sense.[97] To be sure, the common end of eliminating force and fraud as means is implied by Parsons's (and Hobbes's) account, but this is a "procedural" end, so to speak, and need not entail that other ends are held in common and thus overcome the general condition of "randomness" of ends that Parsons imputes to the Utilitarians.

Such a loose "individualistic" society held together only by conformity to negative procedural norms is a far cry from the wide and deep normative consensus penetrating and molding the very motivational springs of human action that is the hallmark of Parsons's social theory. This theory achieved its fullest and most explicit formulation in his later work, but the emphasis on common ends and "ultimate values" was present in *Structure*, going far beyond what would appear by his own account to be the minimal requirements for avoiding the war of all against all and thereby "solving" the problem of order.[98] Parsons fails to distinguish between two things both of which are of vital importance to his overall conception, most fully developed in the later work, of a stable, relatively "integrated" social order or system. First, the negative potentiality of the war of all against all must be avoided. This is a precondition for, second, the commitment of the members of society to common ends or collective goals requiring cooperative action on their part. The elimination of the fear and mistrust induced by the war of all against all is a necessary but not a sufficient condition for commitment to common goals and cooperation in their pursuit. The distinction is implicit in the different ways Parsons himself and many of his followers have used the terms "norm" and "value," norms referring to means, some proscribed and others prescribed, while common values shape the specific ends of action and themselves form a system ordered by a commitment to "ultimate values."[99]

In Parsons's later theorizing he anchored the unit act, that is, the means-ends relationship, to the personality system of the actor at one pole and to the cultural system at the other with the social system mediating between them in the form of "role-expectations" to couple together the "need-dispositions" of the personality and the "value-orientations" of the culture. This was the synthesis of Durkheim and Freud that constituted the essence of Parsonsian theory. At the level of action, it assumed actors motivated by a "need-disposition" to seek approval from others by conforming to norms stemming from generalized value-orientations that they shared as a result of having acquired them through "socialization." Hence the famous ego-alter relationship characterized by "complementarity of expectations" that became Parsons's paradigm of the social system.[100] That it advanced too harmonious and fully realized a unity of the personality, cultural, and social systems, of the "individual" and "society," was the essence of the charge that it projected an oversocialized view of man and an overintegrated view of society. Although Parsons's later accounts of the socialization process shaping individual personality and of the structural-functional interlocking of the institutions of the society were only adumbrated in *Structure*, the roots of these conceptions are clearly discernible in his discussion of Hobbes and the problem of order.

One is struck by the degree to which Parsons read norms into the very nature of human action itself: "In terms of the given conceptual scheme there is no such thing as action except as effort to conform with norms just as there is no such thing as motion except as change of location in space."[101] In *Structure*'s concluding chapter, Parsons directly identifies the "teleological character" of action with its "normative orientation."[102] If "normative" includes *any* "selective standard in terms of which the end is related to the situation,"[103] then obviously any and all purposive or goal-directed behavior, any and all action in short as distinct from mere reactive response to stimuli, is by definition normative. Parsons states directly at the beginning of the chapter in which he develops his end-means schema that action is "normative" because it involves a "choice of alternatives," a view that brings him very close to the definition of human action of later post-Wittgensteinian analytic philosophers of action, who did not, at least explicitly, equate choice with choice between conformity or nonconformity to established social norms.[104]

If action necessarily entails goal-direction and choice, it certainly includes the plans and projects of the criminal and the rebel, even the satanic designs of the truly wicked, as well as the dutiful discharge of moral obligations by the well-socialized good citizen.[105] Action guided by a plan, an intention to bring about a particular outcome, is obviously subject to a "selective standard" and to a choice of alternatives, but even if one questionably calls such action "normative," it is not the case that it must necessarily be shaped by what sociologists call "social norms," that is, prevailing norms that are collectively shared and sanctioned. Yet Parsons tended to identify the normative with *shared* standards, with "patterns which are, by the actor and other members of the same collectivity, deemed desirable."[106] Presumably, this equation of the normative with the purposive and voluntaristic nature of human action, stemming from humanity's distinctive capacities for thought and language, is what Jeffrey Alexander has in mind when he criticizes Parsons for conflating action and order.[107]

But additional "conflations," or failures to make necessary distinctions, are also involved. The human capacity to formulate and pursue ends or purposes and to act on them in efforts to change the situation—Parsons's means-ends relationship, in short—is indeed the product of social experience and interaction. The acquisition of such a capacity, a consequence of the mastery of language, is an achievement of the primary socialization through which infants acquire uniquely human attributes such as linguistic competence and self-consciousness. But this process does not necessarily involve the full internalization of the moral norms and values that make up the cultural tradition of the group into which the infant is born. Cognitive and motivational or emotional socialization are distinct and different processes. The impact of social experience on the formation of human capacities is more universal and is a precondition for socialization understood as the learning and internalization of moral norms, including those that temper or direct the impulses and tensions that might threaten social order.[108] Parsons often seems to identify the social *per se* with the normative, as Durkheim did before him.[109]

Parsons's claim that norms are inherent in action appears on the surface to resemble my own argument that latent norms in the form of felt obligations restricting choice are generated spontaneously in the interplay of mutual expectations that constitutes recurrent social interaction. But Parsons's conception is quite different. His basic concern, adapted from economics, is with individual action—the unit act—rather than with social interaction; the actor's normative "selective standard" linking means to ends, though originally socially acquired, is imported into the situation in which he or she acts from the outside rather than emerging in the course of the actor's response to the situation. Even in Parsons's ego-alter model of interaction, the actors bring to their encounter normative orientations derived from their common culture that control their efforts to gain approval from one another. As Parsons's interactionist and phenomenological critics have pointed out, he assumes the preexistence of ready-made norms that have been adopted by the actors as a result of socialization rather than conceiving of norms as negotiated or even constructed in the process of interaction itself. His norms are "given" by the larger society to which the actors belong, specifically by their past acquisition of those norms through socialization, rather than emerging from their interaction.

Parsons's focus on the means-ends relationship stemmed from his salutary effort to assert against the behaviorists the causal efficacy of "subjective" ends in the mind of the actor that were freely chosen by the actor rather than dictated by external pressures or past "conditioning." But as a representation of action, his means-ends schema of unit acts linked in chains evokes, in me at least, a curious recollection of crude early motion pictures showing people jerkily scuttling from place to place, stopping suddenly, and then bobbing forward again in a sequence of spasmodic movements. Parsons's preoccupation with linked purposeful acts reflects his debate with the economists, although one critic has suggested that it represents "a culture-bound approximation to behavior in Western societies."[110] The later "linguistic turn" in social thought, including Wittgenstein's concept of "following a rule," presents a less action-centered and goal-directed view of the "point of view of the actor," in Parsons's oft-repeated phrase. It affirms, rather, that what is distinctively human is the "reflexive monitoring" by consciousness of *all* experience, active, passive, and purely intrapsychic.[111]

Parsons will probably always be identified with an insistence on the significance of the normative in human behavior, an insistence very much worth making at the time he initially made it,[112] but also with carrying it to the point of exaggerating the power of norms and values to control and even extirpate impulsive and self-interested motivations, both in overt action and even more in intrapsychic life.[113] He did not really have a theory of human nature at all, nor even a general "conception of man," whether oversocialized or not, in *Structure,* although in that first and most famous book he introduced the problem of order and his normative solution to it in rejecting the utilitarian individualism of economic theory. There is a sense in which his entire later theorizing, employing a selective interpretation of Freud at the psychological level and an adaptation of anthropological functionalism at the sociological level, is an attempt to buttress his original normative solution, as a number of his critics have noted. His staunchest defenders against the avalanche of often intemperate and unjust criticism to which he was subjected in the late 1960s and the 1970s have argued that his concepts were based on "analytical abstraction" and were not intended to be applied literally to concrete reality,[114] that in his voluminous writings he often qualified them himself, and that his view of human action was actually "multidimensional" in taking into account more fully than other theorists both normative and egoistic motivations.[115] Yet even his most ardent followers usually end up conceding that his work often managed to convey at least the impression of giving pride of place to individual motivations to conform to established norms, and to value consensus as opposed to social conflict in the larger society. Insofar as Parsons's search for a disciplinary mandate for sociology dictated this emphasis, one can argue that, as in the frequent conservative import of his general theory, he was much too ready to find an intellectual rationale for existing academic divisions into separate disciplines in the social sciences.

In a sense none of the theorists considered in this chapter was chiefly concerned with human nature in its own right. Hobbes and Locke were mainly preoccupied with forms of government and invoked human nature to support their preferences. The same was often true of Rousseau, although that strange and fertile genius, arguably the most extraordinary intellectual figure of the past two and a half centuries, tended to become passionately caught up in whatever aroused his interest. Adam Smith had a rich and subtle view of human nature, as did his fellow Scottish moralists, a view often foreshadowing later formulations,[116] but I have dealt with him only briefly and incidentally in passing. Parsons in *Structure* was more concerned with insisting on the significance of the normative in human action than with developing a theory of human nature as such. In his later work he drew on Freud to formulate an elaborate theory and even elevated personality to equal status with culture and society as partially independent "systems" determining human action. Yet for all the importance he accorded to personality, critics have justly charged him with a selective approach that assigns priority to those psychological traits and dispositions sustaining conformity to social norms and the maintenance of cultural patterns, those that, in effect, confirm the normative solution to the problem of order advanced in *Structure*.[117] When we turn to Freud, and much more briefly to some of his followers and revisers, we confront an approach that was first and foremost concerned with a motivational theory of human nature and only secondarily interested in its implications and ramifications for the problem of order or for society in general. That does not mean that it had no such implications and ramifications.

CHAPTER FIVE

THE FREUDIAN SYNTHESIS

Sigmund Freud's theory of human nature was developed in the course of his efforts as a medical doctor to diagnose and cure mental disorders. It had therefore a practical orientation aimed at the alleviation of personal suffering. The medical origins of psychoanalysis also led to its initial conception of the individual as primarily a biological organism subject to disturbances in psychic functioning that were not fundamentally different from bodily ailments and impairments. The focus on the biological individual placed Freud at a far remove from reflections on human society, its variable forms, and the patterns of change to which it has been subject in the course of history, especially the convulsive transformations associated with the birth of the modern world that were still being assimilated in the late nineteenth century. If not utterly at odds with the assumptions of the social and historical thinkers of the time, psychoanalysis at the very least came into being in an intellectual context that appeared remote from their major concerns.

Yet for a good part of the twentieth century, Freud and Marx have been what one writer has called "the two great tutelary deities of the Western intelligentsia."[1] Both were seen as adversarial figures opposed to the dominant beliefs, values, and institutions of the bourgeois capitalist order that had crystallized in the previous century, Freud at the level of personal life, Marx at the level of the larger political and economic system. Both developed their theories outside of the university and initially appealed to extra-academic constituencies, Freud as a controversial member of the medical profession, Marx as a private scholar with ties to radical political parties and sects of intellectuals and workers.

That both theories promised far-reaching changes aimed at vast improvements in the condition of man and society, Freud by an innovative therapeutic treatment of the individual, Marx by creating through revolution a new social order, accounts for the pressures toward closure in their theorizing that often gave their doctrines a dogmatic, catechistic cast reminding their critics of theological creeds. Similarly, the organizations formed by their adherents were often seen as bearing a resemblance to churches and sects. Neither Marxism nor Freudianism could ever be regarded as strictly academic theories, whether in a positive or negative vein. Indeed, both theories were unevenly and incompletely absorbed into the academy until well into the present century, although Freudianism, especially in the United States, for a few decades was the core of medical training in psychiatry. Apart from the medicalization of psychoanalysis, Freud and Marx appealed mainly to several generations of independent intellectuals who defined themselves as unremitting critics of their culture.

Orthodox or "official" Marxists condemned psychoanalysis as a manifestation of bourgeois decadence and self-indulgence. Freud was severely skeptical of the belief that abolition of private property would create a "new man" liberated from the psychological afflictions of the past.[2] But the appeal of both doctrines to dissident intellectuals gave rise to many attempts to synthesize them by combining Freud's concern for the individual sufferers from the personal frustrations imposed by cultural demands with Marx's vision of large-scale historical change culminating in communism. The most famous and comprehensive attempt was that of the Frankfurt School, formed by German intellectuals on the margins of the university in the 1920s and 1930s, but achieving its maximum influence during the campus revolts of the sixties in both Europe and America. The much sought-after union of Marx and Freud represented a particular version of the perennial problem in social theory of the relation between the individual and society, the micro level of everyday life and the macro level of major institutions, personal agency and impersonal structure, to cite just a few of the many nuanced differences in its phrasing. Attempts at a Marx-Freud synthesis do not quite amount to a distinctive rendition of the problem of order because both Marx and Freud are chiefly identified with forces undermining order: class conflict for Marx and individual desires at odds with social norms for Freud. Yet both theorists also tried to account for what sustained order as well as for what challenged it. As a variant of the problem of relating the individual and society, the effort to unite Marx and Freud had special pathos in envisaging the total overcoming of both personal discontent and social conflict.

The late twentieth century has not been kind to either doctrine, both of them following an unmistakable arc of decline in its closing decades. Marxism achieved its widest influence among Western intellectuals in the 1960s and early 1970s when it was finally—one might even say totally—absorbed into the university, even in Britain and the United States where it had not previously been much of a presence. But the radical ferment of the sixties now appears after the collapse of Soviet Communism in Eastern Europe and the Soviet Union in 1989–91 to have been a last flare-up before extinction of the activist revolutionary aspirations of Marxism. Marxism may survive in enclaves of the academy, but shorn of its claim to a special theory-guided "praxis" it becomes just another academic perspective lacking any privileged relation to politics and history.

Nothing quite so sudden and dramatic as the collapse of Communism has befallen psychoanalysis. There has been, nevertheless, a steady erosion of its prestige on several fronts since the 1960s. Psychoanalysis first attracted intellectuals, especially in literary circles, as a doctrine of sexual liberation in the 1920s in America and a decade or so earlier in Europe.[3] It probably achieved its widest influence both as a personal ethic and as a therapy in the 1940s and 1950s, at least in the United States. The therapeutic popularity of full Freudian analysis was greatest at this time; though lengthy, expensive, and alternately demanding and frustrating as a course of treatment, it was widely believed that it truly cured the neuroses and ensured the lasting mental health—in effect, the personal happiness—of patients who submitted to it. Freudian language passed into the popular speech of the educated and even the half-educated and Freud became, in the words of Auden's "In Memory of Sigmund Freud," "No more a person/ Now but a whole climate of opinion/ Under which we conduct our differing lives."* Theories of personality and socialization based on psychoanalysis became prominent in the newer social sciences of sociology and cultural anthropology as well as in social and personality psychology, notably, as we have seen, in the magisterial theorizing of Talcott Parsons. New forms of psychotherapy have flourished since the 1960s, but orthodox psychoanalysis by medically certified psychiatrists has undergone considerable delegitimation in common with other professions claiming to apply arcane expert knowledge. Belief that the traditional therapy achieves greater and more lasting cures has waned considerably, Freud's integrity as a scientist has been challenged, and orthodox psychoanalysis has been accused of rigid conservatism on matters of gender, the family, and sexual morality.

Although efforts to base a radical critique of modern society on a union of Marx and Freud were renewed in the 1960s, they often involved, as Gary Thom wittily puts it, "asking Freud in to clean up the mess Marx made, then telling him to leave immediately afterwards."[4] Politically radical readings of Freud have inevitably shared in the general decline in radicalism capped by the collapse of Communism though under way before it. Psychoanalytic contributions to "countercultural" styles of personal life have also lost much force. Since the 1960s, it has been hard to go on believing that the ills of modern society are caused primarily by sexual repression when the near-total decline of Puritan and Victorian taboos has quite evidently not made people more selfless, loving, and less acquisitive. Freud himself never made large claims for sexual liberation, but to sexual reformers and to many Freudo-Marxist radicals, both sexual freedom in its own right and the conviction that other social evils were rooted in sexual repression became one of the more prominent "uses of faith" after Freud.[5] The prestige of psychoanalysis has suffered, paradoxically, both from the radical upsurge of the sixties when it was seen as too bourgeois and conservative and from the later decline of both the political and the "countercultural" forms of radicalism.

It does not seem likely that either the world-transforming preten-sions of Marxism or the soul-saving promise of Freudianism will be renewed. Even the Marxism that became fashionable among intel-lectuals in the sixties and seventies was a truncated version of the original doctrine, retracing backward the path from Marx to Hegel[6] and substituting revolutionary will or utopian vision for the eco-nomic forces that Marx believed would doom capitalism and ensure the advent of socialism. By 1960 history had already shown itself to be refractory to Marxist predictions, while the state socialism of the Soviet bloc retained appeal as a model only to movements in the more backward regions of the Third World.

Psychotherapy is bound to continue as a major resource for personal troubles and much of the language of psychoanalysis has passed into popular psychological argot. The rigorous, doc-trinaire Freudian form of therapy will, however, probably not win new adherents. Although psychoanalysis was institutional-ized as a branch of medicine, a case can be made that as a theory of human nature it is less tied to its medical practice than Marxism has been to the fortunes of socialist movements and the general course of history followed by industrial societies. In the past, the unique successes achieved by the therapy were often adduced in support of the theory, although there was always a critical minority that doubted whether the alleged cures amount-ed to more than a placebo effect or the efficacy of suggestion. Psychoanalysts themselves were only too ready to dismiss all informed criticism as the result of "negative transference" experi-enced by dissatisfied patients. Now that accumulated evidence suggests that the therapy is no more successful than a variety of less demanding treatments for personal troubles and neurotic dis-orders, the limitations of the therapy are often invoked to reject the theory on which it purports to base itself.

The implications, however, of using the success or failure of the therapy as a test of the theory are seldom fully considered. If the therapy really did achieve thoroughgoing cures that repre-sented unmistakable applications of methods based on the theory, psychoanalysis would be fully comparable to physics, that is, to a theory from which a technology or application possessing real practical value can be derived. In other words, it would have become an applied science having achieved full control of its subject matter, the most advanced stage of science. No other psychological or social studies discipline reputing to be "scientific" has ever been able credibly and lastingly to make such a claim. To assess psychoanalysis solely or even primarily by the successes or failures of its therapy, assuming one could agree upon and "measure" them, is to impose on it a more exacting standard than is customarily applied to any of the other nonbiological human sciences. It is perhaps comparable to evaluating Marxism solely by the Soviet "experiment," although the predictive failures of Marxism more than the Soviet debacle—the coming to power of Marxists in a backward nation such as Russia having itself notoriously not been predicted—have played the leading role in discrediting Marxism as a successful union of theory and practice. But evaluating psychoanalysis by its record as a therapy amounts to judging it by norms of application and control that go beyond even prediction, let alone the mere understanding or logical adequacy of explanation generally used as criteria in the other social sciences. To be sure, psychoanalysts, displaying a self-satisfied pomposity that is not unknown among practitioners of other fully credentialed professions, have often made vast claims for their special expertise, but, as Norman O. Brown once sardonically put it, "the world will find it easier to believe that we are all mad than that the psychoanalysts are not."[7]

FREUD AND SOCIAL THEORY

In the more restricted realm of social theory, Freud and psychoanalysis are nowadays ignored to almost as great an extent as before their influence began to increase in the 1930s. Although Parsonsian structural-functionalism and Frankfurt School Marxism—best represented by the antipodal figures of Parsons himself and Herbert Marcuse, both of whom died within a year of one another—had opposed theoretical and political perspectives on contemporary society, they at least agreed on the crucial importance of Freud as a theorist of human nature and his necessary centrality to any adequate social theory. The present revival of economistic conceptions of human nature in the more sophisticated form of rational choice theory is altogether innocent of psychoanalytic influence. I once remarked to one of the leading advocates of this approach that I thoroughly agreed with his "methodological individualism" but not with his insistence on "rational choice" as the defining feature of human action. He replied, "What's the difference?" But Freud was surely a methodological individualist whom, despite his deep-seated belief in the power of reason, one would hardly think of as a believer in the primacy of rational choice. "Irrational choice" more accurately characterizes both Freudian theory and the popular view of it, or at the very least "nonrational choice." But critics of rational choice theory have not turned to Freud in rebuttal. If anything, they have fallen back on a Kantian, Durkheimian, or Parsonsian insistence on the importance of norms, morality, and altruistic motives in human conduct. Contemporary controversies conducted in these terms have a distinctly pre-Freudian flavor. If still referred to with respect and less misrepresented than he once was, Freud has, except for a few revisionist feminist theorists, largely been relegated to the margins of contemporary theory.

Yet the belief that all social theories at least presuppose an idea of human nature, at the very least an "image of man," has hardly been refuted or abandoned. Nor is it denied by conceiving of human nature as an empty box to be filled with widely varying social and cultural content, or as no more than the site or point of intersection of diverse linguistic systems, power relations networks, or hegemonic ideologies in currently fashionable postmodernist ("pomo") readings. The strange twists and turns of ideological controversy are revealed when the literary theorist Stanley Fish, perceived as a leading postmodernist radical assaulting entrenched social and academic pieties, declares in challenging and provocative tones "Socialization goes all the way down!" He was directly quoting, it so happens, Richard Rorty.[8] Yet it was just such a belief in the nearly total effectiveness of socialization in shaping human character and conduct that was attacked in sociology over thirty years ago as presenting an oversocialized conception of man, a belief that became the target of the widespread assault on the alleged inherent conservatism of "establishment sociology" in general and Parsonsian theory in particular by assorted radicals and dissidents in the 1960s. The attack was directed against the assumption that men are socialized to conform without resistance to the demands of "society" in the sense of the overall status quo, whereas Fish had in mind socialization to selected subgroups within the larger society defined by race, gender, ethnicity, or class.[9] But the two positions involve no significant difference in their views of human nature if, indeed, they acknowledge the existence of such a thing[10] over and above inert biologically given raw material shaped by socialization.

There is a sense in which psychoanalysis is the *only* comprehensive theory of human nature we have, that is, the only one that establishes a plausible link between biological inheritance and life experience and is truly developmental in documenting what Freud called the "vicissitudes of the instincts."[11] More than any other psychology, psychoanalysis takes with full seriousness three propositions that are obviously fundamental to any adequate nonbiological conception of human nature.[12] First, Life begins at zero. Second, In the beginning is the body. And third, The child is father to the man.[13] Freud himself occasionally identified psychoanalysis with the "genetic explanation" of feelings, meaning the tracing of them back to their genesis in infant experience.[14] Even if Freud's particular efforts to show how infancy, bodily drives, and parental authority shape both human nature at large and individual biography are contestable, he was surely right to base his theory on them, to assume, in short, the literal truth of the three propositions I have listed and the necessity of fleshing them out with detailed content.

The reference to the body in the second proposition lends itself to misconstruction as a possible form of biological determinism, as several responses to my citing it in the past indicate despite my explicit disavowal of such a standpoint.[15] Sociologists often seem to believe in a sort of sociological counterpart to Say's Law in economics, refuted by Keynes, to the effect that production, or supply, inevitably creates its own sufficient demand. The equivalent in sociology is the conviction that there can be nothing in human nature that was not first implanted there by socialization, except for a few simple behavioral tendencies that come with inherited bodily traits. Society creates the needs it then attempts to satisfy, just as supply created demand according to Jean-Baptiste Say. Human nature therefore is entirely the product of the social order—"socialization goes all the way down." Today this view is phrased as the "social construction" of self, identity, worldview, and just about everything that human beings are or do that is not obviously of genetic origin. In the 1930s and 1940s it was often expressed as the claim that "personality" was simply—even "nothing but"—the "subjective side of culture."[16]

This conception, or negation, of a human nature, so attractive to sociologists, goes right back to the namer and founder of sociology itself, none other then Auguste Comte, who in his hierarchy of the sciences omitted altogether psychology, leaving nothing between biology and sociology. Society, he implied, confronts no obstacles in shaping the biological material it receives in accordance with social laws governing order and change, or "statics and dynamics" in Comte's terminology. Freud is sometimes seen as having reversed Comte's view in stating that "sociology. . .cannot be anything but applied psychology. Strictly speaking there are only two sciences: psychology, pure and applied, and natural science."[17] But far from taking what sociologists would routinely dismiss as a "reductionist" position, Freud also, as Donald Carveth has rightly pointed out, asserted the "corollary of this view"[18] in maintaining that "In the individual's mental life someone else is invariably involved, as a model, an object, as a helper, as an opponent; and so from the first individual psychology, in this extended but entirely justifiable sense of the word, is at the same time social psychology as well."[19]

What I mean by "In the beginning is the body" is simply that the body and its needs are all that is there at birth and that socialization must necessarily start with and build on them. The echo of the Book of Genesis may seem to suggest otherwise, but no implication is intended that inherited bodily constitution contains *in nuce* or lays down in advance any fixed pattern of later development. I had in mind in formulating the proposition one of John Dollard's criteria for the adequacy of the explanation of individual biography in a now largely forgotten book: "The organic motors of action ascribed must be socially relevant."[20] This suggests both that some organic motors of action *should* be ascribed because the body is what is there at the beginning and that they must *not* be seen as predetermining later development, which is what Dollard meant in contending that they must be "socially relevant," that is, they must be subject to shaping, direction, and even transformation in the course of the individual's social experience. The first proposition stated above, "Life begins at zero," is borrowed directly from Dollard[21] and the third also more or less corresponds to another of his criteria, although I have opted for Wordsworth's version of it.[22] Dollard found, not so incidentally, that one of Freud's case histories met his criteria more adequately than several other life histories examined in the book that were interpreted according to other theoretical doctrines.

Even if Freud had said nothing at all directly about the social arrangements and collective beliefs to which the individuals with whom he was primarily concerned were exposed, his theory of personality development or character formation would have enormous implications for society and culture. But he addressed himself explicitly to social and cultural themes in five books and a number of articles and commentaries. The first book, *Totem and Taboo*, was published in 1912 and the last, *Moses and Monotheism*, in the year of his death, 1939. Both of these works were essentially historical reconstructions (prehistorical in the case of *Totem and Taboo*) and they have not stood up well to the criticism of specialists and later research,[23] although *Totem and Taboo* was based on writings by anthropologists and zoologists that were widely accepted at the time it was written.[24] The three intervening books were broader and more analytical, to that extent more "theoretical," in discussing the general problem of the relation between the individual and society. All of them were written after Freud had first advanced his theory of the death instinct in *Beyond the Pleasure Principle* (1920) and two of them after he had put forward his structural view of the psyche as consisting of id, ego, and superego in *The Ego and the Id* (1923). One of the three more analytical of the "cultural books,"[25] *The Future of an Illusion* (1927), dealt with the psychoanalytic foundations of religious belief; another, *Group Psychology and the Analysis of the Ego* (1921) was mainly devoted to the phenomenon of leadership or authority in group life. That leaves *Civilization and Its Discontents* (1930) as the most comprehensive of Freud's excursions into the realms of society and culture. It has rightly been called "the central text of Freudian social theory."[26] I shall therefore be mainly though not exclusively concerned with it in the present chapter.

Although *Civilization and Its Discontents* is sometimes regarded by professional psychoanalysts and students of psychoanalytic therapy as a marginal, avocational as it were, work of Freud's, it actually contains both the fullest discussion of aggression and the most detailed account of a number of features of the formation of the superego to be found in Freud's writings. Both of these subjects are absolutely central to the problem of order. The fear of universal aggression *defines* the Hobbesian war of all against all while the development of the superego as a permanent part of individual character is the model for sociological versions of the internalization of social norms, for, that is, the normative solution to the problem of order however much its proponents may misconstrue Freud in overextending his concept. There are traces of the more questionable aspects of Freud's anthropology and social theorizing, expressed more fully in earlier writings, to be found in *Civilization*: his belief in the social life of a primal horde antedating culture and of the primal crime of parricide that led to the creation of culture; his assumption of a collective unconscious—more central to Carl Jung's version of psychoanalysis—containing memory traces of past historical events thus implying a Lamarckian inheritance of acquired characteristics long rejected by geneticists; allegiance to the general notion that ontogeny recapitulates phylogeny so cherished by nineteenth-century post-Darwinians; the conviction that primitive or early man was freer from social constraints and ensuing repression than modern "civilized" peoples. These beliefs, central to *Totem and Taboo*, were never repudiated by Freud, although he wryly referred to *Totem and Taboo* as his "just-so story."[27] They do not, however, loom large in *Civilization*. Moreover, it is possible to separate the speculative history Freud indulged in from a more defensible view of recurrent processes of interaction between social demands and individual responses that do not presuppose causation at a temporal distance by doubtful past events.

It does not, for instance, do great violence to Freud's argument if one understands the "civilization" of his title to refer, at least much of the time, to culture and/or society in general rather than to contemporary civilization contrasted with the ways of life of primitive peoples, our early ancestors, or a hypothetical prehistoric man "before the fall," that is, before the primal crime that led to the birth of culture. Freud did not always, either in *Civilization* or in other writings, clearly distinguish among these. Freud was certainly a critic of the belief in progress, often wondering whether civilization was worth the sacrifices in sensual gratification that he thought it exacted, but he did not doubt that there had been a unilinear historical movement sharply separating the primeval past from the civilized present. He assumed that the technical and material gains of civilization were necessarily purchased at the price of tighter controls over both sexuality and aggression. Not only did he notoriously fail to foresee the relaxation of Victorian sexual prohibitions already well under way and the role his own doctrines would play in contributing to its continuation, but in viewing the relation between society and the constraints it imposed in historical or social evolutionary terms he tended to obscure his own valuable general conception and resolution of the problem of order. Yet at several points in *Civilization* he correctly observes that primitive and modern men are alike in being subject to constraints imposed by the necessary preconditions for stable social existence.[28] When he occasionally seems to suggest that early men were not subject to repression, he is clearly referring to the primal horde situation before the parricide and the later filial response to it, the events that brought into being culture with its controls over instinct. One can reject this as unsound speculation and also the view that the progress of civilization requires intensified repression, but still recognize that Freud did not regard primitive and modern men as beings of a fundamentally different kind standing in a fundamentally different relation to their societies.[29]

Freud's thought, like that of everyone else, was influenced by the prevailing intellectual traditions and general culture of his time and place. Freud's *Trieb* is certainly more accurately translated as "drive" and the rendition of it as "instinct" unfortunately coincided in time with the revolt of American psychologists and social scientists against post-Darwinian biologism in general and instinct theory in particular. The misleading translation, therefore, needlessly predisposed American social science to reject psychoanalysis or to modify it virtually out of existence from the outset. Nevertheless, Freud *did* think in the post-Darwinian biologistic terms in which he had been trained; although not guilty of confusing elemental human motivations with fixed animal instincts, he did conceive of them as biological energies existing in finite quantities that antedated the impact of experience on the new organism and continued to exercise a hidden influence throughout the individual's lifetime.[30] He also often tried to explain their existence in terms of natural selection and even more general nonbiological physical laws. At a broader cultural level, the Viennese bourgeois milieu of his time undoubtedly led him to overestimate the role of the father in psychic development; the more crucial role played by the "pre-Oedipal" mother is now generally accepted after having been emphasized and insisted upon by feminist psychoanalytic theorists most recently. The task of interpreting Freud necessarily involves trying to separate his ideas that have enduring value from those that are now primarily of interest to intellectual and cultural historians. Many efforts have been made to cleanse psychoanalysis of its biologistic assumptions, not infrequently at the price of weakening or abandoning its most valuable and distinctive tenets such as the primacy of infant experience, the roots of the psychic in the physical, and, most of all, the "primal ambivalence" at the core of human emotional life.

Three distinct but obviously interrelated sources of "contamination" of Freud's theorizing can be identified. First and most important is his materialistic, positivistic, antisociologistic biologism, which assumed a number of different forms and from which he never completely freed himself. Second is the inescapable ethnocentrism stemming from his time, place, and social location: the educated bourgeoisie of Central Europe in the late nineteenth and early twentieth centuries to which he, his colleagues, and nearly all his patients belonged.[31] Third, the misleading translations of so many of his key concepts are probably worthy of mention in their own right.[32]

It may seem questionable and insensitive to the objections of feminists to call the first source of distortion the most important in light of the relative neglect of pre-Oedipal infant experience, the inadequate psychology of women, and the centrality long attributed to the Oedipus complex, all of which can be seen as reflecting an ethnocentric assumption that the late Victorian patriarchal bourgeois family is the human norm. However, the Oedipus complex is essentially a theory of how the drives (or "instincts") are shaped in the course of their contacts, or collisions, with other persons within this type of nuclear family structure. Freud may have overgeneralized the type in assuming it was universally human and even misrepresented it in minimizing the role of the pre-oedipal mother, but essentially his account of individual development is a particular application, a special case, of a broader and more basic conception of the encounter between drives and objects of the external world that transforms and gives content to the former. This was cogently stated some time ago by Anne Parsons in addressing herself to early criticisms, especially Malinowski's, of the alleged universality of the Oedipus complex.[33]

Freud's terminology, at least in the English translations of the Standard Edition of his works, has been criticized for "reifying" psychological processes for as long as I can remember, which is for some time before it became fashionable to deconstruct *all* words as obfuscating reifications. At least one recent writer has taken to heart Bruno Bettelheim's criticisms and suggestions for alternative translations and chosen to call instincts "drives," the psyche the "soul," the ego the "I," the id the "It," and so forth.[34] Doubtless it would be a good thing if this practice were to catch on, but until it does I have decided, perhaps cravenly, to stick to the tainted old language.

It is difficult to thread a path between restatement of Freud's ideas in a form that is more acceptable to contemporaries and the irreparable modification or even abandonment of many of the

most valuable of them in the course of doing so. I shall nevertheless make such an effort in exploring Freud's version of the problem of order.

FREUD AND THE PROBLEM OF ORDER

The parallels between Freud's theory of the origin of culture and
the ideas of the social contract theorists, especially Hobbes, have
often been pointed out. The agreement to renounce instinctual
freedom by Freud's band of brothers comes after their experiencing and recoiling from violence, just as Hobbes's inhabitants of
the state of nature contract to surrender their natural right to
resort to force and fraud in their dealings with one another in
order to escape a life that is nasty, brutish, and short. For Hobbes
it is the insecurity of the war of all against all, for Freud the murder of the father and the threat of further violence raised by the
prospect of unlimited sexual promiscuity in the absence of his
authority, that motivates the renunciation of unlimited conflict.
Freud's conception of the primal horde, based on reports of the
mode of life of gorillas and chimpanzees that have turned out not
to be accurate, resembles, however, Hobbes's *solution* to the
problem of order rather than his account of the state of nature
preceding the social contract: the rule of an authority strong
enough to coerce his subjects to obey while at the same time providing them with security. Freud's primal horde situation is
precultural but not presocial like Hobbes's state of nature.
External power in both cases preserves social peace.

Freud's insistence on the primal crime as a real historical event
leading to the imposition of the incest taboo in reaction to it is
closer to Rousseau's proto-evolutionist theory of social origins
than to Hobbes's or even Locke's conception of a social contract
instituting "civil society." If Rousseau stood at the pre-Darwinian
beginnings of stage theories of social and historical evolution,
Freud over a century and a half later was writing under their
influence at the very moment when such theories were falling
into disrepute among social theorists. As we saw in previous
chapters, it is not hard to interpret Hobbes as a model-builder, a
constructor of ideal types, for whom the state of nature and the

social contract were mental experiments designed to accentuate universal truths about the relations between human nature and society or government. Credible attempts have been made by Géza Roheim, Margaret Mead, and others to reformulate *Totem and Taboo* as at least "symbolically" true in its insights into recurrent psychological experiences within the family, even if it must be rejected as a speculative narrative of doubtful historical events that left even more doubtful memory traces inherited by later generations.[35] But considerable reformulation is clearly necessary in light of Freud's refusal to abandon his historical-evolutionist thesis, whereas Hobbes's social contract is more easily read as a conceptual construct even in Hobbes's own terms than as a historical reconstruction. The difference certainly results considerably from the fact that Hobbes and Locke, modeling their theorizing partly on the examples of geometry and classical mechanics, were concerned with general ahistorical truths, while Freud wrote in the afterglow of Darwin and the overextended application of biological evolutionism to human life in general.

Freud's concept of the superego appealed to Talcott Parsons because it described the conversion of initially external constraints on the individual into internalized motivations. Almost self-evidently, such motivations provide a much more reliable foundation for social order than Hobbesian fear of coercion or Lockean mutuality of rational self-interest which, as Parsons put it, do not necessarily "generalize" beyond particular instances of their effectiveness. Parsons argued in a famous chapter in *The Structure of Social Action* entitled "The Changing Meaning of Constraint" that Durkheim had moved from regarding social constraint as the control of individuals by legal sanctions to conceiving of it quite differently as their collective acceptance of moral obligation to conform to norms sustaining social order. Social norms, Parsons concluded, are therefore "constitutive" rather than merely "regulative" of human nature.[36] Freud's conception of superego formation as the introjection of parental injunctions became the model for the process of how external constraints are internalized to form an enduring part of individual character. Parsons went on to broaden greatly the scope of such internalization and largely to ignore the resistance to the internalized norms that was central to the Freudian conception of repression.[37] This virtual elimination of conflict between individual desires and the demands of society resulted in an oversocialized conception of man that seemed to dismiss rather than resolve the very problem of order that had been Parsons's starting point; his theory now virtually denied the existential reality of the problem of order in defining it merely as conceptual error.[38]

Some recent theoretical standpoints have minimized the difference between Hobbes, Freud, and Parsons on human nature on the grounds that all of them give priority to external forces that successfully constrain the individual, the sovereign for Hobbes, parental authority for Freud, and the normative order for Parsons. All amount to "socialization from the outside" in Ian Craib's phrase.[39] Freud explicitly compared the superego to a garrison installed within a conquered city, which indicates its external source but also suggests the latent opposition to it of the forces it has subdued. Recent writers have interpreted the superego as a reflection within the individual psyche of Bentham's Panopticon, the paradigm in Michel Foucault's most influential book of the pervasive supervision and surveillance to which citizens of modern societies are held to be habitually subjected.[40] Foucault's view, in conjunction with his famous denial of the "subject," might be regarded as a cynical rather than a eudaemonistic version of an oversocialized conception of man, seeing individuals as mere ciphers or puppets readily controlled by the constraints of a vast web of power relations, rather than shaped to the requirements of a smoothly functioning integrated social system as in Parsonsian structural-functionalism. This could indeed apply to postmodernism in general with its readiness to understand Rorty's "socialization goes all the way down" as a bold radical assertion, a debunking anti-individualistic version of the conformist inclination of human beings that differs markedly in tone from the more positive view of the same tendency associated in the 1940s and 1950s with Parsons, the "end of ideology," and some forms of post-Wittgensteinian language philosophy.[41] Despite obvious differences in spirit and context, Foucaultian poststructuralism is a reaction against the individualism affirmed in existentialism and various forms of humanist Marxism, just as

Parsonsian normativism was a reaction against economic individualism half a century earlier.[42]

These critics have been primarily concerned with challenging the internal/external (or subject/object) dichotomy itself, crucial for Hobbes, Freud, Durkheim, and Parsons albeit in different ways. The problem of order, however, assumes the existence of two partly independent and opposed forces or entities: individual and society, human nature and the requirements of social life, instinct and culture, the desired and the desirable, however one chooses to characterize them. They may produce modifications in one another as a result of their interaction, but they remain partially independent and antagonistic. Freud is a major theorist of social order because he developed a theory of human nature endowing it *both* with motivations offering resistance to the easy acquisition of patterns of behavior conforming to social demands *and* with motivations creating and sustaining stable and peaceable social bonds. The terms in which he formulated the problem of order may not be acceptable any more than those favored by Hobbes or, for that matter, Parsons, but his sense of the fundamental and enduring nature of the problem remains superior to that of more up-to-date thinkers disposed to minimize or ignore it.

Freud was in the early decades of the century hailed by his supporters as a liberator of humanity from excessive sexual constraint and at the same time damned by his opponents as a subverter of morality and social order. But it eventually became evident, and nowhere more so than in *Civilization*, that he was basically a skeptical upholder of the necessity of order who nevertheless refused to minimize the often excessive costs it imposed on the individual. If in some ultimate sense he was a conservative, a partisan of society against the individual, of culture against instinct, as was widely asserted in the 1960s, he never took a pious or Panglossian view of *any* existing social order, refusing to gloss over its irrationalities and the toll in human suffering it exacted. As he said in the penultimate paragraph of *Civilization*, the book's epilogue in effect: "I have not the courage to rise up before my fellow-men as prophet, and I bow to their reproach that I can offer them no consolation: for at bottom that is what they are all demanding—the wildest revolutionaries no less passionately than the most virtuous believers."[43] This attitude of stoic pessimism, bearing some resemblance, if less volcanic or agonized, to that of Max Weber, envisions no ultimate triumph of good over evil, reason over unreason, freedom over domination, the ennobling in human nature over the base, but sees them as locked in persisting conflict, the boundaries between them often blurred both within individuals and in the interaction between individual strivings and the demands of society. The endurance of conflict in diverse forms never leading to resolution through the final victory of one side over the other was central to Freud's vision. To call it a "synthesis," as I have in the title of this chapter, is in no way to suggest a harmonious blend of potentially discordant forces; it is rather a synthesis or balance of conflicting elements in perpetual tension with one another.

There are many perspectives that deny the reality or at least the persistence of the problem of order by accentuating one of its terms at the expense of the other, becoming partisans intellectually or ideologically, and often enough both at once, of either the individual or of society.[44] Oversocialized conceptions of human nature are examples of the latter; Parsons represents probably the most complex and credible version precisely because he initially recognized and defined the problem of order and eventually drew on Freud to solve it. But there are both oversocialized and undersocialized—perhaps overindividualized would be a more suitable term—views that pay no attention at all to Freud and psychoanalysis, just as Freud has been invoked in various selective and revised versions on behalf of quite different intellectual and ideological positions. A brief general summary of the range of views denying or qualifying the problem of order, with particular attention given to those making use of psychoanalysis, seems indicated.

Emersonian and Nietzschean celebrations of individual freedom and self-creation have tended simply to extol the value of the individual against society, ignoring or bypassing the problem of order altogether. Several recent antisociological sociologists have regarded any emphasis on external social constraints as a social determinism that negates human "agency" or free will.[45] The emphasis on self-realization in German Idealist philosophy going back to Kant, Fichte, and Hegel, which sees true freedom as the freedom of the individual to create and abide by his own law subject to no external constraints whatever is an important source of this outlook with roots in Protestantism; it was a primary influence on Marx, most saliently in his early work and in his sparse utopian reflections.[46] More recently and at a much lower intellectual level, the critique of the oversocialized conception of man in sociology was assimilated to the strictures against "conformity" so prevalent in the 1950s and countered with affirmations of the right of the individual "to do his or her own thing" widely proclaimed in the 1960s. One even found sociologists in tune with the times so interpreting the critique, despite the partial responsibility of sociology itself for the object of criticism.[47] Also, despite the fact that the critique drew on Freud whose bedrock insistence on a common human nature grounded in the universal experience of infancy does not encourage enthusiasm for the ineffable creative individuality of human beings.[48] With greater ingenuity and originality, theorists, including a number of feminists who are of the "party of Narcissus,"[49] have adopted what their critics have questionably branded as a Rousseauian or neo-Rousseauian outlook that pictures human nature as basically loving and unaggressive but distorted by repression, social injustice, and patriarchal domination.[50] This view at times verges on a biologization of the problem of order that sides with instinct against culture, so defining the former that there would be no problem of order if the instincts were given free rein—just the converse of the egoistic instinctivism of the Social Darwinists.

In a rather different vein, Freud has been seen by a number of writers as a defender of the ultimate integrity of the individual for insisting on an inviolable biological core resistant to society's efforts to shape men and women in its own image. This view is not necessarily a denial of the problem of order and the necessity of some socialization, but rather a rejection of certain kinds of far-reaching encroachments by society on the individual: the claims of "greedy institutions,"[51] the aspirations of twentieth-century totalitarian regimes to reshape human nature itself, the increasingly wide and deep diffusion and penetration of the mass media, and the general seductiveness of "mass society" imposing standardized modes of behavior on everyone. Figures as diverse as Lionel Trilling, David Riesman, Herbert Marcuse, and Philip Rieff have at times seen Freud's instinct theory as a last ditch defense against socially "imperialistic" assaults on the individual. This outlook was particularly attuned to the *Zeitgeist* of the 1950s when awareness of the full horrors of Auschwitz and Stalinism was fresh, fears abounded about a totalitarian potential in the politics of all modern societies, and the extent of the pervasiveness of "consumerism" and popular culture was beginning to be fully perceived.

When a view of human nature as potentially benign is combined with a conception of history that envisages the ultimate liberation of the psyche from the shackles placed upon it by socially imposed repressions, we have a much broader version of what I called in Chapter 3 with specific reference to Hobbes the historical relativization of the problem of order. Norman Brown's identification of history with the gradual return of the repressed is a psychoanalytic eschatology consciously patterned on theological, especially Christian, models, with echoes of an antinomian and Dionysian anarchism in its rejection of the claims on the individual of state and society. Herbert Marcuse adopted a more familiar Marxist reading of history, introducing psychoanalysis into it by "historicizing" Freud's view of human nature as a response to economic scarcity, a nature which therefore becomes alterable if and when improvements in the forces of production eliminate scarcity and make possible the abolition of repression and the free reign of Eros.

Such a union of Marx and Freud, characteristic of the Frankfurt School, is a special case of a more widely held Western or humanist Marxist perspective. The problem of order is historically relativized by questioning the inevitability of opposition between individual and society on the grounds that society is a human creation that men can aspire to understand and collectively recreate in a more "rational" form closer to their hearts' desire. This view, of which Georg Lukács was the most influential exponent, stemmed from Hegelian readings of Marx stressing Marx's early writings. Humanist Marxists argued for a "dialectical" relation between individual and society in which their opposition to one another would be overcome (*aufgehoben*) in a higher synthesis when men freed themselves from "false consciousness" and alienation by forging through rational collective action or "praxis" a new conflict-free social order in which, in Marx and Engels's words in *The Communist Manifesto,* "the free development of each becomes the condition for the free development of all." Marx's vision of a fully socialized humanity is to be realized only in the future after the revolution, but in solving the problem of order by overcoming all conflict between individual and society—and with the abolition of classes all group conflicts as well—it is not without resemblance to the minimization of conflict in the Parsonsian conception of the social system. One might say of Marx, paraphrasing what Engels said of Hegel's conservatism, that he is only relatively a conflict theorist but absolutely a consensus theorist. In contrast to Parsons, however, who tends to subordinate the individual to social imperatives, Marx, as Gary Thom notes,

> displays thoroughgoing opposition to any social influence or dependence, to anything that hints of social transcendence or the *sui generis* character of society. . . The notion that communist men and women would collectively control their social destiny is fused with the notion that individual destinies are individually controlled.

Thom aptly concludes that "Marx was a sociologist to end all sociology."[52]

These views tend to reflect partisanship on behalf of a distinctive and generic human nature, a capitalized Humanity of unrealized potentialities seen as a collective historical actor, and to ignore or suppress the existence of social imperatives, what Benjamin Nelson called the "social reality principle,"[53] or what used to be called the "functional prerequisites of society."[54] As Parsons and Shils put it, in what is the problem of order of *The Structure of Social Action* transmuted into the language of structural-functionalism adopted by Parsons in the early 1940s: "Order—peaceful coexistence under conditions of scarcity—is one of the very first functional imperatives of social systems."[55]

Utopias, on the other hand, are images or visions of social arrangements, sets of interrelated social institutions, that achieve a timeless stability by eliminating individual deviation and social conflict. They present human nature as totally plastic and thus easily molded to conform to the requirements of social order. The beehive or the ant colony often appears to be their ideal model; Hobbes himself noted the absence of the very possibility of a war of all against all in insect societies in Chapter 17 of *Leviathan*. In the present century such utopias have for the most part been unfavorably regarded as producing human beings who are nothing but "happy helots" or "cheerful robots,"[56] mere cogs in a "soulless" social machine, which, despite the fulfillment of all desires and the absence of social conflict, is seen as denying some infinitely valuable human essence. Aldous Huxley's *Brave New World* is the prototype of such negative utopias, or dystopias as they have been called.

In a foreword to a later edition of the book published after the regimes of Hitler and Stalin had seemed to give it new relevance, Huxley wrote of it as describing "a population of slaves who do not have to be coerced, because they love their servitude."[57] In contrast to Orwell's *Nineteen Eighty-Four* with which it is so often compared, Huxley's dystopia is based on the planned satiation of all wants, whereas Orwell's rests on frustration and the manipulated direction of the resulting hatred and aggressiveness against the regimes's external enemies.[58] Although Orwell and his admirers have emphasized time and again that the novel was in no way intended as the historical prediction it was widely taken to be, his Oceania is not a true utopia, for, although revolt and social change are effectively prevented, there is no elimination of the problem of order by reducing "the discrepancy between what men want to do and what they ought to do" to a minimum.[59] Huxley's ruler, on the other hand, describes the rationale of the society he controls as "you're so conditioned that you can't help doing what you ought to do. And what you ought to do is on the whole so pleasant, so many of the natural impulses are allowed free play, that there really aren't any temptations to resist."[60]

Orwell's implicit conception of human nature and its limits is, perhaps not incidentally, more consonant with psychoanalysis than the equivalent assumptions of Huxley, who imagined his dystopian society to be founded on what we would today call genetic engineering, chemical stimulants, and a rather mechanistic kind of behaviorist conditioning, techniques serving to produce docile subjects. A quarter of a century after the publication of *Brave New World,* Huxley observed that he had been prescient in anticipating the widespread use of such techniques for controlling human behavior[61] and from the vantage point of the 1990s he appears even more far-seeing with respect especially to drugs and genetic engineering. But he was essentially concerned with methods of changing human nature, in contrast to Orwell whose dystopia was based on the manipulation of a constant human nature.

The elimination of the gap between desire and obligation, or the desired and the desirable, is the essence of utopia. In more sociological terms, it can be formulated as the successful socialization of individuals so that they want to do what the maintenance or "reproduction" of their social order requires them to do. It was a happy and perceptive stroke of Ralf Dahrendorf to suggest in a famous article that marked the real beginnings of what came to be labeled "conflict theory" in sociology that Parsons's self-equilibrating social system resembled accounts of utopias in which everyone dutifully and happily played his or her role and neither deviation nor conflict existed.[62] Dahrendorf's concern was not so much with human nature or the psychology of the individual, as with the inevitability in all societies of "structurally generated conflict." It was the Parsonsian overintegrated conception of society, ruled by procedures ensuring universal consensus and resulting equilibrium, against which Dahrendorf leveled his criticism rather than a conformist social psychology.

A few years later, I conceived of an oversocialized conception of man or human nature as the psychological counterpart to the sociological emphasis on integration through consensus on values.[63] Although Parsons had to his credit realized the enormous importance of Freud to social theory, he had bowdlerized Freud by broadening the process of internalization and superego formation to extend to the entire personality, eliminating the resistance to morality, that is, to the demands of society, offered by the Freudian id and even by the rational calculating ego. Since Parsons was by no means my only critical target, I did not cite his uses of Freud in detail beyond noting their adumbration in *The Structure of Social Action*, but it was in his 1952 article "The Superego and the Theory of Social Systems" that his conversion of Freud into a kind of learning theorist was most evident; subsequent critics pursuing the same line of argument—such as Christopher Lasch, Robert Endleman, Philip Slater, Robert Bocock, Ian Craib, and Howard Kaye[64]—have frequently cited this article, whose major ideas Parsons reiterated in his 1962 response to my article.[65] It is time to look more specifically at the terms of Freud's theory of human nature and its bearing on the preconditions of social life.

FREUD'S TWO INSTINCTS AND THE DEMANDS OF REALITY

Freud identified three major forces that in combination shape human character and gave them Greek names: Ananke, Eros, and Thanatos. Ananke refers to Necessity, the requirements for the survival of the species imposed by nature. Necessity is apprehended by the individual through the psychic agency of the ego, which is oriented to the reality principle.[66] At the level of the individual, reality or the external world includes in addition to nature the society and culture entered at birth and exhibiting the traits of "exteriority and constraint" in Durkheim's well-known words.[67] Freud's other two forces are the two basic instincts or drives internal to the organism that together constitute the id. Eros, which is simply the Greek word for desire, is the drive for life or love aiming "to establish ever greater unities and to preserve them thus—in short, to bind together." The Greek term Thanatos has been widely used by commentators, but was scarcely used by Freud himself; he wrote most often of the "death" or "destructive instinct" and attributed to it the contrary of the aim of Eros, namely, "to undo connections and so to destroy things."[68]

"Eros and Ananke have become the parents of human civilization," Freud wrote.[69] This statement alone is sufficient to dispel the view that Freud is essentially a latter-day Hobbesian (at least what is thought to be Hobbesian), a view often promulgated by sociologists and recently properly criticized by Howard Kaye.[70] Clearly, the claim that Eros is a force creating human society— "Eros, builder of cities" (Auden)—amounts to "socialization from the inside," to invert Ian Craib's objection to oversocialized readings of Freud. As Philip Rieff interprets Freud, "The natural man is instinctually libidinal, a creature born into a hierarchy of love—which goes a long way toward modifying the Hobbesian view."[71] It is surprising how often sociological commentators, going to the opposite extreme from Parsons's domestication of Freud, ignore Freud's view of Eros as a positive motivational force binding men together that has no real counterpart in Hobbes nor, for that matter, in Locke or Rousseau. Yet in *Civilization and Its Discontents*, the book that is most often cited as evidence of Freud's "pessimistic" antisociological Hobbesianism, he devotes three chapters to a discussion of Eros *before* he even introduces more than halfway through the book the idea of innate human aggressiveness. Even such social theorists as Neil Smelser, Leszek Kolakowski, and Michael and Deena Weinstein,[72] who have a sophisticated understanding of Freud, make him out to be a Hobbesian by laying exclusive stress on the role of coercive external authority in making human society possible. But Freud was a thoroughgoing dualist, insisting on irreconcilable conflict between the two opposed instinctual drives: love and hate, life and death, creation and destruction, both of which are, he contended, fused in varying unstable compounds in all concrete motivations and actions, thus accounting for what Rieff calls "the law of primal ambivalence" governing human experience.

Freud's view, however, is more subtle and complex than simply depicting a deadly conflict within the human breast between "good" Eros and "evil" Thanatos, the one leading to the creation of society and the control of nature while the other undermines and destroys all positive and stable relations to the world. For Eros itself, Freud argues, cannot be permitted untrammeled expression if there is to be an enduring social order, even though it motivates the creation and maintenance of the social bond as such. The full gratification of Eros would fail to meet the conditions imposed by Ananke, that is, the requirements for survival dictated by nature. The relevant conditions are the need to form large groups or collectivities based on cooperative work relations among individuals organized to pursue the collective goal of extracting subsistence from the environment and protecting themselves from its dangers. Eros, Freud argued, while encouraging love between men and women and the formation of families, is likely to stop fully satiated at that point, whereas civilization requires wider relations that go beyond sexual or familial ties. Since Eros aims at complete sensual satisfaction, limits must be set to such satisfaction in order to promote aim-inhibited erotic bonds of friendship, affection, and solidarity among individuals so that they can work together in the productive and protective enterprise of building civilization.

This is Freud's primary and most general explanation for the sexual repression he had long before identified clinically as the major cause of neurotic disorders in the individual. It is scarcely an exaggeration to say that psychoanalysis virtually originated with the discovery of the psychoneurotic effects of sexual repression, which made psychoanalysis famous or infamous as a new therapeutic doctrine. Freud from the beginning, most notably in his influential 1908 article "'Civilized' Sexual Morality and Modern Nervousness,"[73] regarded prevailing sexual mores as far stricter than they needed to be and favored their relaxation, a conviction he reiterated in *Civilization*. He did not, however, go so far as to envisage the possibility of the elimination of all restrictions on Eros; some degree of sexual repression was, he thought, a precondition for the very existence of culture and society. At various points in his writing he acknowledged the necessity of specific sexual regulations in much the same terms as those emphasized by sociologists:[74] the need for population replacement justifies the prohibition of sexual "perversions"; the lowered infant mortality in modern civilization necessitates contraceptive or abstinent forms of birth control that reduce sexual pleasure;[75] monogamy—the establishment of sexual property rights—prevents sexual rivalry that might threaten cooperation; and, most important of all, the incest taboo is essential to the weaning of the child from ingrown dependence on the family, its introduction marking for Freud the very beginnings of culture itself as a set of collectively self-imposed rather than coercively enforced restrictions on individual freedom.

The idea of wider ties and attachments being forms of sublimation drawing on aim-inhibited sexual energy that would not be available if Eros were able to achieve full expression in more limited dyadic or familial relations, is Freud's broadest and most definitive explanation for sexual repression. In effect, it makes opposition between individual desire and the requirements of society universal, inescapable, and unalterable if the dissolution of society itself is to be avoided, although existing repression may go far beyond the limits imposed by necessity. Freud advanced his much-cited declaration in *Civilization* that "civilization is built upon the renunciation of instinct" in connection with the necessary limits on Eros before he had even mentioned the concept of an aggressive instinct. Yet the argument for the universal need to repress Eros to maintain society is palpably less obvious than the need to repress aggression. Psychoanalytic revisionists, anxious to reject Freud's pessimism and implicit conservatism about the possibility of great improvements in the human lot, have dealt with it in different ways. The neo-Freudians of the 1930s and 1940s simply desexualized Eros, solving the problem by denying it, as they also did in the case of the destructive instinct. But the "Left Freudians" who became ideological fathers of the "sexual revolution" of the 1960s, most notably Marcuse and Brown, accepted Freud's instinct theory in its most radical and uncompromising form up to and including the death instinct. If the latter posed the greatest obstacle to their utopian vision of the abolition of repression, Freud's case for the repression of Eros was most obviously vulnerable to criticism and provided them with a point of departure. An example is Marcuse's neo-Marxist argument that our industrial economy of relative abundance has overcome the historical necessity of repression for the sake of collective work, the "performance principle," to control the natural environment; continuing repression, therefore, is largely "surplus repression" from which we can now be liberated.[76] This challenge to the

necessity of sexual repression under modern conditions of relative affluence was the most popular of Marcuse's arguments in
the 1960s when he was a hero of the counterculture, although
he also attempted to provide an alternative in his *Eros and
Civilization* to Freud's interpretation of the death instinct.[77]

Philip Slater is one of the very few sociologists to have made
suggestive use of Freud's theory that the unity and stability of
society depends on the repression and sublimation of the energy
of Eros.[78] As all sociologists are wont to do, and perhaps *must*
do, he redefines Freud's two instincts as altogether indeterminate
drives or generalized impulses lodged in the body but in no way
biologically determined or limited in their operation by that fact.
He notes that for Freud both instincts are initially identified in
The Ego and the Id (also earlier in *Beyond the Pleasure Principle*)
with biological processes—the rejuvenation and dissolution of
cells—which Freud then psychologizes by converting into psychic
drives. Slater redefines them as the associative and dissociative
inclinations of the libido, the basic motivational energy of the
organism, toward objects. Since society consists of a network of
groups and institutions imposing specific normative and role
obligations on individuals, the threat of withdrawal from the network into a "world of one's own" arouses "social anxiety."
Three forms of withdrawal lead to the development of norms and
institutions designed to prevent them: familial withdrawal is
deterred by the incest taboo; the narcissistic withdrawal of the
individual, psychosis in its most extreme form, is prevented by
socialization with psychotherapy aiming at reintegration should
it nevertheless occur; finally, dyadic withdrawal, the form to
which Slater devotes greatest attention, is limited by the institution of marriage, for "libidinal contraction must be permitted to
go far enough to ensure sexual union and procreation but not far
enough to threaten the existence of suprafamilial collectivities."[79]

I know of no more brilliant effort than Slater's to link basic
psychoanalytic motivational categories to specific social norms
and institutions, serving both to bind them to the requirements of
orderly social life while recognizing their potential threat to these
requirements. If there is ever to be a full integration of psychoanalysis and sociology, this is the direction it must follow. Slater

briefly alludes to cultural and historical variations in the degree to which particular societies may strive to control withdrawal, especially dyadic withdrawal, mentioning in this connection various utopian communities of the past and twentieth-century totalitarian regimes as extreme cases of "imperialistic" controls. But neither Slater himself, nor anyone else, has followed up on this approach. One wonders, for instance, what larger or deeper changes in social structure and therefore in the nature of the demands upon individuals made possible the "sexual revolution" since the 1960s which overthrew laws, mores, and gender role-expectations bearing on all kinds of sexual expression that had seemed virtually impregnable a few years earlier. This revolution, and for once the appellation is justified in view of the short time in which it took place, greatly reduced the incidence, permanence, and centrality of marriage itself as an institution. A lot more was surely involved in these changes than simply an autonomous cultural trend allowing for greater individual freedom and rights to privacy.[80]

This last consideration leads us back to the limitations of Freud's analysis. If much of the time one can equate Freud's "civilization" with human society and culture as such, it is nevertheless not possible to overlook that he also at times intended it more narrowly in identifying its growth with the progressive widening and consequent thinning of ties among individuals that required ever-increasing drafts upon the energies of Eros. Hence the progress of civilization is necessarily purchased at the price of greater repression, an intensification of the "discontents" of individuals, and an increase in neurosis. Freud not only did not anticipate anything like the sexual revolution for which his own doctrines helped prepare the ground, but in common with just about all other social theorists, including Marxists, he failed to foresee that technological changes driven by and consistent with an economy that remained capitalist might largely dispense with the incentives and deprivations linked to the bourgeois institutions and values of marriage, the family, private property, and the work ethic.[81]

A more fundamental criticism of Freud is that his theory of the necessary repression of Eros presupposes his "hydraulic" conception of psychic energy. If the individual possesses only a limited quantum of libidinal energy, clearly it must be rationed among the various tasks and objects to which he or she is committed or attached. If it is fully discharged in pleasurable sexual relations or in family attachments, there will not be enough left over for the wider public obligations entailed by membership in a larger society. Such a view of a limited supply of available energy is a relic of Freud's nineteenth-century physicalism or materialism.

Yet Freud may have been right in substance even if the doctrinaire terms of his metapsychological theory are no longer convincing. His brilliant ironic analysis in the fifth chapter of *Civilization* of the golden rule that "Thou shalt love thy neighbor as thyself," which concludes that the ideal is psychologically unattainable, need not depend on the mechanistic notion of a finite amount of psychic energy. The limits of time and the conservative tenacity and particularity or individuality of human attachments are quite sufficient to account for the unrealism of the ideal, even granting, as Freud does in an earlier chapter, that there are a few men who are genuinely capable of sublimating Eros to the extent of truly loving Humanity at large. But then, as Orwell memorably observed, most men do not even aspire to saintliness.[82] If, as the British philosopher of ethics J. L. Mackie contends, morality has to be invented to cope with the endemic human condition of "limited resources and limited sympathies,"[83] Freud reveals the inherent limits to our sympathies. The familiar bewailing the loss of the "community" manifest in the close-knit rural villages of the past that goes back to Rousseau is consistent with Freud's view, although he himself was not given to historical nostalgia or what Lasch has dubbed *Gemeinschaftschmerz*.[84]

THE DEATH INSTINCT AND AGGRESSION

But there is worse to come. After arguing against the possibility of living up to the hallowed commandment to love one's neighbor and remarking that the belief in it by an idealistic few may actually encourage the wicked to persist in their ways, Freud suddenly introduces the view that men are not merely indifferent to the fate of their neighbors but often cherish a marked "inclination to aggression" directed against them. His initial account of this inclination is eloquent and historically prescient, and has probably been cited more often than any other statement of his as evidence of his Hobbesianism. Indeed, he quotes the same Latin maxim, "man is a wolf to other men," that Hobbes himself cited nearly three centuries earlier. The full paragraph in which Freud introduces the aggressive instinct deserves reproduction:

> Men are not gentle creatures who want to be loved, and who at the most can defend themselves if attacked; they are, on the contrary, creatures among whose instinctual endowments is to be reckoned a powerful share of aggressiveness. As a result, their neighbour is for them not only a potential helper or sexual object, but also someone who tempts them to satisfy their aggressiveness on him, to exploit his capacity for work without compensation, to use him sexually without his consent, to seize his possessions, to humiliate him, to cause him pain, to torture and to kill him. *Homo homini lupus.* Who, in the face of all his experience of life and of history, will have the courage to dispute this assertion? As a rule this cruel aggressiveness waits for some provocation or puts itself at the service of some other purpose, whose goal might also have been reached by milder measures. In circumstances that are favorable to it, when the mental counter-forces which ordinarily inhibit it are out of action, it also manifests itself spontaneously and reveals man as a savage beast to whom consideration towards his own kind is something alien. Anyone who calls to mind the atrocities committed during the racial migrations or the invasion of the Huns, or by the people known as Mongols under Jenghiz Khan and Tamerlane, or at the capture of Jerusalem by the pious Crusaders, or even, indeed, the horrors of the recent World War— anyone who calls these things to mind will have to bow humbly before the truth of this view.[85]

Written in 1929, one immediately adds the Shoah, the Gulag, the horrors of aerial bombing during the Second World War, mass murder in Cambodia, and various brutal local colonial and tribal wars and insurrections to Freud's list of human cruelties, and marvels at how much the subsequent history of the monstrous and bloody twentieth century seems to confirm him. The pessimism of *Civilization* is sometimes attributed to Freud's fore-bodings over Hitler's growing support, but he actually wrote most of the book in 1929 before the election in which Hitler first surprised with a strong showing. In any event, this is Freud on human nature at his most pessimistic and Hobbesian.

He out-Hobbeses Hobbes, moreover. We saw in the previous chapter that Hobbes did not view men as seeking a "more intensive delight" in the perpetual pursuit and exercise of power, but as being forced for defensive reasons to strive to augment their power in order to protect what they already possessed. Even the "children of pride" who do crave more power seek it essentially for the sake of riches or glory rather than as a source of intrinsic satisfaction. Power for Hobbes, in short, is valued largely as a means to security, material possessions, and reputation, not as an end in itself. But Freud asserts just the contrary: to him, aggression is the consummatory or terminal gratification of an instinctual motive in exactly the same way that sexual release satisfies the rival instinct. People want to inflict pain and injury on others because they find it inherently pleasurable to do so and this pleasure is as inborn as the erotic pleasures directly linked to the body. This is a far darker and more disheartening prospect than any envisaged by Hobbes, but it is what the cited passage directly and unambiguously contends. Hobbes's state of nature and war of all against all seem positively benign in comparison.

The starkness and prescience of the passage I have cited evidently mesmerizes many readers into forgetting entirely what Freud had written in the previous fifty or so pages of *Civilization*. For the passage is habitually quoted in part or in full as decisive evidence of Freud's inveterate Hobbesianism, his alleged conception of a human nature so deeply and innately anti-social that only a punitive external authority could possibly check it and allow for the always precarious existence of society. Eros and the bonds of love it forges drop out of the picture altogether. Also forgotten is the rational recognition of necessity, or Ananke, that leads to the mobilization of aim-inhibited Eros to form large cooperative groups to cope with the hostile natural environment. Reason may for Freud be insufficient by itself to create society without the emotional propulsion of Eros, but it is able to see the advantages, nay, the necessity, of cooperation to pursue collective goals, whereas for Hobbes reason initially perceives only the negative gain of security from violent death in devising the social contract. For Hobbes, the contract is, to be sure, a precondition for "commodious Building; instruments of moving and removing such things as require much force" and the other achievements of culture lacking in the state of nature that he enumerates in Chapter 13 of *Leviathan*, but the prospect of these is not what inspires men initially to make the contract. For Freud, however, reason directly apprehends the advantages of cooperation, not just the relief of escaping from the insecurities of conflict. Freud's qualified faith in the powers of reason was expressed most strongly in *The Future of an Illusion* written two years before *Civilization*.

Most accounts of Freud as the heir of Hobbes also simplify his view of aggression. He indeed speaks of "a powerful share of aggressiveness" as an "instinctual endowment." But the original form of the instinct is a death instinct, a wish to die, to end the tensions of life and lapse back into the insensibility of the inorganic world. Freud does not mention this in *Civilization* until the chapter after his initial introduction of the theme of aggression, when he summarizes the history of his instinct theory up to and including his introduction and detailed exposition of the death instinct in *Beyond the Pleasure Principle*.[86] He notes that the death instinct "is diverted towards the external world and comes to light as an instinct of aggressiveness and destructiveness."[87] He refers to it sometimes as the death instinct but more frequently in *Civilization* and in other writings as the "destructive" or "aggressive" instinct, which does not separate the self from other people as possible objects of aggression. Nor are self and others distinguished when Freud concludes that "the inclination to aggression is an original, self-subsisting instinctual disposition in man. . .and constitutes the greatest impediment to civilization."[88]

If the death instinct were given free rein, there would not only be no society but no species; indeed, the instinct would achieve its aim of destroying all life and restoring a purely inorganic world. For Freud defines it in *Beyond the Pleasure Principle* as a biological tendency toward entropy present in protozoa and all living cells. Thus it is "pressed into the service of Eros" in being directed outward in accordance with Freud's view that both instincts are fused in varying proportions in all motivated activity. But if the aggressiveness that is the form taken by the externalized death instinct were allowed full expression, there could be no society, for this would create precisely the Hobbesian war of all against all that is the negation of society. And, as I argued above, it suggests an even more deadly war than Hobbes's, since aggression is not simply a preemptive defense against anticipated attack or a means to the fulfillment of other ends or passions, but a source of direct sadistic gratification in its own right. Freud does not find it necessary to argue as he did at some length in the case of Eros why the aggressive instinct must be repressed if society is to exist, regarding it as self-evident that it "constitutes the greatest impediment to civilization."

THE SUPEREGO AND ITS FORMATION

Aggressiveness is repressed and society made possible by the displacement of the aggressive drive from external objects—specifically, other people—and its reflexive direction against the self. In thus turning back inward it manifests itself intrapsychically as self-criticism, self-reproach, and even self-condemnation generating the painful emotion of guilt, a response to the ego not being loved and even being hated by that part of it which now evaluates it reflexively. The part in question is what Freud calls the superego, literally the "over" or "above" the "I."[89] The individual's

> aggressiveness is introjected, internalized; it is, in point of fact, sent back to where it came from—that is, directed towards his own ego. . .Civilization, therefore, obtains mastery over the individual's dangerous desire for aggression by weakening and disarming it and by setting up an agency within him to watch over it, like a garrison in a conquered city.[90]

The death instinct, then, undergoes a two-step process of development. An infusion of Eros first directs it outward as aggressiveness and hostility toward the outside world. Then, in a second reorientation, it turns back upon the ego as self-judgment leading to guilt and inner division but without regressing all the way back to its original self-destructiveness, although this may happen in extreme cases of melancholia in which "a pure culture of the death instinct"[91] leads to actual suicide. (For Freud as for Durkheim suicide becomes an important indicator of the human condition.) The first step is a prerequisite for life and the reproduction of the species, and presumably occurs at the biological or biochemical level; the second step in avoiding the war of all against all constitutes at least a necessary condition for social life and is an achievement of socialization.

Since the superego consists of parental commands and directives that the ego now imposes upon itself from within, it is easy to see why introjection is the favorite psychoanalytic mechanism of sociologists and often the only one to which they pay much attention.[92] For the parents uphold the norms of the larger society, social constraints that were originally external are internalized when "the crucial obstacles to my acting on my own desires have become part of myself, my superego,"[93] the macro and micro social worlds are linked, and the normative solution to the problem of order is instantiated. The superego induces guilt over motives to deviant behavior even if they never lead to action; its unique and ubiquitous access as a faculty of the mind to the mind's contents is what makes it so effective an agent of social control. In contrast to benign or at least neutral accounts of the superego, the "critical theory" of the Frankfurt School and its heirs interprets it as the conversion of the tyranny of a society founded on class domination into self-denial, oppression by external authorities becomes repression from within, and the complicity of individuals in their own victimization explains the endless delay in the making of the revolution that will liberate mankind.[94] More limited melioristic visions of the possible tempering or elimination of conflict between individual and society attribute the punitiveness of the superego to one or another remediable or removable feature of the socialization of the child: later weaning, less harsh toilet training, permissiveness with regard to infant sexuality, more demonstrative mother love, greater use of rewards rather than punishments, dual parenting, noncompetitive evaluations of performance, and the like. A host of such nostrums, many though by no means all claiming psychoanalytic legitimation, have won brief if transient popularity in the present century, often succeeding one another with the rapidity of changes in fashion.

All of these approaches conceive of the superego as simply reproducing in relation to the self the treatment to which the child has been subjected. Not that this is not a major influence, but Freud pointed out in *Civilization*, citing Melanie Klein in support, that children who have been raised permissively may also develop harshly judgmental superegos. In conjunction with his previous observation that the most upright and moral, that is, the most repressed, persons are often the most racked with guilt, he concluded that the individual's own repressed aggressiveness, not just the aggressiveness experienced at the hands of others, is a source of the superego's severity. The well-loved and indulged child is blocked by those very facts from directing aggression outward and the highly moral person also suffers from repressed hostility. The doctrines mentioned above all hold in one way or another that aggression is a response to the frustration of non-aggressive desires and that conflict between the individual and society, internalized as the division between ego and superego, can therefore be eliminated if those desires are satisfied by a more indulgent regimen of socialization. Such a view not only denies Freud's claim that aggression is a "self-subsisting" instinctual disposition, but also tends toward a conception of human nature as, potentially at least, entirely loving, life-affirming, and naturally sociable.

But if belief in an innate or deeply rooted aggressive drive is the major ground for attributing an antisocial Hobbesianism to Freud, it overlooks his instinctual dualism and his repeated insistence that all motivation involves a fusion of the two instincts. Why does the superego pattern itself upon the parents, selecting their injunctions as the basis for its self-evaluations? It does so because the parents are the child's first love-objects and fear of loss of their love leads to identification with them, the modeling of self upon the image of them, and self-judgment according to the standards by which they granted or withheld their love. The superego is as much a product of this love based on identification as it is of the aggressiveness deflected onto it; both Eros and the destructive instinct enter into its constitution.

THE SELF AS A UNIQUE OBJECT OF APPRAISAL

"Identification. . .is the source of the social tie."[95] The superego originates in an identification with the parents reflecting the child's love for them. The contribution of Eros in the form of identification to the formation of the superego is evident even in *Civilization*, universally recognized as Freud's most "sombre" and pessimistic book,[96] in which he fails even to mention his earlier discussion of the "ego-ideal" as the ideal self aspired to by part of the superego that is distinct from its punitive restrictive side.[97] The distinction corresponds roughly to Kant's "the Good" as an ideal striven for as a goal, as opposed to "Duty" which is by definition restrictive and self-denying since for Kant it is necessarily totally independent of inclination or desire.[98] Freud emphasizes identification upward, initially with the parents, which is then transferred, as recounted in *Group Psychology and the Analysis of the Ego*, to other leader figures rather than extended horizontally to one's peers as fellow human beings facing a common plight. This emphasis follows less from a predilection for authoritarianism supposedly shared with Hobbes than from Freud's genetic approach that always gives primacy to the earliest experiences and love-objects. It raises, however, problems in his theorizing as to how love and affection, with the reciprocity and implicit equality they so often involve, become dissociated from submissive gratitude for the protection and satisfactions provided by the more powerful beings on whom one is or has been dependent.[99]

Identification is a complex phenomenon in psychoanalytic theory and I shall foreswear a review of its four distinct forms, its relation to narcissism and object-cathexis, and its frequent confusion with such recent widely popularized notions as "identity."[100] As a mode of psychological relatedness to other people that creates likenesses and emotional bonding among them, it plays something of the same role as "suggestion," "imitation," "sympathy," "empathy," "consciousness of kind," "herd instinct" and similar concepts in various late nineteenth- and early twentieth-century social psychologies, all of these notions being descendants of Rousseau's belief in compassion as a human trait. Like them, identification seems to encompass both affective and cognitive qualities. Since Freud was always concerned primarily if not exclusively with affect and motive, his concept of identification, except in its infantile "anaclitic" form before the development of the distinction between ego and external world, evidently presupposes the uniquely human cognitive capacities for "taking the role of the other," reflexively looking back on oneself, and emulating the other that follow from language according to George Herbert Mead and Jürgen Habermas.[101] Emphasis on the cognitive powers of language nicely *complements* rather than merely restates in a different conceptual vocabulary, let alone stands in opposition to, identification as the source of the emotional bond to others in psychoanalysis. Even though identification, apart from its primary narcissistic form, is in psychoanalytic theory a compensation, a substitute, for object loss, in creating wider social unities it is clearly an agent of Eros that has no counterpart in Hobbes.

The capacity to project oneself into the mental life of others, reflexively to imagine how one appears in their eyes, and to remodel oneself in line with their standards and expectations is the product of language with its duality of signifying reference to the experience of both self and other. I argued in Chapter 3 that it is essentially a cognitive achievement with no necessary affective accompaniments, as Mead repeatedly asserted despite occasional lapses into inconsistency. If language makes possible the emergence of the self as an object of experience capable of arousing the full variety of attitudes and emotions toward it that other objects may elicit, the self possesses nevertheless certain unique properties as an object. All human beings who speak a language have selves as objects of cognition, although cultures vary enormously in the degree to which they place a value on the unique qualities of individual selfhood, ranging from the pronounced individualism of the modern West to primitive societies that

define the individual almost entirely by his or her group member-
ships and social identities.

Like the body to which it is attached, one can't get rid of the
self except through loss of consciousness. Human consciousness
is self-consciousness. Since you have to lug this object around
with you wherever you go and whatever you do, and cannot even
fully escape it in sleep, to hate it is to be always in the presence of
something that induces pain and aversion. That is how Freud saw
the guilt resulting from the superego's negative judgment of the
self or ego.[102] Hence the attraction of intoxicants that "take one
out of oneself," commented on in an early chapter of
Civilization. As Freud observed, they are only the crudest of a
number of expedients for achieving a partial and temporary loss
of self. It is important, accordingly, to be able to think well of, to
feel at ease with, this thing that sticks to one like glue. The self as
object emerges in experience *after* experiencing other people as
objects and it is constructed out of an awareness of the responses
of others to one's presence that eventually grasps their self-refer-
ential or deictic nature. It is not surprising therefore that not only
cognition of self as an object but one's affective attitude toward it
should be shaped by the attitudes of others. However deeply
internalized the image of the other may be, self-appraisal never
becomes totally independent of the evaluations of others,
although this condition may be approximated in extreme schizo-
phrenic withdrawal. The degree of independence is highly variable, both among individual personalities and among whole cultures. Abram Kardiner conceptualized this variability as the
"tonicity of the superego."[103]

Thus people cannot just live contentedly in solitude cherishing
exalted notions of themselves, as was rightly noted by several
Hobbes scholars whom I cited in the previous chapter on
Hobbes's idea of "vainglory." In any case, since people cannot
escape the presence of others, the "presentation of self" in everyday social life is unavoidable. So ensuring that others think well
of one becomes a major preventive strategy against the pain of
guilt, shame, and self-doubt. It may take the form of modestly
seeking no more than the liking and approval of others by pas-

sively conforming to their expectations, or it may become a determination to excel in the eyes of others and therefore in one's own eyes, to win admiration as an exceptional being— Machiavelli and Hobbes's desire for glory, Rousseau's vanity or *amour propre*. Erving Goffman's sociology of the presentation of self in face-to-face encounters vividly documents the maneuvers people adopt to avoid the pain of rejection, censure, or even mild "loss of face." In Goffman's world, people are constantly hugging protectively to their bosoms this precious vulnerable object they cannot get rid of. Or to change the metaphor, they hold up in front of their faces carefully crafted and ornamented but fragile masks, made perhaps of papier-mâché, displaying them to others and cautiously jousting for position while avoiding clashes and collisions that would damage them.[104]

If the self is an object that is acquired only as the product of language, it is absent at birth. Social psychologies that give priority to self-linked motivations fail therefore to satisfy the criteria that life begins at zero and that in the beginning is the body. This applies to the early philosophers on glory and vanity, to sociologists who treat the desire for the approval of others as sufficient to resolve or dispose of the problem of order, and to Goffman's micro-sociology of interaction considered as a fully adequate social psychology, as it is by some self-professed "symbolic interactionists."[105] The wish to maintain a favorable, or at least nonpainful, attitude toward that adhesive object, one's self, may be a motive—called the "self-dynamism" by Harry Stack Sullivan[106]— that underlies a great deal of human experience, but it is not a primary or elemental motive there at the start of life. By the time it emerges, the instincts have already undergone quite a few vicissitudes. Currently fashionable pan-linguistic theories of the human subject ignore the fact that infants are born without language and that there are at least some continuities of experience between humans and animals incapable of symbolic communication.

Freud's neglect of language and the transformation of consciousness it brings about, however, adds ambiguity to his concept of identification. On the one hand, identification is equated with the most primitive form of narcissism, existing before the infant

then converted into a psychological drive. Indeed, biological entropy is a manifestation in living matter of a physical process, the Second Law of Thermodynamics or the dissipation of energy. A kind of reverse anthropomorphism is at work here, with cosmic laws of the inorganic universe being read first into living matter and then into human motivations as instincts activating human beings.

It is not hard today to reject all this as a kind of Heraclitean metaphysics couched in the language of nineteenth-century positivist materialism. But Freud's fundamental effort to define human life as ridden with conflict and ambivalence needs to be kept in mind as the source of his "tragic vision" that has so often appealed to writers who are not professional social or psychological scientists. These writers have often admired Freud for his profound and subtle grasp of the mixture of triumph and tragedy, of ephemeral joy and ultimate defeat, that constitutes human life and is most vividly expressed in great literature, so often cited by Freud and matched by his own superb prose that won him the Goethe prize in Germany and the accolade of Thomas Mann.[112] Such writers, most of them literary intellectuals, have, accordingly, sided with the more orthodox brands of psychoanalysis against the revisionists who, motivated by left-wing political hopes, have so often been banally idealistic in their emphasis on human spiritual and altruistic qualities and ready to sacrifice Freud's most disturbing insights in order to affirm these qualities.[113] I confess that I responded to what I felt to be Freud's superior "pessimistic" wisdom at a time when I found the instinctivist and apparently antisociological cast of his argument altogether unacceptable in contrast to the intellectually more congenial sociologism or culturalism of the neo-Freudian revisionists.

It is possible, however, to accept the substance of Freud's emphasis on conflict and ambivalence, and therefore on the reality and universality of the problem of order, while rejecting many of the specific terms of his argument. To say that man is by nature a social and cultural animal is in itself a statement that challenges the "nature or instinct versus culture" formulation that is so often advanced as the essence and summation of

Freud's argument and finds its strongest support in passages of *Civilization*. This formulation is in any case a simplification for, as we have seen, nature or instinct is in Freud's view itself a realm torn by conflict that invades the less intractable conflict between individual desire and the reality principle embodied in the requirements for social life. Moreover, identifications with social objects may come into conflict with one another; Freud emphasized the intrafamilial conflict of the Oedipus complex and also conflict between more immediate erotic and familial identifications and wider group and institutional ties. Nor, even if he conceived of them in too psychologically reductionist a fashion as is argued in the next chapter, did he neglect conflicts between larger groups, as his two essays on war and his perceptive remarks in *Civilization* on the "narcissism of minor differences" with reference to neighboring small nations, ethnic groups, and even village communities attest.

The definition of instinct as an expression of nature, the body, and heredity remains a stumbling block. Freud's concept is, as I previously noted, unmistakably different from the biologist's concept of animal instinct. It even fulfills a contrary explanatory function: instinct as species-specific inherited predisposition is invoked by biologists to explain the unvarying detailed sameness of many animal responses, whereas the Freudian concept indicates highly generalized motivational energies that underlie the immense variety exhibited by concrete human behavior. One purports to account for unvarying specificity, the other provides a common measure for bewildering diversity. Still, the aura of the biological clings to the Freudian concept and unavoidably seems to set limits to human freedom and variability.

Are there such limits? The hermeneutic or interpretive reading of psychoanalysis that redefines all of its terms as meanings dependent on language rather than as motives and affects that are causally effective goes too far in severing human nature from any realm of necessity or intrapsychic obstacles to freedom. Human beings are certainly not born with specific hereditary behavior patterns beyond a few simple reflexes and they are capable of resisting even the most urgent demands of the body; they can deliberately starve themselves or eat to excess, perform extraordinary feats of resistance to fatigue, and, of course, choose to terminate their own lives.[114] Yet these overcomings of instinct and bodily need are at the level of behavior. Motives, emotions, even affect-laden ideas, possess a "compulsive" or "obsessive" quality that cannot be willed away, put out of mind, or expunged by sheer determination, even if they can be blocked from direct expression in action. This is the central fact on which psychoanalysis is founded and which has given it credibility from the beginning. Put as simply as possible, feelings and desires are harder to conquer and transform than ideas or actions. And, as Darwin noted, men are most like animals in their emotions and passions, even in the bodily expressions these assume. There is a sense in which this was recognized long ago by the ancients, the Church fathers, and some thinkers of the Enlightenment such as Hobbes, Locke, and Rousseau, as well as by the great non-Western world religions. One should not identify human nature as such solely with those aspects of it—language, reason, purposive choice—that are peculiarly or distinctively human, as hermeneutic and pan-linguistic theorists are inclined to do, although one can recognize that man's superior gifts or "higher" nature can control his "lower" animal nature without effacing it.[115]

Both nature and culture are riven with conflicts that cut across one another, so the simple dichotomy of nature versus culture so often represented as the essence of Freud's social theory is not tenable. Nor need nature be identified with instinct. Jessica Benjamin is right to argue that the intrapsychic and the intersubjective should be seen as influencing one another.[116] Freud's conception of the death instinct as a "self-subsisting" entity goes too far in stressing projection from the inside as opposed to the introjection from the outside that errs in the other direction in the thought of both the Parsonsians who take a benign view of it and the neo-Marxist critical theorists for whom external oppression is converted into inner psychic repression.

But if aggression is not the result of an instinctual aim redirected outward, one need not go to the opposite extreme of affirming a facile environmentalist version of the frustration-aggression hypothesis and seeing aggression as easily eliminated by more permissive child-rearing practices. For the frustration that generates aggressive feelings may nevertheless be rooted in the human biological condition even if, indeed precisely *because*, that condition is characterized by the absence of instincts rather than their presence as causes of behavior. I have in mind the condition of infantile dependency, the "premature" thrusting into the world of "red and wrinkled lumps of flesh"[117] in what would be still a fetal state even among the the primates, man's closest animal relatives, and human survival in that state for a period of several years during which the world and the parents in all of their fearsome uncertainty impinge upon the helpless organism, generating a tumultuous emotional life of terror, yearning, and occasional fulfillment. (No wonder social scientists have been so prone to identify the problem of order with sheer unpredictability rather than with violent conflict—undoubtedly they are still subject to the unconscious "separation anxiety" of infancy.)

The notion that human nature is shaped by prolonged postnatal infantilization was first developed by Géza Roheim in his "ontogenetic theory of culture."[118] It has been most fully elaborated by Weston LaBarre and Robert Endleman, who have traced the detailed connections between the biological evolution of the human species and such cultural emergents as the family (LaBarre) and language with all its powers of spatio-temporal displacement, negation, and repression giving rise to the Freudian tripartite character structure (Endleman).[119] But a number of separate schools of thought have tended to converge in stressing the priority of infancy in shaping human nature, reflecting precisely the instinct-less condition that is the prerequisite for culture and society: Heinz Hartman's ego psychology, Jacques Lacan's linguistic Freudianism, Melanie Klein's psychoanalysis of children, Norman Brown's metaphysical psychoanalytic vision, existential psychology, the phenomenological philosophical anthropology that has found an American spokesman in Peter Berger, Parsonsian action theory, and, most of all, British object-relations psychoanalytic theory and its adaptations by recent American feminist analysts.[120] These schools differ, often ferociously, among themselves, but they agree in rejecting Freud's instinctivism and emphasis on phylogenetic heredity. Some of them, to be sure, as I have previousdly argued, go too far in the opposite direction in denying or minimizing the discontents that Freud rightly thought were inherent in human existence.

"Infancy versus adulthood or maturity" would be a better way of phrasing the conflict-ridden, anxiety-prone human condition than "nature or instinct versus culture." It does not neglect human biology in the manner of so many oversocialized, socially constructionist, and pan-linguistic versions of human nature, since the helpless, infantilized condition of the newborn human being is itself a product of a long process of evolution through natural selection. Yet it affirms that man is a "naturally" social animal without equating the shaping power of the social with socialization into acquiescent conformity to prevailing norms, roles, and institutions. The conflict between human wishes and the imperatives of social life—both universal and historically specific—that defines the social psychological aspect of the problem of order is a conflict *within* the realm of the social and cultural, between what is early and later in social experience, between what is intended and its unintended and undesired psychological consequences, between, to put it in more technical psychoanalytic language, "the precipitate of the child's pre-Oedipal object relations with its significant others"[121] and the cultural demands and role obligations of later life that are transmitted through and make up most of the content of purposive or directed socialization. What is repressed and is the source of so much human conflict and misery is not biological instinct but infancy, the character of which is determined by the very absence of biological instincts giving it form and direction that defines the human species.

CHAPTER SIX

THE DISPARITY BETWEEN INDIVIDUAL AND GROUP

U nderstanding human nature requires consideration of the relation of the individual, his and her dispositions, capacities, and developmental history, to society. This aspect of the problem of order might be called the "problem of socialization" or the "hobbesian problem" since Hobbes was the first thinker to formulate it in secular or nontheological terms. Or one might call it the "hobbesian/freudian problem" because of Freud's account of the superego and its formation which addresses the central issues. Freud's theory of human nature does justice both to the readiness for and the resistance to socialization of human beings born in a helpless undeveloped state requiring prolonged dependence on others. The use of lowercase for "hobbesian" and "freudian" tacitly acknowledges that neither thinker's solution to the problem of order is completely satisfactory, although they deserve credit for having properly defined it.

Assessment of the views of Hobbes and Freud on human nature is a separate issue from their failure adequately to deal with conflict among groups, a reality distinct from how individuals are shaped by socialization to become at least minimally conforming members of society. They both, though living nearly three centuries apart, treated group conflict, or often avoided treating it, in similar ways. Sometimes they did no more than draw analogies between the behavior of individuals and of groups; sometimes they viewed groups simply as individuals writ large; more frequently, they confined themselves to regarding the existence of groups and their collective behavior patterns as given realities providing opportunities for individuals to pursue their ends or find outlets for their impulses.

The threat posed by group conflict to social order might be called the "marxian problem," the use of lowercase suggesting, as in the case of Hobbes and Freud on socialization, that Marx identified and gave prominence to the problem even if the terms in which he discussed it are not fully acceptable.[1] In so labeling it, I have no intention of affirming the famous opening sentence of *The Communist Manifesto* proclaiming that conflicts between classes are the only significant kinds of social conflict in history, indeed the very content of history itself as a process. Despite the fact that the sentence refers sweepingly to "all hitherto existing societies"—the *Manifesto* was, after all, an agitational pamphlet—Marx's generalization obviously was meant to apply only to societies that were divided into classes, societies sufficiently large and technically advanced to have evolved beyond the stage that he elsewhere called "primitive communism." Even if one widens the notion of group conflict to include groups other than classes—groups differentiated by religion, ethnicity, occupation, locality, political ideology—group conflict in overt or covert form is endemic to societies characterized by social heterogeneity, a high degree of internal differentiation, and social inequalities among large groups or social aggregates. The study of revolutions, insurrections, and internal revolts has been a major preoccupation of sociologists for the last two decades, especially of sociologists engaged in comparative-historical research.[2]

Students of international relations deal with wars between nation-states which obviously fall under the general category of group conflicts even if they do not directly involve the problem of order in posing an internal threat to the survival of the warring societies. The interaction between internal order and external threats from other societies, however, can hardly be ignored. Sociologists have in recent decades, with the illustrious exception of Raymond Aron and a few others, not paid much attention to international relations, wars, and militarism, but there are signs that they have at last begun to realize that no understanding of individual societies is complete without consideration of their relation to other societies as members of a larger competitive interstate system.[3]

The distinction between the "hobbesian/freudian" and the "marxian" problem is a distinction between the "relevant units" that need to be integrated if there is to be a stable social order. The first refers to individual human beings, the second to social groups. The first necessarily centers on the nature of individuals and their receptivity to socialization, the second on the structure of society as a complex of differentiated groups and institutions and their relative integration to form a larger partially bounded unit that is customarily identified as a "society" in the singular. The first is an issue for social psychology and for the recently popular study of micro-social interaction, the second for sociology, that is, for interpretation at the "structural" level of institutional and intergroup analysis, including relations among whole societies or nation-states forming an international order or world system. The distinction is an obvious one, but it is surprising how rarely it is explicitly made in discussions of the problem of order. Descriptions of the absence of order habitually run together anarchy and anomie, regarded as conditions in which individuals are not fully "integrated" into society, and conflicts between groups ranging from civil wars to various forms of collective violence involving more loosely organized and relatively impermanent groups.

Durkheim, the classical theorist of the normative solution to the problem of order, did not adequately distinguish between its hobbesian and marxian forms.[4] He saw the negation of order as the breakdown of normative consensus leading to "anomie"—literally, the absence of norms—as a general social condition.[5] The anomic individual recognizes no moral limits to his or her desires and appetites, which as a result become boundless and insatiable. Universal anomie is Durkheim's equivalent to a Hobbesian war of all against all. To Hobbes, this "state of nature" was both prepolitical and presocial; to Durkheim, on the other hand, general anomie was the outcome of a process of *de*socialization, the breakdown of an established society with a stable normative order. The difference may account for why Hobbes's masterless men are prone to kill each other, while Durkheim's anomic individuals are more likely to kill themselves. Durkheim's sufferers from anomie commit suicide because they experience a loss of meaning when deprived of a moral regulation that both limited and gave legitimacy to their aims and achievements.[6] For Hobbes, social order becomes possible only after the creation of a sovereign political authority, and Hobbesian men living in prepolitical anarchy are freely aggressive toward one another. For Durkheim, the normative order of society so enters into and shapes the fundamental psychological constitution of human beings that the descent into a postsocial state of anomic deregulation causes them to lose any sense of purpose in life and to turn against themselves in despair. Deprived of close attachments to others, the aggressive component of their superegos comes to the fore and they become suicidal, although to employ Freudian terms in this connection is to be guilty of anachronism with respect to Durkheim's theory.

Just as Hobbes's anarchic state of nature led to the social contract that abolished it, Durkheim's state of anomic deregulation generates a collective ferment that gives birth to a new order centered on new norms and values. Durkheim's implicit and occasionally explicit example was the French Revolution; the political thrust of his sociology was to promote the final realization of the ideals of the Revolution by stabilizing the still insecure institutions of the Third Republic. But, as David Lockwood has shown in detail, just *how* the passage from anomie to a new normative order is actually achieved was only vaguely suggested. Durkheim's virtual equation of anomic disorder with the Hobbesian war of all against all makes the transition a far from credible one.[7] Lockwood's major argument is that Durkheim ignores the alternative possibility of a disintegration of society, not into the amoral state of universal anomie, but into two rival moral communities engaged in conflict with one another for ultimate supremacy. This is, of course, the Marxist situation of revolutionary class war between "oppressors and oppressed," each side upholding rival norms and values (or ideologies). Lockwood contrasts Durkheim's monolithic normative order with the schism of the Marxist conflict between two classes, each possessing its own distinctive set of values and ideals. Group conflict may involve more than two contending groups, although the Marxist revolutionary situation dividing society into two main camps is Lockwood's major concern. Lockwood also points out that Parsons is guilty of exactly the same conflation as Durkheim in identifying anomie with "the complete breakdown of normative order" and explicitly including "extreme class conflict to the point of civil war" as an instance of it, although as early as *The Structure of Social Action* he recognized that the Marxist class struggle was a clash between groups with rival value-systems. Nevertheless, in Parsons's major theoretical statements, he both persistently described class conflict as anomie and identified anomie with the Hobbesian situation.[8]

Durkheim and Parsons, in short, the major advocates of the normative solution to the problem of order, conflated the hobbesian and marxian aspects of order from a society-centered or sociologistic perspective, collapsing the marxian problem of group conflict into the hobbesian problem of socializing an unruly human nature. Hobbes and Freud, on the other hand, are guilty of the same conflation from the reverse pole of an individual-centered or psychologistic perspective, projecting the elements of human nature resistant to socialization upon groups locked in conflict.

A contemporary writer, James Rule, in his valuable comprehensive survey of theories of what he calls "collective" or "civil violence," makes the same error as Durkheim and Parsons despite his critical rejection of normativist theories of order. Rule defines his object of study as "the deliberate destruction of persons or property by people acting together."[9] He then proceeds to relate civil violence to the problem of order as initially stated by Hobbes whom he also identifies as the initiator of one of the theoretical traditions striving to explain the civil violence his book examines. He notes that the problem of order has often been seen as "*the* fundamental question of all social science" (his emphasis).[10] There can be no question that civil violence as Rule defines it amounts to a serious disruption of social order. Moreover, it is part of Rule's intention to challenge both psychological and individualistic explanations of civil violence, whether they take the form of rational choice theories or several theories that have in common the explanation of collective violence as resulting from the aggregation of psychological states of individuals such as frustration, anxiety, relative deprivation, or withdrawal of commitment to existing institutions.

Yet in referring to Hobbes, Parsons, and the problem of order, Rule fails to note that the war of all against all was explicitly defined by Hobbes as interindividual rather than intergroup conflict. Rule identifies the problem of order entirely with the control of group conflict, at least the "disruptive" forms of it represented by collective violence, ignoring altogether the problem of human nature and socialization. He reverses, in effect, the selective perspective of Hobbes and Freud who read group conflict as essentially a manifestation in the aggregate of the human nature present in single individuals. Each approach suppresses a different side or aspect of the problem of order—Rule the "hobbesian problem," Hobbes and Freud the "marxian problem."

Rule's blurring of the individual and group levels of the problem of order repeats that of Durkheim and Parsons, despite his rejection of their normative theories. Parsons is a major target of criticism by Rule for first overstating the commitment of individuals to shared "ultimate values" and collective goals and then hedging his statements to a point where his more qualified claims would no longer suffice to overcome the Hobbesian war of all against all that his introduction of collective goals, and ultimate values had been intended to resolve in the first place.[11] However, the internalization of norms proscribing resort to force and fraud as means in pursuit of any ends *would* suffice to overcome the war of all against all, but is not equivalent to internalizing collective ends requiring cooperation or the sharing of ultimate values as ends-in-themselves transcending self-interest. Parsons's ambiguity indeed stems from his concept of the "randomness of ends," rightly criticized by Rule, which leads him to blur the distinction between ends and means in offering his normative solution to the problem of order.[12] The elimination of fear and suspicion among individuals is a precondition for their affirming common goals and cooperating to realize them, but it is not the same thing as the achievement of such consensus and cooperation.

Parsons did not adequately distinguish between them in present-ing his oversocialized view of human nature, but he was right in seeing that the internalization by individuals of rules forbidding force and fraud suffices to eliminate the Hobbesian problem understood as a war of all against all among unsocialized individuals subject to no such constraint. Rule declines to concede even this much to Parsons in focusing on Parsons's overintegrated view of society that minimizes group conflict, which is Rule's *explanandum* in his search for genuinely falsifiable theories purporting to explain the most spontaneous and violent forms of conflict. Both Parsons and Rule conflate the problem of avoiding violent conflict among individuals with that of generating positive commitments to common goals, although they adopt opposed positions on the nature and importance of the latter.

HOBBES AND GROUP CONFLICT

Hobbes described the absence of order as it existed in the state of nature as a condition "where Every man is Enemy to every man," and where men are "apt to invade and destroy one another."[13] These passages and many others from *De Corpore Politico*, *De Cive*, and *Leviathan* unmistakably refer to conflict among *individuals* rather than to conflict among *groups*. Sometimes Hobbes seems to conceive of the war of all against all as a conflict among families rather than individuals, and families, though based on biological kinship, are one kind of social group. Rousseau suggested that if humans really were as Hobbes described them, then the war of all against all would apply to the family as well as the larger society:

> The wicked man, he [Hobbes] said, is a robust child. It remains to be seen whether man in a state of nature is this robust child. Even if we conceded as much to Hobbes, what would he conclude from it? That if this man were as dependent on others when he is robust as when he is feeble, there is no kind of excess to which he would not resort: that he would assault his mother when she was slow in giving him to suck, that he would strangle

a younger brother who got in his way, or bite the leg of another if he was bothered or disturbed by him.[14]

Doubtless Melanie Klein and her followers would regard Rousseau's inference as to what Hobbes's view implied about the infant at the breast as no more than the truth!

Belief that the family, that is, the nuclear family, was in some sense a "natural" unit was an Aristotelian assumption that Hobbes failed to abandon in remarking that the "concord" of "small Families" depended on "naturall lust."[15] He frequently did not distinguish between individuals and families in his accounts of the war of all against all, although he clearly regarded all non-familial groups as "artificiall" creations. That this is more than a minor caveat is suggested by Edward Banfield's analysis in his well-known study of a Calabrian village in Italy of "amoral familism" as a major cause of economic backwardness; he chose Hobbes's famous description of the state of nature as the epigraph for his book.[16] Banfield had in mind the nuclear or "small" families often referred to by Hobbes as warring units,[17] although Banfield clearly regarded their prominence as part of the culture of Southern Italy and not a reflection of "nature." Banfield also noted that the behavior of his villagers presupposed in true Hobbesian fashion the existence of the state to check the "war of all against all," that is, of nuclear families with one another.[18] He identified Hobbes's account of the accoutrements of civilization lacking in the state of nature with the economic backwardness of Southern Italy.

Yet it was collective violence on a scale threatening and eventually bringing about civil war rather than violent relations among individuals that moved Hobbes to create his political theory. Moreover, he often referred to wars between nations as evidence supporting his view that the war of all against all is latent even among peoples who have surmounted it by creating a stable political authority. This exemplifies his practice, later followed by Locke as well, of regarding the state of nature as a relation among any units not subject to a common law or authority rather than as a general social or historical condition of universal conflict among individuals. Hobbes clearly recognized the difference between the war of all against all and wars between states in contending that

> though there had never been any time, wherein particular men were in a condition of warre one against another; yet in all times, Kings, and Persons of Soveraigne authority, because of their Independency, are in continual jealousies, and in the state and posture of Gladiators; having their weapons pointing, and their eyes fixed on one another; that is, their Forts, Garrisons, and Guns upon the Frontiers of their Kingdomes; and continuall Spyes upon their neighbours; which is a posture of War.

That Hobbes was consciously drawing an analogy or describing an abstract juridical relation—or at least the absence of one—rather than conflating the two distinct levels of individual and group conflict is indicated by his immediately following comment that kings "because they uphold thereby, the Industry of their Subjects; there does not follow from it [their wars with each other], that misery, which accompanies the Liberty of particular men."[19] In other words, the state of nature has been overcome *within* warring kingdoms but not between them. Immediately before the passage cited above on interstate conflicts, Hobbes argued that while a state of nature may never have existed anywhere, at least in America "savage people" who have no government except that of "Small Families" still live "in that brutish manner." This particular passage exhibits both Hobbes's tendency to regard the state of nature as a hypothetical model and his assumption that families were natural rather than artificial or "political" (in Aristotle's comprehensive sense) creations. At a later point in *Leviathan*, Hobbes passes more quickly from the war of all against all to conflict among "small Families" to conflict between "Cities and Kingdomes which are but greater Familyes."[20] Four chapters further on, he again asserts his clear recognition that the liberty of nations "is not the Liberties of Particular men; but the Liberties of the Common-wealth: which is the same with that, which every man should have, if there were no Civil Laws, nor Common-wealth at all."[21] He proceeds to note the similarity of the state of "perpetuall war" among "masterlesse men" and the condition of Commonwealths "with their frontiers armed, and canons planted against their neighbours round about." Obviously, he was quite consciously drawing an analogy.

Hobbes, then, fully recognized the difference between nations (or "Common-wealths") that had overcome the war of all against all within their boundaries though remaining in a state of "perpetuall war" with one another and individuals still mired in the state of nature. But except for his ambiguity as to whether the war of all against all is a war between individuals or families, he ignores the existence of organized social groups within nations. This omission reflects his presociological failure to distinguish between the state and society. C. B Macpherson has seen this clearly in remarking on a major difference between Hobbes's model of society and the "possessive market society" to which, in Macpherson's view, it largely corresponds.[22] Hobbes insisted that the sovereign must be self-perpetuating in that the person or persons holding sovereign power must have the right to appoint his or their successors. Locke and Harrington, Macpherson's other major theoreticians of bourgeois society, disagreed with Hobbes on this point, vesting the choice of succession in the public or an elective legislature. Macpherson contends that Hobbes "did not allow for the existence of politically significant unequal classes"[23] or "the centripetal force of a cohesive bourgeois class within the society."[24] Hobbes saw society as so "completely fragmented" that in the absence of a self-perpetuating sovereign or group it would revert to the state of nature whenever the succession became an issue. But he overlooked the existence of "class cohesion," specifically that of a "cohesive possessing class," namely, the bourgeoisie, capable of deciding who should succeed to sovereign power.[25] One need not accept Macpherson's Marxist conviction that the major or only relevant groups are classes defined by the possession or lack of possession of economic resources, but he clearly recognizes Hobbes's failure to perceive the existence of a society organized into persisting social groups independently of the supreme political power of the sovereign.

The adjective "Hobbesian" has by now been freely applied to

so many different conflict situations—Banfield's "amoral familism," warring teenage gangs, economic competition in a capitalist market economy, the American ethos of individualism,[26] ethnic
conflicts in troubled nation-states, outright civil war, international power politics and wars, the Nazi death camps, life in most
"carceral" institutions—that it has become virtually a dead
metaphor. The units in conflict in these examples range from
truly isolated individuals, as in Primo Levi's searing account of
Auschwitz,[27] to organized states ruling over tens or even hundreds of millions. The individual/group distinction becomes thoroughly blurred in such promiscuous use of the "Hobbesian"
label.

Hobbes did acknowledge that individuals would sometimes
band together.[28] He saw such possible unions combining the powers of weaker men against single stronger individuals as ultimate
evidence of the fundamental equality of all men based on their
equal capacity to kill one another.[29] This equality is a central and
radical assumption of his political theory contributing to his
deserved reputation as a founder of liberalism despite his preference for authoritarian government. But he clearly did not regard
such groups as more than transitory alliances based on the strictly expedient self-interested purposes of the moment held in common by their members. In the absence of subservience to an overarching sovereign authority, only precarious *ad hoc* bonds might
temporarily unite men. Hobbes does not even recognize what
James Rule calls "divisible self-interest" as a basis for the formation of stable collectivities in such examples as Mancur Olson's
"small groups" that do not have to confront the "free rider"
problem and the members of Olson's larger groups who are motivated by what he calls "selective incentives."[30] Macpherson's
cohesive bourgeoisie and "class-conscious" classes (Marxist
Klasse für sich) in general would fall into the latter category.

Hobbes has often been read as a theorist of international relations, notably of "realist" theories of "politics among the
nations" (the title of Hans Morgenthau's famous textbook).[31] His
references to the expansionist aspirations of kings and the wars
that result justify such a reading. But its fundamental justification
lies in the analogy he drew between "masterless men" in a state

of nature, and the "anarchical order"[32] of international politics where force is the *ultima ratio* and no independent power capable of overriding the actions of sovereign nations exists. In Aron's "century of total war"[33] it is hardly surprising that the analogy between international relations and Hobbes's famous description of life in his imagined state of nature has been repeatedly drawn. Attempts to create supranational authorities like the League of Nations and the United Nations plainly resemble Hobbes's social contract in which individuals surrender some of their "natural rights" to an authority empowered to enforce peace.

It remains an analogy or at best an abstract juridical relation between units—individuals, on the one hand, and nations, or large politically organized groups, on the other—that are substantively quite dissimilar. Law codifies such abstract relations, treating persons and various kinds of groups as identical for numerous purposes,[34] and one can see why Hobbes and Locke after him subsumed individuals and nations under the "state of nature" rubric in recognizing that both conditions involve an absence of binding laws restricting freedom of action. But substantively, that is to say sociologically and psychologically, unsocialized "natural men" and nations subject to no international authority are units of a quite different kind, the first involving largely nonexistent or hypothetical entities. The limits of the analogical reasoning involved in equating them are well brought out by Hedley Bull, who notes that the basic equality of men in the state of nature so insisted on by Hobbes is in no way duplicated in the world of nations where inequality resulting from differences in power is the fundamental reality in relations among states.[35]

In a brilliant article, Alan Ryan has reversed the analogy or metaphor by using nuclear deterrence theory to illuminate Hobbes's conception of the state of nature rather than indulging in the more familiar practice of invoking Hobbes's war of all against all to describe the anarchy of nations.[36] The creation of the sovereign state as a result of a social contract successfully deters the aggression of individuals against each another by giving each person the equivalent of a "second-strike capacity." Just as the superpowers refrained from launching nuclear war out of fear of the retaliatory capacity of their adversary even after absorbing a first strike, the individual in civil society knows that assaults on fellow citizens expose him to punishment by the sovereign, given the vigilance of the police or Hobbes's "publike Officers, armed, to revenge all injuries shall bee done him."[37] The conviction that possible victims possess secure second-strike capacity prevents the war of all against all just as nuclear war was averted during the forty years of cold war between the United States and the Soviet Union.

Although Hobbes clearly recognized the difference between conflict among Commonwealths that have instituted the social contract eliminating the war of all against all within their borders and the precontractual war among individuals in the state of nature, he on occasion tended to individualize conflict between states by equating it with the personal ambitions of kings. This was perhaps understandable in the seventeenth century when "the state" as a public, impersonal institutional structure had not yet been fully differentiated from the person of its monarchical ruler, and what Gerhard Lenski calls "the proprietary theory of the state"[38] still prevailed. (In a sense the English Civil War that inspired Hobbes's theory was over just this issue and Hobbes is himself regarded as a major early theorist of the state.) Hobbes, for instance, sometimes describes kings as individuals dominated by a desire to increase their riches, honor, and power, the kind of ambitious men who in the state of nature imposed on everyone else the need to seek power for purely defensive purposes.[39]

Hobbes failed to discuss group conflict because he was primarily concerned with the nature and limits of the citizen-subject's obligations to the state and with making a case for what Weber over two centuries later described as the state's monopoly over the legitimate use of violence. In concentrating on the relation between state and citizen, Hobbes ignored the complex network of social ties which spontaneously creates a normative order that exists independently of the political and legal system and antedates its foundation. In this respect he was a typical presociological thinker writing before the "discovery of society."[40] Yet many of his incidental observations suggest that sociologists and Marxists have in their polemics against individualism exaggerated the degree to which Hobbes saw societies as no more than aggregates of preformed and isolated individuals. He had virtually nothing to say, however, about the "war of group against group" within complex politically organized societies—except occasionally to deplore it—despite his often suggestive analogies between warring individuals and independent Commonwealths or nations. He saw group conflict within Commonwealths as remaining relatively subdued or regulated because its overt expressions are suppressed by the state whose *raison d'être* under Hobbes's social contract is to check all acts of violence within its domain except its own. But Hobbes did not regard human nature as transformed after the creation of Leviathan: the disposition to the war of all against all survives in latent form. This obviously could and surely would be likely to apply to the social groups Hobbes ignores as well as to individuals subject to a common power.

FREUD AND PSYCHOLOGICAL INTERPRETATIONS OF GROUP CONFLICT

A psychologist rather than a political theorist, Freud was concerned with individual character rather than with the nature and source of political authority. Nevertheless, like Hobbes, he often drew analogies between individuals and collectivities. Also like Hobbes, he was quite aware when he was drawing an analogy rather than assuming an identity between group and individual behavior and the forces determining them. This needs to be stressed because the most egregious efforts to "psychoanalyze" not just groups but whole national societies have come from epigones rather than from Freud himself. They have deservedly given psychoanalysis a bad name among historians and sociologists. I have in mind such purported explanations of complex events and social processes as attributing wars to outbreaks of repressed aggression, the Russian Revolution to a revolt against "the national father image," German National Socialism to a "paranoid culture," and the like. Even the image of a "sick society" applied to collective practices branded pathological in psychiatric terms involves treating "society as the patient,"[41] as if society were an individual suffering from a neurotic disorder. References to contemporary society as a "sick society" were commonplace in left-wing circles as long ago as the 1930s and 1940s, several decades before Philip Rieff reported the "triumph of the therapeutic."[42]

All of these examples are based on analogies between individual and collective behavior. "Analogy," which implies a reasonably precise point-by-point similarity, may even be too strong a term for them—they are usually no more than loose, at best possibly suggestive, metaphors. Insofar as they are offered as explanations of specific social processes or historical events, they are plainly subject to the objection that one cannot explain a variable by a constant. Wars, revolutions, and regimes like the Nazis are not everyday occurrences, although repressed aggression, Oedipal revolts against the father, and paranoid themes in German culture presumably are relatively enduring presences. If one wants to understand the causes of particular wars, revolutions, or totalitarian mass movements, it is not much help to be told that people have a potential for aggression, parricide, or persecutory delusions.

It does not necessarily follow, however, that reference to such psychological potentials makes no contribution at all to a full explanation of a variable social phenomenon. Hobbes insisted that "the nature of War, consisteth not in actuall fighting; but in the known disposition thereto."[43] In the long quotation from *Civilization and Its Discontents* where Freud introduces the theme of an aggressive instinct, he contended that "this cruel aggressiveness waits for some provocation or puts itself at the service of some other purpose."[44] The explanation of anything entails reference to both the necessary and the sufficient conditions for its occurrence. This may be elementary logic, but it often appears to be overlooked by sociologists who indulge in conventional strictures against "psychologism," citing in support Durkheim's famous dictum that social facts can only be explained by other social facts.[45] Human nature, whatever its sources, may not serve as an "independent variable" accounting for the kinds of social facts that sociologists want to explain, but it may well be an implicit component in their explanations even if they fail to make explicit reference to it. The arguments of sociologists against "psychological reductionism" are generally sound, but they often overshoot their mark.

Some kinds of psychological analysis, more subtle and elaborate than the rather crude examples I have given above, do not go beyond the detection of common psychological themes and motifs in social and cultural phenomena. A case in point is the kind of psychocultural interpretation of popular literature, the products of the entertainment industry, and the rhetorical imagery of public debate that was widespread in the 1940s and 1950s.[46] The historian Christopher Lasch has been one of its few more recent practitioners.[47] Another example is national character analysis, which selects a range of cultural expressions and social practices and treats them as manifestations of an underlying national or social character or basic personality structure allegedly formed by a common process of socialization in childhood.[48] Essentially, such an approach involves considering collective patterns of belief or expression *as if* they were produced by individuals, treating them as symptomatic of an underlying psychological condition presumed to be shared by an aggregate of individuals, but without ascertaining the presence of the condition by direct psychological examination of individuals by means of psychodiagnostic tests, or questionnaires, or clinical examination.[49]

Psychocultural interpretation that identifies universal psychological themes in collectively shared beliefs or customs is a venerable practice. Freud himself engaged in it with respect to the rituals of primitive peoples, jokes and humor, religious beliefs, and mythological themes. All human expressions, individual or collective, can be expected to exhibit universal psychological dispositions. To try to locate them in any human expression, individual or collective, violates no methodological canon, although such a practice is obviously highly susceptible to empirical abuse. Analogical reasoning from individual to group behavior is another matter. When collective beliefs or practices are treated as expressions of a particular psychological condition or personality type without the presentation of any evidence drawn from direct observation of individuals and such an interpretation is thought to explain the existence of the beliefs and practices, argument by analogy, or the confusion of the metaphorical with the real, is at issue. This error has afflicted studies of national character or group personality structure from the beginning and largely accounts for the disrepute into which such inquiries have fallen.[50] A number of students of "culture and personality" have converged on the conclusion that only the direct psychodiagnostic identification of "modal" personality types, that is, the types most frequently represented within the population of a given society sharing a common culture, can justify the imputation of a dominant social or national character, let alone a pathological psychiatric condition, to the population in question.[51] This approach recognizes both the diversity of character types bound to exist in any society, certainly in large and heterogeneous societies, and the presence of commonalities leading to the greater frequency of some types rather than others.

Freud wrote on several occasions on the specific subject of group conflict. He was appalled by the spirit of brutal chauvinism unleashed by the Great War and wrote "Thoughts for the Times on War and Death" in reaction against it as early as 1915, before the horrors of trench warfare had been fully revealed. "The state," he wrote,

> has forbidden the practice of wrong-doing, not because it desired to abolish it, but because it desires to monopolize it, like salt and tobacco. The warring state permits itself every such misdeed, every such act of violence, as would disgrace the individual man.[52]

If less obviously metaphorical, this assertion is the equivalent of Nietzsche's calling the state a "cold monster," and, for that matter, of Hobbes's likening it to Leviathan, the great aquatic beast of the Book of Job. Freud was clearly drawing an analogy between the behavior of individuals and states, not "reducing" the latter to the former. He did not, however, proceed in the vein of Machiavelli to recount the strategic requirements of conflict between states that override the rules of morality governing personal relations. His disgust at the war's revelation of the lower depths of human nature was uppermost—his theory of an independent aggressive instinct, first put forward in 1920 in *Beyond the Pleasure Principle*, has sometimes been attributed to his disillusionment caused by the experience of the war. Freud's view resembles that of Reinhold Niebuhr on the disparity between "moral man" and "immoral society," a disparity exhibited when validation by the group permits all sorts of actions that individuals would refrain from undertaking on their own initiative.[53] After a review of his theory of instincts and their repression by civilization, Freud returns to the subject of the war and concludes on the "uncivilized behavior of our world-compatriots" that

> In reality our fellow-citizens have not sunk so low as we feared, because they had never risen so high as we believed. That the greater units of humanity, the peoples and states, have mutually abrogated their moral restraints naturally prompted these individuals to permit themselves relief for a while from the heavy pressure of civilization and to grant a passing satisfaction to the instincts it holds in check.[54]

Freud's essay generally justifies Philip Rieff's judgment that to Freud "wars and revolutions are outbreaks of archaic attitudes. . .even tribal or national interest. . .is at best the consequence of deeper motives characteristic of all societies."[55] Rieff goes on to argue that "by presuming that the superego counts for little in war, he often misses the more terrifying fact that mass murder often presupposes a strong superego and positive identification with national ideals."[56] One is initially reminded of the mild, dutiful, thoroughly unassertive man, almost a stock figure in some depictions of war though certainly based on real models, who is nevertheless courageous and resourceful to the point of heroism under fire. Modern technological warfare increasingly involves killing at a distance and undoubtedly offers less direct satisfaction to the aggressive drive than a punch on the nose in a barroom brawl, at the same time that it makes aggression against a remote and sometimes invisible enemy easier because of its greater impersonality.

Although Freud, and Rieff in criticizing him, were concerned with war, their judgments apply to *all* forms of group conflict. Freud extends his explanation of war to the petty competitive rivalries between families, villages, and regions that he labels "the narcissism of minor differences," observing that they provide "a convenient and relatively harmless satisfaction of the inclination to aggression."[57] He mentions anti-Semitism in this connection, anticipating a whole genre of literature, of which *The Authoritarian Personality* was the most famous representative,[58] that flourished in the 1940s and 1950s.

The significance of Rieff's statement about the role of the superego in war can hardly be exaggerated, for it pinpoints the limitations both of Freud's "psychologism" or "psychological reductionism" and his instinctivism. Murder sanctioned by the group, Rieff concludes, is not necessarily motivated by the release it provides for aggression but may reflect a disjunction between "public" and "private" morality. The implications of this for the at least partial understanding of Auschwitz, first fully perceived and articulated by Hannah Arendt in her great book *The Origins of Totalitarianism*, are crucial; Rieff's reference to mass murder shows his sensitivity to them.

Freud's second essay on war was written seventeen years after the first in the form of a letter to Albert Einstein.[59] Unlike the 1915 essay, it was written in 1932 after his major writings in social theory and his tripartite division of the psyche into id, ego, and superego. Rieff's contention that "collective action is for Freud the major expression of man's barbarism,"[60] which is supported primarily by citations from the earlier essay on war and from *Totem and Taboo,* seems much less applicable to "Why War?" Freud begins with an account of the formation of groups differing in ideals and collective interests, the pacification of overt conflict among them by the state, and the persisting hostilities among states that lead to wars. He expresses his agreement with Einstein that wars will be prevented only by the creation of an international authority endowed with Hobbesian—or Weberian—powers, and comments that the League of Nations unfortunately lacks the requisite power so long as its member states maintain their absolute sovereignty. This section of the essay, if not particularly original, is unexceptionable from a sociological standpoint.

Freud then summarizes for Einstein his dualistic instinct theory, dwelling in particular on the death instinct, and concludes that "there is no use trying to get rid of men's aggressive inclinations."[61] In a passage reminiscent of the closing paragraphs of *Civilization and Its Discontents*, he suggests reducing the prospect of war by strengthening Eros through achieving wider emotional identifications of men with one another. He also refers in tones reminiscent of *The Future of an Illusion* to a possible dictatorship of reason, but concedes that "in all probability that is a Utopian expectation." He then ruefully remarks of his "indirect" suggestion for the prevention of war by creating more inclusive solidary groups that "an unpleasant picture comes to one's mind of mills that grind so slowly that people may starve before they get their flour."[62] He calls himself an "unworldly theoretician," but qualifies this by suggesting that Einstein's and his own opposition to war, shared with many others, reflects the technical reality that modern war renders obsolete old ideals of heroism and raises the specter of the "possible extermination of one or perhaps both of the antagonists." His prescience here, reiterating what he had written two years earlier in the closing paragraph of *Civilization and Its Discontents*, is evident.

Wars may activate the aggressive drives, but Freud also recognizes the solidarity of groups based on mutual identification which is a product of Eros. Freud then turns to a theme previously introduced in Chapter 7 of *Civilization and Its Discontents*: the possible parallels between the history of civilization and the development of the individual. He is so obviously aware of the speculative and strictly analogical nature of this effort that it would be supererogatory to charge him with reductionism or the methodological error of extrapolating from individuals not merely to groups but to civilizations and whole historical epochs. He warned in *Civilization* that "we should have to be very cautious and not forget that, after all, *we are only dealing with analogies* and that it is dangerous, not only with men but also with concepts, to tear them from the sphere in which they have originated and been evolved."[63] Acknowledging that there is no empirical basis for treating the entire history of humanity as if it conformed to the vicissitudes of an individual psyche, he nevertheless considered it an intellectual venture worth embarking upon as an imaginative exercise.

Norman O. Brown picked up more incautiously where Freud had left off in *Life against Death*,[64] viewing history itself as reproducing the developmental pattern of a neurosis in equating the Reformation with a Swiftian "excremental vision," capitalism with an anal fixation, the Nazis with "a pure culture of the death instinct," and history itself—at least Western history—with the progressive "return of the repressed." Actually, such an effort differs only in its all-embracing scope from psychocultural interpretations that note the similarities between religious rituals and obsessional neuroses or report the presence of Oedipal themes in popular culture. Brown was certainly not engaged in sober social scientific analysis, but the illuminating fertility of his insights is not to be doubted. Such bold analogizing is suggestive because it does not compare utterly incommensurable phenomena: individual and collective behavior both reflect the depths and potentialities of human nature,[65] even though the collective pattern predates the existence of any particular individual.

In *Group Psychology and the Analysis of the Ego*, the book Freud devoted directly to the psychological basis of groups, he developed fully his conception that groups are formed by the mutual identifications of individuals with one another. But in relatively stable and organized groups these identifications are not lateral based on perceptions of their similarity by individuals, but indirect, resulting from the like identifications of individuals with a common leader. Their perceived similarity is thus a byproduct of their individual identifications with an authority figure. Here Freud is not analogizing from the individual to the group but from the family, that is, the patriarchal family, to all groups. His later writings on mutual identifications stemming from aim-inhibited Eros as the foundation of social life place less emphasis on this theme of the essentially authoritarian foundation of group life. Doubtless it partly reflects Freud's belief in the necessary centrality of the father in the bourgeois family, as do his criticisms in *Civilization and Its Discontents* of the American tendency to minimize the importance of leadership, remarks that anticipate

David Riesman's theory that "inner-direction" shaped by a super-ego internalizing the parental injunctions of childhood is being increasingly supplanted by "other-direction" based on the contemporary social pressures of the peer group.[66]

Freud's view of all groups as essentially authoritarian partly follows from his liberal suspicion of the encroachments of the collective on individual freedom, as Rieff has pointed out.[67] But it more fundamentally reflects Freud's genetic perspective—too facilely labeled "reductionist" by many of his critics—that sees the earliest social experience, subjection to parental power, as the model and prototype of all later group experiences. He buttresses his claims about the psychology of groups in *Group Psychology* with the dubious anthropology of *Totem and Taboo*, regarding all groups as regressions to the precultural primal horde situation, the more stable kind to the father-dominated horde, the more transitory groups of Gustave Le Bon and the crowd psychologists to the band of brothers after their parricidal act but before their renunciation of the father's former prerogatives.

Group Psychology is not concerned with the subject of group conflict as such, apart from the general psychological foundations of group life. Freud does draw on Le Bon's crowd psychology, which viewed crowds and mobs, epitomized as Freud noted by those of the French Revolution, as reversions to barbarism in which otherwise rational and moral individuals are overpowered by irrational emotions often spurring them to acts of reckless violence. Crowds suddenly gripped by a single impulse to act are the kinds of collectivities that most obviously embody the aggregation of the psychological states of individuals, an aggregation produced by the milling about and emotional contagion within a confined space stressed by the crowd psychologists and the sociologists influenced by them in the "collective behavior" tradition developed at the University of Chicago by Robert Park and his students. Such groups at one time lent a superficial plausibility to the thoroughly questionable idea of a "group mind," although, as Freud argued, drawing on William McDougall, relatively stable organized groups cannot be equated with transitory crowds and mobs. Nevertheless, Freud regarded all behavior of individuals in groups as psychologically regressive. Le Bon's insensate crowd fired by the excitation its members induce in one another describes only "rapidly formed and transient groups."[68] The existence of a leader on whom the group members are dependent reproduces in more permanent organized groups, including the major institutions of society, the dominance of the father in the family before the formation of the superego. The commands of the leader supplant those of the superego just as the authority of the father preceded and became the model for the superego. The family and parental authority over the child are seen as the paradigms for all groups subject to hierarchical authority. A number of political psychologists have found this interpretation helpful in accounting for the *Führerprinzip* and the "cult of personality" successfully promoted by modern dictators.[69]

The actions of individuals shaped by past or present social influences reflect complex mixtures of motivation. Freud, as we have seen, regarded all action as motivated by some combination of "instinctual" drives. Clearly, this applies to violence sanctioned by social approval, whether it involves primarily the displacement of repressed aggression, passive habitual conformity with group norms, or dutiful obedience to the commands of legitimate authorities. The superego itself, after all, is formed both out of identifications based on Eros and out of aggressive drives redirected back upon the self. The death instinct is first directed outward against the world, ensuring the survival of the species, and then deflected back against the self as a sense of guilt making possible the existence of society by avoiding a Hobbesian war of all against all. The redirection outward yet again of aggressive drives against a socially defined external enemy of the group constitutes a possible third step in the transformations undergone by Freud's destructive instinct. If Freud sometimes seemed to regard war and group conflict as simply providing opportunities for permitted acting out of the crude aggressive drives of individuals, at other times he seemed to recognize that group-sanctioned aggression represented a higher, sublimated form of aggression, an at least tacit recognition of the role of the superego in war that Rieff claimed he overlooked. Nietzsche had earlier perceived that severity of moral judgment often serves as a mask for sadism in personal relations.

The attribution of intrapsychic affects or impulses to external objects constitutes *projection*,[70] the inverse of the psychic mechanism of introjection so favored by sociologists anxious to solve the hobbesian problem by postulating the "internalization of social norms." Howard Kaye has recently complained that sociologists ignore the psychic mechanisms identified by Freud with the single exception of introjection, slighting in particular projection, which may play a major role in the rise of new cultural movements like the Protestant Reformation.[71] Sublimated aggression as a source of ideological fanaticism, aggressive nationalism, and what Erik H. Erikson has called the "pseudo-speciation" of group enemies[72] are cases in point involving ferocious conflicts between groups. The insight that socially defined enemies may provide targets for the displacement of pent-up individual aggressive drives has greatly increased understanding of the durability and intensity of ethnic and racial prejudice. The main empirical contribution to social science of Freudo-Marxism was the *Studies in Prejudice* Series, three of whose five volumes were authored or coauthored by members of the original Frankfurt Institute for Social Research, while the entire series was edited by Max Horkheimer, the Director of the Institute in both Frankfurt and New York.[73] Displacement and projection were the major Freudian mechanisms these studies invoked to explain prejudice.

Freud is only occasionally guilty of lapsing into the crude attribution to groups of properties that can only belong to individuals, the kind of reductionism or confusion of analogy with identity exhibited by some of his more dogmatic followers who have ventured into social theory. And, as I have tried to show, his analysis of the psychological foundations of group attachments is often illuminating and even profound. Yet his contribution to the understanding of group conflict remains a limited though not insignificant one. Even the Frankfurt School's projective theory of prejudice, a sophisticated version of what has often been popularly known as the "scapegoating" theory, has been criticized for failure to account for the selection of the particular object of prejudice in the first place.[74] This is in fact a special case of the general failure of psychoanalysis to give sufficient weight to the objective social and historical processes that generate group differences and conflicts, a special case that loomed large in the heyday of psychoanalytic influence in the social sciences back in the 1940s and 1950s. When interest shifted from anti-Semitism to racial discrimination embodied in institutionalized practices as opposed to shadowy subjective projections reflecting archaic stereotypes, psychoanalytic interpretations of prejudice—and of social behavior in general—suffered decline. Conflicts between classes, political parties, religions, ethnic groups, and nations have "objective" roots in opposed values and interests, although such conflicts may also be invested with "private" displaced affects.

INDIVIDUAL MOTIVATIONS AND GROUP CONFLICT

The most significant difference between the hobbesian and the marxian versions of the problem of order is that the overcoming of conflict among individuals is a prerequisite for conflict at the group level. Groups, apart from transitory crowds and audiences, can only come into being and survive, let alone mobilize their members against other groups, if the individuals composing them have achieved solidarity and consensus with one another and a degree of organization. The individual members therefore have to have been socialized to avoid violent conflicts within their own ranks, to commit themselves to the collective goal of the continued existence and advancement of their group, and to adhere to norms of cooperation in coordinating their actions, perhaps especially if directed against other groups perceived as adversaries. They must be able to communicate symbolically, correctly gauge the expectations of others, internalize at least some norms, and possess selves sensitive to the appraisals of others. Whatever the formal or analogical similarities between the hobbesian war of all against all and the marxian war of group against group, the units involved are quite different socially and psychologically. Conflict between stable and organized groups occurs on a supra-individual level, activating in individuals both elemental drives and thoroughly sublimated modifications of them produced by socialization. This is the import of Rieff's statement about the role of the superego in war and he is right that Freud with his anticollectivist individualistic bias frequently failed to recognize it.

Not only is a mixture of motives likely to underlie the individual's participation in group conflict, but different individuals will be actuated by different motives. This applies, needless to say, not only to group conflict but to motives for the participation of individuals in any collective actions and institutionalized behavior, that is, behavior conforming to established social norms. The only relevant difference is that group conflict risks disruption of the larger social order or system of which the groups are part—except where conflict is against an external enemy as in war. Since the emotions mobilized in group conflict often permit the acting out of aggressive drives deeply rooted in human nature, the relation between such conflict and the potential for hobbesian war of all against all at the individual level cannot be overlooked, however fallacious the practice of extrapolating directly from individual to group.

Most groups and especially conflict groups depend on some degree of underlying solidarity uniting their members. Freud was correct in seeing mutual identifications, whether based on the members' perceptions of their many similarities to one another or only on their sharing a common identification with an authority figure, as the psychological foundation of the solidarity of groups. Solidarity based on likeness may be the initial basis for the formation of any group that achieves a more permanent existence than the ephemeral mobs and crowds of Le Bon and his fellow nineteenth-century crowd psychologists. Nor need such solidarity draw only on the irrational and regressive drives disruptive of social order that the crowd psychologists chose to emphasize. The temporary unity achieved by a rioting mob or expressive crowd is a concentrated form of the solidarity based on mutual identification present in more permanent groups. It is approximated in the early formative phase of those groups classified as social movements, the phase long given greatest attention by past students of social movements.[75] A primary interest in this phase and the fact that social movements, like the revolutionary mobs of the crowd psychologists, are conflict groups engaged in protest against existing authorities has led to their inclusion as objects of study under the rubric of "collective behavior." Recent students have directed more attention to later stages of development in striving to dissociate social movements from the irrationalism and destructive violence associated with the collective behavior tradition, although such a perspective blurs the distinction between social movements and formal organizations, especially conventional interest groups.[76]

Durkheim, who was a major intellectual adversary of the crowd psychologists—most notably of Gabriel Tarde—attached major importance, especially in *The Elementary Forms of the Religious Life*, to the same processes of mutual interstimulation and collective excitation described by the crowd psychologists.[77] In striking contrast to them, however, he saw these processes as generators of social order itself, both the reaffirmation of the individual's dedication to society with its norms as the all-powerful entity transcending his or her finite existence and as the source of new values after the disintegration into universal anomie of an old order.[78] This conception is clearly opposed to that of the crowd psychologists who saw collective ferment as subversive of order in inducing the individual to abandon the moral principles by which he or she customarily lived. Yet Raymond Aron reports in his memoirs that in the 1930s Marcel Mauss, Durkheim's nephew and collaborator as well as an important sociologist in his own right, expressed dismay over the hateful potential of the collective ferment exhibited at Nazi Party Day rallies at Nuremberg, remarking that in their dramatized worship of the group they were a perfect realization of Durkheim's theory of religion.[79] The ceremonies of the Australian aborigines described by Durkheim consisted of ritual dances previously known to the participants and the Nuremberg pageants were planned and orchestrated by their Nazi organizers in contrast to the insensate mobs gripped by spontaneous antinomian passions described by the crowd psychologists. Nevertheless, the emotional contagion inducing a common mood of anger or ecstasy and loss of customary self-consciousness is much the same in all three cases. Moreover, Durkheim saw collective excitation as a source of *new* values as well as the reaffirmation of old ones, rather than like the crowd psychologists as simply subversive of social order. Their contrasting evaluations of the revolutionary mobs of 1789–94 are evident.

Relatively permanent and organized groups engaged in prosaic routine activities do not necessarily depend on a single dominant motive or mood common to their members. An organized group consists of a plurality of roles, possesses a differentiated social structure (as sociologists like to say), and the roles are likely to activate different individual motives. Freud saw this—at least minimally—in imputing in *Group Psychology* markedly different psychological constitutions to leaders and followers.[80] Mancur Olson, Jr., the rational choice theorist of collective action, also recognizes it in noting the necessity of "selective incentives" to attract leaders and organizers of large groups that have to cope with the free rider problem.[81] The members of milling crowds, rioting mobs, and fascinated audiences may be powerfully seized by a single purpose or emotion, but they are apt to be ephemeral and atypical collectivities for just that reason. Groups engaged in a regular activity on a routine basis are likely to develop a more complex structure and therefore to draw on a range of individual motives to attract and keep members, or in the case of ascriptive groups activate them.

Solidarity based on shared norms, commitment to collective goals, and the maintenance of a system of differentiated roles, are defining criteria of *all* stable organized groups, including groups whose *raison d'être* may be conflict with other groups. The basic identity of a group implies the recognition of a boundary between it and other groups, an in-group/out-group distinction in William Graham Sumner's terms. The awareness of *difference* from other groups contains at least a potential for defining them as enemies and engaging in conflict with them. Conflict with another group may, as Simmel and Coser have stressed, serve to increase the in-group solidarity of both groups thereby intensifying the conflict between them.[82] Group conflict is in this sense implicit in the very existence of a plurality of groups within a larger social unit. Awareness of their likeness to one another may have been the initial basis for the formation of the group; after the group has been created and stabilized, the members' sense of difference from other groups becomes salient; if conflict with another group erupts, unity against the common enemy may become the order of the day and greatly enhance a solidarity originally based on similarities among its members altogether unrelated to the grounds of conflict.[83]

Once a group has already been formed and organized, its existence as a group, symbols representing it, its organizational structure, or its particular rituals and rules of procedure may become independent objects of attraction to individuals. Group membership itself creates a new social identity apart from the original similarities leading to the mutual identifications that were the basis for the original formation of the group. Some members may fetishize the group as a value over and above its individual members, recalling the proverbial lover of humanity who has little affection for individual human beings. In the case of conflict groups, a hate-obsessed preoccupation with the enemy may predominate over both the mutual identifications on which the primary solidarity of the group was founded and the valued shared identity forged by group membership itself.

An existing group and its attributes become part of the social environment of the individuals who encounter it. It confronts them as a common object, but like any other common object they may adopt a wide diversity of attitudes toward it. This obvious consideration is what makes it illegitimate to impute a single motivation or attitude to the individuals who belong to the group, despite the fact that its original founders may have felt strong bonds of solidarity with one another and passionate dedication to a common goal. An established group may be defined by the goal it is organized to pursue, but the individual members, though cooperating to promote the common goal and publicly affirming it, may nevertheless do so out of a variety of motives—strong commitment to the goal as embodying a cherished value, a sense of duty, long-run or short-run self-interest, personal attachment to a member or members of the group, the inertia of mere habit. Though a human creation and social construction, once securely established the group becomes an external condition of action exercising constraint over the individuals who encounter it, whether outsiders or the group's own members whose actions and interactions constitute it as a group. Accordingly, individuals may manifest the full repertory of possible human attitudes and motives toward it. This is the essential meaning of Durkheim's famous claim that society is "a reality *sui generis*": an entity transcending individual psychology that cannot be understood as a reflection or manifestation of any single element of that psychology. All stable groups, including groups engaged in conflict, must draw on a whole range of motivations to retain their members' commitment and to achieve the goal or goals that are their *raison d'être*. The group and its goals may exist minimally as common objects of perception and cognition, while at the same time they may have widely different meanings and evoke quite diverse attitudes on the part of both members and outsiders.

These are sociological commonplaces. They are most likely to be overlooked by imputing too great uniformity of outlook to group members in the case of groups formed for the express purpose of waging unrestrained conflict with other groups. First, because conflict groups may commit violent acts that are strongly condemned in intragroup as opposed to intergroup personal relations and partly for this very reason they place a premium on unquestioning obedience to orders. Group members may be expected to undergo what can only be called a process of *resocialization* designed to overcome the inhibitions on the use of violence they had previously acquired.[84] Second, because groups organized for violent conflict in which the very lives of their members may be at stake are compelled to place an especially high value on both solidarity and obedience to leaders. Armies are the obvious case in point, and not only have military metaphors been widely used to describe groups engaged in less violent forms of conflict, but such groups have often imitated military forms of hierarchical organization. Hierarchical organization is imposed by the exigencies of conflict that require quick decision-making and action. The genocide of the Jews committed by the Nazi state has raised issues of individual and collective motivation in a particularly concrete form, issues that are of transcendent moral significance but that also cast light on broader questions about the legitimation of collective goals in conflict situations and the scope and efficacy of socialization.

Germans and their allies on trial after the Second World War for "war crimes" or "crimes against humanity" often pleaded that they were "only following orders." The plea was frequently meant to suggest that they were subject to coercion, that disobedience would have led to severe punishment and even death at the hands of the Nazi authorities. Whether this was so or not—and there is evidence against it with respect to the mass murder of Jews[85]—the claim also presumed that they were obeying a norm of obedience to authority which brought them into conflict with values such as kindness, mercy, compassion, and respect for human life. For soldiers, especially in wartime, and to a lesser extent for members of paramilitary and police units, the plea that they had taken an oath of allegiance imposing an obligation to obey orders issued by the proper authority in a legitimate hierarchical chain of command may have seemed to have exculpatory weight with regard to their indictment for criminal actions against civilians or members of enemy armed forces. Far from acting in an impulsive or personally willful manner, the defendants wished to suggest that they were confronted with a conflict of norms and values posing a real moral dilemma. They were certainly aware of and intended to communicate to the courts judging them that "an act carried out under command is, psychologically, of a profoundly different character than action that is spontaneous."[86]

The quotation is from the first paragraph of the preface to Stanley Milgram's *Obedience to Authority*, the report on a series of psychological experiments he conducted in the early 1960s at Yale University. He asked his subjects, who were volunteers, to administer anonymously painful electric shocks to other pretended volunteers, not directly visible, who gave incorrect answers on a verbal test and then cried out when shocked. Milgram's results have been much discussed in connection with the Nazi destruction of the Jews, his study even becoming known as the "Eichmann Experiment."[87] As he himself indicates, the wish to understand the motivation of German officials who claimed to be carrying out the orders of their superiors provided the stimulus for his research. He wanted to discover how far people would go in obeying orders directing them to commit acts that violated their previous "training in ethics, sympathy, and moral conduct."[88] He framed the question not as a conflict between "instinctual" id impulses and the dictates of the superego, but as one between contradictory norms both possessing moral legitimacy. "After witnessing hundreds of ordinary people submit to the authority in our own experiments," Milgram wrote, "I must conclude that Arendt's concept of the *banality of evil* comes closer to the truth than one might dare imagine. The ordinary person who shocked the victim did so out of a sense of obligation—a conception of his duties as a subject—and not from any peculiarly aggressive tendency" (his emphasis).[89] I am unable to resist pointing out that if the subjects trusted the experimenters who were clothed in the benevolent authority of Science, their trust was not altogether unfounded, for the shocks were bogus, the supposed victims' screaming feigned, and no one was actually hurt.[90] The issues raised by conflict between the orders of a legitimate authority and moral values, however, remain real ones.

Hannah Arendt's famous phrase "the banality of evil" was meant to describe the evil-doers, not their deeds.[91] She wished to emphasize the disproportion between the mediocrity and unimaginative conformity of the Nazi functionaries who carried out the genocide of the Jews and the monstrousness of what they did all in a day's work. The phrase itself may have been first suggested to her by her friend and teacher the philosopher Karl Jaspers,[92] but the idea that the Nazis, including Hitler himself,[93] were vulgar philistines bearing little resemblance to Iago or Macbeth was not a new one. However, Arendt was not concerned to make a quasi-aesthetic point about the unrefined and shallow sensibilities exhibited by the likes of Adolf Eichmann, but to insist that the true horror of totalitarianism lay in its creation of a social system in which ordinary, banal, no-better-than-they-ought-to-be careerists like Eichmann carried out tasks that were "radically evil"[94] by what had long been understood as "civilized" moral standards. Whether or not Eichmann as an individual was actually an undistinguished *homme moyen sensuel*, though properly contested in the debate Arendt's discussion of the case inspired, was a secondary issue. She chose to treat Eichmann as representative of the new totalitarian order whose ultimate triumph she had feared and envisioned in her earlier book, where she contended that the "mass man" of the future "will have more in common with the meticulous, calculated correctness of Himmler than with the hysterical fanaticism of Hitler, will more resemble the stubborn dullness of Molotov than the sensual vindictive cruelty of Stalin."[95] Clearly, over a decade later she saw Eichmann as a replica of the first-named individuals.

The Nazis are often described as barbarians. But, as most observers grasped at least implicitly, they were far from being uncomplicated tribesmen so totally identified with their own group that they had no inhibitions about inflicting excruciating tortures and painful death on enemies from other tribes with whom they recognized no common humanity. Herbert Luethy shared Arendt's awareness of the uniqueness of the Nazis when he asserted at roughly the same time, less than a decade after the Final Solution, that "they marked an absolute zero in human history, far below all barbarism, below all horrors of war and revolution, below Stalin's slave camps."[96] The "barbarism" label has been so often applied to individuals, groups, and conditions regarded as at odds with contemporary ideals and values that it amounts to little more than an expletive expressing strong moral disapproval. Even the appropriateness of calling "evil" such relatively common premodern practices as cannibalism, human sacrifice, infanticide, torture, capital punishment by drawing and quartering,[97] and the mass slaughter in war of populations, including women and children, is open to question. Arendt's famous phrase and Luethy's judgment[98] surely presuppose that the men who carried out the Final Solution *could have and should have known better*, indeed that they *did* know better in some corner of their minds and souls. The Nazis may have striven to indoctrinate their subjects with a new code that directly inverted the Christian ideals of Western civilization,[99] but they were in power for only twelve years, not long enough for even a single generation to have grown up socialized to conform to and internalize only Nazi values. All Nazi subjects and servants had therefore been socialized, their superegos had been formed, under the old moral order by whose unambiguous judgment the mass murder of innocent human beings was totally sinful, evil, and criminal.

Whether active perpetrators or "desk murderers" like Eichmann who did not see what happened "at the end of the telegraph line,"[100] the Nazis knew what they were doing both cognitively at the level of moral awareness and emotionally in the form of guilt, unconscious and masked by their overt behavior though the awareness and the guilt may have been.[101] If they were not barbarians, neither were many of them clinical psychopaths or sociopaths. Philip Rieff's reference to a conflict between "public" and "personal" morality states it too abstractly.[102] A conflict between the norms of present associates, accepted at least at a superficial cognitive-emotional level, and norms internalized in earlier childhood better describes the situation. Whether one chooses to call it evil or merely moral weakness, the culpability of the Nazi murderers lay in their submission to immediate situational pressures that overrode the voice of conscience. This judgment applies whether the norms obeyed were those of Nazi ideology affirmed by the individual or simply the commands of an authority perceived as legitimate.[103] One might contend that submission to authority involves, as Freud argued in *Group Psychology*, regression to infantile dependence on the father before the formation of the superego, but, while this may have some relevance to adoration of the *Führer* and acceptance of his will as an ultimate value,[104] it hardly seems to apply to compliance with orders from "human-all-too-human" superiors in the field by "ordinary men" who were not even Nazis.[105] Both aggression and submission to authority may be human dispositions deeply rooted in universal infantile experience, but both are also regularly enacted in moderated, sublimated forms in routine social life.

The terrible and unprecedented extreme situations of the Final Solution revealed new modalities and combinations of the universally human and the effects of historically specific socialization experiences, rather than fearsome elemental depths of human nature in the raw. The Nazis could succeed in killing so many people and creating such hellish mass institutions as death camps only by utilizing the distinctively modern instrumentally rational techniques of applied science, industrial production, and bureaucratic social organization.[106] Undoubtedly, the "banality" of the quotidian performance of genocidal tasks lay in the use of these techniques on which modern societies and economies are so dependent. And the impersonal mechanical routinization of the tasks helped dull the moral sensibilities of their agents, especially after the gas chambers were introduced, by eliminating any personal relation between murderer and victim. All of these conditions made it easier for ordinary men to do extraordinarily cruel things without apparently suffering any qualms. But the evil was not primarily a matter of means or methods, nor even of the scale on which the genocide was implemented. The evil lay rather in how the perpetrators resolved the conflict between what they were ordered to do and the values they had absorbed in the childhood socialization under which their superegos had developed. The resolution of this conflict in favor of mass murder, however reluctantly or distastefully carried out, is what was uniquely evil about the Nazis, not a reversion to barbarism, nor the eruption of innately antisocial aggressive drives, nor a disproportionate representation of deviant psychopathic personalities in their ranks, nor reliance on the techniques of modern instrumental rationality on a mass scale that made possible such an unprecedented number of victims.

That the deeds of the Nazis were carried out in a situation of deadly group conflict, and justified by an ideology that extolled and indeed brought about that conflict, is hardly incidental. The Nazi crimes were historically unique and cannot be reduced to instances of abstract sociological generalization. Nevertheless, at the risk of bathos, it can be pointed out that they starkly illustrate the proposition that group conflict may legitimate and even obligate behavior toward enemies that is totally prohibited within the group. Such a prohibition is a necessary condition for the formation and continuing existence of the group as a solidary unit signifying the overcoming within its own ranks of the hobbesian problem of order, even though the group's very *raison d'être* may be to wage unrestrained conflict against other groups defined as enemies.

EGOISM/ALTRUISM AND CONFLICT/CONSENSUS

The first pair of concepts in the heading refers to the motives and interests of individuals, the second to relations within or among groups. The two sets of paired concepts are another way of drawing the distinction between the levels of the individual and of the group indicated in the title of this chapter that I have also equated with the hobbesian and the marxian versions of the problem of order. The problem of order is the need to control the individual dispositions and group relations named successively by the first term of each pair if social order is to be securely established and maintained.

The terms referring to individual motivations, or synonyms for them, are, to be sure, occasionally extended by partial analogy to groups in phrases like "the selfishness of groups," a selfishness sometimes even contrasted with the allegedly greater altruism of individuals acting autonomously, as in Niebuhr's "moral man/immoral society" dichotomy, the antinomianism of mobs depicted by the crowd psychologists, and some interpretations of participation in the Nazi genocide reviewed in the preceding section. Yet egoism and altruism, literally "self..ism" and "other..ism," refer primarily to individual attitudes. "Altruism" was, surprisingly, not coined until the nineteenth century and by none other than Auguste Comte—surprisingly, because the conflict in human nature between egoistic and altruistic interests and motivations, variously defined, is a venerable theme in social and philosophical thought. "Altruism" connotes motives that give priority to the interests of other persons over the interests of the acting self. Sometimes it is applied merely to actions that in fact benefit others, whether or not they were intended to do so and whether or not they also benefit the self as well.

The conflict/consensus opposition, on the other hand, refers to the major controversies among sociologists in the 1960s and 1970s over Parsonsian normative functionalism as a theory of social integration at what is sometimes called the "societal" as distinct from the "social" level of action.[107] Parsons's critics were not primarily concerned with individual deviations from norma-

tive consensus but with the determinants of conflict among large
groups within a single society. Their focus was on what Ralf
Dahrendorf, the major proponent of what came to be called
"conflict theory," described as "structurally generated" conflicts
at the level of the whole society. The class conflicts central to
Marxism were only one such conflict, reinterpeted by
Dahrendorf as resulting from inequalities of power rather than of
property.[108] I shall postpone discussion of group conflict at the
societal level until the next chapter.

The reality of altruistic motivations has often been denied.
Hobbes himself made a point of denying that humans ever acted
in a truly altruistic fashion and the real or apparent exceptions
have long been invoked and debated. Such denials almost invariably result in formulations to the effect that all human actions
are basically motivated by a quest for pleasure, material self-
interest, or utility. This underlies the classical economist's famous
paradox of the "invisible hand" of the market producing outcomes that are to the benefit of all despite the fact that each individual actor is motivated solely by the desire to maximize his or
her own pleasure, interest, or utility. That the all-embracing
nature of the economist's "utility" as the object of human striving renders it vacuous, even tautological, for explanatory purposes has been cogently argued by Amitai Etzioni.[109] All purposive or
goal-directed action is indeed action *of* a self, but that does not
necessarily mean that it is action serving only the interests of the
self and remaining indifferent or oblivious to the interests and
feelings of others.

The self becomes an object in experience as a result of the
acquisition of language, which employs the same symbols or
signs to denote the actions of both ego and alter.[110] The self as
object, therefore, is formed by identifications with other "social
objects"—that is, other real or imagined people—in the external
world. Once formed, it becomes a uniquely precious object; great
effort is devoted to its protection and aggrandizement. The explanation for its unique importance lies in the fact of its omnipres-
ence: like the body to which it is attached, it is always there,
escaped from only by loss of consciousness. The cultivation of a
positive or favorable image of and attitude toward one's self

avoids the pain of being constantly in the presence of something that arouses aversion. This would seem to be a universal feature of the human condition, despite the enormous cultural variation in the value placed on the individuality of the self, and in the degree to which its uniqueness as a particular ensemble of personal qualities is celebrated or even recognized.

The self is an object constituted out of identifications with other objects and it retains the capability of wholly identifying itself cognitively, affectively, and in purposive action with other objects: persons, imaginary beings, groups, institutions, whole societies, collective projects or causes, ideas and ideals, moral principles, value-systems or ideologies, even places and material things. The wish to promote and maximize the interests of the self as object can readily be transferred to other objects, despite their externality and less durable presence in psychic experience. James Rule is entirely right to assert "the futility. . .of seeking a rigorous distinction between self-interest and other kinds of interest." After citing several ambiguous cases combining elements of egoistic and altruistic motivation, he observes of them that

> they illustrate something quite basic about social motivation—that people can and do identify with a variety of interests at varying distances from the narrowest of divisible self-interest. . .To try to partition these interests into either-or categories of self-interest versus altruism or philanthropy distracts attention from a reality that has much more nuance.[111]

Entirely altruistic actions that serve the interests of another person or a group, even conformity to a norm demanding self-denial, are not unknown or all that uncommon, as Etzioni has documented from a wide range of empirical studies undertaken by economists and social psychologists.[112]

The longstanding debate between economists and sociologists over the egoism or altruism of human behavior has been vigorously renewed in recent years, largely as a result of the emergence within sociology of a school of rational choice theorists whose stated aim is to extend the economic model of a rational utility-maximizing actor to noneconomic areas of human choice traditionally studied by sociologists. Too often this debate degenerates into a confrontation between rival caricatures: a cold, calculating egoist toting up across the breakfast table the costs and benefits of continuing his or her marriage versus an oversocialized "goody two-shoes" programmed to conform to norms internalized in childhood that serve the collective interest, or common good, in sustaining social order.[113] There is an antiquated, distinctly pre-Freudian flavor to this debate, as if psychoanalysis, the only comprehensive developmental theory of human nature that we have, had not shown systematically both the mixture of motives manifest in the ambivalence or overdetermination of all human action and the development of the individual from the total egocentrism of the infant to later introjection of a wide range of objects that becomes the very foundation of character structure itself.

That attitudes toward objects form a continuum rather than the either/or alternative rejected by Rule is consistent with psychoanalysis, although neither Rule nor Etzioni draw on it in criticizing rational choice models that give absolute primacy to the maximization of self-interest. The self may become a privileged object constantly present in intrapsychic life, but it is not the first object confronted in the individual's experience. As emphasized by Melanie Klein and the British "object-relations" school of psychoanalysis, attitudes toward the earliest objects encountered in infancy shape the deepest motivations of the individual.[114] When with the full mastery of language the self emerges as a cognitive object, it may trap or capture earlier affects and motives centered on the body with their source in bodily tensions. But the care and feeding of the self as object is not a primary or foundational datum of human nature grounded in biologically determined hedonism, as some versions of rational egoism assume.

The utilitarian rational choice model is not, to be sure, oriented even implicitly to any form of biological determinism. In stressing the purposiveness and rationality of human action it attaches primary significance to distinctively human qualities that presuppose language and self-consciousness. It does not therefore *necessarily* deny the social origins of the very capacity to make rational choices. Yet in starting from the basic premise of the instrumental rationality of human actions in the service of strictly egoistic ends, it projects an individualistic bias that ignores the fundamental role played by cognitive and emotional identification with others in shaping the very self whose interests become the mainspring of human motivation and action. Even if all purposive action is mediated by the self, the desires and interests of the self as object need not always take precedence over other objects, some of which were introjected before the self had been fully formed. Internalization of norms and the expectations of others enter into the formation of the very capabilities of the actors enabling them to reflect in advance on the consequences of their actions whether those consequences advance the interests of the self, of others, or simply conform to a norm or value for its own sake. An inability to form stable object attachments inspiring altruistic concerns and to overcome preoccupation with the impact of anything and everything on the self does not reflect an unusually strong self but rather the reverse, as analysts of narcissistic personality traits have maintained.[115]

Rational choice theorists typically justify their model on heuristic grounds, acknowledging that it does not necessarily accurately describe most actual human actions. This is true even of the most sociologically sophisticated and knowledgeable version of the model, that of James S. Coleman. Coleman argues that "much sociological theory takes social norms as given and proceeds to examine individual behavior or the behavior of social systems when norms exist. . .without raising. . .the question of why and how norms come into existence [thus] forsak[ing] the more important sociological problem in order to address the less important."[116] Coleman here cleverly reverses the familiar charge of individualist bias so often leveled by sociologists at economists' accounts of human action in general and rational choice theories in particular. He specifies Talcott Parsons as a case in point, claiming that the proposition that "Persons behave in accordance with social norms" is Parsons's equivalent of the basic assumption of "maximising utility in rational choice theory." Indeed, Coleman's massive *Foundations of Social Theory* is a rejoinder over half a century later in defense of utilitarian individualism to Parsons's famous rejection of it in *The Structure of*

Social Action. Coleman argues the superiority of the rational choice model in explaining the transition from micro to macro collective action as well as its greater usefulness in designing *new* social institutions,[117] both of which preclude simply taking for granted the existence of given norms however adequately such norms may account for the behavior of particular individuals in particular social contexts. Coleman does ultimately concede that there is an "individual-level deficiency" in rational choice theory,[118] but he clearly considers this to be no more than a minor blemish in light of the theory's potential for both intellectual rigor and application to issues of social policy.

Far from assuming norms as given, I maintain that the expectations of others, even when not explicitly formulated at the level of what Giddens calls "discursive consciousness," acquire a force of obligation, a normative weight or presumption, for an actor who is sensitized to them. This presupposes that actors wish (much though not necessarily all of the time) to win the approval of others, or at least to avoid their manifest disapproval. *Why* approval, or the avoidance of disapproval, is so important to humans is not explored by the interactionist sociologies: they tend to take for granted and accept as given the motivation for seeking approval, although they do not assume the preexistence of norms that Coleman attributes to Parsons and Durkheim. Both cognitive Meadian and affective/ motivational Freudian socialization are necessary to produce actors who generate expectations in the course of their interaction that acquire a normatively binding character and may crystallize into full-fledged social norms.

Coleman does not mention either Mead or Freud until more than halfway through his book of nearly a thousand pages and then both of them only once on the same page.[119] He insists that rational choice theory necessarily assumes "persons who are. . .not only rational but also unconstrained by norms and purely self-interested."[120] Infants and small children are not appropriately described as "rational," but they certainly possess the other two attributes of being unconstrained by norms and motivated by pure egoism. But Coleman thinks that rational choice theory must assume stable rather than changing interests.[121] Social systems may change but actors cannot be treated as historical—that is, life-historical or biographical—units. This intentionally unrealistic assumption lends a static quality as well as a certain remoteness from human reality to Coleman's theory, as Charles Tilly has pointed out.[122] Parsons may have exaggerated the extent of the internalization of norms achieved in the course of socialization, but in his later work influenced by Freud he at least took a developmental view of human character that met the three criteria of starting with birth, noting the organic bases of social behavior, and assigning causal priority to childhood.[123]

People identify with objects—primarily with other people—that become incorporated into an expanded conception of self and consequently an enlarged sense of their self-interest, which comes to encompass a changing array of objects as they pursue their life-course. Goals cannot therefore unambiguously, let alone permanently, be tagged as egoistic *or* altruistic. Most of them are clearly both, as James Rule properly recognizes in the passage cited above. Coleman himself goes some distance toward acknowledging this in writing:

> It can be argued that an important process that occurs throughout life is an expansion of the object self to include larger and larger sets of objects. . .Acts of apparent altruism, acts which derive from sentimental attachments and appear to be against the actor's interests narrowly defined, are explicable through such an addition to the theory, the use of the notion of an expanded object self.[124]

Yet the reference to "apparent altruism" and to "interests narrowly defined" savors of old and familiar efforts by proponents of universal egoism to, at the risk of tautology, assimilate behavior that is not obviously selfish to their fundamental assumptions. And Coleman goes on to try to assess the possible ultimate benefits to self of behavior that manifestly serves in the first instance the interests of others.[125]

Coleman's methodological individualism is sound enough, but he complements it with an ontological individualism that he defends on heuristic grounds. As Tilly observes, "He does not. . .take the leap toward which his more decisive small steps seem to be leading: abandoning the individualism for an analysis in which durable social relations form the starting point, rather than merely the means, of solving individually defined problems."[126] Coleman is properly critical of the Durkheim-Parsons tendency to equate the social with the normative,[127] but he then proceeds to presuppose that equation himself in choosing to base his analysis on the starting point of a completely nonsocial individual rather than on norms assumed to be present at the outset. Coleman's model of the actor as rational egoist resembles one of the three "libidinal types" identified by Freud: the "strong-ego" version of what Freud called the ego-centered "narcissistic" type as distinct from the id-dominated "erotic" type and the superego-ruled "obsessional" type.[128] Philip Slater indeed describes this type as "the complete 'economic' man, motivated solely by self-interest."[129]

Whatever the serviceability of rational choice theory in devising social policies or designing new social institutions tailored to the lowest common denominator of the large numbers of individuals who will be affected by them in modern societies, are we likely to rest content with such parsimonious "black box" assumptions? Max Weber too thought that instrumental rationality (*Zweckrationalität*) was the most instantly comprehensible and presumptively most common kind of action, but that did not prevent him from identifying three additional distinctly different kinds of action; much of his scholarship was devoted to trying to unravel and understand the complex web of meanings that inspired actions manifesting or affirming values (*Wertrationalität*), as Richard Münch has pointed out in criticism of Coleman's reinterpretation of Weber's Protestant ethic thesis.[130] Coleman, on the other hand, insists that "what is ordinarily described as nonrational or irrational is merely so because the observers have not discovered the point of view of the actor, from which the action *is* rational."[131] All behavior, then, can ultimately be construed as rational if we try hard enough to do so. Doing so will facilitate the application of formal theoretical models which can provide premises for social policy and the design of new institutions in a modern world in which "primordial" institutions are disappearing.[132]

Are we likely to rest content with a theory that makes a purely pragmatic case for itself and takes for granted the superiority of a nomological-deductive mode of reasoning? Are we not likely at some point to be driven to ask "but what are human beings *really* like and how do they get that way?" Our interest in human nature and in human life generally differs from our much more utilitarian concern with nonhuman things, which is why the nomothetic model of the natural sciences, so long dominant in sociology, has come to seem so utterly inappropriate and inapplicable to the study of human affairs.[133]

The egoism/altruism polarity is too simple and artificial to do justice to the subtle and changing mixtures and developmental transformations to which human motivations are subject—the "vicissitudes of the instincts" in Freud's phrase. In undergoing a socialization process that begins at birth, all human beings, with the exception of the little-understood category of "sociopaths,"[134] arrive at a balance between egoistic impulses and internalized social norms setting limits to acting directly on those impulses. Such a balance is a prerequisite for the achievement of a self capable of forming attachments to social objects that are not sources of direct bodily gratification or material self-interest.[135] Identification with groups larger than the nuclear family is a fundamental case in point if the transition from infantile egocentrism is to be made.[136] Such attachments and identifications may foster group conflicts threatening the stability and integration of a society containing a multitude of different groups. The resulting marxian problem of order, however, presupposes a prior solution to the hobbesian problem of socialization. Group conflict is chiefly waged between individuals who have been socialized, who possess superegos, which enables them to form groups characterized by a degree of consensus, solidarity, and organization that may be strengthened by antagonistic relations with other groups.

CHAPTER SEVEN

GROUP CONFLICT, ORDER, AND DISORDER

Wars, revolutions, rebellions, riots, protest demonstrations—all are instances of group conflict, sometimes involving millions of people. Recent scholarship has powerfully confirmed that revolutions usually occur in the aftermath of wars, especially following defeat in war, at the very least when states have been weakened as a result of successive wars.[1] The twentieth century began in historical as distinct from chronological time with the Great War of 1914-18.[2] A consequence of that war was the later seizure of state power by Communist, Fascist, and National Socialist movements that led to the even deadlier Second World War. That war was followed by over forty years of "cold war" between the United States and the Soviet Union, the two remaining great powers or "superpowers" as they came to be called. It is possible to hope that this disastrous sequence of events, this "history that we did not want,"[3] came to an end in 1989-91 with the collapse of Communism in Russia and Eastern Europe.

As recently as a decade ago I used to argue with Marxists that the two world wars of the present century had a greater impact upon our lives than all the class struggles since the very beginnings of modern capitalism. The waning of intense class struggles in the late twentieth century and the decline of classes themselves as cohesive if loosely bounded conflict groups are today undeniable as the century draws to a close. Yet at the same time ethnic and religious conflicts within and between divided nation states have by no means disappeared and have even become more salient with the end of the nuclear deadlock between the super-powers. Group conflict and the threat it poses to the order and even the survival of societies organized into nation-states are hardly things of the past.

Nations, classes, and ethnic and religious communities are all large-scale "macro" groups that may under certain conditions be transformed into and increasingly come to define themselves as conflict groups. The presence of some line of demarcation between members and nonmembers is a defining criterion of a social group as distinct from a mere aggregate of individuals or a network linked through intersecting chains of interaction. As is true of virtually all sociological concepts, there are ambiguous borderline cases, both as to whether particular persons are or are not members of a given group and as to whether or not a particular aggregate of persons, some of whom interact regularly with others, can properly be considered a group. But a degree of shared consciousness of boundaries including some persons and excluding others amounts to the collective self-definition by an assemblage of individuals that they compose a group.

The existence of a group also provides its individual members with a new social identity as well as creating the negative identity of outsider for nonmembers. The difference between member and nonmember may be purely nominal and of little significance, but it also contains the potentiality of invidious distinction. Whether or not a prospective new member should really be considered "one of us" may become an issue even in the case of such groups as families based primarily on hereditary membership but which can be entered through marriage. A Jules Feiffer cartoon depicts an unpopular high school "nerd" who with a few others of his kind forms a club of nerds; they still feel like isolated deviants until a new unambiguously "nerdy" individual appears and the group votes not to accept him as a member. The last panel of the cartoon shows the original member beaming happily while declaring that they now have a *real* club since "it's not real until you reject someone."[4] This nicely illustrates how the exclusion of someone else may succeed in enhancing the perceived value of a group to its members. Such a sense of invidious distinction may conceivably lead to conflict with excluded groups but may also coexist peaceably with the "nesting" of smaller groups within larger ones that create wider allegiances and more inclusive social identities.[5] There is a continuum from the sheer difference between members and nonmembers implied by group boundaries to invidious distinction, to intergroup hostility, to overt conflict. Only the conversion of a sense of difference into conflict poses a possible threat to the social order that includes the rival parties.

Conflict itself is obviously a matter of degree. Some conflicts may crystallize into ritualized forms of expression that provide emotional satisfactions to participants without producing much in the way of further consequences. Other conflicts may be over real issues that are at stake and yet be regulated according to approved procedures with the result that their outcome is accepted by the contesting parties whose conflict therefore poses no threat to social order. Conflict may reinforce rather than undermine stability, which is the major argument of Lewis Coser in his examination of its many forms and effects.[6] Social conflicts can be located along a continuum from ritualized gesture, through various forms of negotiation and bargaining, to the nonviolent use of force, to all-out violence subject to little or no restraint. The latter, amounting to a war of group against group as distinct from a Hobbesian war of all against all, is what is frequently imagined in menacing images of society disintegrating or falling into "disorder."

Even violent conflict may lead to deadlock or stalemate directly on the field of battle, as in the trench warfare of 1914-18, or a balance of power in which both sides are able to threaten sufficient force to deter each other from the actual use of force, as in the more than forty years of cold war between the West and the Soviet bloc.[7] Conflict may also, of course, be a source of social change, as asserted in Marx's famous claim for class struggle in the opening sentence of *The Communist Manifesto* and also in Leon Trotsky's statement that "war is the locomotive of history." Trotsky's dictum might be regarded as asserting a rival claim to Marx's because it elevates to the major cause of change "external" wars between separate nation-states or political units rather than the internal conflicts between classes produced by the contradiction between the forces and the relations of production. Recent studies of revolution suggest that Trotsky was closer to being right. Both statements, however, treat conflict as a transforming social and historical process. Conflict most obviously leads to social change when one side wins and imposes its exclusive control over a society or social situation that was previously partly shaped by the power, interests, and values of the defeated party. In extreme cases the victor may even eliminate the other side altogether.

THE DEBATE OVER CONFLICT AND CONSENSUS

Conflict, then, *may* promote social change, but it need not do so and may even contribute to stability. This was often overlooked or minimized by sociologists who espoused what came to be called "conflict theory" in polemicizing against the normative functionalism of Talcott Parsons in the 1960s and 1970s.[8] Conflict and change were even sometimes used almost interchangeably, although not only may conflict lead to a stable balance of conflicting forces but social change may occur in the relative absence of conflict. The virtual identification by normative functionalists of social order itself with consensus on norms and values excluded social conflict, whether it produced change or stability.[9] Insofar as functionalists laid stress on institutions and social practices that contribute to the "boundary-maintaining" equilibrium of a given society, they could be charged with neglecting the instabilities, innovations, and "contradictions" that transform societies. Since persistent social conflicts at least contain an obvious potential for change, the criticisms that the functionalists ignored conflict and that they were preoccupied with persistence rather than with change tended to be conflated.

Control over the means of production and consumption by one group reducing others to dependence on it for subsistence under conditions of economic scarcity is the classical Marxist situation giving rise to class conflict. Differences in power between groups, however, need not derive solely from inequalities in control of scarce economic resources. Any exercise of power by one group over another may be experienced as oppressive and lead to open or latent resistance by the subordinate group. Ralf Dahrendorf forcefully made the argument that the conflict of economic interests so central to Marxism was a special case of the broader category of conflict between holders of power and their subjects.[10] There may also be conflicts over values which are often enough the most ferocious kind, but they were less emphasized by Parsons's critics, who wished to minimize or at least qualify the preeminent role he assigned to values and sometimes to represent values as no more than reflections of more basic underlying interests. The Marxist preoccupation with economic interests and the older emphasis on the role of force in society going back at least to Thrasymachus in Plato's *Republic*, revived polemically by Dahrendorf in the 1950s,[11] became the source of the opposition of material interests to values and of coercion to legitimate authority in the conceptual armory of Parsons's critics. Stability, consensus, values, and legitimate authority tended to be grouped together and contrasted with change, conflict, material interests, and coercion as a counterconceptual set. The latter emphasis was labeled "conflict theory" and seen as originating in the critical reaction to Parsonsian structural-functionalism; it still is presented under that label in current textbooks of contemporary theory although often broadened to include Marxism or "neo-Marxism" as well.

The original conflict theorists were not Marxists, although several of them had been in their youth. They are more accurately described as "post-Marxists," or perhaps as "left Weberians," to use a term that came into use at a later date. Frank Parkin quipped that "inside every neo-Marxist there seems to be a Weberian struggling to get out."[12] He had in mind the generation that was politically radicalized in the 1960s, but it applied also to the earlier generation of conflict theorists whose Weberianism had become quite manifest. With only minor qualifications this profile fits even C. Wright Mills, who went on to become an intellectual and ideological father of the student New Left before his early death in 1962. The first conflict theorists were essentially a cosmopolitan, politically sophisticated group whose own direct experience of unexpected and disruptive historical events— wars, revolutions, economic depression, the rise of Fascism and

Stalinism, political exile—led them to feel that Parsonsian normative functionalism, virtually all of whose supporters were
Americans, was a one-sided theoretical perspective that down-
graded or simply omitted from its purview huge slices of social
and historical reality, especially contemporary social and historical reality.[13] Rather than being primarily motivated by ideological
convictions, let alone by a commitment to left-wing political
activism, the rejection by the early conflict theorists of the com-
placent implicit conservatism they detected in Parsonsian normative functionalism was rooted in a common sensibility shaped by
experience with the politics of the Left and the historical castas-
trophes of the 1930s and 1940s.

Despite its origins in political and historical experience, the
criticism of the early conflict theorists was essentially intellectual
and was usually framed in general theoretical terms, often,
though not always, at the same abstract level as Parsonsian theory itself.[14] This was especially true of Dahrendorf, who presented
"conflict" or "coercion" theory as the direct opposite of "integration" theory, arguing that each theory was appropriate to different empirical problems but that they did not lend themselves
in any form to combination or synthesis.[15] The other conflict theorists resisted such a "never the twain shall meet" conception of
the difference and tried with limited success to combine conflict
and consensus, interests and values, power and authority in single theoretical formulations.[16] Conflict theory in general was for a
long time regarded as simply a counterstatement to functionalism, fundamentally parasitic on the more coherent and self-sufficient formulations of the latter to which it stood in opposition.
The naming of "consensus" as the opposite of conflict reflected
the fact that *normative* functionalism, specifically associated with
Parsons's theoretical works of the 1950s, was the major target.[17]
Parsons himself observed somewhat complacently in 1962 that
"the 'Opposition' has much less of a coherent theory than the
'Establishment,'"[18] meaning by the latter his own "systematic theory," as he liked to call it. The entire conflict versus consensus
debate has quite often been treated as a single theoretical unit,
the two rival views seen as representing opposite sides of the
same coin.

The student-centered radical left movements of the 1960s initiated a revival of Marxism, especially after their political decline
in the early 1970s when their more intellectual followers
entrenched themselves in the universities. An academic or "pro-
fessorial" Marxism flourished through the 1970s and 1980s in
the major Western nations.[19] Among sociologists, "conflict theory" sometimes seemed to operate, especially in the United States,
as a code word for Marxism. Those who defined themselves
forthrightly as Marxists adopted a rather patronizing attitude
toward it, seeing it as simply the "other face" of a discredited
Parsonsian structural-functionalism, at best as a halfway house
toward a full commitment to Marxism. In some circles "critical
theory" became an alternative label, one which had originally
been quite consciously adopted as a code word for Marxism by
the refugee scholars of the Frankfurt School during their sojourn
in America. Paradoxically, "conflict theory" provided for some
intellectuals a route back to the Marxism that its earliest expo-
nents had either abandoned or tried to revise along Weberian
lines. This was also true of the Frankfurt School, which had initially taken shape as a pessimistic, even despairing, response to
the political defeats of the Left and to Stalinist totalitarianism in
the 1930s. It too in its solidly academic ambience provided a
road back to some rather old-fashioned Marxist assumptions. It
is too soon to tell what lasting effects the collapse of Soviet
Communism will have on social theory, but it is hardly likely that
even the most cloistered academic varieties of Marxism will
escape unscathed. There are already some indications of a return
to more generalized versions of conflict theory that seem less vulnerable to the discrediting of Marxism.

The terminology deployed in this debate was far from consistent. "Conflict" was opposed to "consensus" in the most frequent binary opposition, although "cooperation" is the obvious
and literal opposite of conflict and was so regarded by earlier
sociologists,[20] as is "dissensus" of consensus. The opposition of
"coercion" and "consensus" makes better sense in suggesting a
contrast between power based on force and the "consent of the
governed" celebrated in the American Constitution, or what sociologists usually call legitimate authority. The asserted polarity of

conflict and "equilibrium" or "integration" presumes that conflict cannot be a source of stability, the view rejected by Coser. Despite frequent allusions to the Hobbesian problem, both conflict and consensus were clearly employed by the debaters with virtually exclusive reference to groups rather than to individuals, that is, at the level of what I have called the marxian as distinct from the hobbesian problem. But the very existence of organized groups mobilized for conflict indicates the achievement of consensus within them, so conflict and consensus can hardly be regarded as absolute contraries in any ultimate sense. The most thoroughgoing conflict theorist was surely Hobbes and the archetypical conflict situation the Hobbesian war of all against all, but such a war amounts to the absence of *any* society, the total negation of social order, rather than representing an alternative "model" of, or "perspective" on, actually existing societies, which is how the opposition between conflict and consensus has usually been characterized. Conflict *between* groups cannot exist unless there is consensus *within* groups, so the former condition directly entails the presence of the latter,[21] Dahrendorf's argument to the contrary that they are mutually exclusive theoretical approaches notwithstanding.

The priority ascribed by normative functionalists to consensus as the source of social order resulted in their projecting an oversocialized conception of the individual and an overintegrated conception of society.[22] Clearly, conflict, whether resulting from divergent economic interests or values, or from coercive power relations, is excluded by a theory that virtually identifies society itself with consensus on norms and values. Conflict conceived of as a Hobbesian war of all against all or as universal anomie becomes the contrary of society, the mark of disorder, of failure to resolve the problem of order. Despite their justified insistence on the undeniable existence of social order, the presence of recurrent, smoldering, ever-potential conflict either making for change or contributing to stability is ignored or minimized by normative functionalists. The roots of such tendencies to conflict in the individual or in human nature was the theme of my 1961 article criticizing "the oversocialized conception of man in modern sociology." At the group level, the conflict theorists, influenced by Marx and Weber, had earlier made a parallel case against Parsons's overintegrated view of society.

The problem for normative functionalism in understanding complex modern societies was to identify a status order that legitimated social inequalities by "defining the differential worth of social functions."[23] Social stratification was equated with the unequal evaluation of occupations and achievements according to a hierarchical scale held to be implicit in the value-system of the society. Conflict between unequal groups was clearly excluded from such a conception, or seen as at most a secondary matter, as in Durkheim's anomic and forced divisions of labor that he characterized as "abnormal." Inequality was viewed as the basic source of group conflict not only by Marxists but by other theorists of conflict as well; the "consensual" interpretation of social hierarchy therefore starkly pointed up the implicit conservativism of normative functionalism, however appropriate its basic assumption of consensus on values might have been to the "simpler" nonstratified societies studied by the cultural anthropologists who were the original founders of functionalism. Functionalists were led to contend that the lower classes or strata in class-divided societies accepted their subordinate position as justified by a value-system they shared with their superiors, rather than at least passively resisting or at most fatalistically resigning themselves to a more or less permanent location at the bottom of the social hierarchy or the class structure.[24] The assumption of universal normative consensus thus became the major target of the critics, although not all versions of functionalism were necessarily committed to it.[25] The conflict/consensus debate, however, as the very identification of consensus as the opposite of conflict indicates, habitually equated functionalism in general with normative functionalism. The debate has been popularized in these terms in numerous introductory textbooks and remains a standard topic to the present day, but functionalism in the large raises additional issues.

Marx is usually seen as the quintessential theorist of social conflict. Certainly, class conflict stands at the very center of his conception of class-divided societies and is identified as the motor of the historical process in which different types of societies succeed one another. The socialist revolution, however, will constitute the last of such successions, for it will usher in a new communist society that will be classless and therefore conflict-free. Conflict, in short, occurs only in the period that Marx called prehistory; when history proper begins with the overthrow of bourgeois society, universal consensus will be achieved. Communist society will transcend both the egoism/altruism and the conflict/consensus oppositions since it will abolish the conditions of scarcity and class conflict in which they are rooted.

It would not be accurate, however, to classify Marx as a conflict theorist with respect to "all hitherto existing societies" and a consensus theorist with respect to society "after the revolution." For the communist society of the future is not sustained by the kind of normative socialization shaping and disciplining individuals to conform to its requirements envisaged by Durkheim and Parsons. It represents rather the full expression of man's "species-being," effacing any conflict either within or between individuals or groups. Marx's communism at the end of history (or prehistory) is a true utopia eliminating any possible tension between desire and obligation, what human beings are motivated to do and what they need to do in order to sustain a viable social order. Nor would it be right to suggest that Marx held an oversocialized view of human nature, or even of an as yet unrealized potential in human nature. For he had, as Gary Thom maintains, "no integrated, coherent view of man" apart from "a number of adjectives in search of a noun."[26] The adjectives were all positive ones: "creative," "dynamic," "productive," and the like, but none of them refers specifically to social behavior. "For Marx species man was something of a substitute for a vision of man with explicit normative dimensions."[27] Just as Marx is thought to be the prime sociologist of conflict but actually is not a conflict theorist at all if one takes into account his "immanent utopianism,"[28] he is ultimately less committed to belief in the "social nature" of man than to "the liberal fantasy that there must be some institutional arrangements that will allow each and everyone to have his way."[29]

Insofar as normative functionalists treat individuals as completely molded to conform to and exemplify existing norms. values, and institutions, they too project a utopian vision of the abolition of any possible conflict between individual wants and social demands, as Dahrendorf perceived in his original influential criticism of Parsons.[30] However, the individual becomes in this version entirely the product of society, whereas to Marx society is nothing but a free expression of man's generic human nature or species-being,[31] the "end of alienation" having abolished the need for any apparatus of social control whatever and therefore for any process of socialization. The consensus prevailing in the commumist utopia that Marx notoriously failed to describe in any detail is essentially a byproduct of the flowering of a human nature suppressed under conditions of scarcity and economic exploitation rather than the secure institutionalization of a normative order. Because the new society will be free of classes, the state, the division of labor, and the market, it will be able to dispense with "ideology," the agency that produces at least temporary and limited consensus in class society by obscuring through false representation the true nature of things. Such misrepresentation will no longer be necessary under communism, since social relations will become "transparent" rather than opaque.[32] Marx cannot therefore be properly classified as either a conflict theorist *tout simple* or a consensus theorist, even though he often engaged in functionalist reasoning in analyzing capitalist society and anticipated the absence of any conflict in the communist society of the future.

NORMATIVE, SYSTEMIC, AND MARXIAN FUNCTIONALISM

If normative functionalism exaggerates both the extent and the depth of integration based on value-consensus in large-scale heterogeneous societies, it is nevertheless not obviously vulnerable to what has been a major charge against functionalism in general: the imputation of a hidden teleology to a reified conception of societies as relatively closed social systems. The normative functionalists tended to conceive of societies as groups, as "imagined communities" vastly larger than families or small face-to-face "micro-social" or "primary" groups,[33] but as solidary groups nonetheless. No logical or conceptual error of reification or illegitimate teleology is necessarily involved in attributing collective needs or goals to unitary groups even if normative functionalists greatly overstated empirically the solidarity of large-scale differentiated societies presumptively based on the commitment of their members to shared values and collective goals. The argument of illegitimate teleology is directed less against the conception of societies as groups writ large united by common values and goals while minimizing internal conflicts than against the conception of societies as holistic systems sustained by the operation of a teleology not of the actual ends pursued by individual actors but of the unintended consequences of their actions.[34] These are regarded as smoothly interlocking in such a way as to maintain the society as a system. It is contended, in effect, that societies successfully achieve integration and self-maintenance by processes operating independently of the consciousness of their members. Society has its reasons, as it were, that are distinct from the reasons of its individual members.[35]

In an exceedingly influential article originally published in 1964 and reprinted in his recent book, David Lockwood may have been one of the first writers to *name* normative functionalism as "a special version of functionalism" to be distinguished from what he called "general" functionalism, which he identified with Merton rather than with Parsons.[36] The qualifying adjective suggests the existence of a nonnormative functionalism, both varieties sharing common traits that justify subsuming them under the general label. Following Lockwood's own distinction between "social" and "system" integration, the nonnormative kind might usefully be called "systemic" functionalism, since the notion that societies are systems does not necessarily assume that their systemic character is the primary result of their members' common beliefs and values.

If normative functionalism is not inherently vulnerable to the charge of postulating a hidden teleology, versions of functionalism that do not consider value consensus to be the foundation of the integration of society are not guilty of assuming an oversocialized conception of man. They continue, however, to presuppose the overintegrated view of society that is common to all versions of functionalism. For normative functionalism, value-consensus serves at least implicitly as a single dominant factor producing the integration of a society, playing much the same role that the economy, or the forces and relations of production, play in classical Marxism, as a number of critics have pointed out.[37] Normative functionalism therefore lends itself to being seen as an "idealistic" one-factor theory opposed to though paralleling in form the one-factor "materialistic" theory of Marxism. Systemic functionalism, however, is more consonant with the pluralistic or multidimensional view of social causation that has often been seen as a major feature of functionalism *per se*, differentiating it from the various single-factor theories that loomed so large in nineteenth-century social theory. This was certainly a source of its original appeal. Systemic functionalism, moreover, can incorporate a degree of social conflict into its general conception of the functional integration of society as the application of the label "conflict functionalism," not intended as an oxymoron, to Coser's theory indicates.[38] It is not therefore vulnerable to the attacks by conflict theorists on the consensual assumptions of normative functionalism.

"The intellectual fundament of functional theory in sociology," Alvin Gouldner maintained, "is the concept of a 'system.'" "Organisms," he went on, "are *examples* of systems. . .the organism was a paradigmatic case of a system."[39] The organicist model or metaphor of society is, of course, an ancient one long antedating functionalism. It is present in the Vedic texts justifying the Hindu caste system, in Plato's *Republic*, and in the Medieval theory of the Great Chain of Being embracing both nature and human society. Its conservative pedigree is unquestionable, as critics of functionalism have been quick to point out. Yet the immense prestige of post-Darwinian biology rather than any commitment to political conservatism in itself accounts considerably for the influence of organic analogies on nineteenth- and early twentieth-century social theory. In the 1920s, 1930s, and 1940s, the dictum that "the whole is greater than the sum of its parts" was widely proclaimed in support of developments in a number of different fields: anti-mechanistic views of the organism in biological theory, *Gestalt* psychology in the study of perception, organismic conceptions of personality in the theories of many psychologists and psychiatrists, Kurt Goldstein's work on the structure of the brain, the concept of "totality" in the dissident neo-Hegelian Marxism of Georg Lukács,[40] and various uses of the notions of "structure" or "system" with reference to cultural materials patterned on structural linguistics.[41] The first prime minister of the Union of South Africa, General Jan Christian Smuts, was also the author of a philosophy he called "holism"; Alfred North Whitehead's "philosophy of organism" was widely cited, influencing, among others, sociologists as different as Talcott Parsons and Erving Goffman.[42] Functionalism, as an image of society that emphasized its similarity to an organism in the self-regulated interdependence of its parts contributing to the survival of the whole, was entirely consistent with this prevailing intellectual *Zeitgeist* affirming holism.

In any case, from Herbert Spencer through Durkheim and the anthropological functionalists to Parsons, the influence of biology as a model for society has been manifest. Even though I have argued that the normative functionalists essentially conceived of societies as if they were unitary social groups writ large, they too have often drawn on biological imagery to describe social processes: the very terms structure and function are derived from the difference between the anatomy and the physiology of an organism. Durkheim was influenced by the work of the French physiologist Claude Bernard and his theorizing is replete with biological metaphors and analogies. The physiologist L. J. Henderson was a well-known early influence on Parsons at Harvard and the work of another Harvard biologist, Walter B. Cannon's *The Wisdom of the Body*,[43] was much admired and cited by both Parsons and Merton. The very title of Cannon's book highlights the issue of hidden teleology: Cannon obviously was consciously using a metaphor in imputing "wisdom" to the body's self-regulating processes. But to suggest that society exhibits an analogous wisdom not only lends itself to conservative Burkean or antistatist argument, but raises the issue of the relation between actors who are capable of real, nonmetaphorical "wisdom" and the social structures and processes their actions are alleged "unintentionally" to produce.[44]

Another model for systemic functionalism of only slightly less importance than the organism was the market. Adam Smith's famous "invisible hand" is a paradigm of the aggregation of the unintended social consequences of narrowly self-interested actions to produce a result beneficial to all in the form of an equilibrium between production and consumption or supply and demand. Smith's emphasis on the self-interest of the actors clearly differentiates the market model from the easily caricatured image of society as a solidary group of oversocialized altruists projected by the normative functionalists. Indeed, Durkheim's "noncontractual element in contract," pointing to the presence of a normative order or *conscience collective* as the precondition for the functioning of market exchanges, was developed in the polemic against Herbert Spencer that was the major theme of Durkheim's first book, *The Division of Labor in Society*. Over fifty years later, Parsons too advanced his conception of a normative order in opposition to the utilitarian individualism of the economists; his own academic background, however, had been in economics and the neoclassicists' concept of equiliibrium certainly influenced his later attraction to sociological functionalism and systems theory, foreshadowed in *The Structure of Social Action* by his discussion of Alfred Marshall and his selection of Vilfredo Pareto, a major economic theorist turned social theorist, as one of his three central figures. Both Durkheim and Parsons drew on nonnormative models of systems, including organisms and markets, for their conceptions of societies as unitary, *sui generis* entities.

It has been argued, most fully by Jürgen Habermas,[45] that Parsons moved in his later work from the priority given to culture in the form of the normative order in *The Social System* and other writings of the same period to his later elaboration, first advanced in *Economy and Society* (coauthored with Neil Smelser), of a biocybernetic model of society as a set of subsystems and media permitting interchanges between them. This approach was later more fully developed by Parsons's student Niklas Luhmann, who cannot plausibly be described as a normative functionalist. But there has never been an absolute dividing line between normative and systemic versions of functionalism; if less inclined to emphasize "invisible" processes achieving integration "behind the backs" or "over the heads" of the actors, normative functionalists have nevertheless regarded the social scientist as the expert diagnostician of the presence and crucial importance of solidarity resulting from normative consensus as the defining criterion of a stable society. In one of his later works Parsons declared himself to be a "cultural determinist, rather than a social determinist" and went on to add, "I believe that within the social system, the normative elements are more important for social change than the 'material interests' of constitutive units."[46] One can read this statement as an insistence on the preeminence "in the last instance" of the normative after Parsons's detour through the theory of subsystems, media, and interchanges, an insistence that is comparable to that of Marxists when after having introduced many qualifications they affirm once again the ultimate priority of the economy. Parsons's treatment of normative order in *The Structure of Social Action* predates his espousal of functionalism, first learned from his students Robert Merton and Kingsley Davis.[47] If Parsons is the very prototype of a normative functionalist and *The Social System* what Lockwood calls the "key work" of that persuasion, neither Merton nor Davis can properly be described as normative functionalists at all. One might even argue that both of them advanced versions of functionalism that ended up undermining it, Merton by stating that social practices might be functional for groups with possibly conflicting interests rather than for the society as a whole,[48] Davis by arguing that functionalism was no more than the attempt to establish causal interdependencies between different institutional activities, which was the presumptive aim of sociological analysis as such.[49]

The distinction between the two kinds of functionalism is a matter of degree. Both assume that societies, including far-flung agrarian empires and large-scale socially heterogeneous modern societies, are unitary entities or systems. If, as Gouldner contended, "system" is the basic concept of functionalism and "organism" a subspecies of it, the notion of system clearly requires further examination. It is, like its near-synonym "structure," what Alfred Korzybski once called a "multiordinal" term used with reference to quite different contents in many sciences and intellectual disciplines.[50] Not only have functionalists, both normative and systemic, conceived of societies as systems, but so have Marxists and some if by no means all conflict theorists. To the functionalists they are self-maintaining systems; to Marxists, neo-Marxists, and selected non-Marxist conflict theorists, they are "contradictory" systems that inevitably generate over time conflict between major social groups, that is, groups that cut across the entire society, that are society-wide or "societal," to use one of the few neologisms coined by sociologists that conveys a necessary meaning even if it should not be taken to imply, as it often is, the existence of a single homeostatic "bounded totality" underlying or distinct from a nation-state.[51] Marx may have been "the master sociologist of disorder" and Durkheim "the master sociologist of order,"[52] but both of them thought of societies as systems, as wholes containing interrelated parts subject to system-level determinants. For Marx, the capitalist system was self-destroying or self-transforming, driven by its inherent "contradictions"; for both normative and systemic functionalists, societies are self-reproducing systems governed by processes that are equilibrating, "boundary-maintaining," or homeostatic.

Independently of the old conflict/consensus debate, Marxists—including Marx himself—have increasingly been seen as engaging in functionalist reasoning with respect to both the stabilizing and the destabilizing of capitalism as a system. Marxism is vulnerable therefore to the same criticisms of implicit teleology as systemic functionalists. Marxism also assumes that the "mode of production," or, more abstractly, History, has "its" reasons that operate independently of the reasons of concrete actors who are usually mired in "false consciousness."[53] One can even find among the varieties of Marxism differences mirroring those between normative and systemic functionalism: the Gramscian concept of hegemony, so popular among sociological Marxists since the 1960s, corresponds to and echoes the Durkheimian-Parsonsian emphasis on normative consensus.[54] There are clear parallels between Parsons's normative solution to the problem of order and the power attributed to "ideology" by latter-day "Western" Marxists seeking to account for the nonoccurrence of proletarian revolution in the advanced capitalist nations.[55] Parsons maintained that social order exists and the potentiality of a Hobbesian war of all against all is averted by a consensus on norms and values proscribing general resort to force and fraud. Western Marxists contend that class conflict leading to revolution and the victory of the subordinate class has been prevented by the proletariat's acceptance of an ideology upholding the existing capitalist system, based though it is on the class domination of the bourgeoisie. Parsons conflated the hobbesian/freudian problem of socializing an unruly human nature and the marxian problem of controlling group conflict; latter-day Western Marxists who ascribe importance to a "hegemonic ideology" are concerned primarily with explaining the apparent dampening down of the revolutionary class conflict that Marx thought would doom capitalism. Those Marxists who have drawn on Freud to explain the absence of proletarian revolution have tended to present an oversocialized conception of human nature under capitalism, though declining, as in the case of the Frankfurt School theorists, to equate it with human nature as such.

Marx, as we have seen, thought that all conflict would be eliminated in the communist society of the future in which man's species-being would find full expression and later Marxist social theorists have not disavowed this utopian prospect.[56] Their emphasis on the power of norms and values to sustain capitalism justifies John H. Goldthorpe's characterization of their point of view as "Parsons through the looking glass."[57] Marx himself argued on systemic economic rather than normative sociological grounds that the free market of the classical economists is contradictory in its operation and eventually subject to crisis and collapse. Late twentieth-century Western Marxists, aware of the failure of Marx's predictions about the future of capitalism and of the antiquated nature of his economic categories, have stressed some version of "legitimation crisis" rather than economic contradictions as the Achilles' heel of capitalism. Consequently, they often end up sounding like normative functionalists diagnosing tendencies to anomie. The shift from systemic economic to normative ideological crisis enables them to maintain their unyielding conviction that the contradictions of capitalism will inevitably produce social conflict that will ultimately spell the end of capitalism.

The implication of a hidden harmony of interlocking unintended consequences that sustains the systemic character of society appears to impute a mystifying aura to the very notion of unintended consequences. But unintended consequences are an altogether familiar and even commonplace happening at the level of personal life. Much of the stuff of individual biography consists of choices and actions, often taken casually under highly particular circumstances, that turn out to have unintended and unforeseen consequences of a far-reaching nature. That is what Milan Kundera meant by "the unbearable lightness of being" in his brilliant and profound novel of that title. One's life is changed by the happenstance of having met a certain person, stumbled on an opportunity for a particular job, gone in one direction rather than another on a journey. Kundera applies an old German saying *Einmal ist Keinmal*—"What happens but once might as well not have happened at all"—to choices and actions taken under circumstances that will never recur. What is true of an individual life, he observes, is also true of history:

> If the French Revolution were to recur eternally, French historians would be less proud of Robespierre. . .There is an infinite difference between a Robespierre who occurs only once in history and a Robespierre who eternally returns, chopping off French heads...*Einmal ist Keinmal. . .* History is as light as individual human life, unbearably light, light as a feather, as dust swirling into the air, as whatever will no longer exist tomorrow.[58]

Systemic functionalism is concerned only with the unintended and unforeseen[59] consequences of collective rather than individual actions that are *recurrent* unlike the events of once in a lifetime or the narrative sequences of history. One is led to wonder for just how long recurrent collective actions might be expected to continue to have unanticipated consequences. Surely, their consequences will be perceived and publicized eventually by at least some of the actors. In modern societies experts are required to understand the full consequences of the inevitably short-sighted and routinized mass responses of millions of people, but the findings of the experts, that is, of social scientists, do not remain indefinitely sealed off from the public whose actions they record: especially under conditions of political democracy, they enter into public and political discourse and become issues of common understanding or misunderstanding, sometimes even becoming incorporated into "common sense."[60] There are collective actions that create situations that react back upon the actors in such a way as to cause them to repeat the initial action thus setting the whole process in motion once again. This is the phenomenon of causal "feedback loops" whose existence is conceded even by critics of functionalism and functionalist reasoning.[61] Yet the very recurrence of such loops or cycles makes it likely that they will be recognized sooner or later by social scientists, if not immediately by the actors themselves, and thus cease to be *unforeseen* consequences producing "hidden" functional or dysfunctional effects. Self-conscious awareness of such causal loops removes them from the category of "blind" homeostatic processes even if unintended but foreseen effects are accepted as unavoidable costs of, or trade-offs for, the intended and desired effects.[62] The most obvious examples are to be found in market behavior, in the interaction of wages, costs, savings, and prices, achieving or failing to achieve an "equilibrium" between supply and demand. Economists may be perceived as guardians of an esoteric body of knowledge capable of foreseeing and even through deliberate policy controlling to a limited degree the mass actions of millions of producers, wage earners, and consumers. But increasingly, as the politics of democracies revolve around success in manipulating the economy, even the arcana of professional economists become matters of public debate.[63] The unintended consequences so heavily stressed by the systemic functionalist are a highly relative matter likely to remain unintended, or at least unforeseen, for a relatively short time in light of the reflexive consciousness about social processes that prevails in modern societies, including the social sciences as a major manifestation.

A fundamental reason why Max Weber has not figured as prominently as Durkheim and Marx in discussions of the problem of order—in the present book, for example—is because he was primarily neither a consensualist nor a conflict theorist, nor did he see societies as systems driven by a "logic" of their own. As Collins and Makowsky write:

> Weber did not find it necessary to ask the general question of what holds society together. He saw that societies over the sweep of history were always coming together and falling apart, shifting and changing from one set of institutions to another. History shows nothing permanent but continual war, conflict and change: states conquering and disintegrating, trade and finance spreading and shrinking, religion and arts slowly shifting from one theme to its opposite. What does remain beneath the change, the concrete basis of human society, are groups of people bound by ties of common feeling and belief: families, households, kinsmen, church and cult members, friends, communities. The core of Weber's theory of stratification is thus a theory of group formation, a set of hypotheses about the conditions that bring men together into solidary groups. These conditions are found in the way men relate to the institutional orders that link groups together into a society.[64]

In an earlier publication, Collins declared that Weber provides "an alternative to all social-system models, be they functionalist, Marxist, or a combination of the two."[65] In the same vein Lockwood observes of Weber, with specific reference to social theory and the problem of order:

> Weber, unlike Durkheim, offered no general theory of society that could found a distinctive school of thought. Thus normative functionalism, in basing itself on Durkheim's theory of society. . .is oriented to the problem of order, whose conceptual limits are set by the ideas of solidarity and anomie. This is a problematic into which Weber's sociology does not easily fit. . .As such his theories have no ready-made applicability to the problem of order (which is not the same thing as saying that they do not have the most important potential relevance.)[66]

Weber saw both conflict and consensus everywhere, but he did not privilege one over the other since they clearly entailed each other. Nor did he see either as products of an overarching system subject to its own imperatives causing either stability "within the system" or conflict leading to change "of the system."

If "system" is understood in a general sense as any set of interdependent units exhibiting recurrent patterns of interaction, then all social analysis presupposes its existence. It becomes no more than a synonym for "order" as observed regularity which was discussed in Chapter 3 above.[67] Since all efforts to find and explain regularities in social life involve a search for system or order so broadly defined, not only Weber but all social scientists are necessarily committed to a belief in societies as systems understood in this comprehensive sense.[68] But when it is asserted that Weber—or anyone else—is not a "systems theorist," a more restricted sense of system is clearly intended. Systems are seen as tightly bounded wholes or totalities that are in some sense "greater than the sum of their parts" and whose needs or necessary conditions of existence regulate the behavior of their parts. Social systems are seen as entities that may react to internal and external stresses in ways that transcend the consciousness of the individuals who compose them. To deny that societies are systems of this kind is not to deny that people act in regular, highly predictable ways most of the time, or that they are often unaware of the wider social consequences of their intentional acts. Their actions form sets of interaction chains that are not infinitely extended but that overlap and lack clear-cut boundaries. Individuals, groups, and patterns of interaction may vary a good deal over time within what may be conceptually delimited as separate systems, although the boundaries of such systems vis-a-vis one another are shifting and porous, obliterating hard and fast distinctions between what is "internal" or "external" to a given social system. If a systems theorist is one who identifies inbuilt "system-level" or holistic tendencies transcending and tightly constraining the multiple interactions of persons and groups so that they either perpetuate the structure and boundaries of the system or inescapably undermine and alter them in a determinate direction, then Weber was not a systems theorist nor are most nonfunctionalist and non-Marxist sociologists. As Lockwood observes of Weber, "his methodological individualism precluded thinking about societies as systems."[69] Weber considered the "parts" making up a society as at most only loosely and indeterminately connected; they constitute "detachable structural bits" forming a "mosaic" rather than a coherent integrated system that can be described as an organic whole.[70]

A mosaic or a collage of unrelated objects consists of disparate objects or pieces that are brought together into a single ordered whole by the unifying vision of the fabricator or artist, as in the Braque painting on the cover of this book. Societies are perhaps more like this than like the biological organisms that have so often been employed as a model for social systems, especially by all breeds of functionalists. But the artist is entirely external to the fragments he brings together in his creation. I do not mean to claim that societies as large-scale units within which social order prevails are simply the mental constructions of social theorists who, perhaps, succeed in convincing princes and peoples of their reality. W. J. H. Sprott once suggested that the first sociologist was the first administrator, possibly a tribal chieftain, who tried to see a mass of overlapping social relationships as a coherent system that might be subject to a set of decisions or policies designed to influence it.[71] This suggests political organization and an unambiguous political center—Machiavelli's Prince shaping and manipulating the body politic like a Renaissance artist moulding base materials into objects of enduring beauty.[72] The prince, unlike the artist, is not outside the frame—in the Goffmanian sense—of the materials with which he works. And indeed the idea of separate societies forming integrated and bounded social systems has often seemed to take for granted a correspondence between such systems and political units, specificially nation-states in the modern world.[73] The dubiousness of such an assumption has recently come under increasing fire with the growing awareness among historians and social scientists of the novelty of the nation-state as a peculiarly modern political form, the result of a complex process of state-building. Its fragility and the difficulties and strains to which it has been subject when extended to parts of the world outside of the West where it originated have also become altogether visible, not to speak of current divisions within Western nations themselves.

There is a certain irony in the fact that sociology as a distinctive perspective on the world first arose in the nineteenth century when "society" in the generic sense was recognized as having an existence independent of and antecedent to the state and formal political-legal institutions. Sociologists proceeded then to individualize the notion of society and to conceive of single societies as holistic or systemic entities, even as quasi-organisms, subject to internal regulative principles of their own. It now appears that they were illegitimately reifying complexes of groups and institutions that were held together and given a certain visibility, coherence, and boundedness mainly by the state as a centralizing force. This is increasingly evident at the present time with the break-up of the Soviet Union, Yugoslavia, and Czechoslovakia where it was obviously only the existence of a centralized state that made it credible to regard these now divided nations as in any sense constituting unitary individual societies subject to autonomous processes of self-regulation.

Like the authors previously quoted, Michael Mann has also observed that "of major theorists only Weber showed a wariness of the *systemic* or *unitary* conception of society" (Mann's emphasis), although he notes that "neo-Weberians" have not always shared Weber's caution on this score. Mann asserts in perhaps too apodictic a fashion that "human beings are social, but not societal," declaring that human beings have "no need to create a society, a bounded and patterned social totality" and that "'society' adds nothing to words like social group or social aggregate or association."[74] Humans, he contends, have "restless drives" that generate a need "to enter into social power relations," thereby creating "organized power networks."[75] One may doubt, however, that human beings have a need for organized power networks any more than for societies as complex totalities. They *do* have a need for social interaction, including cooperation with others to achieve common goals, and this necessarily results in power relations which are inherent in even the most limited dyadic social interactions.[76] But universally human needs do not include any presumptive need for association or identification with large social aggregates.

Mann's major subject in his ambitious and still incomplete projected multivolume work is power relations on a macro scale in the history of civilization, that is, large-scale hierarchical institutional networks based on the unequal distribution and control of ideological, economic, military, and political resources.[77] While Mann is right to reject all forms of society-level systems theory, his organized power networks are essentially a byproduct of primary human needs for whose satisfaction they constitute an "institutional" or "organizational means" in Mann's own characterization of them. The macro scale of his emphasis on power networks should be noted in order to separate it from the fashionable Foucaultian insistence on the ubiquity of a "microphysics" of power with the overtones of repression that inescapably cling to it despite Foucault's later denial of the purely negative character of power.[78] Mann is right that human beings do not "need" large, heterogeneous collectivities, nor do they spontaneously identify with them. Rarely if ever do they create such collectivities *intentionally* as conscious collective projects—except perhaps for proselytizing religions and would-be empire-builders—despite the fact that their actions and interactions bring into being as unintended consequences far-flung time and space networks of interdependent persons and groups that today encompass the entire globe. "Globalization" as a continuing process has clearly not been the goal or result of any calculated design, but this is also true of lesser territorial associations conventionally identified as separate individual societies. Far from being in some sense "primordial," nationalism as an ideology affirming identification with nation-states may be, as Ernest Gellner has argued,[79] a creation of the state rather than a precondition for its existence.

SOCIAL AND SYSTEM INTEGRATION

David Lockwood introduced the distinction between social and system integration in connection with the debate over functionalism of several decades ago. The distinction, however, has since been picked up and elaborated by a number of influential theorists, most notably by Anthony Giddens and Jürgen Habermas, independently of the functionalism debate that has long been moribund.[80] Clearly, one need not treat societies as tightly bounded unitary systems governed by autonomous self-regulating principles to recognize that human beings manage much of the time to routinize their activities, to integrate them in some fashion so that they do not obstruct one another, and to develop fairly stable cooperative relations with their fellows.

As we have seen, people develop firm expectations about one another's behavior that tend to be self-fulfilling, thus endowing their interactions with a recurrent and predictable character. The resulting regularities presuppose, as I argued in earlier chapters, a desire for reliable, more or less conflict-free interaction, whether the desire stems from a need for the approval of others—at least for the avoidance of their disapproval—or from a more general human need for order or "ontological security."[81] Groups, institutions, and societies are nothing but concentrations of recurrent interactions among individuals. They can be identified as clusters in more-or-less continuous fields or chains of interaction, some of them sharply demarcated, others less clearly set apart, but all of them creating densities of interactions distinguishable within their larger context.

Social integration refers to the normative solution to the problem of order in both its hobbesian and marxian versions. It connotes the relatively secure achievement of "consensus, solidarity or cohesion"[82] among interacting individuals. System integration essentially involves utilitarian and/or coercive relations of interdependence among individuals, groups, and social aggregates, although this attitudinal or motivational aspect of it has been less clearly spelled out by those who have made use of the distinction than the identification of social integration with normative consensus.[83] System integration therefore refers to the coercive and economic exchange solutions to the problem of order first advanced by Hobbes and Locke, respectively. In Lockwood's original statement he held that "the focus" of social integration is on "relations between *actors*" and of system integration on "relations between *parts*" of a social system.[84] Lockwood identified system integration with the economy or the "material base" of society, adopting a position closer to Marxism than he came to hold in later writings. The notion of "parts" is vague, even ambiguous, and could be taken to presuppose that societies are holistic systems in which system-level determinants transcend the motives and intentions of individual actors, an idea that, as we have seen, no longer seems defensible.

Giddens initially interpreted the distinction to mean that "in social integration, the 'parts' are purposive actors. In system integration, the 'parts' are collectivities."[85] This virtually equates the distinction with the integration of individuals into society through socialization on the one hand and the elimination or regulation of conflict among groups on the other: social integration solves the hobbesian problem of order and system integration the marxian problem. In a later work, however, Giddens explicitly rejects his previous interpretation of the distinction. He replaces it with the contention that "social integration means systemness on the level of face-to-face interaction. System interaction refers to connections with those who are physically absent in time or space."[86] He observes that the two kinds of integration are fused in "tribal societies" in which the "village community" is the primary locale of all social life.[87] One recalls a much earlier and less abstract contrast drawn by the anthropologist Robert Redfield between the "moral order" and the "technical order" in premodern societies; Redfield argued that the two orders become increasingly dissociated in the course of the transition from precivilized "folk" communities to societies in which even rural villages are deeply influenced by the presence of urban centers.[88] At this point the old pathos-laden opposition between *Gemeinschaft* and *Gesellschaft* is evoked by the distinction. It is at least echoed in Habermas's elaborate theory of the encroachment in the modern world of instrumentally rational "systems" upon the "lifeworld" where normative consensus is forged through communicative interaction,[89] although Habermas essentially affirms modernity and explicitly rejects nostalgia for the past.[90]

Both Giddens and Habermas link social integration to face-to-face interaction in primary groups or social relations at the level of "everyday life." If face-to-face is qualified to take into account direct communication at a distance by electronic means, *all* social causation is mediated through face-to-face interaction, including the forces making for system integration in which a dominant role is played by chains or networks of interaction that both transcend and connect delimited spatial and temporal face-to-face encounters. This is the valid meaning of Randall Collins's insistence on the "microfoundations of macrosociology."[91] Giddens argues that "time-space distanciation," which he sees as a crucial variable attribute of social life, characterizes *both* micro- and macro-social structures.[92] He insists that the distinction between social and system integration is *not* equivalent to the micro/macro dichotomy currently so fashionable among sociological theorists. Yet both Giddens and Habermas lay such stress on face-to-face interaction in social integration that they *seem* to confine it to the micro-sociology of everyday life or the lifeworld. But Benedict Anderson's "imagined communities," which he identifies with nations that may include tens or even hundreds of millions of people, and Edward Lehman's "macro-solidary groups," a phrase that defines itself, are also, surely, major foci of social integration in modern societies.

Social integration needs to be conceived of more comprehensively, without giving definitional priority either to individuals over groups as the units to be integrated or face-to-face interaction over interaction subject to greater time-space distanciation. It includes both the integration of individuals into society at the level of the hobbesian/freudian problem and the achievement of relatively conflict-free coexistence by the many subunits into which complex modern societies are divided.[93] Social integration refers to the formation of social identities by individuals which encourage acceptance of others and the legitimacy of their needs and demands, if not a positive solidarity with them, that supports social order; it implies the allegiances of individuals to other persons, primary groups, and special-purpose associations, as well as to such larger and more remote social aggregates as churches, social classes, social movements, ethnic groups, and nations, which may be represented primarily by symbols to which strong sentiments become attached.

Insofar as nation-states have been the largest collectivities with

which individuals have forged strong identifications, it is not surprising that nationalism has played such a crucial role in social
integration at the level of the nation-state while at the same time
it has often promoted deadly conflicts between nations. It has
long been recognized that in the modern age nationalism has provided much the most successful and enduring alternative to traditional religion as a deeply rooted commitment represented by
symbols that have become objects of reverence and ritual celebration.[94] The sacralization of the nation has not been unrelated to
the fact that nations are not primary groups. As Peter Laslett has
remarked of nationalism:

> It would seem that the features of human psychology which make
> possible collaboration between individuals who are not in compa-
> ny with each other are the same as those which give rise to reli-
> gious activity. There is the same sense of community with others
> unseen and unknown, the same identification with a supreme
> source of authority and security, the same play upon symbols.[95]

Durkheim went so far as to identify God with society in claiming that the object of religious worship was actually a "camou-
flaged image" of society, in Ernest Gellner's words.[96] Several of
the best contemporary illustrations of the Durkheimian theme of
affirming and strengthening social solidarity through collective
ceremonies ritualizing "sacred" sentiments have been interpretive
accounts of patriotic celebrations.[97] Yet, curiously, neither normative functionalists nor their critics[98] have paid much attention to
nationalism, which has at least until recently been relatively
neglected by sociologists. Durkheim's failure to discuss it perhaps
stems from the fact that he was a Dreyfusard and man of the
Left, whereas in late nineteenth-century and early twentieth-century France fervent nationalism was the primary cause and political weapon of the Right, namely, the anti-Dreyfusards, *Action
Française*, and the followers of Maurice Barrès and Charles
Maurras.[99] Nor have Parsons and his followers, for all their stress
on societal consensus on norms and values, had much to say
about nationalism, in which a particular society itself is the main
object of value. Sociologists have tended to consign it as a topic

for study to political scientists and historians in line with their readiness to demarcate "societies" in the singular as their objects of study, conceiving of them as entities that are in some sense more fundamental than mere nation-states. I have referred critically to this practice above; it undoubtedly stems from the nineteenth-century conceptual differentiation between society and the state that provided an initial mandate for the emergence of sociology as a distinct intellectual perspective and its later institutionalization as an academic discipline. Marxists also, both in theory and in practice, have notoriously minimized the importance of nationalism as an allegiance taking precedence over identification with economically based classes.

Social integration at the level of an entire large-scale society need not presuppose the consensus and solidarity, most saliently represented by nationalism, that was so questioned by conflict theorists in the old conflict/consensus debate. It does assume at least the relative reduction and control of divisive group conflicts. The social units with which individuals identify and which become the source of valued social identities, whether they are nations or smaller subunits, exist as realities "in the social consciousness"[100]—in the "hearts and minds of men" (and women) as the cliché has it. The generation of norms out of the interplay of mutual expectations in "free" or spontaneous communicative interaction, as well as the celebration of established norms and values, is the source and continuing locus of social integration in contrast to commands or directives handed down from above or from afar that create system integration through mediated chain interaction.

System integration is not necessarily limited to hierarchical social relations as the previous sentence may seem to imply. The division of labor and exchange relations in the market, classically described by Adam Smith, are also forms of system integration[101] which involve "formally" and sometimes substantively equal relations among individuals and groups. The division of labor, the "invisible hand" of the market, bureaucracy, big-city life, and the interdependencies they create are the essence of system integration. Increasingly, they extend beyond the limits of even the largest social units that become the focus of identity formation.

Unforeseen and apparently threatening impersonal "social forces" typically emerge at the level of system integration, often producing reactions of uncomprehending anger or fatalistic alienation on the part of the ordinary citizens whose life routines they disrupt.

Marx, according to Lockwood, was unique among classical social theorists "in seeking to establish a coherent relationship between social and system integration,"[102] although Lockwood finds his effort to do so far from adequate.[103] The breakdown of system integration in the crisis produced by the final working through of the contradictions of capitalism results in social revolution initiated by the proletariat. System disintegration produces social disintegration leading to the eventual creation of a new system free of the contradictions that had given rise to the class conflicts dooming all previous systems in the course of history. It is worth noting that Marx thought it would take the total collapse of the capitalist market economy, plunging a majority of the population into unemployment and material immiseration, for the proletariat to be moved to revolt. The late "economistic" Marx may well have been more realistic in his grasp of the necessary conditions for successful revolution than latter-day "voluntaristic" Marxists, more attracted to the early Marx, who have wistfully believed that protest against inequality, social injustice, and even mere "alienation" would suffice to bring about revolution in societies that, whatever their deficiencies, were far from breaking down insofar as they continued to satisfy, even if stingily, elementary human needs. But despite his greater realism, Marx failed to provide a credible account of just how what Lockwood calls "the revolutionary end-shift"[104] of the previously acquiescent or at most reformist proletariat would come about and later Marxists have done no better. Marx deduced the inevitability of system breakdown from his theoretical manipulation of the abstract concepts of classical political economy. Joseph Schumpeter praised him for the ingenuity and originality of his economic theory despite its obsolescence and for his stalwart refusal to resort to sociological explanations for either the origin or the predicted collapse of capitalism.[105] Yet the failure to put sufficient political and social flesh on the bare bones of his economic categories taken over from classical economics has always been the major weakness of Marxism as a social theory.

Marx's notion of system breakdown was based on the abstractions of economic theory, but the dependence of modern men and women on time-space distanciated systems staffed by experts and specialists is a thoroughly concrete datum of everyday life. Max Weber recognized some time ago that dependence on such systems is a force working against social disintegration. He wrote in a letter to his friend and student Robert Michels, at that time a radical socialist: "He who wishes to live as modern man, even if this be only in the sense that he has his daily paper, railways, electricity, etc., must resign himself to the loss of ideals of radical revolutionary change: indeed he must abandon the *conceivability* of such a goal."[106] Barrington Moore, Jr., reflecting on the possibility of revolution in advanced urban-industrial societies, came to essentially the same conclusion over half a century later.[107] Dependence on heat and light supplied by electricity, on plumbing linked to water supply systems, on automobiles and the unobstructed roadways they require, on telephonic communications, on regular garbage collection and disposal, to mention only the most obvious examples long antedating the products of recent electronic technology, binds people to myriads of others in far-flung systemic networks. System integration sustains rather than subverts social order by inducing a fear of violent conflict and discouraging support for violent adversaries of the status quo.

Reliance on the very great regularity and predictability of human behavior in modern technologically advanced societies is based on a trust in often unseen experts who understand and operate what Giddens calls the "abstract systems" on which the routines of everyday life are so heavily dependent.[108] Giddens contrasts trust in personal relations with the characteristically modern trust in the impersonal "faceless commitments" of experts who may rarely if ever be encountered in the flesh. He clearly specifies the difference between social integration and the modern form of system integration:

> With the development of abstract systems, trust in impersonal principles, as well as in anonymous others, becomes indispensable

to social existence. Nonpersonalized trust of this sort is discrepant from basic trust. There is a strong psychological need to find others to trust, but institutionally organized personal connections are lacking, relative to pre-modern social situations. . .Routines which were previously part of everyday life or the "lifeworld" become drawn off and incorporated into abstract systems. . .Routines which are structured by abstract systems have an empty, unmoralised character—this much is valid in the idea that the impersonal increasingly swamps the personal.[109]

Highly trained experts are not the sole repositories of such trust: it is also extended to relatively unskilled functionaries and suppliers of goods and services such as busdrivers, shopkeepers, garbage collectors, and policemen. Most of my examples of the extreme predictability of human actions cited in Chapter 3 involved "abstract systems" that constitute a special case or outgrowth of the self-fulfilling nature of mutual expectations in social interaction—even if "discrepant with the basic trust" present in direct personal relations—which was the major theme of that chapter. Social integration depends on a normatively grounded belief and trust in social relations extending even to imagined communities of strangers with whom a social identification is claimed, but system integration involves a more mundane, prosaic, and profane (in Durkheim's sense) trust in the often distant and anonymous representatives of technical and administrative systems.

Giddens identifies with precision the unique qualities of modern life that make "alienation" endemic to it and produce the ubiquitous "quests for community" and "identity" that have loomed so large in contemporary discourse.[110] In his famous essay "Science as a Vocation," Weber saw passive dependence on technical systems as the very essence of the "disenchantment of the world" that characterized modernity. After mentioning the motion of streetcars and the use of money as examples, he went on to conclude:

The increasing intellectualization and rationalization do *not*, therefore, indicate an increased and general knowledge of the conditions under which one lives. . .It means something else, namely, the knowledge or belief that if one but wished one *could* learn it at any time. Hence it means that principally there are no mysterious incalculable forces that come into play but rather that we can, in principle, master all things by calculation. This means that the world is disenchanted.[111]

Alienation and disenchantment have on occasion, most notably in the 1930s, produced fanatical identifications with revolutionary ideological movements of a potentially totalitarian character that have stood for the utopian prospect of a deeper and more satifying social integration. In the 1960s and 1970s, radical intellectuals in a number of countries were attracted to Maoism because of its emphasis on peasants as a potentially revolutionary class uncorrupted by the "softness" of urban life bred by dependence on technical amenities and the "consumerism" fostered by the market.[112] This same dependence was perceived a few years later by "urban guerillas" as increasing the vulnerability of urban populations to terrorist actions.[113] The very efficacy of far-reaching and impersonal system integration may breed alienation, boredom, and a sense of meaninglessness that under particular political circumstances is capable of threatening existing forms of social integration.[114] Yet more commonly, as Weber perceived, system integration at least negatively sustains social integration by arousing fears of its breakdown that set limits to support for insurrectional movements.

The "globalization" of the world economy and the accompanying spread of communications and transportation systems to embrace most of the world represent an unprecedented increase in the dissociation of system from social integration, a process that began long ago with the passage from tribal societies to civilization. Yet the prospect of general identification with humanity at large in what has become, in Marshall McLuhan's phrase, a "global village" seems as remote and utopian as it ever did. Given the persistence both of economic scarcity and the limited capacity of human beings for sympathy with others emphasized by Hobbes and Freud, fears of disorder become more acute in a more interdependent world even though the threat of nuclear holocaust has been removed with the ending of the Cold War. Ecological catastrophe remains a real threat regularly invoked by those seeking to encourage the universal identification of all peoples with each other as fellow residents of "Planet Earth." At the same time, the resurfacing of aggressive ethnic nationalism in an Eastern Europe free of Soviet domination as well as in the former Soviet Union itself and the rise of fundamentalist religious movements in the Islamic world have raised new fears of tension between social integration at the level of the nation-state and system integration at the international level.

VISIONS AND VERSIONS OF DISORDER

In the 1990s Bosnia has come to symbolize the fear of a future of violent conflicts between ethnic groups of fearsome intensity threatening a more economically and technically integrated world. Lebanon played a similar role in the 1980s. The conflicts that have torn apart these nations have been religio-ethnic nationalism in the case of the former Yugoslavia and religious communalism in the case of Lebanon. Both have been seen as dangerous eruptions of ancient "primordial" forces at odds with the conditions of modern life and posing a threat to its stability. The relative neglect by social science scholarship of nationalism as a potent force and general belief in the ongoing secularization of the modern world have contributed to reactions of surprise and dismay to these small-scale but brutal conflicts. Memories of the Nazis and of the origins of both world wars in ethnic conflicts in Eastern Europe account for a widespread mood of dark foreboding about the future of the world in the wake of the Cold War.

Yet as a number of recent scholars have emphasized, the nation-state is as much a product of modernity as capitalism, the world market, bureaucratic social organization, representative government, science and its yield in technological progress. Nationalism has widened the range of mutual identification in modern populations, overcoming local and parochial loyalties and grievances. It is not therefore a "primordial" or "atavistic" force at all and to regard it as such is to give too much credence to those late nineteenth- and early twentieth-century right-wing and crypto-fascist ideologues of *Blut und Boden* and *la terre et les morts* who so defined it in forging it into an antidemocratic weapon against the internationalist Left and the "petty" materialistic contestation of political parties under democracy.[115] The emergence of the nation-state as the dominant political unit of the modern world has coincided with the rise of the city, market economies based on common monetary media of exchange, the mobility of populations both in internal and international migrations and socially within the occupational division of labor, and centralized educational systems universalizing within large national units literacy in a common language as well as other minimal cognitive skills.[116] The idea of the nation itself as an entity embracing peoples of quite different ranks and life circumstances is very much a "constitutive principle of modernity"[117] that has since the fifteenth century undergone a long and varied process of development in the West.

Nationalism has been such a successful ideology in modern history because it has often managed to appeal to the earliest individual memories of childhood—turns of phrase, catches of song, sights and smells—and link them to the idea of the historical continuity of a people, its culture, and land. Biography and history, individual and collective identity are welded together. One recalls sentimental popular poetry in a debased Whitmanesque mode, guilty of what a literary critic once called the "fallacy of enumeration," that rapturously asserts something like "America is apple pie, the roar of the crowd at Yankee Stadium, the blaze of autumn foliage in New England, the sun sinking into the Pacific," and so on.[118] But there is no *necessary* connection between deep and cherished childhood memories and identification with an imagined community of strangers all of whom happen to live within the borders of a particular nation-state. Rilke wrote that "poetry is the past that breaks out in our hearts" and it has been said that literary greatness has its roots in the fullness of the artist's remembrance of things past, especially his or her childhood. But this has little to do with collective as distinct from individual identity, let alone with sentimental patriotism. Both Rilke and Joyce were, it so happens, voluntary exiles.

Nor need nationalist loyalties necessarily assume a specifically ethnic form. Liah Greenfeld distinguishes between ethnic and civic nationalism, the first implying a mythicized spiritual kinship based on language, religion, ritualized memories of a remote historical past, and not infrequently supposed racial ties of "blood," the latter on identification with an actual territory, set of political institutions, and, sometimes, a written constitution.[119] Her distinction is reminiscent of the older and darker one drawn by Hannah Arendt in *The Origins of Totalitarianism* between the inward-looking "tribal nationalism" of the nineteenth-century pan-German and pan-Slav movements, and the "objectified" nationalism of the older European nations based on an actually existing set of political institutions, a clearly bounded territory, and real shared historical memories.[120] Monstrosities such as policies of "ethnic cleansing" are most likely to find support in situations where there has been no separate state with a long history of development uniting all who have actually lived under its authority and contributed to the nation's history.[121]

The horrors of civil war in the former Yugoslavia and the Caucasus, as well as terrorist violence in the Middle East and on the Indian subcontinent fueled by nationalist or religious fundamentalist fanaticisms, should not distract our attention from the surprisingly little violence that attended the liberation of Eastern Europe from Soviet control and the breakup of the Soviet Union itself. One estimate places at slightly over three thousand the loss of life in the former Soviet empire, most of it in Georgia, Tadzhikistan, and in the continuing war between Armenia and Azerbaijan.[122] This is surely a remarkably low figure measured against what might reasonably have been expected, let alone against the enormous casualty list for wars, revolutions, and insurrections in the "blood-dimmed" twentieth century as a whole. Obviously, the totals for Yugoslavia are considerably higher, but even there, as Tom Nairn rightly observes, "if some worst-possible case scenario were to unfold. . .the consequences would not, by the standards of 1948 to 1988, be all that serious. Nobody would have to worry about taking refuge on another planet."[123] The brutal "ethnic cleansing" by the Serbs in Bosnia-Herzegovina has understandably elicited comparisons with Nazi genocide, but Germany was a great power capable of exporting its murderous racial policies through ambitious territorial expansion while Serbia threatens only a small area of the former Yugoslavia.

The collapse of Soviet Communism has resulted in loss of faith in universalist secular ideologies and a retreat into passionate identifications with ethnic and religious group allegiances that had been latent for generations. And, of course, the rebirth of apparently ancient values and group attachments involves newly *invented* "traditions," despite claims of continuity with the past that underlie what is described in positive terms as "primordial" and in negative terms as "atavistic" loyalties, as Susanne Hoeber Rudolph and Lloyd I. Rudolph point out in detail with reference to recent communal violence in India. They proceed to generalize beyond India:

> As political ideology recedes with the collapse of communism, the politics of identity and community, of religion, ethnicity, and gender have begun to occupy the space vacated by political ideology. . .The doctrine of ancient hatreds may become the post-cold war's most robust mystification, a way of having an enemy and knowing evil that deceives as it satisfies. The hatred is modern and may be closer than we think.[124]

The Rudolphs do not fail to note the presence in much milder form of such tendencies in the United States expressed in contemporary controversies over "multiculturalism" and "diversity."[125]

The nation-state remains the largest object of identification and focus of social integration in the modern world at the same time as system integration expands far beyond the boundaries of even the largest nations. If it is unrealistic to expect a global identification to override national identifications by a process similar to the gradual subsumption of local loyalties under national patriotisms in the course of industrialization and modernization, it is scarcely beyond the bounds of possibility—or, indeed, actuality—for different social groups to coexist peacefully within a larger society. Individuals, after all, are entirely capable of maintaining in stable balance multiple role commitments within a variety of different groups and social contexts without suffering paralyzing losses or confusions of identity.[126] The existence of group pluralism often takes the form of the "nesting" of smaller groups within larger ones forming "concentric circles of allegiance."[127] The tensions resulting from the invidious overtones of in-group/out-group distinctions, so often seen as essential to the very constitution of social groups, may even survive in the form of Freud's "narcissism of minor differences."[128] Moreover, it has long been argued that individual membership in different groups produces a pattern of cross-cutting allegiances that reduces the intensity of group conflict.[129]

The breakup of old multi-national empires in the twentieth century, culminating in the possibly still incomplete fragmentation of Russia, raises the prospect of multiple small wars that risk cumulation into larger ones.[130] Yet this is occurring today simultaneously with expanding system integration at a global level. Whatever the ferocious historic rivalries that may once have divided previously stateless ethnic groups and that have now been reactivated by struggles for independence, small nations replacing larger ones are in the end less likely to start wars and cherish expansionist ambitions in a more interdependent world in which their limited size increases their awareness of dependence on others. Greater system integration can thus be seen as limiting group conflict at the international as well as as the intrasocietal level, or at the very least reducing the risk of the actual and feared world wars that have indelibly branded the twentieth century.

The wars, revolutions, and rebellions of the twentieth century in conjunction with the expanding and tightening system integration that has increased the vulnerability to disruption of everyday routines have inspired widespread fears of social disorder. These fears have certainly contributed to recognition of the problem of order as a central if not *the* central issue of social theory. At the same time, apparently contrary fears have been aroused of an excess of order imposed from above by the coercive powers of the state as well as by the expansion of its persuasive powers by means of new technologies of communication. The conception of totalitarianism as a distinctively modern "union of terror and propaganda" (Arendt), the characterization of Stalin as "Genghis Khan with a field telephone," the more recent wide acceptance of

Foucault's concept of all-pervasive "surveillance" as grounds for rejecting the original promise of the Enlightenment—all of these notions point to a fear of a hierarchical imposed order rather than of disorder. George Orwell's *Nineteen Eighty-Four* projects the best-known and most horrific image of such a totalitarian future.

But fears of disorder and of a totalitarian excess of order are not mere opposites, for the threat or reality of the former is both dreaded in its own right and as lending attraction to the latter as a corrective. They are dialectically related, to employ a once fashionable way of putting it, both in reality and in the general awareness of it. The promise to restore and impose order becomes a mobilizing appeal by authoritarian political movements even when they themselves have contributed to the conflicts posing a threat to order. Weimar Germany is the classic case. Both fears appeared well founded in the early history of the present century, but there are signs that they may have begun to lose credibility. Consider such post-Orwellian literary images of the future, meant to be negative if not fully dystopian, as Anthony Burgess's *A Clockwork Orange* and Walker Percy's *Love in the Ruins*, one about an imagined Britain, the other an imagined United States.[131]

Burgess's vision is of a semisocialist Britain in which the streets are taken over after dark by teenage gangs of hoodlums who freely engage in vandalism, theft, rape, and violent assaults for sheer pleasure on innocent citizens whom they encounter in public or whose houses they invade by deceptive means. Burgess paints a thoroughly unpleasant picture, one that is only too suggestive of crime-ridden inner-city neighborhoods in the West today, but the disorder he depicts is temporally and spatially confined and is initiated by the age-group most prone to criminal activity.

Percy depicts an America in which near-civil war prevails in certain regions of the country between blacks and whites, and, overlapping this conflict, leftists and rightists, the religious and the godless, in the course of an unpopular minor foreign war obviously suggested by Vietnam—the novel was published in 1971—waged by a government that still controls most of the country and derives its authority from regular elections. Percy invokes biblical images of social decay—the lion and the lizard languishing in the courtyard, grass growing in the streets—and is profuse in imagining specifically modern equivalents: turtles sunning themselves on the diving boards of abandoned motel pools, electronic belfries sounding in deserted suburban squares, vines sprouting through the roofs of rusting Cadillacs—the breakdown, in short, of modern forms of system integration. But the breakdown is only partial and is overcome by the end of the book without the disappearance of many of the differences that led to civil violence, although black anger has dissolved owing to the *deus ex machina* of the discovery of oil under their lands.

The query "what holds society together?" is metaphorical. Household objects may be held together by the makeshift use of such homely materials as Scotch tape, bent paper clips, pieces of string. One is tempted to answer the question in kind, as it were, by pointing to internal plumbing, electricity, telephone lines, and unobstructed roadways as what holds modern societies together. Perhaps there is more truth than poetry, as they say, in this answer, which asserts the predominance of system integration over social integration in securing social order under modern conditions. George Homans once said "People may value democracy, but do they value it as much as their dinner?"[132] If this seems cynical, it is at least congruent with the present diminution of idealistic expectations in the aftermath of the collapse of Soviet Communism.[133] The vogue of what is called "postmodernism," besides simply providing academics with something apparently new to hold forth on, is another version of what was, perhaps prematurely, identified several decades ago as the "end of ideology."[134] It signals the loss of faith in redemptive secular social and political ideologies; the insistence of postmodernists that science and reason are simply possible perspectives on the world among many others is reminiscent of the arguments in the recent past of religious believers whose faith was challenged by the disenchantment of the world promoted by a scientific worldview. Outraged defenders of both reason and tradition may brand as "nihilism" the refusal to make a "foundational" commitment to anything beyond one's dinner, confidence that the trains will run on time, or trust in one's immediate personal associates, but these may suffice to keep society going.

Societies never fall apart to the extent of literally lapsing into a war of all against all.[135] Nation-states may fragment, dividing into two warring camps as in the classic Marxian vision of revolution, or into several hostile groups controlling different localities even if they are only urban neighborhoods as in Beirut in the 1980s. De-urbanization marked by reversion to agrarian life may also occur as a result of external "barbarian" invasions destroying loosely centralized empires, as in the example of European feudalism after the fall of the Roman Empire.[136] But underneath these processes social order survives at least at a micro-sociological level—the level of families, small groups, and networks of interacting individuals cooperating in the pursuit of common goals. In at least this limited sense, social order is indestructible so long as human beings remain alive.

NOTES

Chapter 1　The Many-Sided Problem of Order

1.　Aristotle, *Politics and Poetics,* Book 1, Chapters 1–6, Cleveland: Fine Editions Press, 1952, pp. 3–11. The references to Aristotle all come from these pages.

2.　Talcott Parsons, *The Structure of Social Action*, New York: McGraw-Hill, 1937, pp. 89–94.

3.　Georg Simmel, "How Is Society Possible?" *American Journal of Sociology,*16 (November 1910), pp. 372–391.

4.　Benedict Anderson, *Imagined Communities: Reflections on the Origin and Spread of Nationalism*, London: Verso, 1983.

5.　Gianfranco Poggi observes with reference to the problem of order "What is ultimately in question is the nature of the units to be ordered" and goes on to note the significant difference between individuals and groups as units, *Images of Society*, Stanford, Calif.: Stanford University Press, 1972, p. 148.

6.　Primo Levi, *The Drowned and The Saved*, London: Abacus, [1986] 1988, p. 108.

7.　Michael Walzer, "The Idea of Civil Society," *Dissent* (Spring 1991), p. 293.

8.　Hobbes did try to argue that the authority of parents over their children was analogous to the authority of the state over its citizens and was similarly a product of at least an implicit covenant. See Hobbes, *De Cive or The Citizen,* New York: Appleton-Century Crofts, [1642] 1949, Chapter 9, pp. 105–113, and *Leviathan*, Harmondsworth, Middlesex, England: Penguin Books, [1651] 1968, pp. 253–257. The difficulty of regarding infants as in any conceivable sense parties to a covenant or contract has always posed major problems to such a view, as Hobbes himself was aware. See the discussion by Gordon J. Schochet, "Intending (Political) Obligation: Hobbes and the Voluntary Basis of Society," in Mary G. Dietz, editor, *Thomas Hobbes and Political Theory*, Lawrence, Kansas: University of Kansas Press, 1990, p. 55. Much of the time, however, Hobbes seems to assume the existence at least of families in the state of nature, depicting it, as Michael Hechter notes, as "that imaginary territory free from any social obligations save perhaps those emanating from the nuclear family." See Hechter, "From Exchange to Structure," in Joan Huber, editor, *Macro-Micro Linkages in Sociology*, Newbury Park, Calif.: Sage Publications, 1991, p. 47.

9. Michael Mann, *The Sources of Social Power*, Volume One, *A History of Power: from the Beginning to A.D. 1756*, Cambridge: Cambridge University Press, 1986, pp. 13–17.

10. Percy S. Cohen provides an admirably clear account of the three solutions, though without associating each of them with one of the three classical social contract theorists, in *Modern Social Theory*, New York: Basic Books, 1968, pp. 21–31. Cohen adds a fourth solution, "inertia," but devotes only half a page to it since it essentially tries to explain the persistence of order rather than the forces that bring it about in the first place (p. 31). See also the useful review and discussion of the three solutions by Robert Dowse and John Hughes, *Political Sociology*, New York: John Wiley and Sons, 1972, Chapter 2, pp. 16–50. The three solutions correspond to the three kinds of resources—coercive, material, and normative—available to power holders to induce the cooperation of others discussed by Amitai Etzioni in *A Comparative Analysis of Complex Organizations*, New York: The Free Press, 1961, pp. 5–6. See also Desmond Ellis, "The Hobbesian Problem of Order," *American Sociological Review*, 36 (August 1971), pp. 692–703.

11. The reference is to the new social contract based on the "general will" meant to remedy the inequality and oppression legitimated by the old and "false" social contract described in the *Second Discourse* on inequality, in *The Social Contract*, Harmondsworth, Middlesex, England: Penguin Books, [1762] 1968.

12. Dennis H. Wrong, "The Oversocialized Conception of Man in Modern Sociology," *American Sociological Review*, 26 (April 1961), pp. 183–193.

13. Gary B. Thom remarked in the early 1980s: "Were modern-day Lebanon to descend to a genuinely Hobbesian state of nature, without social and religious differences and factions, it might well be less dangerous and no more anarchic." *The Human Nature of Social Discontent*, Totowa, N.J.: Rowman and Allanheld, 1983, p. 85.

14. Jeffrey Alexander, *Theoretical Logic in Sociology, Volume One, Positivism, Presuppositions, and Current Controversies*, Berkeley and Los Angeles: University of California Press, 1982, p. 92.

15. Hobbes, *Leviathan*, p.185.
16. Jon Elster, *The Cement of Society: A Study of Social Order*, Cambridge: Cambridge University Press, 1989, pp. 1–2.
17. After noting that "persistence and change" are simultaneously present in all societies, Percy Cohen goes on to observe that this "does not appear to be obvious to those who constantly proclaim that it is in the nature of societies to be riven by conflicts of interest and principle and to be in a constant process of change, while overlooking the fact that it is equally in their nature to be orderly and persistent." *Modern Social Theory*, p. 21.

Chapter 2   The Problem of Order from Hobbes to the Present

1. Thomas Hobbes, *Leviathan*, Harmondsworth, Middlesex, England: Penguin Books, [1651] 1962, p. 223.
2. Ibid., p. 185.
3. Ibid., p. 186.
4. That Hobbes was engaged in "model-building," as it might be called today, is emphasized by one of the most careful recent readings of his political thought. See M. M. Goldsmith, *Hobbes's Science of Politics*, New York: Columbia University Press, 1966, p. 92.
5. Richard S. Peters, *Hobbes*, Harmondsworth, Middlesex, England: Penguin Books, 1956, p. 158.
6. Thomas Hobbes, *De Cive or The Citizen*, New York: Appleton-Century Crofts, [1642] 1949, p. 100.
7. *A Discourse on Inequality*, Harmondsworth, Middlesex, England: Penguin Books, [1755] 1984. This famous long essay is often known as "the second discourse." Its full original title was "Discourse on the Origins and Functions of Inequality among Men."
8. Bertrand de Jouvenel, "Rousseau's Theory of the Forms of Government," in Maurice Cranston and Richard S. Peters, editors, *Hobbes and Rousseau*, Garden City, N.Y.: Doubleday Anchor Books, 1972, p. 484. See also Roger D. Masters, "The Structure of Rousseau's Political Thought," in Cranston and Peters, eds., p. 405; Maurice Cranston, "Introduction" to *A Discourse on Inequality*, p. 36.
9. See the very succinct account of Rousseau's sequence of historical stages reported by the editor, Maurice Cranston, summarizing Jean Starobinski's commentary on the French edition of Rousseau's collected works, "Editor's Notes," p. 182, n. 19, *A Discourse on Inequality*.

10. Claude Lévi-Strauss, however, in acclaiming Rousseau as the "father of anthropology," describes Rousseau's account as "a theoretical model of human society that does not correspond to any observable reality, but with the aid of which we can succeed in distinguishing between what is primordial and what is artificial in man's present nature." He goes on to observe that "Natural man did not precede society, nor is he outside it." *Tristes Tropiques*, New York: Atheneum, 1974, p. 392. He, not surprisingly in view of his structuralist orientation, minimizes the historical-evolutionist overtones of Rousseau's work in emphasizing its value as an effort to disclose what is permanent and unchanging in man's nature.

11. Robert Nisbet, *The Sociological Tradition*, New York: Basic Books, 1966.

12. C. B. Macpherson, *The Political Theory of Possessive Individualism: Hobbes to Locke*, Oxford: Oxford University Press, l962. See also Macpherson's earlier "Hobbes's Bourgeois Man" in K. C. Brown, editor, *Hobbes Studies*, Oxford: Basil Blackwell, 1965, pp. 168–183. (This article was originally published in 1945.)

13. Hobbes, *Leviathan*, pp. 186–187.

14. Keith Thomas, "The Social Origins of Hobbes' Political Thought," in K. C. Brown, editor, *Hobbes Studies*, pp. 185–236. See also Alan Ryan, "Hobbes and Individualism," in G. A. J. Rogers and Alan Ryan, editors, *Perspectives on Thomas Hobbes*, Oxford: The Clarendon Press, 1988, pp. 100–102.

15. William Letwin, "The Economic Foundation of Hobbes's Politics," in Cranston and Peters, eds., *Hobbes and Rousseau*, pp. 143–164.

16. D. D. Raphael, *Hobbes: Morals and Politics*, London: Allen and Unwin, 1977, p. 93.

17. Ryan, "Hobbes and Individualism," pp. 92–93, 98, 102. Ryan writes: "To have been an articulate defender of capitalism, Hobbes would have had to have had a much more calculating, accounting outlook than he actually possessed" (p. 102).

18. Albert O. Hirschmann, *The Passions and the Interests*, Princeton, N.J.: Princeton University Press, 1977.

19. John Plamenatz, "Introduction," to Hobbes, *Leviathan*, London: Collins, Fontana, 1962, pp. 54–55.

20. Hobbes, *Leviathan*, (Penguin Book edition), p. 185.

21. As is cogently stated by Ryan in "Hobbes and Individualism," pp. 92–93, which makes more authoritatively, that is, with greater

knowledge of Hobbes scholarship, this point that I first made in "Hobbes, Darwinism, and the Problem of Order," in Walter A. Powell and Richard Robbins, editors, *Conflict and Consensus: A Festschrift in Honor of Lewis A. Coser*, New York: The Free Press, 1984, pp. 204–217.

22. Lawrence Stone, *The Family, Sex and Marriage in England, 1500–1800*, New York: Harper and Row, 1977, pp. 93, 98.

23. Ibid., p. 99.

24. Alan MacFarlane, *The Origins of English Individualism*, Cambridge: Cambridge University Press, 1977, p. 111.

25. Reo F. Fortune, *The Sorcerers of Dobu*, New York: E. P. Dutton, 1932.

26. Ruth Benedict, *Patterns of Culture*, Boston: Houghton Mifflin, 1934, pp. 130–172. The cited passage is from p. 172.

27. Colin Turnbull, *The Mountain People*, New York: Simon and Schuster, 1972. But see Robert B. Edgerton, who reports doubts by other ethnographers about Turnbull's account, in *Sick Societies: Challenging the Myth of Primitive Harmony*, New York, The Free Press, 1993, pp. 6–8.

28. Cora Du Bois, *The People of Alor*, Minneapolis: University of Minnesota Press, 1945.

29. Abram Kardiner, *The Psychological Frontiers of Society*, New York: Columbia University Press, 1945, p. 256.

30. Alan MacFarlane, review-essay, *History and Theory*, 18 (1979), pp. 103–126.

31. Stone, *The Family, Sex and Marriage in England*, pp. 258–259.

32. Ibid., pp. 234, 259.

33. Ibid., pp. 97–98. Used in the singular, "friend" did, Stone tells us, tend to mean someone to whom one had a personal attachment, much as it still does.

34. MacFarlane, *The Origins of English Individualism*.

35. MacFarlane, review-essay, pp. 111, 118.

36. Peter Laslett, *New Society*, December 14, 1978, pp. 649–650; Lawrence Stone, *New York Review of Books*, 26 (April 19, 1979), pp. 40–41; George Homans, *Contemporary Sociology*, 9 (March 1980), pp. 262–263.

37. Macpherson, *The Political Theory of Possessive Individualism*, pp. 13, 48.

38. William Letwin, "The Economic Foundation of Hobbes's Politics," p. 157.

39. Richard Hofstader, *Social Darwinism in American Thought*, Boston: The Beacon Press, 1955.

40. Lewis Feuer, "Marx and Engels as Sociobiologists," *Survey*, 23 (Autumn 1977–1978), pp. 109–136.

41. Talcott Parsons, *The Structure of Social Action*, New York: McGraw Hill, 1937, p. 113.

42. Jürgen Habermas, *Theory and Practice*, Boston: The Beacon Press, 1973, pp. 65–67; Raphael, *Hobbes: Morals and Politics*, pp. 69–71.

43. Habermas, *Theory and Practice*, p. 65.

44. Gertrude Himmelfarb, *Darwin and the Darwinian Revolution*, Garden City, N.Y.: Doubleday Anchor Books, 1962, pp. 426–430.

45. Hofstadter, *Social Darwinism in American Thought*, pp. 159–161.

46. Ibid., pp. 64–104.

47. I have deliberately cited popular phrases from a number of different periods.

48. Budd Schulberg, *What Makes Sammy Run?* New York: Bantam Books, [1941]1944, p. 9.

49. Robert Bierstedt, who was himself a graduate student at Harvard at this time, told me he thought it highly unlikely that Schulberg could have heard about Parsons's book during his Dartmouth years.

50. Henry Hughes, *Treatise on Sociology*, Philadelphia, 1854; George Fitzhugh, *Sociology of the South*, Richmond, Va., 1854.

51. Louis Hartz, *The Liberal Tradition in America*, New York: Harcourt, Brace and World, 1955, p. 180. See also Arthur J. Vidich and Stanford Lyman, *American Sociology*, New Haven: Yale University Press, 1985, pp. 9–19.

52. Eugene Genovese, *The World the Slaveholders Made*, New York: Pantheon Books, 1969, pp. 117–244.

53. An earlier writer has even speculated that Fitzhugh might have read and been influenced by *The Communist Manifesto*, published only six years before his own major work, but Genovese (pp. 182–184) argues that this could not have been the case.

54. H. Stuart Hughes, *The Sea Change: The Migration of Social Thought*, New York: Harper and Row, 1975, pp. 187–188. Also J. G. Merquior, *Rousseau and Weber: Two Studies in the Theory of Legitimacy*, London: Routledge and Kegan Paul, 1980, p. 74.

55. Macpherson, *The Political Theory of Possessive Individualism*, p. 50.

56. Leo Strauss, *Natural Right and History*, Chicago: University of Chicago Press, 1953, pp. 169, 183–184, 266, 268–271, 277–279, 292–294. Presumably, Allen Bloom sees himself as following his mentor Strauss when he makes the preposterous statement that, as against Aristotle's claim that man is a social animal, "the hidden

premise underlying modern social science [is] that man is by nature a solitary being." *The Closing of the American Mind,* New York: Simon and Schuster, 1987, p. 366. He goes on to refer—dubiously—to Marx, Freud, and Weber and a few sentences later takes a swipe at Margaret Mead, but nowhere in the entire book does he mention Durkheim, who clearly does not fit his statement and who has equally clearly been a major influence on modern social science. If anything the major premise, at least of modern sociology and anthropology, is that man is essentially social by nature; the doctrinaire rejection of the social contract theorists as "atomistic individualists" stems from this assumption, which is altogether congruent with Strauss's classically conservative view. Undoubtedly, Bloom's totally erroneous reading of David Riesman's *The Lonely Crowd* (New Haven: Yale University Press, 1950) follows also from his animus against the hyperindividualism he falsely imputes to social science: he tells us that Riesman extols "inner-direction" as the admirable *nouvelle vague* outlook derived, supposedly, from Nietzsche that is now supplanting the philistine bourgeois norm of "other-direction" (pp. 144–146, 154–155). Riesman saw it, of course, the other way around with "other-direction" as the new trend (not necessarily to be welcomed for that reason) and "inner-direction" as the classical bourgeois character type now on the wane. See Dennis Wrong, "*The Lonely Crowd* Revisited," *Sociological Forum,* 7 (June 1992), pp. 381–389.

57. Hannah Arendt, *The Origins of Totalitarianism*, New York: Harcourt, Brace, 1951, p. 139.

58. Parsons, *The Structure of Social Action*, p. 97.

59. Charles Camic, "*Structure* after 50 Years: The Anatomy of a Charter," *American Journal of Sociology*, 95 (July 1989), pp. 85–89.

60. Anthony Giddens, *Studies in Social and Political Theory*, New York: Basic Books, 1977, p. 174; Francois Bourricaud, *The Sociology of Talcott Parsons*, Chicago: University of Chicago Press, 1981, p. 99.

61. Hobbes, *Leviathan*, pp. 225–227.

62. Quentin Skinner, "The Context of Hobbes's Theory of Political Obligation," in Cranston and Peters, eds., *Hobbes and Rousseau*, pp. 101–142.

63. Quoted in Robert B. Edgerton, *Rules, Exceptions, and Social Order*, Berkeley and Los Angeles: University of California Press, 1985, p. 246.

64. R. G. Collingwood, *The New Leviathan*, Oxford: The Clarendon Press, 1942, p. 183.

65. Ibid., pp. 182–184; Wrong, "The Oversocialized Conception of Man in Modern Sociology," pp. 184–186.
66. J. L. Mackie, *Ethics: Inventing Right and Wrong*, Harmondsworth, Middlesex: Penguin Books, 1977, p. 111.

Chapter 3   Order as Regularity and as Rule

1. Talcott Parsons, *The Structure of Social Action*, New York: McGraw-Hill, 1937, pp. 91–92. Parsons distinguishes the two kinds of order clearly and unambiguously. The distinction is so often blurred in discussions of the problem of order that neverthe-less cite Parsons that it is worth quoting him at length: "The antithesis of the latter [factual order] is randomness or chance in the strict sense of phenomena conforming to the statistical laws of probability. Factual order, then, connotes essentially accessibility to understanding in terms of logical theory, especially of science. Chance variations are in these terms impossible to understand or reduce to law. Chance or randomness is the name for that which is incomprehensible, not capable of intelligible analysis. Normative order, on the other hand, is always relative to a given system of norms. . . .The breakdown of any given normative order, that is a state of chaos from a normative point of view, may well result in an order in the factual sense, that is a state of affairs susceptible to a scientific analysis" (p. 91). Parsons adds in foot-note 2 appended to the second sentence in the above quotation: "The limits of science are, then, to the positivist, the absolute lim-its of human comprehension."

   It is surprising that so many writers on the problem of order, including leading interpreters of Parsons like Jeffrey Alexander, have explicitly or implicitly equated randomness, irregularity, and unpredictability *per se*, or the absence of factual order, with the war of all against all, or the absence of normative order, which need not in the least be inconsistent with a high degree of factual order according to Parsons. See Alexander, *Theoretical Logic in Sociology*, Volume One, *Positivism, Presuppositions, and Current Controversies*, Berkeley and Los Angeles: University of California Press, 1982, p. 92.

2. It was often argued in the 1960s that Parsons had abandoned the voluntarism of his "theory of action" in *The Structure of Social Action* for social determinism when he embraced functionalism in his later works. This argument has always seemed to me to have little merit, for the voluntarism of the theory of action was intend-

ed to characterize not concrete individual actors but humanity at large in suggesting that collective values were not reducible to extra-social hereditary or environmental determinants or to the mechanical conditioning of the behaviorists. Marion Levy, Jr., was consistent with his teacher Parsons in defining "social action" as a "residual category," referring to behavior that could not be explained by biological or nonhuman environmental factors in his *The Structure of Society*, Princeton, N.J.: Princeton University Press, 1952, pp. 7–10. Only biological and environmental, not cultural or social, determinants are here excluded. My "oversocialized conception of man" thesis won unmerited popularity when it was understood as asserting the autonomy, creativity and "free will" of the individual in spite of the fact that it drew heavily on Freud whose psychic determinism was certainly at odds with a belief in free will or the creative individuality of the self. Christopher Lasch notes this misreading in *Haven in a Heartless World: The Family Besieged*, New York: Harper and Row, 1977, pp. 216–217. For a particularly egregious recent misreading of my argument, assuming that it intends to affirm free will but charging it with actually doing so in too qualified a fashion, see Richard Hilbert, *The Classical Roots of Ethnomethodology*, Chapel Hill, N.C.: University of North Carolina Press, 1991, p. 34. Hilbert also, consistent with his espousal of ethnomethodology, misidentifies the problem of order as conceived of by both Hobbes and Parsons as the avoidance of cognitive chaos rather than of violent conflict; he sees the problem of order as an entirely cognitive issue for both thinkers: the problem of finding regularities in human behavior comparable to "the motions of the stars and planets for astronomers" (pp. 19–20). This was *not* Parsons's problem of order, let alone Hobbes's.

3. Jeffrey Alexander, *Positivism, Presuppositions, and Current Controversies*, pp. 115–122, 199–200, n. 113. Also *Theoretical Logic in Sociology*, Volume Four, *The Modern Reconstruction of Classical Thought: Talcott Parsons*, Berkeley and Los Angeles: University of California Press, 1983, pp. 213–219.

4. Stuart Hampshire, "Can There Be a General Science of Man?" *Commentary*, 24 (August 1957), pp. 164–167.

5. Anthony Giddens, *Central Problems in Social Theory*, Berkeley and Los Angeles: University of California Press, 1979, pp. 248–250.

6. Anthony Giddens, *The Constitution of Society*, Cambridge: The Polity Press, 1984, p. 344. Actually, the frequency with which

actors conform to a social norm or law *was* at one time advanced as an instance of a social law and the behavior of motorists stopping at traffic lights was the major empirical and statistical evidence cited in favor of the law, which was in its day widely cited. See F. H. Allport, "The J-curve Hypothesis of Conforming Behavior," *Journal of Social Psychology*, 5(1934), pp. 141–183.

7. This is what Anthony Giddens calls "the double hermeneutic" of social science in *New Rules of Sociological Method*, New York: Basic Books, 1976, p. 162.

8. Alfred Schutz was the most forceful exponent of this view that all sociological or social science concepts are "meta" or "second-order" concepts.

9. Giddens, *The Constitution of Society*, p. 285.

10. Richard Grathoff, *The Theory of Social Action: The Correspondence of Alfred Schutz and Talcott Parsons*, Bloomington, Ind.: Indiana University Press, 1978, p. 36.

11. The phrase is Carl Friedrich's. See the discussion in Dennis H. Wrong, *Power: Its Forms, Bases, and Uses*, New York: Harper and Row, 1979, and Chicago: University of Chicago Press, 1988, pp. 7–10.

12. The ambiguity of the term "expectations" is indicated by Robert Cooley Angell, from whom I have also borrowed my second example here. See his *Free Society and Moral Crisis,* Ann Arbor: University of Michigan Press, 1958, p. 34.

13. Talcott Parsons, *Politics and Social Structure*, New York: The Free Press, 1969, p. 363.

14. The different forms of power and their combinations are reviewed at length in Wrong, *Power*, pp. 21–83.

15. Robert K. Merton, *Social Theory and Social Structure*, Revised and Enlarged Edition, New York: The Free Press, 1957, pp. 421–436.

16. Goffman writes: "We lean on these anticipations that we have, transforming them into normative expectations, into righteously presented demands." Erving Goffman, *Stigma*, Englewood Cliffs, N.J.: Prentice-Hall, 1963, p. 2.

17. Peter L. Berger and Thomas Luckmann, *The Social Construction of Reality*, Garden City, N.Y.: Doubleday Anchor Books, 1967.

18. Giddens attributes these to "practical" as distinct from "discursive" consciousness in *Central Problems in Social Theory*, pp. 24–25.

19. Erving Goffman, "The Interaction Order," *American Sociological Review*, 48 (February 1983), pp.1–17.

20. As suggested by the quotation from Goffman in note 16 above.

21. Herbert Blumer, *Symbolic Interaction: Perspective and Method*, Englewood Cliffs, N.J.: Prentice-Hall, 1969, p. 19.

22. The literary uses of the desert island situation are discussed by Morroe Berger in *Real and Imagined Worlds: The Novel and Social Science*, Cambridge, Mass.: Harvard University Press, 1977, pp. 46–60.

23. Judith Blake and Kingsley Davis, "Norms, Values, and Sanctions," in Robert E. L. Faris, editor, *Handbook of Modern Sociology*, Chicago: Rand-McNally, 1964, pp. 461–464.

24. I have elaborated considerably on an example suggested by W. J. H. Sprott, *Science and Social Action*, Glencoe, Ill.: The Free Press, 1954, pp. 10–11. In general, I am much indebted to Sprott's lucid analysis of social action, which is reprinted in Dennis H. Wrong and Harry L. Gracey, editors, *Readings in Introductory Sociology*, Third Edition, New York: Macmillan, 1977, pp. 53–61.

25. William Foote Whyte, *Street Corner Society*, Chicago: University of Chicago Press, 1943.

26. I have also borrowed this example from Sprott, *Science and Social Action*, pp. 12–14. See also Snow's "Appendix" on the history of Oxford and Cambridge colleges in C. P. Snow's novel *The Masters*, Harmondsworth, Middlesex, England: Penguin Books, 1956, pp. 300–312.

27. George Homans notes Chester Barnard's concept of a "zone of indifference" with reference to commands in Barnard's discussion of leadership and comments that what is true of commands is also true of norms, although his main concern in this section of his book is with leadership and authority. Homans, *The Human Group*, New York: Harcourt, Brace, 1950, pp. 425–426. My "zone of conformity" is the equivalent with reference to norms of Barnard's "zone of indifference." The zone is undoubtedly even wider with respect to norms than with respect to commands, that is, leaves greater latitude to individual interpretation of the norm where surveillance is more diffuse since it is vested in a group, often an indeterminately bounded one, rather than in a specific authority.

28. This is a feature of language particularly associated with the theories of Noam Chomsky.

29. Whyte, *Street Corner Society*, p. x.

30. Max Weber, *Economy and Society*, three volumes, translated and edited by Guenther Roth and Claus Wittich, Volume One, Totowa, N.J.: The Bedminster Press, 1968, pp. 26–27.

31. Jonathan Turner mentions the neglect of motivation as one of
     "the limits of interactionism" in *The Structure of Sociological
     Theory*, Fourth Edition, Chicago: The Dorsey Press, 1989, p. 459,
     although he then proceeds in the conventional fashion of sociolo-
     gists to dismiss psychoanalytic theory as "mysticism."

     Commenting on Talcott Parsons's frequent use of "expecta-
     tion," the philosopher Max Black remarked "Expectations fall on
     the side of the 'cognitive'" and went on to note the predominant
     cognitivism of both G. H. Mead and Parsons, although his criti-
     cism applies only to an aspect of Parsons's theory and he erred in
     attributing it to the influence of Mead, who was not "the
     acknowledged progenitor of this segment of Parsons's theory" and
     who, as I note below, explicitly described his own conception of
     the self as a cognitive one. See Black, "Some Questions about
     Parsons's Theories,"in Black, editor, *The Social Theories of
     Talcott Parsons*, Englewood Cliffs, N.J.: Prentice-Hall, 1961, p.
     255. See also note 34 below.

32. Wrong, "The Oversocialized Conception of Man in Modern
     Sociology," *American Sociological Review*, 26 (April 1961), pp.
     183–193.

33. However, as Charles Camic has pointed out, Parsons does *not*
     deal with motivation in *The Structure of Social Action*. See Camic,
     "The Utilitarians Revisited," *American Journal of Sociology*, 85
     (November 1979), pp. 520–523, 544–545; also Camic, "*Structure
     after 50 Years: The Anatomy of a Charter*," *American Journal of
     Sociology*, 95 (July 1989), pp. 80–81. Parsons's discussion stresses
     rather the *intentionality* of action and the importance of what
     would today be called *agency* in human behavior as opposed to
     passive response to external stimuli. His focus on the "unit act"
     and its linkage of means and ends bypasses motivation altogether,
     which narrows and distorts his conception of the Hobbesian prob-
     lem of order (see Chapter 4 below, pp. 99–102). In Parsons's *later*
     work, on the other hand, after he had incorporated Freud into his
     theorizing, starting with some of the papers in *Essays in
     Sociological Theory*, Glencoe, Ill.: The Free Press, 1949 and in
     Parsons and Edward A. Shils, editors, *Toward A General Theory
     of Action*. Cambridge: Harvard University Press, 1951, and *The
     Social System*, Glencoe: The Free Press, 1951, he strongly empha-
     sizes the actor's underlying motivation and its roots in his or her
     personality or character structure. In the "Preface to the Second
     Edition" of *The Structure of Social Action*, Glencoe, Ill.: The Free
     Press, 1949, p. B, he mentions the neglect of psychology in general

and of Freud in particular as a weakness that he sees his more recent work as having rectified. Whether his conception of human motivation is acceptable is another issue altogether. That it is not was the brunt of my argument against Parsons in "The Oversocialized Conception of Man."

34. Ian Craib, however, insists that "what he [Parsons] does is concentrate on the cognitive and role-learning processes and describe them in Freudian language." He then asserts that Parsons associates Freud with G. H. Mead, "who is solely concerned with the conscious processes of role-learning, a matter of socialization from the outside," *Psychoanalysis and Social Theory: The Limits of Sociology,* New York and London: Harvester Wheatsheaf, 1989, p. 74. This is the same error made by Max Black nearly three decades earlier. See note 31 above. I agree fully that Parsons "sociologises Freud," which is what I argued in "The Oversocialized Conception of Man," but he did not do this under the influence of Mead, who, as I maintain below, explicitly characterized the process of self-formation through what he called the "interiorization of the social process" as one of cognitive learning. Parsons's model of internalization was borrowed directly from Freud, granting that he flattened it out, so to speak, in tending to equate it with a learning process that encountered no deep motivational resistance.

35. Thomas Hobbes, *Leviathan,* Harmondsworth, Middlesex, England, Penguin Books, [1651] 1962, p. 185.

36. For example, in Peter L. Berger, *The Sacred Canopy,* Garden City, N.Y.: Doubleday Anchor Books, 1969.

37. As argued by Donald L. Carveth, "The Disembodied Dialectic: A Psychoanalytic Critique of Sociological Relativism," *Theory and Society,* 4 (1977), pp. 73–102, and "Sociology and Psychoanalysis: The Hobbesian Problem Revisited,"*Canadian Journal of Sociology,* 7 (Spring 1982), pp. 201–228. Also Carveth, *Sociologism and Psychoanalysis: A Study of Implicit Theories of Human Nature in "Symbolic Interactionism," "Reality Constructionism," and Psychoanalysis,* Unpublished doctoral dissertation, Department of Sociology, University of Toronto, 1977. See also Gary B. Thom, *The Human Nature of Social Discontent,* Totowa, N.J.: Rowman and Allanheld, 1983, pp. 30–40. Although Berger is cool toward psychoanalysis, Weston LaBarre, one of the few social scientists who has both been strongly sympathetic to Freudian psychoanalysis and has attempted to relate its conception of human nature to man's distinctive biological evolu-

tionary history, acknowledges a debt to Arnold Gehlen who is the major progenitor of Berger's notion of man's distinctive "world openness." See LaBarre, *The Human Animal*, Chicago: University of Chicago Press, 1954, p. 343.

38.   Herminio Martins suggests that they have "miniaturized" the problem of order as it was formulated by Parsons. See Martins, "Time and Theory in Sociology," in John Rex, editor, *Approaches to Sociology*, London and Boston: Routledge and Kegan Paul, 1974, p. 251.

39.   Aaron Cicourel, *Cognitive Sociology*, New York: The Free Press, 1974.

40.   Translated by Ted Humphrey, New York: Abaris Press, 1982, p. 73. I acquired this translated passage at third-hand from Norbert Wiley who received it from Lewis W. Beck, Professor Emeritus at the University of Rochester and Kant scholar, who sent him a copy of it with a brief commentary of his own. I had written Wiley inquiring about the source of a different translated version that appeared in Geoffrey Hawthorn, *Enlightenment and Despair: A History of Sociology*, Cambridge: Cambridge University Press, 1976, pp. 31–32. I am grateful to Wiley for having made available to me Beck's communication, with the enclosure of Humphrey's translation of the passage from Kant.

41.   Geoffrey Hawthorn's freer translation renders the rather confusing "the I that I think" as "I, the thinking subject" and "intuition" and "intuit" as "perception" and "perceive." It seems to me that his translation, if less accurate, is more in line with contemporary usage and understanding, at least among sociologists and social psychologists. In any case, it makes the continuity with Mead much more evident.

42.   Kant famously remarked on the dual wonder of the "starry heavens above" and the "moral conscience within us." His sense of wonder over the latter undoubtedly owes something to his belief in the impossibility of explaining the self-observing capacity of the "I" that is implied by the existence of conscience. Freud liked to quote Kant's reference to the wonder of conscience, which Kant thought proved the existence of God. See, for example, Sigmund Freud, *New Introductory Lectures on Psychoanalysis*, New York: W. W. Norton, 1933, pp. 88, 223. Freud plainly thought that he had resolved what was a mystery to Kant with his theory of the superego. Mead, I am here suggesting, also thought that he was clearing up what had been a mystery to Kant in showing that language was the source of the division of the self into an observing

and an observed part. But though related—the division of the self is a precondition for conscience or the superego—they are not the same mystery: self-division is a cognitive capacity, moral obligation is a category of motivation.

43. George Herbert Mead, *Mind, Self and Society*, Chicago: University of Chicago Press, 1934, pp. 106–108.

44. Mead frequently refers to Giddings's "consciousness of kind" and the psychologists' concept of "sympathy," criticizing them for inadequately accounting for the phenomena they identify. See *Mind, Self and Society*, pp. 298–300. Mead was concerned as early as 1914 with the relation between symbolic communication, "taking the role of the other," and the ideas of the psychologists, as well as of the sociologists Franklin Giddings and Charles Horton Cooley, on imitation and sympathy as socializing mechanisms. These subjects are discussed at some length in his previously unpublished "Lectures in Social Psychology" from both 1914 and 1927, *The Individual and the Social Self*, Edited with an Introduction by David L. Miller, Chicago: University of Chicago Press, 1982, pp. 53–72, 136–150, also in the Appendix on "Functional Identity of Response," pp. 197–217.

45. As is recognized by David L. Miller, *George Herbert Mead: Self, Language and The World*, Chicago: University of Chicago Press, 1973. See also Hans Joas, *G. H. Mead: A Contemporary Reexamination of His Thought*, Cambridge: The Polity Press, 1985.

46. Donald L. Carveth specifically disagrees with my contention that Mead's self is essentially a cognitive phenomenon, maintaining that although "this is certainly the self of the Meadians. . . fortunately, just as Freud was not a Freudian, so Mead was not a 'symbolic interactionist,'" "The Hobbesian Microcosm: On the Dialectics of the Self in Social Theory," *Sociological Inquiry*, 47, (1977), p. 8, n. 5. See also Carveth, *Sociologism and Psychoanalysis*, Chapter Three. I agree with Carveth that Mead was not guilty of holding an oversocialized view of man as a result of blurring the difference between cognition and motivation. I am still disposed, however, to insist that Mead's major problematic was the relation between the self as knowing subject and as known object, and that this is essentially an epistemological problem rooted in the Kantian theory of knowledge. Mead was, in short, primarily a philosopher and not a sociologist or social psychologist; he is not, therefore, guilty of the fallacies of the latter, including those of his own followers. Carveth's discussion was

addressed to my article "Human Nature and the Perspective of Sociology," *Social Research*, 30 (Fall 1963), pp. 300–318; reprinted in Wrong, *Skeptical Sociology*, New York: Columbia University Press, 1976, pp. 55–70. In a later article Carveth has explicitly modified his earlier discussion of Mead. See "Sociology and Psychoanalysis: The Hobbesian Problem Revisited," pp. 205–206.

47. Mead, *Mind, Self and Society*, p. 173. I quoted this passage in "Human Nature and the Perspective of Sociology" and I note that a decade later the philosopher and former student of Mead's, David Miller, quotes the same passage to make the same point about the "primarily cognitive" nature of Mead's conception of the self: Miller, *George Herbert Mead*, p. 48.

48. Harry Stack Sullivan, *Conceptions of Modern Psychiatry*, Washington, D.C.: William Alanson White Psychiatric Foundation, 1940 and 1945, pp. 7–10. The sociologists seem to have somehow run together Mead's concept of "significant symbol" and "generalized other" in coming up with "significant other," though the latter is certainly a useful concept.

49. One anthropologist who has fully recognized this is Robert Redfield, *The Primitive World and Its Transformations*, Ithaca, N.Y.: Cornell University Press, 1953, p. 91. Redfield describes Mead's account of the origins of mind and self in social interaction as a "human universal."

50. See, for example, Goffman's brilliant early article "On Cooling the Mark Out," *Psychiatry*, 15 (November 1952), pp. 451–463. As Tom Burns has noted, this second published article of Goffman's was the first to display his unique "deadpan satirical" style of analysis (*Erving Goffman*, London and New York: Routledge, 1992, pp. 13–16). Goffman was notoriously interested in appearances, their manipulation ("impression management"), and their possible discrepancy with underlying reality, the latter including conventionally "appropriate" affects and motivations. Hence his interest in all of his work, both early and late, in "play-acting" or dramaturgy involving systematic feigning or the production of illusion and in such specialists of deception as confidence men and espionage agents. The essence of Goffman's alleged "cynicism" lies in his demonstration that the "presentation of self" is largely a matter of producing particular cognitive appearances that may or may not be attended by the appropriate sincere or authentic underlying motivations and affects. His satiric and ironic effects are produced by his describing ordinary people in ordinary social situations *as if* they were con men coolly calcu-

lating the impressions they make for ulterior self-interested motives. As Giddens has observed, "One of the most striking gaps in Goffman's writings is the absence of an account of motivation." *The Constitution of Society*, p. 86; see also pp. xxiv and 70.

51. In *Civilization and Its Discontents* Freud remarks on the failure of many adults to develop a superego as opposed to refraining from doing a "bad thing" only out of fear of being discovered, remarking cryptically and ominously that "present-day society has to reckon in general with this state of mind" (New York: W. W. Norton, [1930] 1961, p. 72). See the old but still relevant discussion by William M. McCord and Joan McCord, *Psychopathy and Delinquency*, New York: Grune and Stratton, 1954.

52. W.H. Auden, "Get There If You Can and See The Land You Once Were Proud to Own," in Selden Rodman, editor, *A New Anthology of Modern Poetry*, New York: The Modern Library, 1938, p. 375.

Chapter 4   Social and Antisocial Elements in Human Nature

1. Robert Nisbet, *The Sociology of Emile Durkheim*, New York: Oxford University Press, 1974, p. 108.

2. Steven Lukes, *Individualism*, Oxford: Basil Blackwell, 1973, p. 151.

3. John Dewey, *Human Nature and Conduct*, New York: The Modern Library, [1922] 1930, pp. 134–137.

4. See the lengthy passage from Sartre's *Critique of Dialectical Reason*, Volume One, cited (and translated) by George Lichtheim in Lichtheim, "Sartre, Marxism, and History," *Collected Essays*, New York: Viking Press, 1973, pp. 381–383. Lichtheim notes the near-identity of Sartre's view to that of Hobbes, pp. 387, 388. See also Raymond Aron, *Marxism and the Existentialists*, New York: Harper and Row, (1969) p. 169; Mark Poster, *Existential Marxism in Postwar France*, Princeton, N.J.: Princeton University Press, 1975, p. 281.

5. Thomas Hobbes, *Leviathan*, Harmondsworth, Middlesex, England: Penguin Books, [1651] 1962, pp. 184–185.

6. Talcott Parsons, *The Structure of Social Action*, New York: McGraw Hill, 1937, pp. 109–110.

7. By, for example, Gerhard Lenski, *Power and Privilege: A Theory of Social Stratification*, New York: McGraw-Hill, 1966, Chapters 1–3, pp. 1–72. Rousseau more or less anticipated this view in *A Discourse on Inequality*, Harmondsworth, Middlesex, England:

Penguin Books, [1755] 1984, p. 116. He preferred the simple subsistence economy of the state of nature and of "nascent society,"
precisely because of the absence of the inequality and ferocious
conflict over the distribution of the surplus product that characterized more productive economies.

8. Lenski, *Power and Privilege*, pp. 94–112; Robert B. Edgerton,
    Rules, Exceptions, and Social Order, Berkeley and Los Angeles:
    University of California Press, 1985, pp. 239–243.

9. Michael Oakeshott, *Hobbes on Civil Association*, Oxford: Basil
    Blackwell, 1975, p. 34, n. 59.

10. Hobbes, *Leviathan*, p. 161.

11. As Alan Ryan states: "Though Hobbes indeed describes the mech-
    anisms of desire and motivation in terms which suggest that each
    person is indeed bent on *maximizing* his or her own enjoyment, it
    emerges on closer inspection that Hobbes readily envisaged us
    'satisficing.'. . .What Hobbes's individuals maximize in the state of
    nature is *power*. They do not do so because they like power, nor
    because they want to maximize the enjoyment of anything posi-
    tive. They are forced to maximize their power even though they
    would be content with a moderate living. This is because isolated
    individuals have no other means of security; they are not utility-
    maximizing but danger-of-death-minimizing creatures." "Hobbes
    and Individualism," in G. A. J. Rogers and Alan Ryan, editors,
    Perspectives on Thomas Hobbes, Oxford: The Clarendon Press,
    1988, pp. 92–93 (his emphasis). The same point is made by
    Richard Tuck in *Hobbes*, Oxford: Oxford University Press, 1989,
    p. 55.

12. Hobbes, *Leviathan*, p. 150.

13. M. M. Goldsmith clearly specifies the conception of power as a
    generic or universal means to anything in Hobbes's *Science of
    Politics*, New York: Columbia University Press, 1966, p. 67. See
    also S.I. Benn, "Hobbes on Power," in Maurice Cranston and
    Richard S. Peters, editors, *Hobbes and Rousseau*, Garden City,
    N.Y.: Doubleday Anchor Books, 1972, pp. 206–211. Talcott
    Parsons in his writings on power frequently characterized it as a
    "universal means." See, for example, Parsons, *The Structure of
    Social Action*, pp. 262–263; *Politics and Social Structure*, New
    York: The Free Press, 1969, pp. 252–404; *Social Systems and the
    Evolution of Action Theory*, New York: The Free Press, 1977, p.
    209.

14. Bertrand Russell, *Power: A New Social Analysis*, London: Allen &
    Unwin, 1938, p. 25.

15. Dennis H. Wrong, *Power: Its Forms, Bases and Uses,* New York: Harper and Row, 1979, Chicago: University of Chicago Press, 1988, p. 2.

16. Deborah Baumgold, "Hobbes's Political Sensibility: The Menace of Political Ambition," in Mary G. Dietz, editor, *Thomas Hobbes and Political Theory*, Lawrence, Kansas: University of Kansas Press, 1990, pp. 74–90. Also Ryan, "Hobbes and Individualism," pp. 102–104.

17. Thomas Hobbes, *De Cive or The Citizen*, New York: Appleton-Century Crofts, [1642] 1949, p. 26.

18. See my brief discussion of Foucault in "Preface 1988" to *Power: Its Forms, Bases, and Uses*, Chicago: University of Chicago Press, 1988, pp. x–xiii.

19. Hobbes, *De Cive or The Citizen*, p. 24.

20. Ryan, "Hobbes and Individualism," pp. 102–103. This clarifies why commentators like Strauss and Oakeshott give such priority to pride as a source of contention and why so many others have seen it as Hobbes's version or equivalent of "original sin."

21. Niccolo Machiavelli, *The Prince*, Harmondsworth, Middlesex, England: Penguin Books, [1512] 1961, p. 63.

22. John Plamenatz, "Introduction" to Hobbes, *Leviathan*, London: Collins, Fontana Library of Philosophy, 1962, pp. 64–65.

23. Oakeshott, *Hobbes on Civil Association*, p. 82 (his emphasis).

24. Leo Strauss, *The Political Philosophy of Hobbes*, Chicago: University of Chicago Press, [1936] 1952 , p. 20. Goldsmith makes the same point in *Hobbes's Science of Politics,* pp. 78–79.

25. Oakeshott, *Hobbes on Civil Association*, p. 36.

26. Sigmund Freud, *Group Psychology and the Analysis of the Ego*, New York: Bantam Books, [1921] 1960, p. 41; Michael Oakeshott, *Rationalism in Politics and Other Essays*, Indianapolis: Liberty Press, 1991, pp. 460–461.

27. Oakeshott, *Rationalism in Politics*, p. 356. In seeing vanity or pride as the basic source of conflict among men, Oakeshott and Leo Strauss before him come close to Rousseau's view of the corrupting effects of society after the state of nature has been overcome, although neither of them acknowledges this similarity.

28. Sigmund Freud, *Civilization and Its Discontents*, New York: W. W. Norton, [1930] 1961, pp. 47–49.

29. Juan E. Corradi has amply documented this, mentioning Hobbes, with reference to the Southern Cone nations of South America in general and Argentina in particular, in a number of publications. See especially, "Towards Societies without Fear?" Part IV, Corradi,

Patricia Weiss Fagen, and Manuel Antonio Garreton, *Fear at the Edge: State Terror and Resistance in Latin America*, Berkeley and Los Angeles: University of California Press, 1992, pp. 269, 278, 282.

30. Peter Winch, "Man and Society in Hobbes and Rousseau," in Cranston and Peters, editors, *Hobbes and Rousseau*, p. 235.

31. Hobbes, *De Cive or The Citizen*, pp. 1–2.

32. See the references in Chapter 1 of this text, note 8.

33. John Locke, *The Second Treatise of Government*, Indianapolis: Bobbs-Merrill, [l960] 1952, p. 10.

34. Adam Smith, *The Wealth of Nations,* Harmondsworth, Middlesex, England: Penguin Books, [1776] 1974, pp. 117–118.

35. Ruth W. Grant, "Locke's Political Anthropology and Lockean Individualism," pp. 64–86; William G. Batz, "The Historical Anthropology of John Locke," pp. 242–251, both in Richard Ashcraft, editor, *John Locke: Critical Assessments*, Volume Three, London and New York: Routledge, 1991. Grant writes of Locke that he "recognized fully the extent to which human beings are social beings" (p. 65). Batz observes that Locke, in contrast to Hobbes, thought of the state of nature as a historical fact, reporting his comment that "in the beginning all the World was America" (pp. 242–243). He goes on to observe that "Unlike Hobbes. . .Locke considered men in essence to be at least semi-social" (p. 245). These statements by recent Locke scholars not only confirm my own interpretation of his "desert island" scenario, but also indicate that Parsons was correct in claiming in *The Structure of Social Action* that Locke was "factually the more nearly right" than Hobbes, even if "he gave the wrong reasons", pp. 97–98, n. 1. Compare them with Oakeshott's more qualified statement about the social aspects of Hobbes`s state of nature cited on page 000 above.

36. As J. G. Merquior writes of Hobbes: "He shared with the tenets of natural law the idea that political authority is based on a social contract, and civil society rests on the consent of the subjects (note that until Hegel the expression civil society, stemming from ancient political theory, meant the body politic, *not* society as contrasted with the state)." *Rousseau and Weber: Two Studies in the Theory of Legitimacy*, London: Routledge, 1980, p. 26. See also Merquior, *Liberalism, Old and New*, Boston: Twayne Publishers, 1991, pp. 28–29, on the meaning of "civil society" to the thinkers of the Enlightenment.

37. Marshall Sahlins alludes to Smith's "natural propensity to truck

and barter" and calls it a "reduction to biology" in *Culture and Practical Reason*, Chicago: University of Chicago Press, 1976, p. 53. Michael Hechter also refers dismissively to Adam Smith's "natural propensity to truck and barter" in "From Exchange to Structure," in Joan Huber, editor, *Macro-Micro Linkages in Sociology*, Newbury Park, Calif.: Sage Publications, 1991, p. 48. I pick these two examples from quite different writers at random. In a thorough study of Smith's thought, Jerry Z. Muller states that Smith regarded the propensity as "innate," but he does not cite textual evidence for believing this and it seems to me that Smith was at least ambiguous on the issue. See Muller, *Adam Smith in His Time and Ours*, New York: The Free Press, 1993, p. 57. D. D. Raphael notes Smith's vagueness on the question in *Adam Smith*, Oxford: Oxford University Press, 1985, p. 50.

38. Alessandro Pizzorno, "On the Individualistic Theory of Social Order," in Pierre Bourdieu and James S. Coleman, editors, *Social Theory for a Changing Society*, Boulder, San Francisco, Oxford: Westview Press and Russell Sage Foundation, 1991, pp. 209–231.

39. Ibid., p. 215.

40. A similar argument is advanced by Jon Elster, *The Cement of Society: A Study of Social Order*, Cambridge: Cambridge University Press, 1989, pp. 284–285, though specifically with reference to industrial societies characterized by high social and geographical mobility.

41. Pizzorno, "On the Individualistic Theory," p. 218.

42. See the citations attesting to this belief in Dennis H. Wrong, "The Oversocialized Conception of Man in Modern Sociology," *American Sociological Review*, 26 (April 1961), pp. 187–191. The importance attached to the need for approval by others does not seem to have declined among sociologists in recent years. Often it is simply taken for granted, perhaps more often even than in the past with the decline of interest among them in psychoanalysis.

43. Pizzorno, "On the Individualistic Theory," p. 213.

44. For a sociological version of this familiar opposition, see Ralf Dahrendorf, *Essays in the Theory of Society,* Stanford, Calif.: Stanford University Press, 1968, pp. 135–137.

45. Rousseau, *A Discourse on Inequality*, p. 98.

46. Quoted by John McManners, "The Social Contract and Rousseau's Revolt against Society," in Cranston and Peters, editors, *Hobbes and Rousseau*, pp. 296–297.

47. For a recent restatement of the contrast that is heavily loaded in

Hobbes's favor, see Thomas Sowell, *A Conflict of Visions*, New York: William Morrow, 1987, pp. 35–36. Sowell is a prominent conservative polemicist, but liberals and even many radicals are equally likely to disavow belief in the innate goodness of man, partly because conservatives so often charge them with naively believing in it and almost routinely invoke Rousseau in doing so. Sowell's book is a case in point. See my review of it, "Opposites Detract," *New Republic*, February 9, 1987, pp. 46–48.

48.   These writers did not, it should be noted, put forward a general notion of primitives as benign and altruistic, for the central principle of their cultural relativism was the variability of all cultures, including the primitive or nonliterate ones studied by cultural anthropologists. Indeed, the two most famous anthropologists who made use of anthropology as social criticism, Mead and Benedict, also reported on "Hobbesian" primitive societies, as did the influential neo-Freudian theorist Abram Kardiner drawing on the ethnography of Cora Du Bois, and, more recently, Colin Turnbull. See Chapter 2 above, p. 25. See also Robert B. Edgerton, *Sick Societies: Challenging the Myth of Primitive Harmony*, New York: The Free Press, 1993.

49.   So conscientious an intellectual historian as George Lichtheim, for example, writes that to Rousseau "men are sociable by *nature* and possess an inborn inclination to do good to their fellow-men" (*The Origins of Socialism*, New York: Praeger, 1969, pp. 12–13 [his emphasis]). See also Lichtheim, *A Short History of Socialism*, New York: Praeger, 1970, pp. 22–23. A much more accurate account of Rousseau is provided by an earlier intellectual historian of socialism, Alexander Gray, who points out in *The Socialist Tradition* that men have no trouble living in harmony with one another in Rousseau's state of nature because they have as little to do with one another as possible, London: Longmans, Green, [1946] 1963, pp. 76–85.

50.   Hobbes, as noted above, was not entirely consistent on this score.

51.   Rousseau, *A Discourse on Inequality*, pp. 98–99.

52.   Ibid., pp. 161–166. The discussion in the main text is on pp. 102–104.

53.   See in particular his comment referring to both Hobbes and Locke at the end of his endnote criticizing Locke's theory of sexual bonding, ibid., p. 166. Alan Ryan notes that the harmony of Rousseau's state of nature "is possible only because everything that is distinctively human—speech, self-consciousness, individual and social aspiration—is absent." Ryan, "The Nature of Human

Nature in Hobbes and Rousseau," in Jonathan Benthall, editor, *The Limits of Human Nature*, London: Allen Lane, 1972, p. 15.

54. Rousseau, *A Discourse on Inequality*, p. 85.

55. Ibid., p. 101. Kitty Genovese was a Queens cocktail waitress who on returning in the small hours to the apartment complex in Kew Gardens where she lived was stabbed to death in its courtyard. Residents of the buildings hearing her screams did not come to her rescue or even telephone the police. The case became the occasion for a lot of tongue-clucking over the impersonality and inhumanity of modern urban life, including a book by a *New York Times* editor, A. M. Rosenthal, *Thirty-eight Witnesses*, New York: McGraw-Hill, 1964. See the recollection of the case a quarter of a century later as a kind of fateful landmark by Douglas Martin, "Would New York Still Turn Away?" *New York Times*, March 27, 1989, p. B1. But see the interactionist analysis of the situation by John M. Darley and Bibb Latané, suggesting that Kitty's neighbors were perhaps unfairly judged, in "Bystander Intervention in Emergencies,"*Journal of Personality and Social Psychology*, 8 (1968), pp. 377–383. See also the discussion of their analysis by Randall Collins in *Sociological Insight*, New York: Oxford University Press, 1982, pp. 15–16.

56. Rousseau, *A Discourse on Inequality*, p.115.

57. Claude Lévi-Strauss, *Tristes Tropiques*, New York: Atheneum, 1974, p. 391.

58. See Rousseau's very lucid account of this crucial development, essentially the major *fons et origo* of social inequalities, in *A Discourse on Inequality*, p. 118. See also his conclusion about the crucial importance of the valuation of individual differences on p. 132.

59. Ibid., p. 116.

60. Dahrendorf, for example, in *Essays in the Theory of Society*, pp. 158–159. Dahrendorf takes too seriously and literally the famous opening statement of Part Two in *A Discourse on Inequality* in which Rousseau asserts that the first man who fenced off some land and declared it his was the true creator of "civil society" and all the miseries it has brought in its train, p. 109. Like many others, Dahrendorf is anxious to establish a line of continuity between Rousseau and Marx. He ignores Rousseau's argument that property is essentially a result of the combination of individual differences highlighted by improved tool-making and the vanity that results from a more intense social life.

61. One can find in *A Discourse on Inequality* all of the separate

"variables" or "dimensions" that sociologists of inequality or social stratification, simplifying Max Weber, have distinguished. But to Rousseau, wealth and power are sought not for their own sakes but solely in order to achieve preeminence over others. The "haves" enjoy what they have primarily in contemplating others who lack it and envy them.

62. Emile Durkheim, *The Division of Labor in Society*, New York: Macmillan, [1893] 1933, pp. 256–263.

63. Rousseau, *A Discourse on Inequality*, pp. 110, 114, 119, 132–133, 136. The first reference is to "the first stirring of pride" aroused by early man's sense of superiority over other species, which only later involved comparisons of self with fellow humans.

64. Jean Starobinski, *Jean-Jacques Rousseau: Transparency and Obstruction*, Chicago: University of Chicago Press, [1971] 1988. On the history and influence of Starobinski's book on both Rousseau studies and on French intellectual life generally, see Robert Darnton, "A Star Is Born," *New York Review of Books*, October 27, 1988, pp. 84–88. Starobinski clearly states that "the fall [from the innocence of natural life] is nothing other than the introduction of pride" (p. 27).

65. In the penultimate paragraph of *A Discourse on Inequality*, Rousseau writes of the savage's happy ignorance that there could be such a thing as "a class of men who attach importance to the gaze of the rest of the world, and who know how to be happy and satisfied with themselves on the testimony of others rather than on their own." He goes on to declare that "the savage lives within himself; social man lives always outside himself; he knows how to live only in the opinion of others, it is, so to speak, from their judgement alone that he derives the sense of his own existence" (p. 136).

66. Rousseau's *Confessions* provides ample evidence of this, but see the two volumes that have appeared of Maurice Cranston's biography: *Jean-Jacques: The Early Life and Work of Jean-Jacques Rousseau*, London: Allen Lane, 1983, and *The Noble Savage: Jean-Jacques Rousseau 1754–1762*, London: Allen Lane, 1991.

67. Richard S. Peters, *Hobbes*, Harmondsworth, Middlesex, England: Penguin Books, 1956, Chapter 1, pp. 13–42.

68. Dennis H. Wrong, "Identity: Problem and Catchword," in Wrong, *Skeptical Sociology*, New York: Columbia University Press, 1976, pp. 81–94.

69. For Rousseau it is *the* source, for Hobbes *a* source, although, as indicated above, both Strauss and Oakeshott in interpreting

Hobbes emphasize its centrality to him in virtual exclusion of anything else as the source of conflict among men.

70. Elster, *The Cement of Society*, p. 262.

71. Quoted by Edgerton in *Rules, Exceptions, and Social Order*, p. 246.

72. This is undoubtedly why Lévi-Strauss in *Tristes Tropiques* chooses to interpret Rousseau's account of the state of nature as a "theoretical model," for in praising Rousseau as the father of anthropology and the inspiration of his own work, he knows full well that "Natural man did not precede society, nor is he outside it" (p. 392). He interprets Rousseau's account of natural man as an "experiment" to see what might be possible "within society" (pp. 392–393).

73. They most closely resemble the "individualism" of many small-scale foraging or food-gathering tribes reported by Edgerton in *Rules, Exceptions, and Social Order*, pp. 179–189. He describes one such tribe as "extremely individualistic, noncooperative and noncompetitive" (p. 183), which certainly applies both to Rousseau's presocial state of nature and his nascent society.

74. J.G. Merquior points out the inappropriateness of picturing Rousseau as a nostalgic communitarian in *Rousseau and Weber*, p. 74.

75. The *locus classicus* nowadays for alarm over "privatization" and calls for a renewal of "community" is Robert Bellah, et al., *Habits of the Heart,* New York: Harper and Row, 1985 .

76. Edgerton, *Rules, Exceptions, and Social Order*, p. 257.

77. As described in contemporary America, without, however, deploring these attitudes, by Herbert J. Gans, *Middle American Individualism*, New York: The Free Press, 1988, pp. 98–120.

78. As Merquior points out in *Rousseau and Weber*, pp. 84–85.

79. Parsons, *The Structure of Social Action*, pp. 96–97.

80. The standard source remains Louis Hartz, *The Liberal Tradition in America*, New York: Harcourt, Brace and World, 1955.

81. As maintained by Weston LaBarre, *The Human Animal,* Chicago: University of Chicago Press, 1954.

82. Charles Camic has correctly summarized the origins of Parsons's view in his critique of neoclassical economics and his desire to find a mandate for sociology complementing—rather than supplanting—that of economics in "The Utilitarians Revisited," *American Journal of Sociology,* 85 (November 1979), pp. 516–550; "The Making of a Method: A Historical Reinterpretation of the Early Parsons," *American Sociological Review,* 52 (August 1987), pp. 421–439; "*Structure* After 50 Years: The Anatomy of a Charter,"

American Journal of Sociology, 95 (July 1989, pp. 38–107; and "Reputation and Predecessor Selection: Parsons and the Institutionalists," *American Sociological Review*, 57 (August 1992), pp. 421–445.

83. James B. Rule, in *Theories of Civil Violence*, Berkeley and Los Angeles: University of California Press, 1988, p. 134, cogently criticizes the notion of "randomness of ends" for its inherent implausibility, but does not relate it to Parsons's polemic against the assumptions of the economists, although he cites Charles Camic who lays considerable stress on this in "The Utilitarians Revisited," pp. 520–545.

84. Hobbes, *Leviathan*, p. 139.

85. Analytic philosophers have developed careful distinctions between ends or intentions, motives, and reasons. See, for example, G. E. M. Anscombe, "Intention," in Alan R. White, editor, *The Philosophy of Action*, Oxford: Oxford University Press, 1977, pp. 147–148. Anscombe argues that "intention" is "*what* is aimed at" whereas "motive" determines aims or choices and is equivalent to the "cause" of an action. She notes that this distinction is often obscured in popular speech, as when people speak of a "motive of gain." See also Anscombe, *Intention*, Second Edition, Ithaca, N.Y.: Cornell University Press, 1966. Although he does not use the same terminology, the motive/end distinction is equivalent to the distinction between what Alfred Schutz calls "in-order-to" and "because" motives, the former referring to a future condition and constituting therefore the *end* of an action in the sense of both Parsons and John Dewey. Schutz, *Collected Papers*, Volume One, The Hague: Martinus Nijhoff, 1962, pp. 69–72. For Parsons, "an end is. . . a future state of affairs to which action is oriented by virtue of the fact that it is deemed desirable by the actor(s)." *The Structure of Social Action*, p. 75.

86. See Dewey, *Theory of Valuation*, Chicago: University of Chicago Press, 1939, pp. 33–36, 40–41, 52, also Dewey, *Logic: The Theory of Inquiry*, New York: Henry Holt, 1938, pp. 166–168.

87. Parsons, *The Structure of Social Action*, p. 90.

88. As Camic points out in "*Structure* after 50 Years," noting that Parsons was at least aware of Schutz's earlier concern with these distinctions, p. 63.

89. Critics have, it is true, pointed out that Parsons concerns himself with the actor's "orientation" to action rather than with action itself. In this sense he is guilty of a cognitivist, or at least mentalist, bias that neglects not so much motivation but overt behavior.

These critics were referring to Parsons's post-*Structure* writings that do not neglect motivation but that can even be seen as overemphasizing it. See Max Black, "Some Questions about Parsons's Theories," pp. 274–275 and William Foote Whyte, "Parsonian Theory Applied to Organizations," p. 255 in Black, editor, *The Social Theories of Talcott Parsons*, Englewood Cliffs, N.J.: Prentice-Hall, 1961.

90. "There is a problem of allocation of resources not only as between different ends of the same individual, but also as between those of different individuals." Parsons, *Structure*, p. 235.

91. Ibid., p. 59.

92. In his "Preface to the Second Edition" of *Structure,* Parsons ackowledges his inattention to psychology in general and to Freud in particular, thus presumptively to motivation as such. Glencoe, Ill.: The Free Press, 1949, p. B.

93. Robert M. MacIver, *Society: A Textbook of Sociology,* New York: Rinehart, 1937, pp. 28–32, 47–48.

94. Parsons, *Politics and Social Structure*, pp. 252–404. Parsons's interpretation of Hobbes as postulating an inevitable struggle for "power over" others is much the same as C. B. Macpherson's in *The Political Theory of Possessive Individualism: Hobbes to Locke,* New York: Oxford University Press, 1962 and Macpherson's "Introduction" to the Penguin edition of *Leviathan*, 1962, pp. 9–63, although Parsons was describing a hypothetical possibility whereas Macpherson thought Hobbes's account at least prefigured emerging bourgeois or capitalist society. See the discussion of Macpherson's thesis in Chapter 2 above.

95. Parsons does state that "since the passions, the ultimate ends of action, are diverse there is nothing to prevent their pursuit resulting in conflict," *Structure*, p. 89, see also pp. 235–239. One might retort to this that there is equally nothing to prevent their *not* coming into conflict at least most of the time. Indeed, a diversification of ends plays a role in Durkheim's theory of the origins of the division of labor as a response to greater population density and actual or potential competitition for limited resources. See Durkheim, *The Division of Labor in Society*, pp. 267–277. Durkheim cites Darwin and Haeckel in drawing an analogy between the origins of the division of labor and speciation, or the origin of species, when intensified competition for a single limited resource leads to differentiation with new species finding separate niches enabling them to subsist within a common environment instead of entering into a conflict over limited resources that

would either reduce their numbers or lead to dispersion ("segmentation" in Durkheim's language). For Parsons it is less the clashing of ends than conflict over the possession of scarce *means*, over "power" as the generalized term for universal means, that creates the menace of the war of all against all. In a later section of *Structure* he acknowledges more fully than in his initial discussion that *both* the clashing ends of individuals *and* their potential use of one another as means create the problem of order, but here too he emphasizes more strongly the utility of force and fraud as means to most ends, pp. 235–239.

96. Parsons does not use the concept of "internalization" that looms so large in his later theorizing in *Structure,* although he does refer twice to Freud's concept of "introjection" as formative of the "superego," pp. 386, 388.

97. One might argue that normative limitation of means is not likely to be fully effective given the "greater motivating force" (Kecskemeti) of ends over means. See the valuable discussion by Paul Kecskemeti, *Meaning, Communication, and Value*, Chicago; University of Chicago Press, 1952, p. 262–276. Kecskemeti generalizes to all stratified societies the "goal-norm discrepancy" noted by Merton in American society in his famous article "Social Structure and Anomie," reprinted in Robert K. Merton, *Social Theory and Social Structure*, Revised and Enlarged Edition, New York: The Free Press, 1957, pp. 131–160. Kecskemeti argues that at least *some* discrepancy is preferable to a situation in which all those who successfully achieve their ends are able to bask in the odor of sanctity as a result of owing their success entirely to the use of the proper, normatively sanctioned means. Kecskemeti anticipated here a central argument of Michael Young's brilliant *The Rise of the Meritocracy 1870–2033*, New York: Random House, 1959.

98. Rule in *Theories of Civil Violence*, Chapter 5, pp. 132–169, vigorously criticizes Parsons for grossly overrating the role of common values and collective ends in human conduct and argues that Parsons's qualifications of his overstatements actually destroy his "solution" to the problem of order. But Rule does not discuss Parsons's emphasis on the "internalization" of purely negative norms proscribing force and fraud, which would resolve the problem of order as a war of all against all even if it would not suffice to create a consensual society based on shared "ultimate values" and commitments to collective goals.

99. Jon Elster in *The Cement of Society,* pp. 1–3, distinguishes

between two kinds of disorder: lack of predictability exemplified by cognitive chaos, and lack of cooperation which he identifies with the Hobbesian state of nature. This only faintly suggests the distinction I want to make between avoidance of conflict and commitment to collective goals. Cognitive chaos, the absence of what Parsons calls "factual order," is, as I have previously argued, a separate epistemological-linguistic issue from the problem of order as Hobbes and Parsons conceived of it. More important, the absence of cooperation does not necessarily imply universal conflict rather than merely the relative independence of individuals and/or small groups (nuclear families?) from one another, a "state of nature" closer to Rousseau's than to Hobbes's. (I am equating "cooperation" here with commitment to common goals, although if it is defined behaviorally it can of course be compelled by force or purchased by inducement. See Wrong, *Power: Its Forms, Bases, and Uses*, pp. 139–141).

100. Talcott Parsons, *The Social System*, Glencoe, Ill.: The Free Press, 1951, pp. 204–205 and Parsons and Edward A. Shils, editors, *Toward a General Theory of Action*, Cambridge, Mass.: Harvard University Press, 1951, pp. 105–107.

101. Parsons, *Structure*, pp. 76–77. Earlier in the chapter, without drawing the analogy with physics, he wrote: "What is essential to the concept of action is that there should be a normative orientation," p. 45. Both Charles Camic in "*Structure* after 50 Years," pp. 64–67 and Brian Barry in *Sociologists, Economists and Democracy*, Chicago: University of Chicago Press, [1970] 1978, pp. 85–87, 178–179, note the far-reaching and questionable nature of this assumption. Parsons defined "norm" as "a verbal description of the concrete course of action. . .regarded as desirable, combined with an injunction to make certain future actions conform to this course" (p. 75).

102. Parsons, *Structure*, p. 732.

103. Ibid., p.77.

104. Ibid., p. 44. For the analytic philosophy of action see Peter Winch, *The Idea of Social Science and Its Relation to Philosophy*, London: Routledge, 1955, pp. 60–65. J. C Merquior, however, in line with his teacher Ernest Gellner's famous assault in *Words and Things* (Harmondsworth, Middlesex, England: Penguin Books, 1959) on the Oxford analytic philosophers of the 1950s, does charge some social theorists who make use of Wittgenstein's concepts of "language games" and "forms of life" with being "prone to conceive of rule-governed conduct as though it were identical

with established, socially approved behavior." A few pages later he refers to Winch in this connection and links Oxford analysis, the end-of-ideology writers, and Parsons's structural-functionalism together, rather too facilely, as different expressions of 1950s consensual thinking, *Rousseau and Weber,* pp. 158, 160.

105. Parsons has, of course, often been accused of an inability to account for deviance and rebellion, let alone "evil," except under the catch-all rubric of "failures of socialization" which he has sometimes employed in an implicitly tautological way. See my "Human Nature and the Perspective of Sociology," *Social Research,* 30 (Fall 1963), pp. 300–318, reprinted in Wrong, *Skeptical Sociology,* pp. 55–70.

106. Parsons, *Structure,* p. 76.

107. I say "presumably" because, although Alexander frequently refers to this "conflation" (one of his favorite words), he never fully clarifies just what he means by it. See Jeffrey Alexander, *Theoretical Logic in Sociology,* Volume Four, *The Modern Reconstruction of Social Thought: Talcott Parsons,* Berkeley and Los Angeles: University of California Press, 1983, pp. 213–219. Also *Positivism, Presuppositions, and Current Controversies,* Volume One, 1982, p. 119. Alexander manages to discuss the issue on an even more abstract level than Parsons himself in arguing that Parsons "conflates" the two separate polarities of "voluntarism versus determinism" and "individualism versus collectivism," both of them central in Alexander's view to the controversies over "theoretical logic in sociology" that is the focus of his four-volume work.

I certainly agree that the distinctively human capacity for purposive or goal-directed action is not the same thing as the problem of order and need not presuppose the actor's conformity to prevailing social norms, although it does presuppose, surely, the acquisition of language and conceptual thought which are products of socialization, and probably also presupposes selfhood and "identity" (as argued by Alessandro Pizzorno). And the socialization of infants presupposes the overcoming of the war of all against all at least within nuclear families, as Rousseau noted in criticism of Hobbes. In this rather restricted sense at least, action implies order. One might also say that the capacity to conform to norms—"to follow a rule" in Wittgenstein's sense—presupposes the primary socialization through which the child learns language and the resulting capacity for conceptual thought and goal-directed action. But this applies just as much to the capacity to question or violate existing social norms. Perhaps all this is what Alexander has in mind with his "voluntarism/determinism" and "individualism/collectivism" dichotomies that he says Parsons conflates, but I am by no means certain. Giddens briefly distinguishes between action and order in Parsons in *The Constitution of Society*, Cambridge: The Polity Press, 1984, p. xxxvii.

108. My original title for "The Oversocialized Conception of Man in Modern Sociology" was "Social versus Socialized Man," the distinction that is elaborated in the last section of the article, pp. 192–193.

109. As pointed out by Gianfranco Poggi in *Images of Society*, Stanford, Calif.: Stanford University Press, 1972, pp. 242–244, 247, 253. In footnote 3 on p. 244, Poggi anticipates my own argument here in noting that Parsons as well as Durkheim identifies the "normative" with "intentionality" as such.

110. Alvin W. Gouldner, *For Sociology*, New York: Basic Books, 1974, p. 177. Gouldner presumably had in mind the rational purposeful behavior on which the West places a premium.

111. Giddens, *The Constitution of Society*, pp. 3–7.

112. As against the contrary claims of behaviorism, biological determinism, vulgar Marxism, and the kind of narrow and abstracted methodological individualism favored then and now by neoclassical economics. Camic's articles cited in note 82 above are the most accurate accounts available of the intellectual context in which *Structure* was written. Probably in understandable reaction against the many vulgarized sociologies of knowledge to which Parsons has been subjected, Camic perhaps overstresses the Harvard scene and the quest for a disciplinary mandate. He strikes a properly critical note, however, with reference to the latter that is free from the defensiveness of Parsons's latter-day partisans.

113. One of my major arguments in "The Oversocialized Conception of Man" was that Parsons, in contrast to Freud, blurred the distinction between the intrapsychic and overt action.

114. Parsons himself took this line in his response to "The Oversocialized Conception of Man," accusing me of demanding prematurely significant "empirical generalizations" and ignoring the "opportunity for analytical clarification of the operation of a factor." See Parsons, "Individual Autonomy and Social Pressure: A Reply to Dennis H. Wrong," *Psychoanalysis and the Psychoanalytic Review*, 49 (Summer 1962), pp. 70–79. As Camic has much more recently pointed out, Parsons's habitual emphasis on "analytical abstraction" was an effort to apply to theory in

sociology the kind of heuristic *in ceteris paribus* assumptions that had long characterized economic theory, which he persisted in seeing as the essence of theoretical "sophistication." See the citations in note 82 above.

115. This, essentially, is Alexander's view which I am not alone in finding less than convincing. I confess that my reservations about Alexander's formulations are enhanced by the fact that he grossly misstates and misrepresents my own criticism of Parsons in "The Oversocialized Conception of Man" on the several occasions he refers to it in *The Modern Reconstruction of Classic Thought: Talcott Parsons*, pp. 41, 303–304, 376, 446. Critics have pointed out that he has seriously misrepresented other theorists as well: see, for example, James B. Rule, "Out of This World," *Theory and Society*, 12 (1983), pp. 801–814. I find Charles Camic a much more reliable interpreter of both Parsons and his critics and, for that matter, of earlier theorists discussed by Parsons such as the Utilitarians.

116. See the extensive thoughtful review by Muller in *Adam Smith in His Time and Ours*, pp. 89–97. See also Raphael, *Adam Smith*, pp. 29–45, 86–94.

117. Wrong, "The Oversocialized Conception of Man in Modern Sociology"; George C. Homans, "Bringing Men Back In,"*American Sociological Review*, 29 (November 1964), pp. 809–818; Harold Garfinkel, *Studies in Ethnomethodology*, Englewood Cliffs, N.J.: Prentice-Hall, 1967, pp. 66–70.

Chapter 5   The Freudian Synthesis

1. I am fairly certain that the phrase is Susan Sontag's, but I have been unable to locate its exact source.

2. Sigmund Freud, *Civilization and Its Discontents*, New York: W.W. Norton, [1930] 1961, pp. 59–61. See the fuller discussion of Marxism and the "Soviet experiment" in his *New Introductory Lectures on Psychoanalysis*, New York: W. W. Norton, 1933, pp. 241–248.

3. See Martin Green's account of the influence of Otto Gross on Max Weber's circle in Heidelberg and the bohemian colony of Ascona before the Great War in *The von Richthofen Sisters*, New York: Basic Books, 1970.

4. Gary B. Thom, *The Human Nature of Social Discontent*, Totowa, N.J.: Rowman and Allanheld, 1983, p. 57

5. Philip Rieff, *The Triumph of the Therapeutic: Uses of Faith after Freud*, New York: Harper and Row, 1966.

6. See George Lichtheim, *From Marx to Hegel*, New York: Herder and Herder, 1972.

7. Norman O. Brown, *Life against Death: The Psychoanalytical Meaning of History,* Garden City, N.Y.: Doubleday Anchor Books, 1960, p. 312 (original edition: Middletown, Conn.: Wesleyan University Press, 1959.)

8. Richard Rorty, *Contingency, Irony, and Solidarity*, Cambridge and New York: Cambridge University Press, 1989, pp. xiii, 177, 185. Rorty's point was essentially an epistemological one, namely, that all truth claims are necessarily made in language ("discourse"), which is always learned by human beings in a particular historical and cultural context. Language, therefore, does not and cannot reflect some prelinguistic, extrahuman reality. Yet in the utterly different context of his particular philosophical polemic, Rorty comes close to restating various tenets of cultural relativism, the sociology of knowledge, and what I criticized as an oversocialized conception of man that were widely held by sociologists and cultural anthropologists a generation ago. For example, he suggests that the question "'What is it to be a human being?' should be replaced by questions like 'What is it to inhabit a rich twentieth-century democratic society?' and 'How can an inhabitant of such a society be more than the enactor of a role in a previously written script?'" (p. xiii). This last question suggests precisely the view of man as a conformist "role player" that was so roundly assailed by assorted conflict theorists, Blumerians, phenomenologists, ethnomethodologists, and affirmers of human creativity in the 1960s. Nor is it clear why "the ability to use language, and thereby to exchange beliefs and desires with other people" that is acquired through socialization necessarily means that "all we share with all other humans is the same thing we share with all other animals—the ability to feel pain" (p. 185). Even if we live in the Tower of Babel, the fact that we all possess "linguistic competence" is surely of no small consequence.

9. I made this point about the similarity in basic conceptions of the malleability of human nature shared by structural-functionalists and their neo-Marxist, conflict-oriented critics in "Human Nature and the Perspective of Sociology,"*Social Research*, 30 (Fall 1963), pp. 300–318, reprinted in Dennis H. Wrong, *Skeptical Sociology*, New York: Columbia University Press, 1976, pp. 55–70.

10. Indeed, Rorty, as quoted in note 8 above and elsewhere in *Contingency, Irony, and Solidarity,* explicitly denies the existence of a common human nature, identifying, as sociologists have often

done in the past, the idea of "human nature" with some vital essence seen as preceding socialization.

11. The very phrase suggests that Freud's instincts are not the fixed patterns of behavior that biologists define as instinctive but rather labile, indeterminate motivational energies. The phrase as translated from Freud has been roundly criticized by the late Bruno Bettelheim on the grounds that "vicissitudes" is a somewhat esoteric English word that may connote natural events as well as human experiences and, reiterating earlier criticisms by others, that "drive" is a more accurate rendition of Freud's *Trieb* than "instinct" because it lacks the suggestion of a fixed pattern of behavior conveyed by the latter. See Bettelheim, *Freud and Man's Soul*, New York: Alfred A. Knopf, 1983, pp. 103–107.

12. I advanced these propositions as the foundation of the psychoanalytic conception of man in "Postscript 1975," in *Skeptical Sociology*, pp. 47–54. The second proposition about the body was asserted, in italics no less, in "The Oversocialized Conception of Man in Modern Sociology," *American Sociological Review*, 26 (April 1961), p. 191 (reprinted in *Skeptical Sociology*, pp. 31–46).

13. Wordsworth clearly phrased this in what would today be considered a blatantly sexist way. How about "the child is parent to the person?"

14. Freud, *Civilization and Its Discontents*, p. 12.

15. See, for example, Talcott Parsons, "Individual Autonomy and Social Pressure: A Reply to Dennis H. Wrong,"*Psychoanalysis and the Psychoanalytic Review*, 49 (Summer 1962), especially pp. 74–75; Judith Blake and Kingsley Davis, Chapter 13, "Norms, Values, and Sanctions," in R. E. L. Faris, editor, *Handbook of Modern Sociology*, Chicago: Rand McNally, 1964, p. 471. Although he exonerates me from the charge of biologism leveled by Parsons, Donald Carveth complains that I nevertheless remain "dangerously close to the scene of the crime" in advancing this proposition about the body; he also avers that, in referring to the "somatic, animal roots" of motivation in "Postscript 1975," I raise the danger "of slipping back into the old biologism," Donald L. Carveth, *Sociologism and Psychoanalysis: A Study of Implicit Theories of Human Nature in "Symbolic Interactionism," "Reality Constructionism" and Psychoanalysis*, unpublished doctoral dissertation, Department of Sociology, University of Toronto, 1977, p. 175. I agree with him, however, when in a later article he writes after quoting me "we must insist that psychoanalysis is not primarily about the body at all but about *ideas*

about the body, mostly infantile, unconscious, and fantastic ideas in fact" ("Sociology and Psychoanalysis: The Hobbesian Problem Revisited,"*Canadian Journal of Sociology*, 7 (Spring 1982), p. 224 [his italics]).

16. Much the same viewpoint still prevails, if phrased differently, with respect to culture and cultural determinism in anthropology according to Melford E. Spiro, *Culture and Human Nature*, Chicago: University of Chicago Press, 1987, pp. 3–31.

17. Freud, *New Introductory Lectures*, p. 245.

18. Carveth, "Sociology and Psychoanalysis: The Hobbesian Problem Revisited," p. 203. Carveth's discussion of the entire issue of so-called "psychological reductionism" can hardly be improved upon.

19. Sigmund Freud, *Group Psychology and the Analysis of the Ego*, New York: Bantam Books, [1921] 1960, p. 3.

20. John Dollard, *Criteria for the Life History*, New York: Peter Smith, [1935] 1949, pp. 17–18.

21. Ibid., p. 26.

22. My borrowing is at second-hand, mediated by Brown, *Life against Death*, p. 125. I owe a great deal to Brown's brilliant book. Probably, "In the beginning is the body" is also influenced in its formulation by him, for he writes of "the resurrection of the body" and is in general sensitive to the relationship between psychoanalytic and religious-mystical ideas that are often expressed in metaphorical language. Although unable to share Brown's chiliastic view of history as the return of the repressed or his later excursions into a kind of mystical poetry retaining only a loose connection to psychoanalysis, *Life against Death* in conjunction with teaching *Civilization and Its Discontents* to an undergraduate seminar on "Great Books" led me to question the neo-Freudian culturalist revisionists on whose work I had been brought up academically speaking. There is a certain tendency to dismiss Brown as an irrationalist utopian visionary who became a guru of the hippies in the sixties, which ignores his cogent and accurate presentation in *Life against Death* of the more complex and anti-commonsensical of Freud's ideas, e. g. the death instinct, and his pointed criticism of the neo-Freudians for excising from their versions of psychoanalysis its foundation in bodily and infantile experience. I agree with Christopher Lasch, *The Minimal Self*, New York: W. W. Norton, 1984, p. 235, that Brown is superior to Marcuse in his understanding of Freud and that he is also "a more trenchant critic of neo-Freudian revisionism than Marcuse" (p. 236).

23. See the critiques both originally published in *The American Journal of Sociology* by the foremost authorities in the fields of cultural anthropology and the history of the Jews, A. L. Kroeber, "*Totem and Taboo* in Retrospect," pp. 45–49, and Salo W. Baron, "Book Review of *Moses and Monotheism*," pp. 50–55, in Bruce Mazlish, editor, *Psychoanalysis and History*, Englewood Cliffs, N.J.: Prentice-Hall, [1939] 1963.

24. For a valuable recent effort to separate what is untenable in the theory and what can be retained at least in somewhat restructured form, see Robert Endleman, *Psyche and Society: Explorations in Psychoanalytic Sociology*, New York: Columbia University Press, 1981, Chapter 6, pp. 115–127.

25. They are so described with the quotation marks by Robert A. Paul, "Freud's Anthropology: A Reading of the 'Cultural Books,'" in Jerome Neu, editor, *The Cambridge Companion to Freud*, Cambridge: Cambridge University Press, 1991, pp. 267–286.

26. Robert Bocock, *Sigmund Freud*, London and New York: Tavistock Publications, 1983, p. 104.

27. Kroeber reports that Freud himself noted that Kroeber's original review of *Totem and Taboo* in 1920 had "amusingly" characterized it as a "*Just So* story." Kroeber calls it "a felicitous phrase" considering that "Many a tale by Kipling or Anderson contains a profound psychological truth," "*Totem and Taboo* in Retrospect" (p. 145). Freud's reference to Kroeber's original review was in *Group Psychology and the Analysis of the Ego*, p. 69, but was actually in error, for it was the British anthropologist R. R. Marett who had called it a "just-so story," translator's addendum, p. 77.

28. For example he notes on page 33 contemporary hostility to civilization expressed in the belief that "we should be much happier if we gave it up and returned to primitive conditions." But on the very next page he states that Europeans have been mistaken in thinking that contemporary "primitive peoples and races" lead "a simple, happy life with few wants" and that "later experience has corrected some of those judgements." (Quite possibly he had Rousseau's *Discourses* in mind.) On page 42, however, he contends that the "liberty of the individual. . .was greatest before there was any civilization," which certainly suggests belief in a precultural "state of nature." He proceeds on the next page to refer to the persistence of "the remains of. . .original personality, which is still untamed by civilization." Then on pages 47–48 he restates the thesis of *Totem and Taboo* that civilization came into being when the band of brothers slew their despotic father and

thus discovered the superior power of the group over the single individual. (He does not mention here the remorse that led them to impose the incest taboo.) He then proceeds on pages 48–54 to argue the inevitability of conflict between love, sexual desire, and the familial preoccupations of women, on the one hand, and the interests of civilization, on the other. Then on page 62 he mentions the deprivations imposed on the majority by the patriarch during the primal horde era, but then goes on to remark accurately enough that research has shown that contemporary primitive peoples do not enjoy "instinctual freedom" but that their lives "are subject to restrictions of a different kind but perhaps of greater severity than those attaching to modern civilized man." Later on page 74, he suggests that primitive man externalizes the blame for misfortune and is relatively free from the sense of guilt experienced by civilized man. Obviously, there is a partial recognition here that all human societies impose restrictive rules on their members that coexists, however, with the belief that the restrictions tend to become more demanding and painful in the more advanced or civilized societies and the very occasional invocation of the precultural state of nature postulated in *Totem and Taboo*.

29.   Much the same thing can be said of Freud's contemporary D. H. Lawrence, renowned as the great apostle of the superiority of the primitive as opposed to the emptiness and loss of vitality of modern life. But Lawrence too recognized the essential identity of primitive and modern men in rejecting the idea of the greater "spontaneity" of the former in an essay written at about the same time as *Civilization and Its Discontents*, "On Human Destiny," *Selected Essays*, London: William Heinemann, 1930, pp. 203–209. I find it hard to resist the temptation to quote at considerable length, but the following will have to suffice to give something of the flavor: "Since man became a domesticated, thinking animal, long, long ago, a little lower than the angels, he long,long ago left off being a wild instinctive animal.. . .Man is never spontaneous, as we imagine the thrushes or the sparrow-hawk, for example, to be spontaneous. No matter how wild, how savage, how apparently untamed the savage may be, Dyak or Hottentot, you may be sure he is grinding upon his own fixed, peculiar ideas, and he's no more spontaneous than a London bus conductor: probably not as much" (p. 204).

30.   Although, as Carveth notes, I have, along with Parsons and others, strenuously defended Freud in the past from the standard sociological accusation of biologism or instinctivism, I am willing to accept

Carveth's insistence that there is a point at which this becomes a
needlessly quixotic task ("Sociology and Psychoanalysis: The
Hobbesian Problem Revisited," p. 217, n. 11).

31. When I was an undergraduate in the 1940s, one of my teachers
posed the following question on a final examination: "Freud did
some valuable ethnography on middle-class Jewish women in
Vienna at the turn of the century. Discuss." We were expected to
agree that he had indeed done that, but that that was all he had
done, namely, describe a particular culture or subculture at a particular moment in history. The same teacher advised us not to
bother reading Freud because we could read instead Karen
Horney who had corrected him. This was, of course, at the high
tide of cultural relativism in Anglo-American social science,
although it is worth noting that fifty years later such views have
again acquired a following.

32. The most recent thoroughgoing critique of the translations is
Bruno Bettelheim's *Freud and Man's Soul*.

33. Anne Parsons, "Is the Oedipus Complex Universal? The Jones-
Malinowski Debate Revisited and a South Italian Nuclear
Complex," in W. Muensterberger, et al., editors, *The
Psychoanalytic Study of Society*, New York: International
Universities Press, 1964, pp. 278–328. For a useful recent (1991)
account of "the consensus (not unanimity) among analysts about
what is enduring in Freud's formulations" on the Oedipus complex, see Bennett Simon and Rachel B. Blass, "The Development
and Vicissitudes of Freud's Ideas on the Oedipus Complex," in
Jerome Neu, ed., *The Cambridge Companion to Freud*, pp.
173–174.

34. Jonathan Lear, *Love and Its Place in Nature*, New York: Farrar
Straus & Giroux, 1990.

35. Géza Roheim, *The Origin and Function of Culture*, Garden City,
N.Y.: Doubleday Anchor Books, [1943] 1971; Roheim, *The
Riddle of the Sphinx*, New York: Harper and Row, [1934] 1974,
pp. 146–160, 184–196, 266–271; Margaret Mead, "*Totem and
Taboo* Reconsidered with Respect,"*Bulletin of the Menninger
Clinic*, 27 (1963), pp. 185–199.

36. Talcott Parsons, *The Structure of Social Action*, New York:
McGraw-Hill, 1937, p. 382.

37. See especially Parsons, "The Superego and the Theory of Social
Systems" in *Social Structure and Personality*, New York: The Free
Press, 1969, pp. 17–33 (originally published in *Psychiatry*,
February 1952). Other essays in Part One of this collection are
also relevant.

38. Wrong, "The Oversocialized Conception of Man in Modern Sociology;" Ian Craib, *Psychoanalysis and Social Theory: The Limits of Sociology*, New York and London: Harvester Wheatsheaf, 1989, p. 74.

39. Craib, *Psychoanalysis and Social Theory*, p. 74. Craib exempts Freud from the charge he directs against Parsons that the socialization is complete and meets with no resistance, for he accepts the validity of Freud's instinct theory.

40. Michel Foucault, *Discipline and Punish: The Birth of the Prison*, New York: Vintage Books, 1977.

41. J. G. Merquior sees all of these as expressions of the *Zeitgeist* of the 1950s in *Rousseau and Weber: Two Studies in the Theory of Legitimacy*, London: Routledge, 1980, p. 160.

42. Anthony Giddens points out an affinity between Parsons's view of power as a "collective resource" and Foucault's emphasis on its creative potential in *The Constitution of Society*, Cambridge: The Polity Press, 1984, p. 15. See also my own discussion of Foucault on power in "Preface, 1988" to Dennis H. Wrong, *Power: Its Forms, Bases, and Uses*, Chicago: University of Chicago Press, [1979] 1988, pp. x–xiii.

43. Freud, *Civilization*, p. 92.

44. Perhaps it should be noted that I am referring here, as indeed in the entire chapter and its predecessor, to the "Hobbesian" (lowercase "hobbesian" is preferable for reasons to be advanced in the next chapter) or social psychological aspect of the problem of order, human nature and its tractability to social discipline, and not to the "Marxian" (again I prefer the lowercase "marxian") aspect of the problem, or the issue of group conflict within large-scale differentiated societies. Particular group conflicts can, of course, be resolved, or, more commonly, simply decline in intensity and disappear.

45. Dick Atkinson, *Orthodox Consensus and Radical Alternative*, London: Heinemann Educational Books, 1971; Alan Dawe, "The Two Sociologies,"*British Journal of Sociology*, 21 (1970), pp. 207–218; "Theories of Social Action," in Tom Bottomore and Robert A. Nisbet, editors, *A History of Sociological Analysis*, New York: Basic Books, 1978, pp. 362–417.

46. Robert C. Tucker, *Philosophy and Myth in Karl Marx*, Second Edition, Cambridge, Mass: Harvard University Press, 1972.

47. As was recognized by David Riesman, with the assistance of Reuel Denney and Nathan Glazer, *The Lonely Crowd*, New Haven: Yale University Press, 1950; and William H. Whyte, *The Organization Man*, Garden City, N.Y.: Doubleday Anchor Books,

1956, who were the major intellectual figures associated with the "social criticism" of the 1950s that anathematized "conformity."

48. Christopher Lasch notes this misconstruction in *Haven in a Heartless World: The Family Besieged*, New York: Harper and Row, 1977, pp. 149, 216–217, n. 37.

49. The term is Christopher Lasch's from *The Minimal Self*, p. 247.

50. Paul Robinson, *The Freudian Left*, New York: Harper and Row, 1969; Carveth, "Sociology and Psychoanalysis," pp. 207–210

51. Lewis A. Coser, *Greedy Institutions*, New York: The Free Press, 1974.

52. Thom, *The Human Nature of Social Discontent*, pp. 43, 46.

53. Benjamin Nelson and Dennis Wrong, "Perspectives on the Therapeutic in the Context of Contemporary Sociology: A Dialogue between Benjamin Nelson and Dennis Wrong," *Salmagundi*, (Summer-Fall 1972), p. 180; see also my own comments, pp. 188–189.

54. See the once much-cited article by David Aberle and four other young students of Parsons at the time, "The Functional Prerequisites of Society,"*Ethics*, 60 (January 1950), pp. 100–111. Nearly all works written in the late 1940s and 1950s from a functionalist viewpoint, including a number of introductory textbooks, used to start out by listing the universal functional prerequisites or social imperatives to which all societies were held to be subject, the list usually including controlling social conflict (that is, "solving" the problem of order), producing and distributing the material means of subsistence, replacing the population through reproduction, socializing infants, and the like. Ultimately, these lists were boiled down to Parsons's celebrated AGIL scheme of four universal system problems: Adaptation to the natural environment, Goal Attainment, Integration (the old problem of order), and Latent Pattern Maintenance (or the preservation of distinctive cultural patterns). The four-function scheme was first presented in Parsons and Neil J. Smelser, *Economy and Society,* Glencoe, Ill.: The Free Press, 1956, pp. 18–20; it receives its fullest elaboration, being extended to apply not merely to social systems but to everything in the universe from God to the human anus, in Parsons's last nonposthumous book, *Action Theory and the Human Condition,* New York: The Free Press, 1978, pp. 352–433, especially p. 361 and p. 383.

55. Talcott Parsons and Edward A. Shils, *Toward A General Theory of Action*, Cambridge, Mass.: Harvard University Press, 1951, p. 180.

56. A metaphor of C. Wright Mills's in *The Sociological Imagination*, New York, Oxford University Press, 1959, p.171.

57. Aldous Huxley, *Brave New World*, New York: Bantam Books, [1932] 1953, "Foreword," p. xiv.

58. To be sure, the rulers in the end destroy even Winston Smith's inner resistance to the point where in the book's horrific ending he declares he "loves Big Brother." But this is a very special form of treatment applied to a dissident from the Inner Party and is not the regular technique of rule over the general population, which is based on frustration of basic sexual and material needs and planned orgies of hatred directed against the regime's external enemies.

59. George Kateb, *Utopia and Its Enemies*, New York: The Free Press, 1963, p. 166.

60. Huxley, *Brave New World*, p. 244.

61. Aldous Huxley, *Brave New World Revisited*, New York: Harper and Row, 1958.

62. Ralf Dahrendorf, "Out of Utopia: Toward a Re-orientation of Sociological Analysis," *American Journal of Sociology*, 64 (September l958), pp. 115–127.

63. I first compared and distinguished the overintegrated conception of society and the oversocialized conception of man in an earlier article, "The Failure of American Sociology," *Commentary*, 28 (November 1959), pp. 375–380 (reprinted as "C. Wright Mills and the Sociological Imagination" in *Skeptical Sociology*, pp. 21–30).

64. Lasch, *Haven in a Heartless World*, pp. 111–133; Endleman, *Psyche and Society*, pp. 44–50; Philip Slater, "The Social Bases of Personality," in Neil J. Smelser, editor, *Sociology: An Introduction*, New York: John Wiley, 1967, pp. 548–600; Robert Bocock, *Freud and Modern Society*, London: Thomas Nelson, 1976, pp. 31–35; Craib, *Psychoanalysis and Social Theory*, pp. 74–78; Howard L. Kaye, "A False Convergence: Freud and the Hobbesian Problem of Order," *Sociological Theory*, 9 (Spring 1991), pp. 87–105.

65. Parsons, "Individual Autonomy and Social Pressure: A Reply to Dennis H. Wrong."

66. Freud's fullest account of the ego and its relation to the id and the reality principle is in *The Ego and the Id*, New York: W. W. Norton, [1923] 1962, pp. 25–27. He first discussed the reality principle and its opposite or complement the pleasure principle in his 1911 article "Formulations Regarding the Two Principles in

Mental Functioning," in Freud, *General Psychological Theory from The Collected Papers of Sigmund Freud*, edited by Philip Rieff, New York: Collier Books, 1963, pp. 21–28. See also the discussion in Freud, *Beyond the Pleasure Principle*, New York: Bantam Books, [1920] 1959.

67. Early in *Civilization and Its Discontents* Freud lists our bodies, the external world, and our relations with other people as three distinct sources of suffering (p. 24). From the standpoint of the individual, the last two are external and therefore might be regarded as constituting Ananke or outside circumstances that have to be confronted. Hans Meyerhoff, however, sees Ananke as natural necessity, the two instincts of Eros and Thanatos, and the "institutions and ideals developed by society" as forming three "independent variables" whose interaction produces culture, "Freud and the Ambiguity of Culture," in Mazlish, ed., *Psychoanalysis and History*, p. 58 (Meyerhoff's article was originally published in *Partisan Review* 14 [Winter 1957], pp. 117–130.) Since it is Ananke or external necessity that for Freud compels the formation of suprafamilial collectivities pursuing the collective goal of subduing nature, Meyerhoff's "institutions and ideals" are subsumed under Ananke in Freud's original formulation.

68. Sigmund Freud, *An Outline of Psychoanalysis*, New York: W. W. Norton, [1940] 1949, p. 20.

69. *Civilization and Its Discontents*, p. 48. At a later point in the book he asserts that "the process of civilization is a modification which the vital process experiences under the influence of a task that is set by Eros and instigated by Ananke—by the exigencies of reality; and that this task is one of uniting separate individuals into a community bound together by libidinal ties" (p. 86).

70. Kaye, "A False Convergence: Freud and the Hobbesian Problem of Order."

71. Philip Rieff, *Freud: The Mind of the Moralist*, New York: Doubleday Anchor Books, [1959] 1961, p. 243.

72. Neil J. Smelser, "Social Structure," in Smelser, editor, *Handbook of Sociology*, Newbury Park, Calif.: Sage Publications, 1988, pp. 103, 112–113; Kolakowski cited at length by Kaye, "A False Convergence," pp. 90–92; Michael and Deena Weinstein, "Freud on the Problem of Order: The Revival of Hobbes," *Diogenes* (Winter 1983), pp. 39–50. Smelser writes: "Freud. . .remained fundamentally Hobbesian in his formulation" (p. 103).

73. In *Freud: Sexuality and the Psychology of Love*, from *The*

Collected Papers of Sigmund Freud, edited by Philip Rieff, New York: Collier Books, 1963, pp. 20–40.

74. Kingsley Davis's chapter on the family in his advanced sociology textbook *Human Society*, New York: Macmillan, 1949, pp. 392–432, is still as thorough and adequate a discussion as any available.

75. Note his reference to this in *Civilization and Its Discontents*, p. 35.

76. Herbert Marcuse, *Eros and Civilization*, Boston: The Beacon Press, 1955.

77. Ibid., pp. 51–54.

78. Philip Slater, "On Social Regression," *American Sociological Review*, 28 (June 1963), pp. 339–364. Long after the publication of this article, Neil Smelser, the editor of the journal at the time it was published, told me that it was the longest article ever published in the *ASR*, the official journal of the American Sociological Association, and in his view the most profound and original. I agree with him on this.

79. Ibid., p. 342.

80. Bryan S. Turner, "Family, Property and Ideology," in Turner, *For Weber*, London: Routledge, 1981, pp. 289–317.

81. Marcuse, of course, took note of the greater sexual freedom in Western capitalist societies but classified it as "repressive desublimation" in *One-Dimensional Man*, Boston: The Beacon Press, 1964, pp. 56–83.

82. Orwell, "Reflections on Gandhi," in Sonia Orwell and Ian Angus, editors, *The Collected Essays, Journalism and Letters of George Orwell*, Volume Four, 1968, p. 467 (originally published in *Partisan Review*, January 1949).

83. J. L. Mackie, *Ethics: Inventing Right and Wrong*, Harmondsworth, Middlesex, England: Penguin Books, 1977, p. 111.

84. Christopher Lasch, *The True and Only Heaven*, New York: W. W. Norton, 1991, p. 139.

85. Freud, *Civilization*, pp. 58–59.

86. Fuller histories of the evolution of Freud's instinct theory are provided, however, in Chapter 4 of *The Ego and the Id*, pp. 41–47 and *New Introductory Lectures*, pp. 131–144.

87. Freud, *Civilization*, pp. 66.

88. Ibid., p. 69.

89. Freud, *The Ego and the Id*, pp. 28–39. See also the account in Freud, *New Introductory Lectures*, pp. 84–86.

90. Freud, *Civilization*, pp. 70–71.

91. Freud, *The Ego and the Id*, p. 53.
92. As Kaye points out in "A False Convergence," pp. 101–102. See also Kaye, "Rationalization as Sublimation: On the Cultural Analyses of Weber and Freud," *Theory, Culture & Society*, 9 (1992), pp. 45–74.
93. Jeffrey B. Abramson, *Liberation and Its Limits: The Moral and Political Thought of Freud*, New York: The Free Press, 1984, p. 134.
94. Kaye, "A False Convergence," pp. 95–99.
95. Richard Wollheim, *Sigmund Freud*, New York: The Viking Press, 1971, p. 267.
96. See Peter Gay's summary and account of the conditions under which it was written in *Freud: A Life for Our Time*, New York: W. W. Norton, 1988, pp. 543–553.
97. His last full account of the superego in *New Introductory Lectures* again mentions the ego-ideal, which was the starting point of his discussion in *The Ego and the Id*, and distinguishes the two aspects of the superego as striving toward an ideal and as restriction of impulse (pp. 92–95).
98. Abramson in *Liberation and Its Limits* notes the anti-Kantianism implied in Freud's protests against the excessive and psychologically crippling severity of "civilized" superegos, p. 46. See especially Freud's discussion of the "relentless harshness" of the superego in *New Introductory Lectures*, pp. 89–90.
99. See Abramson's critical discussion of Rieff's reading of Freud in this connection, *Liberation and Its Limits*, pp. 22–23. Michael and Deena Weinstein make their ultimately unpersuasive case for Freud's Hobbesianism less on the basis of the destructive instinct than on the argument in *Group Psychology and the Analysis of the Ego* that Freud fails to recognize the existence of direct lateral identifications as a source of group solidarity as opposed to awareness of similitude based on common identifications with an idealized leader, in their "Freud on the Problem of Order," pp. 46–56. They are right, I think, in recognizing that Freud fails adequately to account for lateral identifications, but wrong in stating that such identifications are based on difference rather than likeness and in attributing Freud's failure fully to discuss them to his alleged Hobbesianism. The Weinsteins' argument that identification with peers involves an "appreciation of otherness" (pp. 54–55) strikes me as odd; while it certainly involves "otherness" in the sense of identification with a separate being, it is surely likeness or Franklin Giddings's "consciousness of kind" that causes the identification. Mead's concept of the "generalized other" and

Habermas's claim that language inherently implies equality in its universality of reference certainly give priority to consciousness of similarity between self and other, although, as I have previously argued, both of them are primarily cognitivist in their treatment of communication.

100. Charles Rycroft equates it with three distinct processes of relating onself to someone else and then distinguishes four "types of identification" in *A Critical Dictionary of Psychoanalysis*, Harmondsworth, Middlesex, England: Penguin Books, [1968] 1972, pp. 67–68.

101. Jürgen Habermas, *The Theory of Communicative Action*. Volume 2, *Lifeworld and System: A Critique of Functionalist Reason*, Boston: The Beacon Press, 1987, pp. 1–46.

102. The relation between the idea of the self and Freud's concept of the ego is a debatable issue that need not be considered here. See Giddens, *The Constitution of Society*, p. 51, and C. Fred Alford, *The Self in Social Theory*, New Haven: Yale University Press, 1991, pp. 4–5. Freud's "ego" includes *both* Mead's "I" and "me" as is clear from *New Introductory Lectures*, p. 84. My references to the self as object obviously refer only to the "me" in Mead's sense.

103. Abram Kardiner, *The Individual and His Society*, New York: Columbia University Press, 1939, pp. 65, 72–75.

104. This seems to me a more accurate metaphor to describe much of Goffman's work than the rather overworked dramaturgical one present in his early work but later qualified if not repudiated by him. See the discussion by Tom Burns, *Erving Goffman*, London and New York: Routledge, 1992, pp. 304–310.

105. All these approaches make the mistake of beginning "at about the thirty yard line rather than at the goal line," to use Dollard's football metaphor (*Criteria for the Life History*, p. 41).

106. Harry Stack Sullivan, *Conceptions of Modern Psychiatry*, Washington, D.C.: William Alanson White Psychiatric Foundation, 1940 and 1945, pp. 9–10.

107. See the discussion in Freud, *New Introductory Lectures*, pp. 84–92.

108. Freud discusses this at some length in *The Ego and the Id*, pp. 46–47.

109. Freud, *Civilization*, pp. 87–88. One writer who correctly grasps and reproduces the subtlety of Freud's argument is Abramson, *Liberation and Its Limits*, pp. 33–35.

110. Freud, *Civilization*, p. 66.

111. See the review of opinions on the death instinct by J. LaPlanche

and J.-B. Pontalis, *The Language of Psychoanalysis*, New York: W. W. Norton, [1967] 1973, pp. 97–103.

112. For example, Lionel Trilling, *Freud and the Crisis of Our Culture*, New York: New York Psychoanalytic Society, 1955; Meyerhoff, "Freud and the Ambiguity of Culture"; and the essays by Alfred Kazin, Will Herberg, and Stanley Edgar Hyman in Benjamin Nelson, editor, *Freud and the Twentieth Century*, New York: Meridian Books, 1957; Thomas Mann, *Essays from Three Decades*, New York: Alfred A. Knopf, 1947, pp. 412–417.

113. See the discussion by Daniel Yankelovich and William Barrett, *Ego and Instinct*, New York: Random House, 1970, pp. 452–454. These authors respect Freud's tragic vision but want to transcend the conventional terms of optimism versus pessimism that dominate the debate between psychoanalytic orthodoxy and revisionism.

114. One of the most eloquent and concise assertions of this drawing on Sartre's existential concept of freedom is Carveth, "Sociology and Psychoanalysis," pp. 210–219.

115. I have been influenced here by Russell Keat's critique of Habermas in *The Politics of Social Theory*, Chicago: University of Chicago Press, 1981, pp. 92–93. Keat does not deny that the "higher" capacities, e. g. language, may influence the "lower" instinctual drives. Keat is also valuable on the issue of whether causality plays a part in intentional or purposive actions, concluding that it does, pp. 112–118. Carveth also stresses the frequent dominance of the higher faculties over the lower in "Sociology and Psychoanalysis," pp. 223–224, but does not criticize linguistic-hermeneutic readings of psychoanalysis.

116. Jessica Benjamin, *The Bonds of Love*, New York: Pantheon Books, 1988, pp. 19–24. She writes: "I suggest that the intrapsychic and the intersubjective should not be seen in opposition to each other (as they usually are) but as complementary ways of understanding the psyche" (p. 20).

117. R. G Collingwood, although he was a Hobbesian rather than a Freudian, wrote in *The New Leviathan*, Oxford: The Clarendon Press, 1942, p. 176: "A man is born a red and wrinkled lump of flesh having no will of its own at all, absolutely at the mercy of the parents by whose conspiracy he has been brought into existence. This is what no science of human community must ever forget."

118. Géza Roheim, *The Origin and Function of Culture*, especially Chapter 3, pp. 95–132; *The Riddle of the Sphinx*, Chapter 3, pp. 111–143, 196–222, 266–271.

119. Weston LaBarre, *The Human Animal*, Chicago: University of

Chicago Press, 1954; Endleman, *Psyche and Society*, pp. 67–132.

120. I have expanded somewhat on Carveth's list of convergent intellectual tendencies in "Sociology and Psychoanalysis," p. 117.

121. Carveth, *Sociologism and Psychoanalysis*, p. 61. Carveth puts it succinctly: "Most of the impulses and fantasies that succumb to repression are expressions of diffuse inclinations which have received their aims and objects from largely unintended social learning—but which come to be inhibited by later social learning" (pp. 88–89).

Chapter 6   The Disparity Between Individual and Group

1. I initially referred to the "Hobbesian question" and the "Marxist question," distinguishing them as I do here, in "The Oversocialized Conception of Man in Modern Sociology," *American Sociological Review*, 26 (April 1961), p. 184 (reprinted in *Skeptical Sociology*, New York: Columbia University Press, 1976, pp. 31–46.)

2. All of the major figures in this field—Barrington Moore, Jr., Reinhard Bendix, Charles Tilly, Theda Skocpol, Jack Goldstone—have, in the tradition of Marx, almost exclusively concerned themselves with conflict within large-scale, "class-divided" agrarian or industrial societies, ignoring the undoubtedly much rarer occurrences of social conflict in primitive or tribal societies. (But see Robert B. Edgerton, *Sick Societies: Challenging the Myth of Primitive Harmony*, New York: The Free Press, 1993.) The same applies to theorists of conflict such as Lewis Coser, C. Wright Mills, David Lockwood, Ralf Dahrendorf, John Rex, Randall Collins, and James Rule.

3. For example, Barrington Moore, Jr., *The Social Origins of Democracy and Dictatorship: Lord and Peasant in the Making of the Modern World*, Boston: The Beacon Press, 1966; Reinhard Bendix, *Kings or People: Power and the Mandate to Rule*, Berkeley and Los Angeles: University of California Press, 1978; Theda Skocpol, *States and Social Revolutions*, Cambridge: Cambridge University Press, 1979; Anthony Giddens, *The Nation-State and Violence*, Berkeley and Los Angeles: University of California Press, 1985; Daniel Chirot, *Social Change in the Modern Era*, New York: Harcourt Brace Jovanovich, 1986; Randall Collins, *Weberian Sociological Theory*, Cambridge: Cambridge University Press, 1986; Charles Tilly, *Coercion, Capital, and European States, A.D. 950–1992*, Oxford: Basil Blackwell, 1990 and 1992; Jack A. Goldstone, *Revolution and*

Rebellion in the Early Modern World, Berkeley and Los Angeles: University of California Press, 1991.

4. This is shown in considerable detail, though not, of course, under these labels, by David Lockwood, *Solidarity and Schism: "The Problem of Disorder" in Durkheimian and Marxist Sociology*, Oxford: The Clarendon Press, 1992, pp. 98–129.

5. I do not agree with Anthony Giddens that Durkheim was not concerned with the problem of order as a general problem in social theory but only with the transition from "traditional" to "modern" society. Durkheim's frequent references to primitive and ancient societies suggest that he conceived of order as a problem facing all societies and not just modern ones racked by political and economic revolutions. See Giddens, *Studies in Social and Political Theory*, London: Hutchinson, 1977, pp. 210–211.

6. Emile Durkheim, *Suicide,* Glencoe, Ill.: The Free Press, [1897] 1951.

7. Lockwood, *Solidarity and Schism*, pp. 107–110.

8. For Lockwood's discussion of Parsons in this connection, see Ibid., pp. 103–106.

9. James B. Rule, *Theories of Civil Violence*, Berkeley and Los Angeles: University of California Press, 1988, p. 11.

10. Ibid., p. 224.

11. Rule devotes an entire chapter to severe and unqualified criticism of Parsons in ibid., Chapter 5, pp. 132–169.

12. See Ibid., pp. 165–168.

13. Thomas Hobbes, *Leviathan*, Harmondsworth, Middlesex, England, Penguin Books, [1651] 1968, p. 186.

14. Jean-Jacques Rousseau, *A Discourse on Inequality*, Harmondsworth, Middlesex, England: Penguin Books, [1755] 1984, pp. 98–99.

15. Hobbes, *Leviathan*, p. 187.

16. Edward Banfield, *The Moral Basis of a Backward Society*, New York: The Free Press, 1958.

17. See Banfield's definition of "amoral familism" in ibid., p. 83.

18. Ibid., pp. 155–156.

19. Hobbes, *Leviathan*, p. 188.

20. Ibid., p. 224. I am following the text in rendering "families" as spelled on occasion but not consistently with a *y* in place of the second *i*.

21. Ibid., p. 266.

22. C. B. Macpherson, *The Political Theory of Possessive Individualism: Hobbes to Locke*, Oxford: Oxford University

Press, 1962, pp. 90–95. Macpherson develops his argument even
more fully in his 1968 "Introduction" to the Penguin Book edition
of *Leviathan*, pp. 51–60.

23. Macpherson, *The Political Theory of Possessive Individualism*,
p. 93.

24. Macpherson, "Introduction," p. 56.

25. Macpherson, *The Political Theory of Possessive Individualism*,
pp. 93–95. Macpherson's Marxist assumptions are rather more
salient in his earlier book and in "Hobbes's Bourgeois Man," in
K. C. Brown, editor, *Hobbes Studies*, Oxford: Basil Blackwell,
1965, than in his later introduction, presumably because the latter
was implicitly addressed to a wider audience as an introduction to
an acknowledged classic text.

26. Kenneth Gergen, for example, writes in *The Saturated Self*, New
York: Basic Books, 1992, p. 241: "Others write of how individualism lends itself to a sense of isolation, loneliness, and anomie; promotes forms of economic exploitation; champions a competitive as
opposed to a cooperative view of international relations; and leads
to a relentless plundering of natural resources in the service of competition and self-gratification. As individualism gains ascendance,
social life begins to approximate a Hobbesian condition of all
against all." This kind of polemical rhetoric is familiar to the point
of cliché, which is not necessarily testimony to its truth.

27. Primo Levi, *The Drowned and the Saved*, London: Abacus, [1986]
1988. Much earlier, Hannah Arendt, drawing on the earliest sur-
vivors' accounts, had described life in the camps as equivalent to a
process of *de*socialization, referring to the initial killing of "the
juridical person in man," next "the murder of the moral person in
man," and finally "the killing of man's individuality" or the sense
of "the uniqueness of the human person, in *The Origins of
Totalitarianism*, New York: Harcourt and Brace, 1951, pp.
415–426.

28. After describing the war of all against all in *De Cive*, Hobbes
wrote: "And it so happens, that through fear of each other we
think it fit to rid ourselves of this condition, and to get some fellows; that if there needs must be war, it may not yet be against all
men, nor without some helps" (*De Cive or The Citizen*, New
York: Appleton-Century Crofts, [1642] 1949, pp. 30–31).

29. Hobbes, *Leviathan*, p. 183.

30. Rule defines "divisible self-interest" on p. 33 of *Theories of Civil
Violence*; Mancur Olson, Jr., *The Logic of Collective Action*, New
York: Schocken Books, Revised Edition, 1971.

31. Hans Morganthau, *Politics Among the Nations*, New York: Alfred A. Knopf, 1949.

32. Raymond Aron, "The Anarchical Order of Power," in *History, Truth, Liberty*, Chicago: University of Chicago Press, 1985, pp. 251–273.

33. Raymond Aron, *The Century of Total War*, Garden City, N.Y.: Doubleday, 1954.

34. James S. Coleman treats the legal definition of groups as corporate persons as a momentous step in history in *Foundations of Social Theory*, Cambridge, Mass.: The Belknap Press of Harvard University Press, 1990, pp. 532–542. See also his 1992 presidential address to the American Sociological Association, "The Rational Reconstruction of Society," *American Sociological Review*, 58 (February 1993), pp. 2–4.

35. Hedley Bull, "Hobbes and the International Anarchy," *Social Research*, 48 (Winter 1981), pp. 725–756.

36. Alan Ryan, "The Nature of Human Nature in Hobbes and Rousseau," in Jonathan Benthall, editor, *The Limits of Human Nature*, London: Allen Lane, 1972, p. 11.

37. Hobbes, *Leviathan*, p. 187.

38. Gerhard Lenski, *Power and Privilege: A Theory of Social Stratification*, New York: McGraw-Hill, 1966, pp. 214–216.

39. Hobbes, *Leviathan*, p. 16l.

40. Randall Collins and Michael Makowsky, *The Discovery of Society*, New York: Random House, 1972.

41. The title of a once influential book by Lawrence K. Frank, *Society as the Patient: Essays in Culture and Personality*, New Brunswick, N.J.: Rutgers University Press, 1948.

42. Philip Rieff, *The Triumph of the Therapeutic: Uses of Faith after Freud*, New York: Harper Torchbooks, [1966] 1968. Christopher Lasch recently noted for how long a time political liberals have adopted a therapeutic language in blaming "society" rather than individuals for various social ills. I had a teacher in the early l940s who liked to pontificate repellently that "race prejudice is a sour pimple on the stomach of a sick society." See Lasch, "For Shame," *New Republic*, August 10, 1992, pp. 32–33.

43. Hobbes, *Leviathan*, p. 186.

44. See ibid., p. 237.

45. Michael Hechter ably summarizes the standard sociological position in *Principles of Group Solidarity*, Berkeley and Los Angeles: University of California Press, 1987, pp. 15–17, which he rejects though ultimately favoring a rational choice rather than a psychoanalytic theory of human motivation.

46. For example, Martha Wolfenstein and Nathan Leites, *Movies: A Psychological Study*, Glencoe, Ill.: The Free Press, 1950; many examples are included in Robert Endleman, *Personality and Social Life: A Text and Reader*, New York: Random House, 1967.

47. Notably in Christopher Lasch's *The Culture of Narcissism*, New York: W. W. Norton, 1978, and Lasch, *The Minimal Self*, New York: W. W. Norton, 1984. See my critique of the first book and Lasch's earlier *Haven in a Heartless World: The Family Besieged*, New York: Harper and Row, 1977, "Bourgeois Values without the Bourgeoisie? The Cultural Criticism of Christopher Lasch," *Dissent*, 26 (Summer 1979), pp. 308–314.

48. Erich Fromm and Abram Kardiner were by no means the only but were certainly the two most systematically psychoanalytic theorists and practitioners of this approach in Fromm, *Escape from Freedom*, New York: Farrar and Rinehart, 1941; Kardiner, *The Individual and His Society*, New York: Columbia University Press, 1939, and *The Psychological Frontiers of Society*, New York: Columbia University Press, 1945. David Riesman's *The Lonely Crowd*, New Haven: Yale University Press, 1950 (with the assistance of Reuel Denney and Nathan Glazer) was the most famous and influential book of this genre, although arguably it was less an example of national character analysis than of the broader, looser—and, not incidentally, often more plausible—kind of psychocultural interpretation referred to in the preceding paragraph of the text. See Robert Gutman and Dennis H. Wrong, "Riesman's Typology of Character," in Seymour Martin Lipset and Leo Lowenthal, editors, *Culture and Social Character: The Work of David Riesman Reviewed*, New York: The Free Press, 1961, pp. 295–315.

49. The best critical analysis of this method that I know is Reinhard Bendix, "Individual Personality and Compliant Behavior," *American Journal of Sociology*, 58 (November 1952) pp. 293–303.

50. For further discussion of these issues, see Gutman and Wrong, "Riesman's Typology of Character," pp. 302–311

51. See the discussion and review of the relevant literature by Robert A. LeVine, *Culture, Behavior, and Personality*, Chicago: Aldine, 1973, especially Chapter 3, pp. 43–59.

52. "Reflections upon War and Death" (1915) in Freud, *Character and Culture*, from *The Collected Papers of Sigmund Freud*, edited by Philip Rieff, New York: Collier Books, 1963, p. 112. I have used the original translated title of this essay, "Thoughts for the Times on War and Death," in the text.

53. Reinhold Niebuhr, *Moral Man and Immoral Society*, New York: Scribner's, 1932: "The selfishness of human communities must be regarded as an inevitability" (p. 272).

54. Freud, "Reflections upon War and Death" (1915), p. 112.

55. Philip Rieff, *Freud, The Mind of the Moralist*, New York: Doubleday Anchor Books, [1959] 1961, pp. 272–273.

56. Ibid., pp. 273–274.

57. Sigmund Freud, *Civilization and Its Discontents*, New York: W. W. Norton, [1930] 1961, pp. 61–62; see also Freud, *Group Psychology and the Analysis of the Ego*, New York: Bantam Books, [1921] 1960, p. 42.

58. Theodore Adorno, Else Frenkel-Brunswick, Daniel J. Levinson, and R. Nevitt Sanford, *The Authoritarian Personality*, New York: Harper and Row, 1950.

59. Sigmund Freud, "Why War?" (1932) in Freud, *Character and Culture*, pp. 134–147.

60. Rieff, *Freud: The Mind of the Moralist*, p. 273.

61. Freud, "Why War?" p. 143.

62. Ibid., p. 145.

63. Freud, *Civilization and its Discontents*, p. 91 (my emphasis).

64. Norman O. Brown, *Life against Death*, New York: Doubleday Anchor Books, 1960.

65. In a book concerned with the current condition of the humanities, David Bromwich writes of David Hume, Edmund Burke, William James, and Michael Oakeshott, his major examplars of the proper approach to cultural and intellectual tradition (all of them pre- or, in Oakeshott's case, non-Freudian): "What these thinkers share is an interest in human nature and a belief that *every discussion of individual or collective identity implies a reading of human nature.*" *Politics by Other Means: Higher Education and Group Thinking*, New Haven: Yale University Press, 1992 (my emphasis).

66. Riesman, *The Lonely Crowd*. For a full discussion of Freud's attitude to America see Howard L. Kaye, "Why Freud Hated America," *The Wilson Quarterly*, 17 (Spring 1993), pp. 118–125.

67. Rieff, *Freud: The Mind of the Moralist*, pp. 270–275.

68. Freud, *Group Psychology*, p. 78. See also pp. 21–25.

69. Franz Neumann, "Anxiety and Politics," pp. 269–290 and E. V. Walter, "The Politics of Decivilization," pp. 291–308, in Morris R. Stein, Arthur J. Vidich, and David Manning White, editors, *Identity and Anxiety: Survival of the Person in Mass Society*, Glencoe, Ill.: The Free Press, 1960. Also Rieff, *Freud: The Mind of the Moralist*, pp. 252–260.

70. J. LaPlanche and J.-B. Pontalis, *The Language of Psychoanalysis*, New York: W. W. Norton, [1964] 1973, pp. 349–356.

71. Howard L. Kaye, "A False Convergence: Freud and the Hobbesian Problem of Order," *Sociological Theory*, 9 (Spring 1991), pp. 101–102.

72. Erik H. Erikson, *Identity: Youth and Crisis*, New York: W. W. Norton, 1968, pp. 298–299.

73. Max Horkheimer and Samuel H. Flowerman, editors, *Studies in Prejudice*, Vols. 1–5, New York: Harper and Bros., 1950–1952.

74. See Dennis H. Wrong, "The Psychology of Prejudice and the Future of Anti-Semitism in America," *European Journal of Sociology*, 6 (1965), pp. 314–315.

75. See Doug McAdam, John D. McCarthy, and Mayer N. Zald, "Social Movements," in Neil J. Smelser, editor, *Handbook of Sociology*, Newbury Park, Calif.: Sage Publications, 1990, pp. 697–698.

76. Anthony Giddens, *Sociology*, New York: W. W. Norton, 1991, pp. 769–770; see also the distinctions drawn by Edward W. Lehman, *The Viable Polity*, Philadelphia: Temple University Press, 1992, p. 49.

77. This has recently been pointed out by Charles Lindholm in *Charisma*, London and New York: Basil Blackwell, 1990. See my review of this book, "The Magic Touch," *New Republic*, April 5, 1991, pp. 41–43.

78. Lindholm, *Charisma*, pp. 27–33; Lockwood, *Solidarity and Schism*, pp. 34–35.

79. Raymond Aron, *Memoires*, Paris: Juilliard, 1983, p. 94.

80. Note Freud's description of the leader, the father figure at the beginning of history, in *Group Psychology*, pp. 71–72.

81. Olson, *The Logic of Collective Action*, pp. 60–65, 133–134.

82. Georg Simmel, *Conflict and the Web of Group-Affiliations*, Glencoe, Ill.: The Free Press, [1922 and 1923] 1955, pp. 14–123; Lewis A. Coser, *The Functions of Social Conflict*, Glencoe, Ill.: The Free Press, 1956, pp. 87–110.

83. I am here following John Torrance's discussion of what he calls primary, secondary, and tertiary forms of solidarity in *Estrangement, Alienation and Exploitation: A Sociological Approach to Historical Materialism*, New York: Columbia University Press, 1977, pp. 126–128. See also Dennis H. Wrong, *Power: Its Forms, Bases and Uses*, Chicago: University of Chicago Press, [1979] 1988, pp. 146–156.

84. Edward W. Lehman suggested this point to me with military training in mind.

85. Christopher B. Browning, *Ordinary Men: Reserve Police Battalion 101 and the Final Solution in Poland,* New York: Harper/Collins, 1992, p. 170. The historian István Deák writes: "In none of the vast literature on the Holocaust is there, so far as I know, the record of a single case of a German policeman or member of the SS having been severely reprimanded, imprisoned, or sent to the front—much less shot—for his refusal to participate in mass murder" ("Strategies of Hell," *New York Review of Books,* October, 1992, p. 10).

86. Stanley Milgram, *Obedience to Authority: An Experimental View,* New York: Harper and Row, 1969, p. xi.

87. Stephen Whitfield, *Into the Dark: Hannah Arendt and Totalitarianism,* Philadelphia: Temple University Press, 1980, p. 226. See also Barrington Moore, Jr., *Injustice: The Social Bases of Obedience and Revolt,* White Plains, N.Y.: M. E. Sharpe, 1978, pp. 94–100; Zygmunt Bauman, *Modernity and the Holocaust,* Cambridge: The Polity Press, 1989, Chapter 6, pp. 151–168.

88. Milgram, *Obedience to Authority,* p. 1.

89. Ibid., p. 6; see also Browning, *Ordinary Men,* p. 216, n. 5; and Bauman, *Modernity and the Holocaust,* pp. 19–20.

90. Barrington Moore, Jr., also expresses some reservations about the artificiality of Milgram's laboratory experiments in *Injustice: The Social Bases of Obedience and Revolt,* pp. 102–103.

91. Hannah Arendt, *Eichmann in Jerusalem: A Report on the Banality of Evil,* Harmondsworth, Middlesex, England: Penguin Books, [1963] 1965.

92. Richard A. Schweder, "Dialogues amid the Deluge," *New York Times Book Review,* September 20, 1992, p. 54.

93. One of the best earlier expressions of it was by Herbert Luethy, "The Wretched Little Demon That Was Hitler," *Commentary,* 17 (February 1954), pp. 129–138. Luethy wrote: "The problem Hitler's German biographers struggle with is. . .how to reconcile the gravity, the catastrophic magnitude of the events, with the vulgar mediocrity of the individual who initiated them; and, if not to explain this, at least to make it conceivable how a great and civilized nation could identify itself with a spiritually and morally retarded being" (p. 131). For other anticipations of the linking of Nazi banality with evil, see Whitfield's survey of them in *Into the Dark,* pp. 212–214.

94. The concept of "radical evil" comes from Kant. See the discussion of Arendt's use of it in *The Origins of Totalitarianism* and its apparent—though not necessarily real—inconsistency with the

"banality of evil" thesis asserted in her *Eichmann in Jerusalem,* by Whitfield, *Into the Dark,* pp. 102–104, 153, 211–219; and by George Kateb, *Hannah Arendt: Politics, Conscience, Evil,* Totowa, N.J.: Rowman and Allanheld, 1983, pp. 78–80.

95. Arendt, *The Origins of Totalitarianism,* p. 319.

96. Luethy, "The Wretched Little Demon That Was Hitler," p. 138.

97. As in the case of Damiens, the failed regicide whose punishment is so unforgettably described in the opening pages of Michel Foucault's *Discipline and Punish: The Birth of the Prison,* New York: Vintage Books, [1975] 1979, pp. 3–6.

98. It is worth citing Arendt and Luethy because both of them wrote less than a decade after the Final Solution when reactions to it were still fresh and not yet mediated by the mass of interpretations, rhetorical formulae, and ritualized condemnations that have since accumulated. Also, although Arendt is today a famous name while Luethy is scarcely remembered, they both were regular contributors to such journals as *Commentary, Partisan Review, Encounter, Der Monat,* and *Preuves* that played a major role in expressing and shaping the outlook of Western intellectuals toward the destruction of the Jews. See my discussion of totalitarianism and the history of the concept in a review-essay on Whitfield's *Into the Dark,* "Books in Review," *Society,* 18 (May/June 1981), pp. 68–71.

99. Arendt, *Eichmann in Jerusalem,* p. 150. Arendt said much the same thing a decade earlier in Carl J. Friedrich, editor, *Totalitarianism,* New York: Grosset and Dunlap, 1954, p. 78, further evidence of the fundamental continuity between *The Origins of Totalitarianism* and *Eichmann in Jerusalem.*

100. Gerald Reitlinger, *The SS, Alibi of a Nation, 1922–1945,* New York: The Viking Press, 1957, p. 288.

101. Christopher Browning describes just such a case among the police officers actually directing the mass murder of Jews in rural Poland. The man in question was in fact one of the few members of the police battalion who was an ardent Nazi, but he managed to acquire acute intestinal ailments that prevented his presence at any actions against Jews (*Ordinary Men,* Chapter 13, "The Strange Health of Captain Hoffman," pp. 114–120). Browning concludes: "If mass murder was giving Hoffman stomach pains, it was a fact that he was deeply ashamed of and sought to overcome to the best of his ability" (p. 120).

102. See ibid., p. 300, citing Rieff, *Freud: The Mind of the Moralist,* pp. 273–274.

103. Arendt, noting situations in which Eichmann tried to frustrate the directives of Himmler, his superior who was trying to make deals at the end of the war to save the lives of Jews, develops a rather tortuous argument to the effect that Eichmann was nevertheless still the faithful, pliant bureaucrat because he saw himself as the servant of the *Führer's* "law" that took precedence over anything else (*Eichmann in Jerusalem*, pp. 146–150). Whitfield points out the questionable nature of this argument, noting that Hitler himself had even shown faint signs of relaxing his order to exterminate all Jews (*Into the Dark*, pp. 219–220.)

104. See the citations in note 93 above.

105. Christopher Browning's *Ordinary Men* is about just such men.

106. Zygmunt Bauman is certainly correct in stating in *Modernity and the Holocaust* that these specific expressions of modernity were necessary conditions for the occurrence of the Final Solution (pp. 7, 9, 13, 15–17). He goes, however, too far in suggesting that its true horror is its congruence with modernity and that this has been systematically overlooked; he goes rather further, I think, than Arendt who strikes the same note "in her more Heideggerian moments," to quote myself in "Books in Review," *Society*, p. 71. The manifestation of specifically modern "instrumental rationality" in the genocide carried out by the Nazis was commented on at the very beginning when the events first became known just after the Second World War—by, for example, Dwight Macdonald in the journal he founded and edited, *Politics*. Yet applied science, industrialism, and bureaucracy are *methods and means* rather than ends or ultimate values in themselves. If they account for the scale of the Nazis' success and even for the possibility of carrying out mass murder in an impersonal way that creates distance between the murderers and their victims, they hardly explain the goal itself. That the instrumental rationality fostered by the Enlightenment found its fullest and ultimate expression in the Final Solution is the thesis of Max Horkheimer and Theodore Adorno in their immensely influential book, originally written in the early 1940s, *The Dialectic of the Enlightenment*, New York: The Seabury Press, [1944] 1969. The thesis has always struck me as a thoroughly perverse and literally reactionary one, a self-indulgent exercise in linking the "absolute zero" of the Shoah to everything the authors happened to dislike about the modern world.

107. Bauman makes a major point of the difference between these levels in explaining the Holocaust, identifying the "societal" level

with a state-directed policy of genocide acting through bureauratic organizations at odds with the "social" essence of human nature, *Modernity and the Holocaust*, pp. 178–179. He also explicitly identifies "the solution of the Hobbesian problem" with the societal level and rejects it as an explanation of "moral tendency." He identifies the problem of order as such exclusively with the control of group conflict in a large-scale society, while acknowledging that "moral capacity" is "conceivable only . . .in a social context." In short, his "Hobbesian problem of order" is equivalent to my "marxian problem" of group conflict and his "social context" of morality is equivalent to my "hobbesian problem" of socialization or the social shaping of human nature. I do not therefore disagree with his insistence on the "pre-societal sources of morality," which does not deny its *social* sources, although as indicated above in note 106 I think he is too inclined to blame "modernity" for the essential evil of the Final Solution.

108. Ralf Dahrendorf, *Class and Class Conflict in Industrial Society*, Stanford, Calif.: Stanford University Press, 1959.

109. Amatai Etzioni, *The Moral Dimension: Toward a New Economics*, New York: The Free Press, 1987, pp. 23–31. See also Michael Hechter, "Should Values Be Written Out of the Social Scientists' Lexicon?" *Sociological Theory*, 10 (Fall 1992), pp. 214–230.

110. What Mead and his followers called "symbol" and distinguished from "sign," Ferdinand de Saussure and the school of structural linguistics that he created called "sign" and divided into the two parts of "signifier" and "signified." For an elaborate formalization of the Meadian distinction, see Charles W. Morris, *Signs, Language and Behavior*, New York: Prentice-Hall, 1946.

111. Rule, *Theories of Civil Violence*, p. 39.

112. Etzioni, *The Moral Dimension*, Chapter 4, pp. 51–66. Etzioni's entire book is essentially devoted to showing with ample citations of the relevant empirical evidence that human motivations are not monolithically dominated by the utility-maximizing instrumental rationality of the economists.

113. Etzioni, while defending the reality of conduct that is not driven solely or even primarily by self-interest, distances himself also from the oversocialized model cherished by some sociologists and traditional conservatives (*The Moral Dimension*, pp. 6–8). The example of the breakfast-table egoist is suggested by Gary Becker's influential *A Treatise on the Family*, Cambridge, Mass.: Harvard University Press, 1981. See also Etzioni's criticism of Becker's argument that the decision to have children resembles the

purchase of "consumer durables" (*The Moral Dimension*, pp. 77–78).

114. "Object" as used by psychoanalysts refers to anything external to the individual psyche, including other persons. The term in no way implies failure to recognize any difference between sentient human beings and material things. For good summaries of the psychoanalytic uses of the term see J. LaPlanche and J.-B. Pontalis, *The Language of Psychoanalysis*, pp. 273–281; also Charles Rycroft, *A Critical Dictionary of Psychoanalysis*, Harmondsworth, Middlesex, England: Penguin Books, [1968] 1972, pp. 100–101.

115. For useful summaries see Christopher Lasch, *The Culture of Narcissism,*. pp. 31–51, 90–94, 178–180; and Lasch, *The Minimal Self*, pp. 180, 182. This applies at least to the "weak" and presumably much more common form of narcissistic personality rather than to the "strong" type mentioned below on p. 000 and in note 128.

116. Coleman, *Foundations of Social Theory*, p. 241.

117. James S. Coleman, "Message from the Chair," *Perspectives*, The Theory Section Newsletter, American Sociological Association, 13 (October 1991), pp. 1–2.

118. Coleman, *Foundations of Social Theory*, pp. 292–293.

119. Ibid., p. 507.

120. Ibid, pp. 31–32.

121. Ibid., pp. 292–293.

122. Charles Tilly, "Individualism Askew," *American Journal of Sociology*, 96 (January 1991), pp. 1007–1011.

123. See pp. 118–119 of this text.

124. Coleman, *Foundations of Social Theory*, pp. 517–518.

125. Ibid., pp. 519–520.

126. Tilly, "Individualism Askew," p. 1008.

127. See the argument above, pp. 000.

128. Sigmund Freud, "Libidinal Types," [1931] 1963, in Freud, *Character and Culture*, pp. 210–214. Philip Slater describes the type as a "strong-ego narcissist" able to carry out a "robust form of narcissistic withdrawal" from social obligations in "On Social Regression," *American Sociological Review*, 28 (June 1963), pp. 345–346.

129. Slater, "On Social Regression," p. 345.

130. Richard Münch, "Rational Choice Theory: A Critical Assessment and Its Explanatory Power," in James S. Coleman and Thomas J. Fararo, editors, *Rational Choice Theory: Advocacy and Critique*,

Newbury Park, Calif.: Sage Publications, 1992, pp. 156–157. For Coleman's rather banal reinterpretation of it, see *Foundations of Social Theory*, pp. 6–10.

131. Coleman, *Foundations of Social Theory*, p. 18 (his emphasis).

132. This is a major theme of Coleman's in *Foundations of Social Theory*, pp. 584–587, and "The Rational Reconstruction of Society," pp. 1–17.

133. As some of his critics have pointed out, it is perhaps "no accident" that Coleman began his professional career as a chemical engineer. For an excellent recent discussion of the inadequacy of "positivism" or nomological-deductive reasoning in social science, see two articles by Joseph M. Bryant in *Canadian Journal of Sociology: "Positivism redivivus?* A Critique of Recent Proposals for Reforming Sociological Theory (and Related Foibles)," 17 (No. 1, 1992), pp. 29–53; and "Towards a Respectable, Reflexive, Scientific Sociology: A Note on the Reformation Required," 17 (No. 3, 1992), pp. 322–331. Bryant's argument is primarily directed against Jonathan Turner's advocacy of a positivistic sociology, but it has relevance also to rational choice theory.

134. See the purely descriptive account based on behavioral criteria alone in the *Diagnostic and Statistical Manual of Mental Disorders*, Third Edition, American Psychiatric Association, 1980, under the heading of "Antisocial Personality Disorder," pp. 45–50. The types exhibiting this "disorder" are distinguished according to combinations of two binary classifications: "Undersocialized/socialized" and "aggressive/nonaggressive." Coleman, despite his model of actors "unconstrained by social norms," notes that some "internalization" of norms is universal except for "sociopaths and small children" (*Foundations of Social Theory*, p. 294).

135. As Freud held in *Civilization and Its Discontents* in contending that society required the partial repression of Eros in order to make possible the "aim-inhibited erotic" bonds that were essential for the formation of extra-familial collectivities (pp. 49–57).

136. Slater writes in his sociological restatement of Freud emphasizing the social necessity of preventing individual, dyadic, and familial withdrawal from obligations to the larger society: "Only when an individual falls in love with a stranger while some of his libido is still harnessed to an incestuous object, will he be inclined to attach himself to a larger agglomeration which embraces them both. In so doing he sacrifices total gratification and gains whatever benefits accrue from societal existence" ("On Social Regression," p. 364).

Chapter 7   Group Conflict, Order, and Disorder

1. Theda Skocpol, *States and Revolutions*, Cambridge: Cambridge University Press, 1979; Jack A. Goldstone, *Revolution and Rebellion in the Early Modern World*, Berkeley and Los Angeles: University of California Press, 1991; Charles Tilly, *Coercion, Capital, and European States, A.D. 950–1992*, Oxford and Cambridge: Blackwell, 1990 and 1992, especially pp. 186–187.

2. In Raymond Aron's lapidary words: "Since, under a July sun, bourgeois Europe entered the century of total war, men have lost control of their history and have been dragged along by the contradictory promptings of techniques and passions." *The Century of Total War*, Garden City, N.Y.: Doubleday, 1954, p. 55.

3. Ibid., p. 164.

4. *Village Voice*, November 24, 1992, p. 5.

5. Freud's "narcissism of minor differences" are a case in point as are Coser's "safety-valve institutions," in Lewis A. Coser, *The Functions of Social Conflict*, Glencoe, Ill.: The Free Press, 1956, pp. 41–48.

6. Lewis A. Coser, *The Functions of Social Conflict*; Coser, *Continuities in the Study of Conflict*, New York: The Free Press, 1967.

7. After contending that conflict is not "a sufficient condition for change," Percy S. Cohen asserts: "The simple point is that conflict may lead to impasse not to change!" Not only does he end this statement with an exclamation point but he also italicizes it (Cohen, *Modern Social Theory*, New York: Basic Books, 1968, p. 184).

8. Jeffrey Alexander describes this controversy as "the most widely acknowledged debate in the recent period" in *Theoretical Logic in Sociology*, Volume 1, *Positivism, Presuppositions and Current Controversies*, Berkeley and Los Angeles: University of California Press, 1982, p. 50.

9. Coser, writing in the 1950s, meant to stress its stabilizing effects as the very title of his book, "the *functions* of social conflict," indicated, but he certainly in no way denied that conflict could also be a motor of change.

10. Ralf Dahrendorf, *Class and Class Conflict in Industrial Society*, Stanford, Calif.: Stanford University Press, 1958. Dahrendorf's earlier essays polemicizing against Parsons and his followers, and which were particularly influential at the time of their publication, are included in his *Essays in the Theory of Society*, Stanford, Calif.: Stanford University Press, 1968.

11. See, for example, in addition to his *Class and Class Conflict in Industrial Society*, Dahrendorf's essay "In Praise of Thrasymachus," in *Essays in the Theory of Society*, pp. 129–150.

12. Frank Parkin, *Marxism and Class Theory: A Bourgeois Critique*, New York: Columbia University Press, 1979, p. 25.

13. Coser was a refugee from Nazi Germany; so was Reinhard Bendix, who should be included among the conflict theorists although he usually isn't; Dahrendorf is German, the son of a leading Social Democrat who had been imprisoned by the Nazis and who himself spent a short time in a concentration camp as a teenager; David Lockwood is British; John Rex is a South African expatriated to Britain. Three Americans are usually listed as conflict theorists: Mills studied and later collaborated with Hans Gerth, a German refugee scholar; Barrington Moore, Jr., was originally a Sovietologist whose first two books were on Soviet politics; Randall Collins, a generation younger than the others, who has done the most in recent years to appropriate and publicize the label "conflict theory," especially in *Conflict Theory: Toward An Explanatory Science*, New York: Academic Press, 1975, studied at Berkeley at a time when the sociology faculty there included not only Bendix, but Seymour Martin Lipset, Philip Selznick, Nathan Glazer, and William Petersen, all of whom had been youthful radicals in a Trotskyist milieu in New York City, and Leo Lowenthal, an original member of the Frankfurt School of revisionist Marxism. I myself fit the pattern as a Canadian, once active in the socialist CCF party, who became much influenced by the New York intellectual circles linked to such journals as *Partisan Review, The New Leader, Politics, Commentary*, and *Dissent*. Alvin Gouldner should also be included among the major conflict theorists, although his relevant writings were for the most part produced in the late sixties and seventies rather than the fifties (especially *The Coming Crisis of Western Sociology*, New York: Basic Books, 1970) despite the fact that he was of the same generation as most of the others. He had been a member of the Communist party in his youth in New York City and continued to affirm a version of Marxism despite his severe criticism of virtually all other versions.(See especially his *The Two Marxisms*, New York: Seabury Press, 1980, and also my article "A Note on Marx and Weber in Gouldner's Thought," *Theory and Society*, 11 [1982], pp. 899–905.) Parsons himself supplied a list of forty-five students who had worked with him at Harvard which includes only four non-Americans (one of the forty-one classified as

American, however, was actually a Canadian who had originally been a German refugee as a teenager); see Nicholas C. Mullins, *Theories and Theory Groups in Contemporary American Sociology*, New York: Harper and Row, 1973, p. 51.

14. Randall Collins notes with approval the concrete, empirical grounding of current "conflict theory," which was less true, he maintains, of the earlier conflict theorists who were responding directly to Parsons. The latter group presumably incudes Coser, Dahrendorf, Lockwood, and Rex, though hardly Moore and Mills. Yet the first-named group were writing essentially out of a sense of social and historical reality that led them to question the abstract harmonies of social order postulated by Parsons. See Collins, "Conflict Theory and the Advance of Macro-Historical Sociology," in George Ritzer, editor, *Frontiers of Social Theory*, New York: Columbia University Press, 1990, p. 73.

15. Percy Cohen presents a highly schematic contrast between "consensus/integration" theory (mainly Parsons) and "conflict/coercion" theory (mainly Dahrendorf) in *Modern Social Theory*, p. 167.

16. The efforts at combination and their inadequacies are cogently discussed by David Lockwood in *Solidarity and Schism: "The Problem of Disorder" in Durkheimian and Marxist Sociology*, Oxford: The Clarendon Press, 1992, pp. 385–392.

17. Lockwood describes Parsons's *The Social System*, published in 1951 (Glencoe, Ill.: The Free Press), as "the key work of normative functionalism" (*Solidarity and Schism*, p. 381).

18. Talcott Parsons, "Individual Autonomy and Social Pressure: A Reply to Dennis H. Wrong," *Psychoanalysis and the Psychoanalytic Review*, 49 (Summer 1962), p. 71. I recall at the American Sociological Association annual meeting in 1963 hearing Alvin Gouldner, after presenting an early version of his criticism of Parsons in *The Coming Crisis of Western Sociology*, report that Parsons had recently observed with apparent surprise that many of the people criticizing him seemed to be doing so from a Marxist point of view. Gouldner asked rhetorically, "Who in the world did he expect to criticize him if not Marxists? Would anybody be surprised to learn that owners of taverns were the leading opponents of Prohibition?"

19. This was the major target of Parkin's *Marxism and Class Theory*.

20. I have in mind the Chicago sociologists of the 1920s and 1930s who, influenced by Simmel and Leopold von Wiese, regarded "conflict," "cooperation," "accommodation," and "assimilation" as the four basic "social processes."

21. This was noted in one of his earlier publications on the subject by Randall Collins, "A Comparative Approach to Political Sociology," in Reinhard Bendix, editor, *State and Society: A Reader in Political Sociology*, Boston: Little, Brown, 1968, p. 51. Despite this, Collins has persisted in describing his own work as "conflict theory," which would seem to privilege conflict over consensus or cooperation as a more basic social process. Yet precisely the establishment of consensus and solidarity through ritualized chains of interaction has been a major theme of Collins's theorizing.

22. I first used the oversocialized/overintegrated duality in "The Oversocialized Conception of Man in Modern Sociology," *American Sociological Review*, 26 (April 1961), pp. 183–193. Lockwood reiterates the phrase with reference to normative functionalists in *Solidarity and Schism*, p. 337.

23. Lockwood, *Solidarity and Schism*, p. 173.

24. Lockwood devotes an entire chapter to "fatalism," which, he argues, is mentioned but then minimized by Durkheim in *Solidarity and Schism*, pp. 38–66.

25. The famous—or infamous—Davis-Moore functional theory of stratification, one of the very earliest uses of functional analysis in sociology, for example, does not rely on a normativist argument that assumes value-consensus. Essentially, it applies a market model assuming only that material satisfactions and prestige are universally desired rewards. This is regularly overlooked by critics of functionalism who often focus on the Davis-Moore theory and read it as a consensual theory of social inequality. See the original, many times reprinted, article by Kingsley Davis and Wilbert E. Moore, "Some Principles of Social Stratification," *American Sociological Review*, 10 (April 1945), pp. 242–249. My criticism of this article, "The Functional Theory of Stratification: Some Neglected Considerations," appeared in *American Sociological Review*, 24 (December 1959), pp. 772–782, and is reprinted in *Skeptical Sociology*, New York: Columbia University Press, 1976, pp. 103–120. For examples of the normative functionalist view of stratification, see Parsons's two essays on social stratification in *Essays in Sociological Theory*, Revised Edition, Glencoe, Ill.: The Free Press, 1954, pp. 69–88, 386–439; and Bernard Barber, *Social Stratification*, New York: Harcourt, Brace and World, 1957, pp. 1–16.

26. Gary Thom, *The Human Nature of Social Discontent*, Totowa, N.J.: Rowman and Allanheld, 1983, p. 45.

27. Ibid., p. 43.

28. Axel van den Berg, *The Immanent Utopia: Marxism on the State and the State of Marxism*, Princeton, N.J.: Princeton University Press, 1988, pp. 43–77.

29. Thom, *The Human Nature of Social Discontent*, p. 47. "Utopian" would be a more appropriate adjective preceding "fantasy" than "liberal" in the quotation. Presumably, Thom has in mind the kind of totally permissive "liberalism" that was popular in some circles in America in the 1960s and after.

30. Ralf Dahrendorf, "Out of Utopia: Towards a Reorientation of Sociological Analysis," *American Journal of Sociology*, 64 (September, 1958), pp. 115–127. (Reprinted in *Essays in the Theory of Society*, Stanford, Calif.: Stanford University Press, 1968.)

31. J. G. Merquior in *Western Marxism*, London: Paladin Books, 1986, pp. 27–29, 56, notes the de-individualizing nature of both Hegel's "generic man" and Marx's version of it as man's "species-being."

32. Louis Althusser, however, maintained that "ideology" would still characterize the layman's understanding in communist society as opposed to the "scientificity" of the Marxist expert's understanding. See Alex Callinicos, *Althusser's Marxism*, London: Pluto Press, 1976, pp. 61–62, 97–101.

33. According to Benedict Anderson, "All communities larger than primordial villages of face-to-face contact (and perhaps even there) are imagined"(*Imagined Communities: Reflections on Nationalism*, London: Verso, 1983, p. 15). Michael Walzer observes, "Beyond the family and neighborhood, all communities are imagined. . ." in "Nationalism and Ethnic Particularism," a symposium, *Tikkun*, 7 (November-December, 1992), p. 55.

34. Jon Elster, *Making Sense of Marx*, Cambridge: Cambridge University Press, 1988, pp. 27–28. Elster writes: "Intentional explanation cites the *intended* consequences of behavior in order to account for it. Functional explanation cites the *actual* consequences. More specifically, to explain behavior functionally involves demonstrating that it has *beneficial* consequences for someone or something" (p. 27).

35. Anthony Giddens's first and fullest description and criticism of this view, which is his fundamental criticism of functionalism restated in many of his writings, is to be found as one of the reprinted essays in *Studies in Social and Political Theory*, London: Hutchinson, 1977, pp. 96–129.

36. David Lockwood, "Appendix: Social Integration and System Integration," in his *Solidarity and Schism*, pp. 399–412.

37. See, for example, Daniel Bell, *The Cultural Contradictions of Capitalism*, New York: Basic Books, 1976, p. 10. Alvin W. Gouldner also pointed out the similarity between the emphasis on norms and values in some varieties of functionalism and single-factor theories that sociologists had widely repudiated in *For Sociology*, New York: Basic Books, 1974, p. 265.

38. By Jonathan H. Turner in *The Structure of Sociological Theory*, Fourth Edition, Chicago: The Dorsey Press, 1989, pp. 165–183. It should be noted of Coser that he did not support the tightly integrated holistic or systemic conception of functionalism, but rather upheld his teacher Robert Merton's much looser view in which functions are seen as possibly contributing to the necessary conditions of existence of groups within a larger social system and not necessarily to the system as a whole. Coser mainly pointed out that conflict often promoted the stability of groups or institutions rather than undermining them, as appeared to be widely assumed at the time he wrote in regarding conflict implicitly as an undesirable phenomenon. In the sixties conflict came to be viewed by left-oriented sociologists as desirable precisely because it was seen as destabilizing.

39. Gouldner, *For Sociology*, p. 190.

40. Martin Jay, *Marxism and Totality*, Berkeley and Los Angeles: University of California Press, 1984. See also Merquior, *Western Marxism*, pp. 76–78.

41. For an acute and valuable review of these, see J. G. Merquior's, *From Prague to Paris: A Critique of Structural and Post-Structural Thought*, London: Verso, 1986, pp. 6–17, 189–192.

42. Goffman, whom I knew briefly as an undergraduate and fellow sociology major at the University of Toronto, was once a strong adherent of Whitehead. His sense that social life should be grasped in its actual "articulation" in experience rather than through the mechanical application of abstract concepts owed something to Whitehead, as did his attraction to Durkheim and functionalism that has been properly stressed by Randall Collins in opposition to the generally held view that Goffman was first and foremost a "symbolic interactionist." See Collins, *Theoretical Sociology*, New York: Harcourt Brace Jovanovich, 1988, pp. 203–205. For the earliest sociological influences on Goffman, see Yves Winkins, "Portrait de Sociologue en Jeune Homme," in *Erving Goffman, Leurs Moments et Leurs Hommes*, collected and edited by Yves Winkins, Paris: Seuil/Minuit, 1988, pp. 21–26. I was actually Winkins's major and for the most part only source for his account of Goffman's year at Toronto when he was first

exposed to sociology. He had been a philosophy major at the University of Manitoba where he had presumably come into contact with Whitehead's work. He frequently used to cite the ideas of Whitehead's magnum opus, *Process and Reality*.

43. Walter B. Cannon, *The Wisdom of the Body*, New York: W. W. Norton, 1932.

44. Giddens's insistence on the "knowledgeability of the actor" as central to the "double hermeneutic" he attributes to social science is crucial to his rejection of functionalism. See especially his fullest criticism of functionalism in *Studies in Social and Political Theory*, pp. 96–129. Many passages from later works could also be cited; his insistence on the "knowledgeability of the actors" who produce social structures as a "skilled accomplishment" is broached at the very beginning of *The Constitution of Society*, Cambridge: The Polity Press, 1984, pp. xxxvii, 2–5; see also pp. 26, 220. "Functionalists. . .discount agents' reasons in favor of society's reasons," as he put it in *A Contemporary Critique of Historical Materialism*, Berkeley and Los Angeles: University of California Press, 1981, p. 18.

45. Jürgen Habermas, *The Theory of Communicative Action*, Volume 2, *Lifeworld and System: A Critique of Instrumental Reason*, Boston: The Beacon Press, 1987, pp. 199–203. Habermas's argument that Parsons moved from a normative to a systems theory should not be identified with the earlier argument, popular in the 1960s, that Parsons abandoned the "voluntarism" of his "theory of action" in *The Structure of Social Action* for social determinism when he embraced functionalism *per se*.

46. Talcott Parsons, *Societies: Evolutionary and Comparative Perspectives*, Englewood Cliffs, N.J.: Prentice-Hall, 1966, p. 113.

47. Jonathan Turner asserts that Merton introduced Parsons to functionalism in *The Structure of Sociological Theory*, p. 81, n. 1. Davis, who was a student at the same time well acquainted with anthropological functionalism, must have played a similar role.

48. Robert K. Merton, *Social Theory and Social Structure*, Revised and Enlarged Edition, New York: The Free Press, 1957, pp. 19–84.

49. Kingsley Davis, "The Myth of Functional Analysis as a Special Method in Sociology and Anthropology," *American Sociological Review*, 24 (December 1959), pp. 757–772.

50. Alfred Korzybski, *Science and Sanity*, Lancaster, Pa.: The International Non-Aristotelian Library Publishing Company, 1933, pp. 14–15, 433–442. See also Merquior's discussion of

structural "transformations" in *From Prague to Paris*, pp. 190–192.

51. Edward W. Lehman uses the term "macro-solidary" to describe such groups, distinguishing them from the myriad small groups such as families, cliques, and other face-to-face, "micro" or "primary," groups that flourish in any and all societies but whose conflict or consensus in their relations with with one another do not bear on the stability or change of the total society. This term has the advantage of recognizing the larger size and complexity of organization of groups that are politically relevant without assuming that they are products of a unitary "society" as a singular entity. See Lehman, *Political Society: A Macrosociology of Politics*, New York: Columbia University Press, 1977, p. 35. The conception of societies or social systems as single, bounded entities is forcefully rejected by Michael Mann, *The Sources of Social Power*, Volume 1, *A History of Power: from the Beginning to A.D. 1756*, Cambridge: Cambridge University Press, 1986, pp. 1–2, 11–17.

52. Lockwood so describes them in *Solidarity and Schism*, p. 309.

53. Anthony Giddens criticizes Marxist functionalism in *A Contemporary Critique of Historical Materialism*, pp. 15–19, 215; see also Jon Elster in *Making Sense of Marx*, pp. 27–37 and R. W. Connell, "A Critique of the Althusserian Approach to Class," in Anthony Giddens and David Held, editors, *Classes, Power and Conflict*, Cambridge: The Polity Press, 1984, pp. 138–143.

54. As Lockwood argues at length in *Solidarity and Schism*, pp. 321–331. He calls Gramsci "the Durkheim of modern Marxism" (p. 337). See also Nicholas Abercrombie, Stephen Hill, and Bryan S. Turner, *The Dominant Ideology Thesis*, London: Allen & Unwin, 1980.

55. The parallels are fully discussed by van den Berg in *The Immanent Utopia*, pp. 419–429, 510–511. See also Nancy Di Tomaso, "'Sociological Reductionism' from Parsons to Althusser: Linking Action and Structure in Social Theory," *American Sociological Review*, 50 (February 1982), pp. 14–28.

56. As demonstrated by van den Berg in *The Immanent Utopia*.

57. John H. Goldthorpe, "Class, Status, and Party in Modern Britain," *European Journal of Sociology*, 13 (1972), p. 359.

58. Milan Kundera, *The Unbearable Lightness of Being*, New York: Harper and Row, 1977, pp. 4, 8, 223. One of Kundera's aims is to explain Nietzsche's "strange" doctrine of "eternal recurrence." Since Kundera wrote, it is worth noting, French historians have

become rather less proud of Robespierre without his having eternally recurred. See Francois Furet and Mona Ozouf, editors, *A Critical Dictionary of the French Revolution*, Cambridge, Mass.:The Belknap Press of Harvard University Press, 1989.

59. The necessity for adding "unforeseen," that is, for distinguishing it from "unintended," is argued by Anthony Giddens in *Studies in Social and Political Theory*, pp. 107–109. See also Dennis H. Wrong, *Power: Its Forms, Bases and Uses*, New Edition, Chicago: University of Chicago Press, [1979] 1988, p. 5.

60. This is one of the major points that Anthony Giddens has stressed again and again as differentiating the social from the natural sciences. See, for example, *Studies in Social and Political Theory*, pp. 27–28 for one of his earliest statements of it. For a more recent statement that refers in particular to economists, see his *The Consequences of Modernity*, Stanford, Calif.: Stanford University Press, 1990, pp. 40–41. See also Dennis Wrong, "The Influence of Sociological Ideas on American Culture," in Herbert J. Gans, editor, *Sociology in America*, Newbury Park, Calif.: Sage Publications, 1990, pp. 19–30.

61. See Arthur L. Stinchcombe, *Constructing Social Theories*, New York: Harcourt, Brace and World, 1968, pp. 87–91; Anthony Giddens, *Central Problems in Social Theory*, Berkeley and Los Angeles: University of California Press, 1979, pp. 73–81; Collins, *Theoretical Sociology*, pp. 46–57.

62. For example, Giddens and Collins in the sources in the previous note.

63. See Anthony Giddens, *Social Theory and Modern Society*, Stanford, Calif.; Stanford University Press, 1987, pp. 191–199. The relatively new "rational expectations" approach centers on the assumption that economic actors successfully anticipate the effects of governmental economic policies and therefore nullify their intended effects by altering their behavior to take them into account. Giddens sees this approach as a recognition by the most advanced social science of his assumption that all social science is reflexive in its influence on its own subject matter, that, as he puts it, "Social science hence 'circles in and out' of what it is about" (p. 191). For interviews with leading economists, including several Nobelists, about the "new classical economics" or "rational expectations" approach, see Arjo Klamer, *Conversations with Economists*, Totowa, N.J.: Rowman and Allanheld, 1984.

64. Randall Collins and Michael Makowsky, *The Discovery of Society*, New York: Random House, 1972, pp. 101–102.

65. Collins, "A Comparative Approach to Political Sociology," p. 56, n. 34.

66. Lockwood, *Solidarity and Schism*, p. 16.

67. Indeed, I used the term "system" in defining "order" at the very beginning of Chapter 3 above. For a detailed account of "system" or "structure" in the more specific sense of a unity of interdependent parts, see Merquior, *From Prague to Paris*, pp. 189–192.

68. Kingsley Davis in effect made this claim for functionalism in "The Myth of Functional Analysis."

69. Lockwood, *Solidarity and Schism*, p. 385.

70. I have drawn here for the two last phrases in quotes from John Rex, *Sociology and the Demystification of the World*, London and Boston: Routledge, 1974, pp. 94–97.

71. W. J. H. Sprott suggested that "the sociologist. . .is the specialist who tries to elaborate and make precise the administrative world-picture."*Science and Social Action*, Glencoe, Ill: The Free Press, 1955, pp. 17–18. Although Sprott does not say as much, such a view suggests a closer connection between tbe state and society than was acknowledged by the nineteenth-century sociologists who asserted the primacy of the latter over the former.

72. The analogy between the artist and the political leader applies to the materials transformed rather than to the objects represented in the artist's creation. But modern art blurs the distinction in making the means and materials of aesthetic creation themselves the primary subject of the work of art as in Braque's collages like the one on the cover. See the brilliant discussion of this modernist tendency in Clement Greenberg's famous early article "Avant-garde and Kitsch," in Philip Rahv and William Phillips, editors, *The Partisan Reader*, New York: Dial Press, 1946, pp. 378–383. (The article originally appeared in *Partisan Review* in 1939.)

73. Michael Mann, *The Sources of Social Power*, p. 2; Anthony Gddens, *The Nation-State and Violence*, Berkeley and Los Angeles: University of California Press, 1986, p. 22. Giddens notes that despite this equation sociologists have until recently paid little attention to the nation-state itself as a distinctive social and political entity. See also Herbert J. Gans's survey and critical assessment of the uses made of the concept of "society" in introductory sociology textbooks in *Middle American Individualism*, New York: The Free Press, 1988, pp. 116–120, 188–189.

74. Michael Mann, *The Sources of Social Power*, pp. 13–14. Mann actually uses the dictum "human beings are social, not societal" as the heading of a chapter section. Zygmunt Bauman's distinction

between the "social" and the "societal" in *Modernity and the Holocaust* (Cambridge: The Polity Press, 1989) appears to be similar, although he places special emphasis on the "societal" as involving centralized bureaucratic control. See note l07 in Chapter 6 above.

75. "Societies as organized power networks" is the title of Michael mann's first chapter in his *Source of Social Power*.

76. See Wrong, *Power*, Chapter 1, especially pp. 3, 10.

77. Michael Mann's notion of four distinct partially overlapping and intersecting but potentially conflicting networks bears some resemblance to Daniel Bell's conception of the "disjunction of the realms" of culture, social structure, and politics in *The Cultural Contradictions of Capitalism*, pp. 9–15. One of Bell's aims in stressing the contradictions between the realms in contemporary capitalist society is to reject the emphasis on the dominance of a single realm in both Marxism and normative functionalism and for this reason he is like Mann an opponent of the view that societies form coherent systems.

78. Michel Foucault, *Power/Knowledge, Selected Interviews and Other Writings, 1972–1977*, New York: Pantheon Books, 1980, p. 119.

79. Ernest Gellner, *Nations and Nationalism*, Ithaca, N.Y.: Cornell University Press, 1983.

80. See Giddens, *Studies in Social and Political Theory*, pp. 123–129; Giddens, *The Constitution of Society*, pp. 139–144; Habermas, *Lifeworld and System*, p. 202. See also Cohen, *Modern Social Theory*, pp. 129–156.

81. Peter Berger postulates a basic human need for "nomos" or order in *The Sacred Canopy*, Garden City, N.Y.: Doubleday Anchor Books, 1969, pp. 21–25, and other works; Anthony Giddens asserts a need for "ontological security" in *The Consequences of Modernity*, pp. 92–100. Giddens insists that this need is an "emotional phenomenon," but Berger, consistently with his phenomenological approach, does not clearly separate the cognitive and emotional components of his need for order, as I argued in Chapter 3, p. 60 above.

82. Cohen, *Modern Social Theory*, p. 170. Cohen writes "either consensus, solidarity, or cohesion" and claims that "Lockwood is not quite clear on this." "Consensus" implies normative agreement while "solidarity" and "cohesion," often used synonymously, are attributes of the interrelations of individuals. Presumably, as three attributes of groups they reinforce one another.

83. But see Abercrombie, Hill and Turner, *The Dominant Ideology hesis*, pp. 154–155. These authors specifically identify system integration with "the dull compulsion of economic relations," a phrase they take from Marx and employ repeatedly in arguing against the normative-consensual conception of social order.

84. Lockwood, *Solidarity and Schism*, p. 399 (his italics).

85. Giddens, *Studies in Social and Political Theory*, p. 125.

86. *The Constitution of Society*, pp. 27–28; he repudiates his earlier identification of the distinction with that of actors as and collectivities on p. 39, n. 32.

87. Ibid., p. 143.

88. Robert Redfield, *The Primitive World and Its Transformations*, Ithaca, N.Y.: Cornell University Press, 1953, pp. 2–25. The whole book deals with the increasing dissociation of the moral and technical orders in the course of the transition from precivilized to civilized societies.

89. As pointed out by Jeffrey Alexander in "Habermas's New Critical Theory: Its Promise and Problems," *American Journal of Sociology*, 91 (September 1985), pp. 400–424. See also Axel van den Berg, "Habermas and Modernity: A Critique of the Communicative Theory of Action," *Working Papers on Social Behavior*, Montreal: Department of Sociology, McGill University, no date, pp. 61–63.

90. Habermas writes that "images of traditional forms of life" possess "the melancholy charm of irretrievable pasts and the radiance of nostalgic remembrance of what had been sacrificed to modernization"(*Lifeworld and System*, p. 329). His affirmation of modernity is most explicit in his *The Philosophical Discourse of Modernity*, Cambridge, Mass.: MIT Press, 1992.

91. Randall Collins, "On the Microfoundations of Macrosociology," *American Journal of Sociology*, 86 (October 1981), pp. 984–1015.

92. Giddens, *The Constitution of Society*, pp. 140–142.

93. In simple "tribal" societies the major subunits are likely to be kinship groups, although, the major conflict theorists who ignored them or dealized their unity to the contrary notwithstanding, this does not mean that they are not confronted with the marxian problem of controlling group conflict even though socioeconomic classes are not the units in conflict. I too have largely identified the marxian problem with large-scale class-divided societies. Robert B. Edgerton in *Sick Societies: Challenging the Myth of Primitive Harmony*, New York: The Free Press, 1993, leaves no doubt that

primitive or "folk" societies are sometimes racked with conflicts between both individuals and groups.

94. As Michael Harrington perceptively observed, "The 'Marseillaise' was the most successful hymn of the nineteenth century, the tricolor its most powerful icon." *The Politics at God's Funeral,* New York: Penguin Books, 1983, p. 38.

95. Peter Laslett, "The Face to Face Society," in Laslett, editor, *Philosophy, Politics and Society,* New York: Macmillan, 1956, p. 177. Benedict Anderson, who lays particular stress on the "imagined" and therefore unseen nature of the object of veneration in nationalism, notes that "the dawn of the age of nationalism" coincided with "the dusk of religious modes of thought" (*Imagined Communities,* p. 19).

96. Gellner, *Nations and Nationalism,* p. 56.

97. See, for example, W. Lloyd Warner's account of Memorial Day observances in Newburyport, Massachusetts, in *American Life, Dream and Reality,* Chicago: University of Chicago Press, 1953; and Michael Young and Edward Shils on the coronation of Elizabeth II in "The Meaning of the Coronation," *Sociological Review,* 1 (December 1953), pp. 63–81.

98. Abercrombie, Hill, and Turner fail to mention it in their assault on normative functionalism and Althusserian Marxism in *The Dominant Ideology Thesis,* as was pointed by Tom Bottomore in his foreword to the book, p. x, and at greater length by me in "Ruling Classes and Ruling Ideas," *Times Literary Supplement,* September 11, 1981, p. 1039.

99. See Anthony Giddens, "Introduction" to Giddens, editor, *Emile Durkheim: Selected Writings,* Cambridge: Cambridge University Press, 1972, pp. 44–48.

100. The phrase is Stanislaw Ossowki's from *Class Structure in the Social Consciousness,* New York: Macmillan, [1956] 1963.

101. Habermas mentions the market as his first and major example of system integration in *Lifeworld and System,* p. 202.

102. Lockwood, *Solidarity and Schism,* pp. 378–379.

103. See especially Lockwood's long critique of the conception of the genesis of revolutionary consciousness by Marx and later Marxists in ibid., pp. 230–275.

104. Ibid., especially pp. 238, 358.

105. Joseph Schumpeter, *Capitalism, Socialism and Democracy, Third Edition,* New York: Harper, 1950, pp. 30, 43–44.

106. Quoted by Anthony Giddens, *Politics and Sociology in the Thought of Max Weber,* London: Macmillan, 1972, p. 46, Weber's emphasis. Giddens's quotation is a partially free transla-

tion from Wolfgang Mommsen's *Max Weber and German Politics, 1890–1920*, first published in Germany in 1959 and in English translation by the University of Chicago Press in 1974. I prefer Giddens's rendition of the relevant phrases in Weber's letter to the version in the translation of Mommsen on p. 104, n. 62.

107. Barrington Moore, Jr., *Reflections on the Causes of Human Misery*, Boston: The Beacon Press, 1972, pp. 179–180, 189–193. Moore states that "Electricity means even more to a modern city than the supply of wheat to eighteenth-century Paris" (p. 190).

108. This is one of Anthony Giddens's central points in *The Consequences of Modernity*. See especially pp. 83–88. See also Giddens, *Modernity and Self-Identity: Self and Society in the Late Modern Age*, Stanford, Calif.: Stanford University Press, 1991, pp. 18, 133–137. Giddens seems to me to be entirely correct in this book in rejecting the fashionable term "postmodernism," preferring to describe the present as "the late modern age."

109. Giddens, *The Consequences of Modernity*, p. 120.

110. See my article "Myths of Alienation," *Partisan Review* (summer 1985), pp. 222–235. Also earlier articles on the ideas of community and identity reprinted in *Skeptical Sociology*, pp. 71–94.

111. Hans Gerth and C. Wright Mills, editors and translators, *From Max Weber: Essays in Sociology*, New York: Oxford University Press, 1946, p. 139. Giddens makes exactly the same point about ignorant dependence with reference to electricity in *The Consequences of Modernity*, p. 135. Much earlier, Weber had used the term *stahlartes Gehäuse* to describe modern man's dependence on a capitalist market economy characterized by a highly developed division of labor. Talcott Parsons translated this phrase as "iron cage," which has become widely used to describe Weber's stoically negative view of the modern world. See Weber, *The Protestant Ethic and the Spirit of Capitalism*, New York: Scribner's, [1905] 1932, p. 181.

112. The two most influential books expressing this outlook were Frantz Fanon, *The Wretched of the Earth*, New York: Grove Press, 1963 and Régis Debray, *Revolution in the Revolution*, New York: Monthly Review Press, 1967.

113. Walter Z. Laqueur, *The Age of Terrorism*, Boston: Little, Brown, 1987, pp. 246–251.

114. This was the condition Weber called "disenchantment of the world" that bears a kinship to (though not an identity with) Marx's "alienation" and Durkheim's "anomie," as has often been noted.

115. See Raymond Aron's brilliant discussion of the Left and Right

oppositions and the "dialectic of the extremes" their competition risks generating in *The Century of Total War,* pp. 241–261. For the invocation by conservatives of nationalism as a weapon against the class appeals of the Left, see Seymour Martin Lipset, *Revolution and Counterrevolution: Persistence and Change in Social Structures,* Revised and Updated Edition, Garden City, N.Y.: Doubleday Anchor Books, [1968] 1970, pp. 209–210. See also Wrong, *Power,* pp. 202–203, 211–215.

116. This is Gellner's major theme in *Nations and Nationalism.* As he wrote elsewhere, "It seems to me obvious that modern nationalism has nothing whatever to do with the reassertion of atavistic loyalties (other than invoking or inventing them for its convenience); it has nothing to do with the Blut und Boden to which it appeals but is, on the contrary, an inescapable consequence of the atomised, mobile and universally literate modern society." *Culture, Identity, and Politics,* Cambridge: Cambridge University Press, 1987, p. 113.

117. Liah Greenfeld, *Nationalism: Five Roads to Modernity,* Cambridge, Mass.: Harvard University Press, 1993, p. 491. This book is likely to remain for some time the major account of the ideological origins of nationalism, at least for Britain, France, Germany, Russia, and the United States.

118. Not that such lyricism cannot be genuinely moving and evocative in the hands of a master like Whitman himself or F. Scott Fitzgerald who wrote: "France was a land, England was a people, but America having about it still the quality of an idea, was harder to utter—it was the graves at Shiloh and the tired, drawn, nervous faces of its great men, and the country boys dying in the Argonne for a phrase that was empty before their bodies withered. It was a willingness of the heart." I am grateful to Robert Benard of CBS Theatrical Films for having written me to correct a mangled version of this statement that I reproduced in *New Republic* ("The Long Trail," July 19 and 26, 1982, p. 36).

119. Greenfeld, *Nationalism: Five Roads to Modernity,* pp. 11–13.

120. Hannah Arendt, *The Origins of Totalitarianism,* New York: Harcourt, Brace, 1951, pp. 226–243.

121. John Breuilly writes: "Nationalism is not the expression of nationality." *Nationalism and the State,* Chicago: University of Chicago Press, 1983, p. 382. Breuilly virtually identifies nationalism as an ideology with the demand for a state by groups lacking one of their own.

122. I cite the figure from Tom Nairn, "Demonising Nationalism," *London Review of Books,* 15 (25 February, 1993), p. 3. Nairn's

article is an eloquent rebuttal of the general alarmism about the resurfacing of national and ethnic rivalries in the postcommunist world, emphasizing the essentially modern rather than atavistic aspects of nationalism and the nation-state.

123. Ibid., p. 3.

124. Susanne Hoeber Rudolph and Lloyd I. Rudolph, "Modern Hate," *New Republic*, March 23, 1993, pp. 24–29 (quotation from p. 29). For the notion of "invented traditions," see Eric Hobsbawm and Terence Ranger, editors, *The Invention of Tradition*, Cambridge: Cambridge University Press, 1983.

125. For a perceptive analysis of these in the context of contemporary American academic and intellectial life, see Todd Gitlin, "The Rise of 'Identity Politics,'" *Dissent* (Spring 1993), pp. 72–77.

126. As shown by Rose L. Coser in arguing that more humane and tolerant citizens are likely to result from such a diversified social experience in a *gesellschaftlich* rather than *gemeinschaftlich* social context in *In Defense of Modernity: Role Complexity and Individual Autonomy*, Stanford, Calif.: Stanford University Press, 1991.

127. Anthony D. Smith, "State-Making and Nation-Building," in John A. Hall, editor, *States in History*, Oxford: Basil Blackwell, 1986, p. 260.

128. H. G. Wells early in the century gave an amusing example of such "nested" or "concentric" group allegiance in describing the successively wide identifications of a botanist with systematic botanists against plant physiologists, with biologists against physicists, natural scientists against social scientists and humanists, educated persons against the working class, Englishmen against Europeans. Cited by Robert Bierstedt, *The Social Order*, New York: McGraw-Hill, 1957, p. 268.

129. Lewis Coser, *The Functions of Social Conflict*, pp. 153–154.

130. The difference, of course, between civil violence in and around Sarajevo today and in 1914 is that there are no great powers linked by alliance to Serbia or its local adversaries that are ready to be activated by the conflict there. The relative stability of the Cold War resulted from the fact that possible superpower involvement, directly or by proxy, in local conflicts risking a nuclear Third World War dampened down such conflicts. The end of the Cold War eliminates such inhibitions. At the time of writing, the unwillingness of the European states and the United States to intervene against Serbian aggression and atrocities in Bosnia has inspired much anguished moral condemnation.

131. Anthony Burgess, *A Clockwork Orange*, New York: W. W.

Norton, 1963 and Walker Percy, *Love in the Ruins,* New York: Farrar, Straus & Giroux, 1971.

132. Quoted by James B. Rule in *Theories of Civil Violence,* Berkeley and Los Angeles: University of California Press, 1988, p. 144.

133. See the remarks of Irving Howe, "The Spirit of the Times," *Dissent* (Spring 1993), pp. 131–133. Howe quotes Theodore Draper as having said to him (as he also did to me) that "the central experience of the twentieth century was communism, like it or hate it." By the time of its collapse, Communism had few supporters left outside of its borders, or, for that matter, inside them, but the speed, manner, and completeness of its collapse certainly have cast a shadow that will take a very long time to dissolve over the very idea of a possible or feasible "alternative society," whether one chooses to call it "socialism" or something else, that will retain the advantages of Western capitalist democracies while doing away with their blemishes. To the extent that this is so, I doubt that even the thoughtful and modest proposal of my old and dear friend, Howe, who died suddenly a few days after I first wrote this note, for a revival of utopian thinking will find many supporters for quite a while.

134. For an accurate statement of what the much-reviled "end of ideology" writers actually meant, see Edward A. Shils, *The Constitution of Society,* Chicago: University of Chicago Press, 1982, pp. 221–223 (originally published in the International Encyclopedia of the Social Sciences, 1968).

135. Herbert Gans writes: "The social and political chaos in which all reciprocity and trust disappear, basic institutions stop functioning, people kill each other, and society disintegrates seems to be found mainly in fictional dystopias." *Middle American Individualism,* p. 116. In a footnote, Gans notes that the view that societies are threatened with actual dissolution seems to presuppose "a holistic, intensely interdependent social system. . .[that] caricatures functionalism" p. 190, n. 41.

136. Rushton Coulborn has written: "A feudal society newly formed after a decline is. . .at rock-bottom in the scale to which the word civilized applies. . .civilized societies in decline have always been caught at the feudal level." Coulborn, editor, *Feudalism in History,* Hamden, Conn.: Archon Books, [1956] 1965, p. 197.

BIBLIOGRAPHY

Abercrombie, Nicholas, Stephen Hill, and Bryan S. Turner. 1980. *The Dominant Ideology Thesis*. London: Allen & Unwin.

Aberle, David, A. K. Cohen, A. K. Davis, Marion J. Levy, Jr., and F. X. Sutton. 1950. "The Functional Prerequisites of Society." *Ethics*, 60 (January): 100–111.

Abramson, Jeffrey B. 1984. *Liberation and Its Limits: The Moral and Political Thought of Freud*. New York: The Free Press.

Adorno, Theodore, Else Frenkel-Brunswick, Daniel J. Levinson, and R. Nevitt Sanford. 1950. *The Authoritarian Personality*. New York: Harper and Brothers.

Alexander, Jeffrey C. 1982. *Theoretical Logic in Sociology*. Volume 1, *Positivism, Presuppositions, and Current Controversies*. Berkeley and Los Angeles: University of California Press.

———. 1983. *Theoretical Logic in Sociology*. Volume 4, *The Modern Reconstruction of Social Thought: Talcott Parsons*. Berkeley and Los Angeles: University of California Press.

———. 1985. "Habermas's New Critical Theory: Its Promise and Problems." *American Journal of Sociology*, 91 (September): 400–424.

Alford, C. Fred. 1991. *The Self in Social Theory*. New Haven: Yale University Press.

Allport, F. H. 1934. "The J-curve Hypothesis of Conforming Behavior." *Journal of Social Psychology*, 5:141–183.

American Psychiatric Association. 1980. *Diagnostic and Statistical Manual of Mental Disorders*, Third Edition. American Psychiatric Association.

Anderson, Benedict. 1983. *Imagined Communities: Reflections on the Origin and Spread of Nationalism*. London: Verso.

Angell, Robert Cooley. 1958. *Free Society and Moral Crisis*. Ann Arbor: University of Michigan Press.

Anscombe, G. E. M. 1966. *Intention,* Second Edition. Ithaca, N.Y.: Cornell University Press.

———. 1977. "Intention." In Alan R. White, ed., *The Philosophy of Action*. Oxford: Oxford University Press.

Arendt, Hannah. 1951. *The Origins of Totalitarianism*. New York: Harcourt, Brace.

———. [1963] 1965. Eichmann in Jerusalem: *A Report on the Banality of Evil*. Harmondsworth, Middlesex, England: Penguin Books.

Aristotle. 1952. *Politics and Poetics*. Cleveland: Fine Editions Press.

Aron, Raymond. 1954. *The Century of Total War*. Garden City, N.Y.: Doubleday.

———. 1969. *Marxism and the Existentialists*. New York: Harper and Row.

———. 1983. *Memoires*. Paris: Juilliard.

———. 1985. *History, Truth, Liberty*. Chicago: University of Chicago Press.

Atkinson, Dick. 1971. *Orthodox Consensus and Radical Alternative*. London: Heinemann Educational Books.

Auden, W. H. 1938. "Get There If You Can and See the Land You Once Were Proud to Own." In Selden Rodman, ed., *A New Anthology of Modern Poetry*. New York: The Modern Library.

Banfield, Edward. 1958. *The Moral Basis of a Backward Society*. New York: The Free Press.

Barber, Bernard. 1957. *Social Stratification*. New York: Harcourt, Brace.

Barnes, Barry. 1988. *The Nature of Power*. Chicago and Urbana: University of Illinois Press.

Baron, Salo W. [1939] 1963. "Book Review of *Moses and Monotheism*." In Bruce Mazlish, ed., *Psychoanalysis and History*. Englewood Cliffs, N.J.: Prentice-Hall.

Barry, Brian. 1978. *Sociologists, Economists, and Democracy*. Chicago: University of Chicago Press.

Batz, William G. 1991. "The Historical Anthropology of John Locke." In Richard Ashcraft, ed., *John Locke: Critical Assessments*, Volume Three. London: Routledge.

Bauman, Zygmunt. 1989. *Modernity and the Holocaust*. Cambridge: The Polity Press.

Baumgold, Deborah. 1988. *Hobbes's Political Theory*. Cambridge: Cambridge University Press.

———. 1990. "Hobbes's Political Sensibility: The Menace of Political Ambition." In Mary G. Dietz, ed., *Thomas Hobbes and Political Theory*. Lawrence, Kansas: University of Kansas Press.

Becker, Gary. 1981. *A Treatise on the Family*. Cambridge, Mass.: Harvard University Press.

Bell, Daniel. 1976. *The Cultural Contradictions of Capitalism*. New York: Basic Books.

Bellah, Robert N., Richard Madsen, William M. Sullivan, Ann Swidler, and Steven M. Tipton. 1985. *Habits of the Heart*. New York: Harper and Row.

Bendix, Reinhard. 1952. "Individual Personality and Compliant Behavior." *American Journal of Sociology,* 58:293–303.

———. 1978. *Kings or People: Power and the Mandate to Rule.* Berkeley and Los Angeles: University of California Press.

Benedict, Ruth. 1934. *Patterns of Culture.* Boston: Houghton-Mifflin.

Benjamin, Jessica. 1988. *The Bonds of Love.* New York: Pantheon Books.

Benn, S. I. 1972. "Hobbes on Power." In Maurice Cranston and Richard S. Peters, eds., *Hobbes and Rousseau: A Collection of Critical Essays.* Garden City, N.Y.: Doubleday Anchor Books.

Berger, Morroe. 1977. *Real and Imagined Worlds: The Novel and Social Science.* Cambridge, Mass.: Harvard University Press.

Berger, Peter L. 1969. *The Sacred Canopy.* Garden City, N.Y.: Doubleday Anchor Books.

Berger, Peter L., and Thomas Luckmann. 1966. *The Social Construction of Reality.* Garden City, N.Y.: Doubleday Anchor Books.

Bettelheim, Bruno. 1983. *Freud and Man's Soul.* New York: Alfred A. Knopf.

Bierstedt, Robert. 1957. *The Social Order.* New York: McGraw-Hill.

Black, Max. 1961. "Some Questions about Parsons's Theories." In Max Black, ed., *The Social Theories of Talcott Parsons,* Englewood Cliffs, N.J.: Prentice Hall.

Blake, Judith, and Kingsley Davis. 1964. "Norms, Values, and Sanctions." In Robert E. L. Faris, ed., *Handbook of Modern Sociology.* Chicago: Rand-McNally.

Bloom, Allen. 1987. *The Closing of the American Mind.* New York: Simon and Schuster.

Blumer, Herbert. 1969. *Symbolic Interaction: Perspective and Method.* Englewood Cliffs, N.J.: Prentice-Hall.

Bocock, Robert. 1976. *Freud and Modern Society.* London: Thomas Nelson and Sons.

———. 1983. *Sigmund Freud.* London and New York: Tavistock Publications.

Bourricaud, François. 1981. *The Sociology of Talcott Parsons.* Chicago: University of Chicago Press.

Breuilly, John. 1983. *Nationalism and the State.* Chicago: University of Chicago Press.

Bromwich, David. 1992. *Politics by Other Means: Higher Education and Group Thinking.* New Haven: Yale University Press.

Brown, Norman O. [1959] 1960. *Life Against Death: The Psychoanalytical Meaning of History.* Garden City, N.Y.: Doubleday.

Browning, Christopher B. 1992. *Ordinary Men: Reserve Police Battalion 101 and the Final Solution in Poland.* New York: HarperCollins.

Bryant, Joseph M. 1992a. "Positivism *redivivus?* A critique of recent proposals for reforming sociological theory (and related foibles)." *Canadian Journal of Sociology,* 17:29–53.

———. 1992b. "Towards a respectable, reflexive, scientific sociology: a note on the reformation required." *Canadian Journal of Sociology,* 17:322–331.

Bull, Hedley. 1981. "Hobbes and the International Anarchy." *Social Research,* 48:725–756.

Burgess, Anthony. 1963. *A Clockwork Orange.* New York: W. W. Norton.

Burns, Tom. 1992. *Erving Goffman.* London and New York: Routledge.

Callinicos, Alex. 1976. *Althusser's Marxism.* London: Pluto Press.

Camic, Charles. 1979. "The Utilitarians Revisited." *American Journal of Sociology,* 85:516–550.

———. 1987. "The Making of a Method: A Historical Reinterpretation of the Early Parsons." *American Sociological Review,* 52:421–439.

———. 1989. "Structure after 50 Years: The Anatomy of a Charter." *American Journal of Sociology,* 95:38–107.

———. 1992. "Reputation and Predecessor Selection: Parsons and the Institutionalists." *American Sociological Review,* 57:421–445.

Cannon, Walter B. 1932. *The Wisdom of the Body.* New York: W. W. Norton.

Carveth, Donald L. 1977a. *Sociologism and Psychoanalysis: A Study of Implicit Theories of Human Nature in "Symbolic Interaction-ism, Reality Constructionism, and Psychoanalysis."* Unpublished doctoral dissertation, Department of Sociology, University of Toronto.

———. 1977b. "The Disembodied Dialectic: A Psychoanalytic Critique of Sociological Relativism." *Theory and Society,* 4:73–102.

———. 1977c. "The Hobbesian Microcosm: On the Dialectics of the Self in Social Theory." *Sociological Inquiry,* 47:2–12.

———. 1982. "Sociology and Psychoanalysis: The Hobbesian Problem Revisited." *Canadian Journal of Sociology,* 7:201–228.

Chirot, Daniel. 1986. *Social Change in the Modern Era.* New York: Harcourt Brace Jovanovich.

Cicourel, Aaron. 1974. *Cognitive Sociology.* New York: The Free Press.

Cohen, Percy S. 1968. *Modern Social Theory.* New York: Basic Books.

Coleman, James S. 1990. *Foundations of Social Theory.* Cambridge, Mass.: The Belknap Press of Harvard University Press.

———. 1991. "Message from the Chair." *Perspectives,* The Theory Section Newsletter. Washington, D.C.: American Sociological

Association, 13:1–2.

———. 1993. "The Rational Reconstruction of Society." *American Sociological Review,* 58 (February):1–15.

Collingwood, R. G. 1942. *The New Leviathan.* Oxford: The Clarendon Press.

Collins, Randall. 1968. "A Comparative Approach to Political Sociology." In Reinhard Bendix, ed., *The State and Society: A Reader in Political Sociology.* Boston: Little, Brown.

———. 1975. *Conflict Sociology: Toward an Explanatory Science.* New York: Academy Press.

———. 1981. "On the Microfoundations of Macrosociology." *American Journal of Sociology,* 86:984–1015.

———. 1982. *Sociological Insight.* New York: Oxford UniversityPress.

———. 1986. *Weberian Sociological Theory.* Cambridge: Cambridge University Press.

———. 1988. *Theoretical Sociology.* New York: Harcourt Brace Jovanovich.

———. 1990. "Conflict Theory and the Advance of Macro-Historical Sociology." In George Ritzer, ed., *Frontiers of Social Theory.* New York: Columbia University Press.

Collins, Randall, and Michael Makowsky. 1972. *The Discovery of Society.* New York: Random House.

Connell, R. W. 1984. "A Critique of the Althusserian Approach to Class." In Anthony Giddens and David Held, eds., *Classes, Power and Conflict.* Cambridge: The Polity Press.

Corradi, Juan E., Patricia Weiss Fagen, and Manuel Antonio Garreton. 1992. *Fear at the Edge: State Terror and Resistance in Latin America.* Berkeley and Los Angeles: University of California Press.

Coser, Lewis A. 1956. *The Functions of Social Conflict.* Glencoe, Ill.: The Free Press.

———. 1967. *Continuities in the Study of Conflict.* Glencoe, Ill.: The Free Press.

———. 1974. *Greedy Institutions: Patterns of Undivided Commitment.* New York: The Free Press.

Coser, Rose L. 1991. *In Defense of Modernity: Role Complexity and Individual Autonomy.* Stanford, Calif.: Stanford University Press.

Coulborn, Rushton, ed. [1956] 1965. *Feudalism in History.* Hamden, Conn.: Archon Books.

Craib, Ian. 1989. *Psychoanalysis and Social Theory: The Limits of Sociology.* New York and London: Harvester Wheatsheaf.

Cranston, Maurice. 1983. *Jean-Jacques: The Early Life and Work of Jean-Jacques Rousseau.* London: Allen Lane.

———. 1984. "Introduction" and "Editor's Notes." In Jean-Jacques

Rousseau, *A Discourse on Inequality*. Harmondsworth, Middlesex, England: Penguin Books.

———. 1991. *The Noble Savage: Jean-Jacques Rousseau 1754–1762*. London: Allen Lane.

Cranston, Maurice, and Richard S. Peters, eds. 1972. *Hobbes and Rousseau: A Collection of Critical Essays*. Garden City, N.Y.: Doubleday Anchor Books.

Dahrendorf, Ralf. 1959. *Class and Class Conflict in Industrial Society*. Stanford, Calif.: Stanford University Press.

———. 1968. *Essays in the Theory of Society*. Stanford, Calif.: Stanford University Press.

Darley, John, and Bibb Latané. 1968. "Bystander Intervention in Emergencies." *Journal of Personality and Social Psychology*, 8:377–383.

Darnton, Robert. 1988. "A Star Is Born," *New York Review of Books*, October 27:84–88.

Davis, Kingsley. 1949. *Human Society*. New York: Macmillan.

———. 1959. "The Myth of Functional Analysis As a Special Method in Sociology and Anthropology." *American Sociological Review*, 24:757–772.

Davis, Kingsley, and Wilbert E. Moore. 1945. "Some Principles of Social Stratification." *American Sociological Review*, 10:242–249.

Deák, István. 1992. "Strategies of Hell." *New York Review of Books*, October 8:10.

Debray, Régis. 1967. *Revolution in the Revolution*. New York: Monthly Review Press.

Dewey, John. [1922] 1930. *Human Nature and Conduct*. New York: Random House.

———. 1938. *Logic: The Theory of Inquiry*. New York: Henry Holt.

———. 1939. *Theory of Valuation*. Chicago: University of Chicago Press.

Di Tomaso, Nancy. 1982. "Sociological Reductionism from Parsons to Althusser: Linking Action and Structure in Social Theory." *American Sociological Review*, 50:14–28.

Dollard, John. [1935] 1949. *Criteria for the Life History*. New York: Peter Smith.

Dowse, Robert E., and John A. Hughes. 1972. *Political Sociology*. New York: John Wiley.

Du Bois, Cora. 1945. *The People of Alor*. Minneapolis: University of Minnesota Press.

Durkheim, Emile. [1893] 1933. *The Division of Labor in Society*. New York: Macmillan.

———. [1911] 1947. *The Elementary Forms of the Religious Life*. New York: The Free Press.

———. [1897] 1951. *Suicide*. Glencoe, Ill.: The Free Press.

Edgerton, Robert B. 1985. *Rules, Exceptions, and Social Order.* Berkeley and Los Angeles: University of California Press.

———. 1993. *Sick Societies: Challenging the Myth of Primitive Harmony.* New York: The Free Press.

Ellis, Desmond. 1971. "The Hobbesian Problem of Order." *American Sociological Review,* 36:692–703.

Elster, Jon. 1988. *Making Sense of Marx.* Cambridge: Cambridge University Press.

———. 1989. *The Cement of Society: A Study of Social Order.* Cambridge: Cambridge University Press.

Endleman, Robert. 1967. *Personality and Social Life.* New York: Random House.

———. 1981. *Psyche and Society: Explorations in Psychoanalytic Sociology.* New York: Columbia University Press.

Erikson, Erik H. 1968. *Identity: Youth and Crisis.* New York: W. W. Norton.

Etzioni, Amitai. 1961. *A Comparative Analysis of Complex Organizations.* New York: The Free Press.

———. 1987. *The Moral Dimension.* New York: The Free Press.

Fanon, Frantz. 1963. *The Wretched of the Earth.* New York: Grove Press.

Feiffer, Jules. 1992. Cartoon. *The Village Voice,* November 24:5.

Feuer, Lewis. 1977–78. "Marx and Engels as Sociobiologists." *Survey,* 23:109–136.

Fitzhugh, George. 1854. *Sociology of the South.* Richmond, Va.

Fortune, Reo F. 1932. *The Sorcerers of Dobu.* New York: E. P. Dutton.

Foucault, Michel. [1975] 1977. *Discipline and Punish: The Birth of the Prison.* New York: Vintage Books.

———. 1980. *Power/Knowledge, Selected Interviews and Other Writings.* New York: Pantheon Books.

Frank, Lawrence K. 1948. *Society as the Patient: Essays in Culture and Personality.* New Brunswick, N.J.: Rutgers University Press.

Freud, Sigmund. 1933. *New Introductory Lectures on Psychoanalysis.* New York: W. W. Norton.

———. [1940] 1949. *An Outline of Psychoanalysis.* New York: W. W. Norton.

———. [1912] 1950. *Totem and Taboo.* New York: W. W. Norton.

———. [1920] 1959. *Beyond the Pleasure Principle.* New York: Bantam Books.

———. [1921] 1960. *Group Psychology and the Analysis of the Ego.* New York: Bantam Books.

———. [1930] 1961. *Civilization and Its Discontents.* New York:W. W. Norton.

———. [1923] 1962. *The Ego and the Id.* New York: W. W. Norton.

———. [1911] 1963a. " 'Civilized' Sexual Morality and Modern Nervousness." In *Sexuality and the Psychology of Love* from *The Collected Papers of Sigmund Freud*, edited by Philip Rieff. New York: Collier Books.

———. [1911] 1963b. "Formulations Regarding the Two Principles in Mental Functioning." In *General Psychological Theory* from *The Collected Papers of Sigmund Freud*, edited by Philip Rieff. New York: Collier Books.

———. [1915] 1963c. "Reflections Upon War and Death." In *Character and Culture* from *The Collected Papers of Sigmund Freud*, edited by Philip Rieff. New York: Collier Books.

———. [1932] 1963d. "Why War?" In *Character and Culture*, edited by Philip Rieff. New York: Collier Books.

———. [1931] 1963e. "Libidinal Types." In *Character and Culture*, edited by Philip Rieff. New York: Collier Books.

———. [1927] 1964. *The Future of an Illusion*. New York: W. W. Norton.

Friedrich, Carl J., ed. 1954. *Totalitarianism*. New York: Grosset and Dunlap.

Fromm, Erich. 1941. *Escape from Freedom*. New York: Farrar and Rinehart.

Furet, François, and Mona Ozouf. 1989. *A Critical Dictionary of the French Revolution*. Cambridge, Mass.: The Belknap Press of Harvard University Press.

Gans, Herbert J. 1988. *Middle American Individualism*. New York: The Free Press.

Garfinkel, Harold. 1967. *Studies in Ethnomethodology*. Englewood Cliffs, N.J.: Prentice-Hall.

Gay, Peter. 1988. Freud: *A Life for Our Time*. New York: W. W. Norton.

Gellner, Ernest. 1959. *Words and Things*. Harmondsworth, Middlesex, England: Penguin Books.

———. 1983. *Nations and Nationalism*. Ithaca, N.Y.: Cornell University Press.

———. 1987. *Culture, Identity, and Politics*. Cambridge: Cambridge University Press.

Genovese, Eugene. 1969. *The World the Slaveholders Made*. New York: Pantheon Books.

Gergen, Kenneth. 1992. *The Saturated Self*. New York: Basic Books.

Gerth, Hans, and C. Wright Mills, eds., 1946. *From Max Weber: Essays in Sociology*. New York: Oxford University Press.

Giddens, Anthony. 1972a. *Politics and Sociology in the Thought of Max Weber*. London: Macmillan.

———. 1972b. "Introduction" to Giddens, ed., *Emile Durkheim: Selected Writings*. Cambridge: Cambridge University Press.

———. 1976. *New Rules of Sociological Method.* New York: Basic Books.

———. 1977. *Studies in Social and Political Theory.* London: Hutchinson.

———. 1979. *Central Problems in Social Theory.* Berkeley and Los Angeles: University of California Press.

———. 1981. *A Contemporary Critique of Historical Materialism.* Berkeley and Los Angeles: University of California Press.

———. 1984. *The Constitution of Society.* Cambridge: The Polity Press.

———. 1986. *The Nation-State and Violence.* Berkeley and Los Angeles: University of California Press.

———. 1987. *Social Theory and Modern Society.* Stanford, Calif.: Stanford University Press.

———. 1990. *The Consequences of Modernity.* Stanford, Calif.: Stanford University Press.

———. 1991a. *Sociology.* New York: W. W. Norton.

———. 1991b. *Modernity and Self-Identity: Self and Society in the Late Modern Age.* Stanford, Calif.: Stanford University Press.

Gitlin, Todd. 1993. "The Rise of 'Identity Politics.' " *Dissent,* Spring: 72–79.

Goffman, Erving. 1952. "On Cooling the Mark Out." *Psychiatry,* 15:451–463.

———. 1963. *Stigma.* Englewood Cliffs, N.J.: Prentice-Hall.

———. 1983. "The Interaction Order." *American Sociological Review,* 48:1–17.

Goldsmith, M. M. 1966. *Hobbes's Science of Politics.* New York: Columbia University Press.

Goldstone, Jack A. 1991. *Revolution and Rebellion in the Early Modern World.* Berkeley and Los Angeles: University of California Press.

Goldthorpe, John H. 1972. "Class, Status, and Party in Modern Britain." *European Journal of Sociology,* 13:342–372.

Gouldner, Alvin W. 1970. *The Coming Crisis of Western Sociology.* New York: Basic Books.

———. 1974. *For Sociology.* New York: Basic Books.

———. 1980. *The Two Marxisms.* New York: The Seabury Press.

Grant, Ruth. 1991. "Locke's Political Anthropology and Lockean Individualism." In Ashcraft, ed., *John Locke: Critical Assessments,* Volume Three. London: Routledge.

Grathoff, Richard. 1978. *The Theory of Social Action: The Correspondence of Alfred Schutz and Talcott Parsons.* Bloomington, Ind.: Indiana University Press.

Gray, Alexander. [1946] 1963. *The Socialist Tradition.* London: Longmans, Green.

Green, Martin. 1970. *The von Richthofen Sisters*. New York: Basic Books.

Greenberg, Clement. 1946. "Avant-garde and Kitsch." In Philip Rahv and William Phillips, eds., *The Partisan Reader*. New York: Dial Press.

Greenfeld, Liah. 1993. *Nationalism: Five Roads to Modernity*. Cambridge, Mass.: Harvard University Press.

Gutman, Robert, and Dennis H. Wrong. 1961. "Riesman's Typology of Character." In Seymour Martin Lipset and Leo Lowenthal, eds., *Culture and Character: The Work of David Riesman Reviewed*. New York: The Free Press.

Habermas, Jürgen. 1973. *Theory and Practice*. Boston: The Beacon Press.

———. 1987. *The Theory of Communicative Action*. Volume 2, *Lifeworld and System: A Critique of Instrumental Reason*. Boston: The Beacon Press.

———. 1991. *The Philosophical Discourse of Modernity*. Cambridge, Mass.: MIT Press.

Harrington, Michael. 1983. *The Politics at God's Funeral*. New York: Penguin Books.

Hartz, Louis. 1955. *The Liberal Tradition in America*. New York: Harcourt Brace and World.

Hawthorn, Geoffrey. 1976. *Enlightenment and Despair: A History of Sociology*, Cambridge: Cambridge University Press.

Hampshire, Stuart. 1957. "Can There Be a General Science of Man?" *Commentary*, 24:164–167.

Hechter, Michael. 1987. *Principles of Group Solidarity*. Berkeley and Los Angeles: University of California Press.

———. 1991. "From Exchange to Structure." In Joan Huber, ed., *Macro-Micro Linkages in Sociology*. Newbury Park, Calif.: Sage Publications.

———. 1992. "Should Values Be Written Out of the Social Scientist's Lexicon?" *Sociological Theory*, 10:214–230.

Hilbert, Richard. 1991. *The Classical Roots of Ethnomethodology*. Chapel Hill, N.C.: University of North Carolina Press.

Himmelfarb, Gertrude. 1962. *Darwin and the Darwinian Revolution*. Garden City, N.Y.: Doubleday.

Hirschmann, Albert O. 1977. *The Passions and the Interests*. Princeton, N.J.: Princeton University Press.

Hobbes, Thomas. [1642] 1949. *De Cive or The Citizen*. New York: Appleton-Century Crofts.

———. [1651] 1968. *Leviathan*. Harmondsworth, Middlesex, England: Penguin Books.

Hobsbawm, Eric, and Terence Ranger, eds., 1983. *The Invention of Tradition*. Cambridge: Cambridge University Press.

Hofstadter, Richard. 1955. *Social Darwinism in American Thought*. Boston: The Beacon Press.

Homans, George. 1950. *The Human Group*. New York: Harcourt Brace.

———. 1964. "Bringing Men Back In." *American Sociological Review*, 29:809–819.

———. 1980. Review of Alan MacFarlane, *The Origins of English Individualism*. *Contemporary Sociology*, 9:262–263.

Horkheimer, Max, and Theodore Adorno. [1944] 1969. *Dialectic of the Enlightenment*. New York: The Seabury Press.

Horkheimer, Max, and Samuel H. Flowerman, eds. 1950–1955. *Studies in Prejudice*, Five Volumes. New York: Harper and Bros.

Howe, Irving. 1993. "The Spirit of the Times," *Dissent* (Spring) 131–133.

Hughes, H. Stuart. 1975. *The Sea Change: The Migration of Social Thought*. New York: Harper and Row.

Hughes, Henry. 1854. *Treatise on Sociology*. Philadelphia.

Huxley, Aldous. [1932] 1953. *Brave New World*. New York: Bantam Books.

———. 1958. *Brave New World Revisited*. New York: Harper and Row.

Jay, Martin. 1984. *Marxism and Totality*. Berkeley and Los Angeles: University of California Press.

Joas, Hans. 1985. *G. H. Mead: A Contemporary Reexamination of His Thought*. Cambridge: The Polity Press.

Jouvenel, Bertrand de. 1972. "Rousseau's Theory of the Forms of Government." In Cranston and Peters, eds., *Hobbes and Rousseau*.

Kardiner, Abram. 1939. *The Individual and His Society*. New York: Columbia University Press.

———. 1945. *The Psychological Frontiers of Society*. New York: Columbia University Press.

Kateb, George. 1963. *Utopia and Its Enemies*. New York: The Free Press.

———. 1983. *Hannah Arendt: Politics, Conscience, Evil*. Totowa, N.J.: Rowman and Allanheld.

Kaye, Howard L. 1991. "A False Convergence: Freud and the Hobbesian Problem of Order." *Sociological Theory*, 9 (Spring):87–105.

———. 1992. "Rationalization as Sublimation: On the Cultural Analyses of Weber and Freud." *Theory Culture & Society*, 9:45–74.

———. 1993. "Why Freud Hated America." *The Wilson Quarterly* (Spring):7:118–125.

Kecskemeti, Paul. 1952. *Meaning, Communication, and Value*. Chicago: University of Chicago Press.

Keat, Russell. 1981. *The Politics of Social Theory*. Chicago: University of Chicago Press.

Klamer, Arjo. 1984. *Conversations with Economists*. Totowa, N.J.: Rowman and Allanheld.

Korzybski, Alfred. 1933. *Science and Sanity*. Lancaster, Pa.: The International Non-Aristotelian Library Publishing Company.

Kroeber, Alfred L. [1939] 1963. "*Totem and Taboo* in Retrospect." In Mazlish, ed., *Psychoanalysis and History*.

Kroeber, Alfred L., and Clyde Kluckhohn. [1952] 1963. *Culture: A Critical Review of Concepts and Definitions*. New York: Vintage Books.

Kundera, Milan. 1977. *The Unbearable Lightness of Being*. New York: Harper and Row.

LaBarre, Weston. 1954. *The Human Animal*. Chicago: University of Chicago Press.

LaPlanche, J., and J.-B. Pontalis. [1967] 1973. *The Language of Psychoanalysis*. New York: W. W. Norton.

Laqueur, Walter Z. 1987. *The Age of Terrorism*. Boston: Little, Brown.

Lasch, Christopher. 1977. *Haven in a Heartless World: The Family Besieged*. New York: Harper and Row.

———. 1978. *The Culture of Narcissism*. New York: W. W. Norton.

———. 1984. *The Minimal Self*. New York: W. W. Norton.

———. 1991. *The True and Only Heaven*. New York: W. W. Norton.

———. 1992. "For Shame." *New Republic* (August) 10:32–33.

Laslett, Peter. 1956. "The Face to Face Society." In Laslett, ed., *Philosophy, Politics and Society*. New York: Macmillan.

———. 1978. Review of Alan MacFarlane, *The Origins of English Individualism*. In New Society (December) 14:649–650.

Lawrence, D. H. 1930. *Selected Essays*. London: William Heinemann.

Lear, Jonathan. 1992. *Love and Its Place in Nature*. New York: Farrar, Straus & Giroux.

Lehman, Edward W. 1977. *Political Society: A Macrosociology of Politics*. New York: Columbia University Press.

———. 1992. *The Viable Polity*. Philadelphia: Temple University Press.

Lenski, Gerhard. 1966. *Power and Privilege: A Theory of Social Stratification*. New York: McGraw-Hill.

Letwin, William. 1972. "The Economic Foundation of Hobbes's Politics." In Cranston and Peters, eds., *Hobbes and Rousseau*.

Levi, Primo. [1986] 1988. *The Drowned and the Saved*. London: Verso.

Lévi-Strauss, Claude. 1974. *Tristes Tropiques*. New York: Atheneum.

LeVine, Robert A. 1973. *Culture, Behavior, and Personality*. Chicago: Aldine.

Levy, Marion J. 1952. *The Structure of Society*. Princeton, N.J.: Princeton University Press.

Lichtheim, George. 1969. *The Origins of Socialism*. New York: Praeger.

———. 1970. *A Short History of Socialism*. New York: Praeger.

———. 1972. *From Marx to Hegel*. New York: Herder and Herder.

———. 1973. *Collected Essays*. New York: Viking Press.

Lindholm, Charles. 1990. *Charisma*. London and New York: Basil Blackwell.

Lipset, Seymour Martin. [1968] 1970. *Revolution and Counter-revolution: Persistence and Change in Social Structures*. Garden City, N.Y.: Doubleday Anchor Books.

Locke, John. [1690] 1952. *The Second Treatise of Government*. Indianapolis: Bobbs-Merrill.

Lockwood, David. 1992. *Solidarity and Schism: "The Problem of Disorder" in Durkheimian and Marxist Sociology*. Oxford: The Clarendon Press.

Luethy, Herbert. 1954. "The Wretched Little Demon That Was Hitler." *Commentary* (February) 17:129–138.

Lukes, Steven. 1973. *Individualism*. Oxford: Basil Blackwell.

McAdam, Doug, John D. McCarthy, and Mayer N. Zald. 1990. "Social Movements." In Neil J. Smelser, ed., *Handbook of Sociology*. Newbury Park, Calif.: Sage Publications.

McCord, William M., and Joan McCord. 1954. *Psychopathy and Delinquency*. New York: Grune and Stratton.

MacFarlane, Alan. 1977. *The Origins of English Individualism*. Cambridge: Cambridge University Press.

———. 1979. Review-essay. *History and Theory*, 18:103–126.

Machiavelli, Niccolo. [1512] 1961. *The Prince*. Harmondsworth, Middlesex, England: Penguin Books.

MacIver, Robert M. 1937. *Society: A Textbook of Sociology*. New York: Rinehart.

Mackie, J. L. 1977. *Ethics: Inventing Right and Wrong*. Harmondsworth, Middlesex, England: Penguin Books.

McManners, John. 1972. "The Social Contract and Rousseau's Revolt Against Society." In Cranston and Peters, eds., *Hobbes and Rousseau*.

Macpherson, C. B. 1962a. *The Political Theory of Possessive Individualism: Hobbes to Locke*. Oxford: Oxford UniversityPress.

———. 1962b. "Introduction" to Hobbes, *Leviathan*. Harmondsworth, Middlesex, England: Penguin Books.

———. 1965. "Hobbes's Bourgeois Man." In K. C. Brown, ed., *Hobbes Studies*. Oxford: Basil Blackwell.

Mann, Michael. 1986. *The Sources of Social Power,* Volume 1, *A History of Power: From the Beginning to A.D. 1756.* Cambridge: Cambridge University Press.

Mann, Thomas. 1947. *Essays from Three Decades.* New York: Alfred A. Knopf.

Marcuse, Herbert. 1955. *Eros and Civilization.* Boston: The Beacon Press.

———. 1964. *One-Dimensional Man.* Boston: The Beacon Press.

Martin, Douglas. 1989. "Would New York Still Turn Away?" *New York Times,* March 27:B1.

Martins, Herminio. 1974. "Time and Theory in Sociology." In John Rex, ed., *Approaches to Sociology.* London and Boston: Routledge.

Masters, Roger D. 1972. "The Structure of Rousseau's Political Thought." In Cranston and Peters, eds., *Hobbes and Rousseau.*

Mazlish, Bruce, ed. 1963. *Psychoanalysis and History.* Englewood Cliffs, N.J.: Prentice-Hall.

Mead, George Herbert. 1934. *Mind, Self and Society.* Chicago: University of Chicago Press.

———. 1982. *The Individual and the Social Self.* Edited with an Introduction by David L. Miller. Chicago: University of Chicago Press.

Mead, Margaret. 1963. "*Totem and Taboo* Reconsidered with Respect." *Bulletin of the Menninger Clinic,* 27:185–189.

Merquior, J. G. 1980. *Rousseau and Weber: Two Studies in the Theory of Legitimacy.* London: Routledge.

———. 1986a. *From Prague to Paris: A Critique of Structural and Post-Structural Thought.* London: Verso.

———. 1986b. *Western Marxism.* London: Paladin Books.

———. 1991. *Liberalism, Old and New.* Boston: Twayne Publishers.

Merton, Robert K. 1957. *Social Theory and Social Structure.* Revised and Enlarged Edition. New York: The Free Press.

Meyerhoff, Hans. [1957] 1963. "Freud and the Ambiguity of Culture." In Mazlish, ed., *Psychoanalysis and History.*

Milgram, Stanley. 1969. *Obedience to Authority: An Experimental View.* New York: Harper and Row.

Miller, David L. 1973. *George Herbert Mead: Self, Language and the World.* Chicago: University of Chicago Press.

Mills, C. Wright. 1959. *The Sociological Imagination.* New York: Oxford University Press.

Mommsen, Wolfgang. [1959] 1974. *Max Weber and German Politics, 1890–1920.* Chicago: University of Chicago Press.

Moore, Barrington, Jr. 1966. *The Social Origins of Democracy and Dictatorship: Lord and Peasant in the Making of the Modern World.* Boston: The Beacon Press.

————. 1972. *Reflections on the Causes of Human Misery*. Boston: The Beacon Press.

————. 1978. *Injustice: The Social Bases of Obedience and Revolt*. White Plains, N.Y.: M. E. Sharpe.

Morgenthau, Hans. 1949. *Politics Among the Nations*. New York: Alfred A. Knopf.

Morris, Charles W. 1946. *Signs, Language and Behavior*. New York: Prentice-Hall.

Muller, Jerry Z. 1993. *Adam Smith in His Time and Ours*. New York: The Free Press.

Mullins, Nicholas C. 1973. *Theories and Theory Groups in Contemporary American Sociology*. New York: Harper and Row.

Münch, Richard. 1992. "Rational Choice Theory: A Critical Assessment and Its Explanatory Power." In James S. Coleman and Thomas J. Fararo, eds., *Rational Choice Theory: Advocacy and Critique*. Newbury Park, Calif.: Sage Publications.

Nairn, Tom. 1993. "Demonising Nationalism." *London Review of Books* (February):15, 25.

Nelson, Benjamin, ed., 1957. *Freud in the Twentieth Century*. New York: Meridian Books.

Nelson, Benjamin, and Dennis Wrong. 1972. "Perspectives on the Therapeutic in the Context of Contemporary Sociology: A Dialogue between Benjamin Nelson and Dennis Wrong." *Salmagundi* (Summer-Fall):160–195.

Neumann, Franz. 1960. "Anxiety and Politics." In Morris R. Stein, Arthur J. Vidich, and David Manning White, eds., *Identity and Anxiety: Survival of the Person in Mass Society*. Glencoe, Ill.: The Free Press.

Niebuhr, Reinhold. 1932. *Moral Man and Immoral Society*. New York: Scribners.

Nisbet, Robert. 1966. *The Sociological Tradition*. New York: Basic Books.

————. 1974. *The Sociology of Emile Durkheim*. New York: Oxford University Press.

Oakeshott, Michael. 1975. *Hobbes on Civil Association*. Oxford: Basil Blackwell.

————. 1991. *Rationalism in Politics and Other Essays*. Indianapolis: Liberty Press.

Olson, Mancur, Jr. 1971. *The Logic of Collective Action*. Revised Edition. New York: Schocken Books.

Orwell, George. 1949. *Nineteen Eighty-Four*. New York: Harcourt, Brace.

————. [1949] 1968. "Reflections on Gandhi." In Sonia Orwell and Ian Angus, eds., *The Collected Essays, Journalism and Letters of*

George Orwell, Volume 4. Harmondsworth, Middlesex, England: Penguin Books.

Ossowski, Stanislaw. [1956] 1963. *Class Structure in the Social Consciousness.* New York: Macmillan.

Parkin, Frank. 1979. *Marxism and Class Theory: A Bourgeois Critique.* New York: Columbia University Press.

Parsons, Anne. 1964. "Is the Oedipus Complex Universal? The Jones-Malinowski Debate Revisited and a South Italian Nuclear Complex." In W. Muensterberg et al., eds., *The Psychoanalytic Study of Society.* New York: International Universities Press.

Parsons, Talcott. 1937. *The Structure of Social Action.* New York: McGraw-Hill.

———. 1949a. *The Structure of Social Action.* Second Edition. Glencoe, Ill.: The Free Press.

———. 1949b. *Essays in Sociological Theory.* Glencoe, Ill.: The Free Press.

———. 1951. *The Social System.* Glencoe, Ill.: The Free Press.

———. 1954. *Essays in Sociological Theory.* Revised Edition. Glencoe, Ill.: The Free Press.

———. 1962. "Individual Autonomy and Social Pressure: A Reply to Dennis H. Wrong." *Psychoanalysis and the Psychoanalytic Review,* 49 (Summer):70–79.

———. 1966. *Societies: Evolutionary and Comparative Perspectives.* Englewood Cliffs, N.J.: Prentice-Hall.

———. 1969a. *Politics and Social Structure.* New York: The Free Press.

———. 1969b. *Social Structure and Personality.* New York: The Free Press.

———. 1977. *Social Systems and the Evolution of Action Theory.* New York: The Free Press.

———. 1978. *Action Theory and the Human Condition.* New York: The Free Press.

Parsons, Talcott, and Edward A. Shils. 1951. *Toward a General Theory of Action.* Cambridge, Mass.: Harvard University Press.

Parsons, Talcott, and Neil J. Smelser. 1956. *Economy and Society.* Glencoe, Ill.: The Free Press.

Paul, Robert A. 1991. "Freud's Anthropology: A Reading of the 'Cultural Books.'" In Jerome A. Neu, ed., *The Cambridge Companion to Freud.* Cambridge: Cambridge University Press.

Percy, Walker. 1971. *Love in the Ruins.* New York: Farrar, Straus & Giroux.

Peters, Richard S. 1956. *Hobbes.* Harmondsworth, Middlesex, England: Penguin Books.

Pizzorno, Alessandro. 1991. "On the Individualistic Theory of Social Order." In Pierre Bourdieu and James S. Coleman, eds., *Social*

Theory for A Changing Society. Boulder, San Francisco, Oxford: Westview Press and Russell Sage Foundation.

Plamenatz, John. 1962. "Introduction" to Hobbes, *Leviathan*. London: Collins, Fontana.

Poggi, Gianfranco. 1972. *Images of Society*. Stanford, Calif.: Stanford University Press.

Poster, Mark. 1975. *Existential Marxism in Postwar France*. Princeton, N.J.: Princeton University Press.

Powell, Walter W., and Richard Robbins, eds. 1984. *Conflict and Consensus: A Festschrift in Honor of Lewis A. Coser*. New York: The Free Press.

Raphael, D. D. 1977. *Hobbes: Morals and Politics*. London: Allen and Unwin.

———. 1985. *Adam Smith*. Oxford: Oxford University Press.

Redfield, Robert. 1953. *The Primitive World and Its Transformations*. Ithaca, N.Y.: Cornell University Press.

Reitlinger, Gerald. 1957. *The SS, Alibi of a Nation, 1922–1945*. New York: The Viking Press.

Rex, John. 1974. *Sociology and the Demystification of the World*. London and Boston: Routledge.

Rieff, Philip. [1959] 1961. *Freud: The Mind of the Moralist*. Garden City, N.Y.: Doubleday Anchor Books.

———. [1966] 1968. *The Triumph of the Therapeutic: Uses of Faith after Freud*. New York: Harper and Row.

Riesman, David. 1950. *The Lonely Crowd*. With the assistance of Reuel Denney and Nathan Glazer. New Haven: Yale University Press.

Robinson, Paul. 1969. *The Freudian Left*. New York: Harper and Row.

Roheim, Géza. [1943] 1971. *The Origin and Function of Culture*. Garden City, N.Y.: Doubleday Anchor Books.

———. [1934] 1974. *The Riddle of the Sphinx*. New York: Harper and Row.

Rorty, Richard. 1989. *Contingency, Irony and Solidarity*. Cambridge and New York: Cambridge University Press.

Rosenthal, A. M. 1964. *Thirty-eight Witnesses*. New York: McGraw-Hill.

Rousseau, Jean-Jacques. [1762] 1968. *The Social Contract*. Harmondsworth, Middlesex, England: Penguin Books.

———. [1755] 1984. *A Discourse on Inequality*. Harmondsworth, Middlesex, England: Penguin Books.

———. n.d. *Confessions of Jean-Jacques Rousseau*. New York: The Modern Library.

Rudolph, Susanne Hoeber, and Lloyd I. Rudolph. 1993. "Modern Hate." *New Republic*, March 23:24–29.

Rule, James B. 1983. "Out of This World." *Theory and Society,* 12:801–814.

———. 1988. *Theories of Civil Violence.* Berkeley and Los Angeles: University of California Press.

Russell, Bertrand. 1938. Power: *A New Social Analysis.* London: Allen & Unwin.

Ryan, Alan. 1972. "The Nature of Human Nature in Hobbes and Rousseau." In Jonathan Benthall, ed., *The Limits of Human Nature.* London: Allen Lane.

———. 1983. "Hobbes, Toleration, and the Inner Life." In David Miller and Larry Siedentop, eds., *The Nature of Political Theory.* Oxford: The Clarendon Press.

———. 1988. "Hobbes and Individualism." In G. A. J. Rogers and Alan Ryan, eds., *Perspectives on Thomas Hobbes.* Oxford: The Clarendon Press.

Rycroft, Charles. [1968] 1972. *A Critical Dictionary of Psychoanalysis.* Harmondsworth, Middlesex, England: Penguin Books.

Sahlins, Marshall. 1976. *Culture and Practical Reason.* Chicago: University of Chicago Press.

Schochet, Gordon J. 1990. "Intending (Political) Obligation: Hobbes and the Voluntary Basis of Society." In Mary G. Dietz, ed., *Thomas Hobbes and Political Theory.* Lawrence, Kans.: University of Kansas Press.

Schulberg, Budd. [1941] 1944. *What Makes Sammy Run?* New York: Bantam Books.

Schumpeter, Joseph. 1950. *Capitalism, Socialism and Democracy,* Third Edition. New York: Harper.

Schutz, Alfred. 1962. Collected Papers, Volume 1, *The Problem of Social Reality.* The Hague: Martinus Nijhoff.

Schweder, Richard A. 1992. "Dialogues amid the Deluge." *New York Times Book Review,* September 20:54.

Shils, Edward A. [1968] 1982. *The Constitution of Society.* Chicago: University of Chicago Press.

Simmel, Georg. 1910. "How Is Society Possible?" *American Journal of Sociology,* 16:372–391.

———. [1922 and 1923] 1955. *Conflict and the Web of Group-Affiliations.* Glencoe, Ill.: The Free Press.

Simon, Bennett, and Rachel B. Blass. 1990. "The Development and Vicissitudes of Freud's Ideas on the Oedipus Complex." In Jerome Neu, ed., *The Cambridge Companion to Freud.* Cambridge: Cambridge University Press.

Skinner, Quentin. 1972. "The Context of Hobbes's Theory of Political Obligation." In Cranston and Peters, eds., *Hobbes and Rousseau.*

Skocpol, Theda. 1979. *States and Social Revolutions*. Cambridge: Cambridge University Press.

Slater, Philip E. 1963. "On Social Regression." *American Sociological Review,* 28:339–364.

———. 1967. "The Social Bases of Personality." In Neil J. Smelser, ed., *Sociology: An Introduction*. New York: John Wiley.

Smelser, Neil J. 1988. "Social Structure." In Smelser, ed., *Handbook of Sociology*. Newbury Park, Calif.: Sage Publications.

Smith, Adam. [1776] 1974. *The Wealth of Nations*. Harmondsworth, Middlesex, England: Penguin Books.

Smith, Anthony D. 1986. "State-Making and Nation-Building." In John A. Hall, ed., *States in History*. Oxford: Basil Blackwell.

Snow, C. P. 1956. *The Masters*. Harmondsworth, Middlesex, England: Penguin Books.

Sowell, Thomas. 1987. *A Conflict of Visions*. New York: William Morrow.

Spiro, Melford E. 1987. *Culture and Human Nature*. Chicago: University of Chicago Press.

Sprott, W. J. H. 1954. *Science and Social Action*. Glencoe, Ill.: The Free Press.

Starobinski, Jean. [1971] 1988. *Jean-Jacques Rousseau: Transparency and Obstruction*. Chicago: University of Chicago Press.

Stinchcombe, Arthur L. 1968. *Constructing Social Theories*. New York: Harcourt, Brace and World.

Stone, Lawrence. 1977. *The Family, Sex and Marriage in England 1500–1800*. New York: Harper and Row.

———. 1979. Review of Alan MacFarlane, *The Origins of En-glish Individualism. New York Review of Books,* April 19:40–41.

Strauss, Leo. [1936] 1952. *The Political Philosophy of Hobbes*. Chicago: University of Chicago Press.

———. 1953. *Natural Right and History*. Chicago: University of Chicago Press.

Sullivan, Harry Stack. 1940 and 1945. *Conceptions of Modern Psychiatry*. Washington, D.C.: William Alanson White Psychiatric Foundation.

Thom, Gary B. 1983. *The Human Nature of Social Discontent*. Totowa, N.J.: Rowman and Allanheld.

Thomas, Keith. 1965. "The Social Origins of Hobbes' Political Thought." In K. C. Brown, ed., *Hobbes Studies*. Cambridge, Mass.: Harvard University Press.

Tilly, Charles. 1990 and 1992. *Coercion, Capital, and European States, A.D. 1950–1992*. Oxford: Basil Blackwell.

———. 1991. "Individualism Askew." *American Journal of Sociology* (January) 96:1007–1011.

Torrance, John. 1977. *Estrangement, Alienation and Exploitation: A Sociological Approach to Historical Materialism*. New York: Columbia University Press.

Trilling, Lionel. 1955. *Freud and the Crisis of Our Culture*. Boston: Beacon Press.

Tuck, Richard. 1989. *Hobbes*. Oxford: Oxford University Press.

Tucker, Robert C. 1972. *Philosophy and Myth in Karl Marx*. Second Edition. Cambridge, Mass.: Harvard University Press.

———. ed., 1978. *The Marx-Engels Reader*. Second Edition. New York: W. W. Norton.

Turnbull, Colin. 1972. *The Mountain People*. New York: Simon & Schuster.

Turner, Bryan S. 1981. *For Weber*. London: Routledge.

Turner, Jonathan H. 1989. *The Structure of Sociological Theory*. Fourth Edition. Chicago: The Dorsey Press.

van den Berg, Axel. 1988. *The Immanent Utopia: Marxism on the State and the State of Marxism*. Princeton, N.J.: Princeton University Press.

———. n.d. "Habermas and Modernity: A Critique of the Communicative Theory of Action." *Working Papers on Social Behavior*. Montreal: Department of Sociology, McGill University.

Vidich, Arthur J., and Stanford Lyman. 1985. *American Sociology*. New Haven: Yale University Press.

Walter, E. V. 1960. "The Politics of Decivilization." In Morris R. Stein, Arthur J. Vidich, and David Manning White, eds., *Identity and Anxiety: Survival of the Person in Mass Society*. Glencoe, Ill.: The Free Press.

Walzer, Michael. 1991. "The Idea of Civil Society." *Dissent* (Spring): 293–304.

———. 1993. Contribution to Symposium, "Nationalism and Ethnic Particularism," *Tikkun*, 7:55.

Warner, W. Lloyd. 1953. *American Life, Dream and Reality*. Chicago: University of Chicago Press.

Weber, Max. [1905] 1932. *The Protestant Ethic and the Spirit of Capitalism*. New York: Scribners.

———. 1968. *Economy and Society*. Volume 1. Translated and edited by Guenther Roth and Claus Wittich. Totowa, N.J.: The Bedminster Press.

Weinstein, Michael, and Deena Weinstein. 1983. "Freud on the Problem of Order: The Revival of Hobbes." *Diogenes* (Winter):39–50.

Whitfield, Stephen. 1980. *Into the Dark: Hannah Arendt and Totalitarianism*. Philadelphia: Temple University Press.

Whyte, William F. 1943. *Street Corner Society*. Chicago: University of Chicago Press.

———. 1961. "Parsonian Theory Applied to Organizations." In Max Black, ed., *The Social Theories of Talcott Parsons*.

Whyte, William H. 1956. *The Organization Man*. Garden City, N.Y.: Doubleday Anchor Books.

Winch, Peter. 1955. *The Idea of Social Science and Its Relation to Philosophy*. London: Routledge.

———. 1972. "Man and Society in Hobbes and Rousseau." In Cranston and Peters, eds., *Hobbes and Rousseau*.

Winkins, Yves. 1988. "Portrait de Sociologue en Jeune Homme." In Erving Goffman, *Leurs Moments et Leurs Hommes*. Collected and edited by Yves Winkins. Paris: Seuil/Minuit.

Wolfenstein, Martha, and Nathan Leites. 1950. *Movies: A Psychological Study*. Glencoe, Ill.: The Free Press.

Wollheim, Richard. 1971. *Freud*. New York: The Viking Press.

Wrong, Dennis H. 1961. "The Oversocialized Conception of Man in Modern Sociology." *American Sociological Review*, 26 (April):183–193.

———. 1965. "The Psychology of Prejudice and the Future of Anti-Semitism in America." *European Journal of Sociology*, 6:311–328.

———. 1976. *Skeptical Sociology*. New York: Columbia University Press.

———. 1979. "Bourgeois Values without the Bourgeoisie? The Cultural Criticism of Christopher Lasch." *Dissent* (Summer): 308–314.

———. 1981a. Review-essay on Stephen Whitfield, *Into the Dark*. *Society* 18 (May/June):68–71.

———. 1981b. "Ruling Classes and Ruling Ideas." *Times Literary Supplement*, September 11:1039.

———. 1982a. "A Note on Marx and Weber in Gouldner's Thought." *Theory and Society*, 11:899–905.

———. 1982b. "The Long Trail." *New Republic*, July 19 and 26:36.

———. 1985. "Myths of Alienation" *Partisan Review* (Summer): 222–235.

———. 1987. "Opposites Detract." *New Republic*, February 9:46–48.

———. [1979] 1988. *Power: Its Forms, Bases and Uses*. New Edition. Chicago: University of Chicago Press.

———. 1990. "The Influence of Sociological Ideas on American Culture." In Herbert J. Gans, ed., *Sociology in America*. Newbury Park, Calif.: Sage Publications.

———. 1991. "The Magic Touch." *New Republic*. April 5:41–43.

———. 1992. *"The Lonely Crowd Revisited."* Sociological Forum. 7 (June):381–389.

Yankelovich, Daniel, and William Barrett. 1970. *Ego and Instinct*. New York: Random House.

Young, Michael. 1959. *The Rise of the Meritocracy, 1870–2033*. New York: Random House.

Young, Michael, and Edward A. Shils. 1953. "The Meaning of the Coronation." *Sociological Review*, 1 (December):63–81.

INDEX